Witness for the Prosecution

The Real Truth of the *Eatock v Bolt* Court Case
and the Injustice of Andrew Bolt's Conviction

by *Roger Karge*

Genealogical Research and a Disclaimer:

All genealogical work presented here has been undertaken in good faith by professional genealogists and archival researchers and is based on publicly available records at the time of the research. It should be noted that genealogical research is not an exact science. Existing records can contain errors and family trees can change if new evidence comes to light. Similarly, this research cannot account for events which may have resulted in Aboriginal ancestry entering into the family line such as via a private or unrecorded adoption of an Aboriginal child into the family, or a relationship out of wedlock between a family member and an Aboriginal person that produced a child of Aboriginal descent who was then incorporated into the family without record, or with a record that did not disclose the Aboriginality of that child.

First Reprint with corrections 2026

ISBN 978-0-646-70553-8

Risdon Cove Publishing, Prahran, Victoria, 3181, Australia

Website: https://www.hidden-histories-tas.org

Email enquiries, comments, corrections to:
hidden.histories.tas@gmail.com

The true events of this
notorious court case
were based
on one original lie.

Preface

*Falsehood flies, and truth comes limping after it, so that
when men come to be undeceived, it is too late; the jest is
over, and the tale hath had its effect.*

Jonathan Swift[1]

In 2011, **Pat Eatock**, a 'fair-skinned' Aboriginal woman took
one of Australia's leading journalists, **Andrew Bolt**, to court.
She accused him, and his employer the *Herald and Weekly
Times*, of publishing offensive messages about her *not being
genuinely* Aboriginal and implying that she only *chose* to identify as Aboriginal to access benefits that were meant for *real*
Aboriginal people. Her resulting spectacular win in the notorious *Eatock v Bolt* case fueled a political and media frenzy
that signified major turning points in both race relations, and
freedom of speech in Australia.

To some, a great injustice had been righted by the presiding judge, **Mordecai 'Mordy' Bromberg** - for too long
they had claimed that 'fair-skinned' Aboriginal people, with
only minor Aboriginal ancestry, had been derided as not being real Aboriginal people. Journalist Andrew Bolt had called
them 'white Aborigines' and Eatock's win humiliated Bolt and
brought him to heel for contravening the Racial Discrimination Act.

Others however, believed the opposite had occurred – a

---

[1] *The Examiner No. XIV*, 9 November 1710.

new injustice had been created and a legal precedent set that would restrict the right to free speech for Australians in general and journalists in particular. They reasoned that Bolt's conviction, as one of Australia's most read and watched current affairs and political commentators, would result in no one else ever again daring to question, or even discuss, a person's public claim to Aboriginal ancestry for fear of being branded, as Bolt had been, a 'racist'.

Since 2018, I have been the editor of *Dark Emu Exposed*, a website that has gained some small notoriety for exposing public figures who claim to be of Aboriginal descent but whose genealogical records show they have no Aboriginal ancestry at all.[2] In August 2024, a short email arrived in my inbox. It was from Andrew Bolt himself and read:

> I was just wondering - have you ever checked on Pat Eatock? I should have, and paid for not doing so. She admitted in court some of her own family didn't identify as Aboriginal and my barrister - who I'd forced to ask the question - refused to ask a follow-up question. How interesting if it turns out she was never Aboriginal in the first place but was successful as the lead plaintiff on getting discussion of identity banned in my case as racial discrimination.

This book *Witness for the Prosecution* answers Bolt's enquiry. It re-examines the polarising court case in the light of startling new evidence that the late Pat Eatock (d. 2015) was mistaken to believe she was of Aboriginal descent. In fact, the genealogical evidence presented here shows she had no Aboriginal ancestry at all - she was a 'fake' and thus would appear to have had no standing as a 'fair-skinned Aboriginal' woman, in bringing the case to court in the first place.

Instead of justice being served by Eatock's win, it now appears that a new injustice was created, not only for Bolt but also for the Australian community as a whole with regard

---

[2]Professor Marcia Langton AO is particularly unsettled by my website which she claims is run by a 'nefarious Trump-like cult group' that produces 'garbage'.[see QR Code on page (xv) for [0.1] from 03.00]. Of course the problem for Langton was that, time and time again, my research turned out to be true.[0.2], [0.3]

to the stifling of free speech for the past thirteen years on the topic of Aboriginal identity.

Whether or not one agrees with the opinions of Andrew Bolt, is not really the point. It is that our society needs commentators like Bolt to freely speak their minds, without fear or favour - just as we need people like Pat Eatock and her supporters to be free to speak up against Bolt and his ideas. Yes, it can be 'humiliating, offensive, insulting or even intimidating' to both sides, but this is how society progresses - by a clash of ideas in the public space and in parliaments where ultimately, and hopefully, the good ideas are legislated and the bad ones rejected. The underlying principle that allows our society to assess, choose or reject ideas as the case may be, is free speech - it is a very important cultural invention. To speak freely and express one's views without fear also operates as a societal safety valve. It allows activist individuals or small groups to express and release their political tensions in small doses, thereby avoiding the build-up of deep-seated resentment that would ultimately explode in mass riots or even revolution. It is no coincidence that the most successful and least politically violent countries in the world tend to have higher levels of free speech, when compared to failed and dictatorial states where dissent is often strictly controlled or ruthlessly suppressed.

Witness for the Prosecution details this tale of mistaken identity and an extravagant $1.5 million, eight-day trial[3] that should never have happened. The tragic consequence of this saga is that the biggest losers of all are the genuine Aboriginal people of Australia. They now have to suffer the indignity caused by this judgement, which gives a cloak of legal protection to any Australian brazen enough to put on an Aboriginal T-shirt, paint their face in ochre, drape themselves in an Aboriginal flag and self-declare, as we constantly hear today, to be 'a proud [insert tribal name(s) here] Aboriginal [wo]man.' It does not matter if these 'New Identifiers' have any Aboriginal

---

[3]Chris Merritt, 'A question of principle rather than money', *The Australian*, 2 Apr 2011.

ancestry or not - after Bolt's defeat no-one has the courage anymore to ask or check. Thus, an 'Aboriginal' reawakening was legally born - that of a new class of Australians, the 'fair-skinned' Aboriginal people - Bolt's 'white Aborigines' - many of whom are nothing more than New-Identifiers, Box-Tickers, or ultimately, the mistaken, the fake or the fraud.[4]

But there is an unexpected upside to this story that I believe no-one has discovered, until now. Justice Bromberg himself, perhaps inadvertently and unknowingly, has given Andrew Bolt a metaphorical 'get out of jail free card' to once again call out the 'fakes' and 'white Aborigines', but this time quite legally. The *pro bono* and progressive commentators, who cheered on Justice Bromberg in a court case that had, with hindsight, all the appearance of being a 'stitch-up', have actually produced a framework now for Bolt to routinely expose high-profile 'fakes' on his *Sky News Australia* 'The Bolt Report'.[5] This would have seemed an impossible outcome in the immediate aftermath of Bolt's loss in court. All it took was a very close reading of Justice Bromberg's 470-paragraph judgment, some guidance from University of Melbourne Law professor Adrienne Stone, and a small group of diligent genealogists and researchers working in good faith.

Ultimately, free speech is back and maybe, in the end, the law isn't always such an ass.

Roger Karge
Melbourne, October 2025

---

[4]See Chapter 11.1 for definitions.
[5]Thirteen high profile fakes so far and counting - see [0.4]

For References link - see QR code on page (xv)

References

[0.1] Marcia Langton. *Comments on Dark Emu Exposed, see YouTube clip here.* 2023.

[0.2] Dark Emu Exposed. *Professor Lisa Jackson Pulver Summary.* 2025.

[0.3] Dark Emu Exposed. *Professor Megan Davis Summary.* 2023.

[0.4] The Bolt Report. *Andrew Bolt calls out those who 'claim' Aboriginal heritage without evidence.* 2024.

Introduction

A new word was in the making to keep Australians blind to the realities: Aboriginalisation.[6] To criticise the cultural suicide and fraud of this new cult was to be called a racist.

Salman Rushdie (paraphrase)[7]

While writing *Witness for the Prosecution* I realised that something very strange was happening to modern Australia. It was just how often it seemed that the 'experts' were stuffing up their projects and predictions. Whether it was as simple as digging a few tunnels for the Snowy 2.0 project, the handling of the COVID-19 pandemic, the court case of Cardinal George Pell, buying French submarines, getting the so-called 'modest proposal' of the Voice referendum through, or even just building a road on time and on budget, Australia's engineering, military, political and legal 'experts' frequently just turned out to be hopeless failures. They seem to have lost the ability to guide the project at hand to success, despite the solutions being hidden in plain sight for anyone to see. The *Eatock v Bolt* court fiasco of 2011 is a case in point for the legal and journalistic professions.

In Part I, I will go right back to 2010 when a well-planned and well-resourced complaint was lodged against Andrew Bolt

---

[6] See Definition in section 11.2.4

[7] This quote is a paraphrase of Salman Rushdie on Islamophobia, cited in Bruckner, P., *An Imaginary Racism – Islamophobia and Guilt*, John Wiley & Sons (UK), 2018, p(ii).

and the *Herald and Weekly Times* (HWT) with the Australian Human Rights Commission (AHRC) by solicitors acting for an elderly Aboriginal activist, Pat Eatock. The solicitors claimed their client was 'offended, insulted and humiliated by Andrew Bolt's articles and blog comments' which he had published in 2009.

Eatock was complaining on behalf of herself and 'a group of Aboriginal people' who claimed Bolt's articles and blog comments contravened the Racial Discrimination Act 1975 (RDA).

Unbeknown to Bolt's legal team, the archives contained the evidence that Pat Eatock wasn't Aboriginal at all. If Bolt's defence had conducted professional genealogy and archival research early on, this miscarriage of justice could have been avoided. They would have been able to quietly inform the applicant's legal team at the outset that their client was not of Aboriginal descent as she claimed. She thus had no *locus standi* - legal standing - to bring the case in the first place as an 'offended, humiliated and insulted Aboriginal person.' The result would have been: 'Case dismissed'.

Unfortunately, Bolt's legal team didn't spend their first week or two researching the archives. Their client was thus destined to endure two years of pre-trial stress followed by eight agonising days in the Federal Court, at a trial cost said to be of some $1.5 million.

Part II examines the aftermath of *Eatock v Bolt* - what Justice Bromberg's judgement has meant for all the parties adversely affected by it, as well as for Australia and Australians in general. In particular, I will show how the chief characters in this legal 'stitch-up', as Bolt himself now calls it, were found to be wanting - Pat Eatock with her false claims, but also her late sister **Joan Eatock**, who wrote a book filled with fabrications to support the modern-day family's claim to Aboriginality; Eatock's counsel, **Ron Merkel QC** supported by Holding Redlich solicitor **Joel Zyngier**, both working *pro bono* and who perhaps naively believed they were 'acting entirely in the public interest' to raise 'very important issues about protecting racial minorities from discrimination';[8] and finally Andrew Bolt's defense counsel, **Neil Young QC**, who in the circumstances seemed to perform at a level that was less than optimal or desirable.

Some commentators have publicly been very critical of the presiding judge's actions as well.[9] Indeed, one notable commentator, Janet Albrechtsen, has described **Justice Bromberg's** style in another court case as 'frolicking' - in an activist sense.[10]

Originally I too had been with the pro-free speech advocates who were critical of his judgment, but on deeper reflection I now think he has done a great service to Australia, given that, as I will explain, that 'service' turned out not to be the politically progressive or activist one he might have envisaged.

An underlying theme of this book revolves around the questions, 'just who is, and who isn't, Aboriginal today?' and, 'should it even matter?' I will draw on the commentary and family histories of a number of prominent and political Aboriginal Australians, as well as several self-proclaimed 'Aboriginal' academics, in exploring these questions.

In the writing of this book, I have come to the view that many of the answers and solutions we seek to help us deal with modern-day issues are 'hidden in plain sight'. For example, the genealogical records of prominent Australians claiming to be Aboriginal, that appeared for the first time on the *Dark Emu Exposed* website, have always been available, in the archives, but no one had ever collated and published these records as complete family trees. A significant number of these prominent Aboriginal people have now turned out to be fakes.

I have also published excerpts from information obtained under Freedom Of Information (FOI) and from Australian Security Intelligence Organisation (ASIO) files. I have communi-

---

[8] *Probono News*, 65, April 2011.
[9] See Chapter 8.1
[10] Janet Albrechtsen, 'Judges on a legal frolic', *The Australian*, 11 Aug 2021.

cated with people who witnessed the 2011 *Eatock v Bolt* trial
in person. All other primary and secondary information obtained was always there, available for anyone to see - the court
and newspaper records, the public commentary of all the main
participants in this saga and, as importantly, records of historical racial precedents which we ignore at our peril. These
precedents, such as repugnant ideas of political censorship,
and classifying a nation's citizens according to race, should
repel us in the same way the policies of apartheid and Nazi
Germany repelled our parents and grandparents. But here we
find ourselves today, in modern Australia, slowly progressing
down the path of officially sanctioned racism and the control of
free speech, whether it be by the various Human Rights Com-
missions giving legal protection to race-based exemptions for
'identified positions'[11], the Federal Court judgments by Justices Bromberg[12] and Merkel[13], or in the creation of a new
class of Aboriginal 'alien' based on race by the High Court[14].
Worryingly, these legal precedents further affirm the desire by
many activists, legislators and jurists to feel it is permissible
to create a new class of Australians based on race.

Part III addresses some of the legacies that may arise from
this reappraisal of *Eatock v Bolt*, such as where, if anywhere,
this case could go now. Does the fact that Pat Eatock was
not of Aboriginal descent alter the court's findings? Could
the case be reopened by an appeal lodged on the basis of the
new evidence presented here?

More broadly, I hope readers will have gained a better
understanding of what statutory Aboriginality is and how it
is being used as a criteria in Aboriginal affairs generally, and
more specifically in constitutional changes, treaty, land hand-
backs, race relations, race-based positive discrimination, and
what is referred to as the politics of social justice and *Clos-*

---

[11]See Queensland Human Rights Commission. Race-based Positive Discrimination -
  FACT SHEET: Aboriginal and Torres Strait Islander Identified Positions.
[12]In *Eatock v Bolt*.
[13]In *Shaw v Wolf*.
[14]In *Love v Commonwealth of Australia*.

ing the Gap initiatives. As importantly, readers should now appreciate that the methodology detailed in *Witness for the Prosecution* gives the public *permission* and a *template* with which to confidently once again exercise their free speech and to challenge, in a civil 'manner' and 'tone', the racial and ethnic claims of others, without being branded a racist.

This case should not have gone to court in the first place. Bolt's employer, the HWT, had offered free newspaper and online access for Pat Eatock and the co-applicants to respond. The debate in this case should have been like a tennis match on the court of free speech, with the Australian public in the stalls, turning their heads from left to right and back again as they watched and listened to the argument 'ball' get hit between Bolt and the 'fair-skinned' Aborigines. Instead, Pat Eatock, ever the militant Communist Party member and activist that she was, rode onto the court on her mobility scooter, along with her legal cohort of 'ball boys', scooped up all the balls and then appealed to the umpire that Bolt's forehand and style were too hurtful and offensive for her and the 'fair-skinned' Aborigines to keep playing. Umpire Bromberg agreed. Bolt was sent off and the public were left to watch as hundreds, if not thousands, of other dubious 'white Aborigines' ran onto the now-free court, faces painted in ochre and hitting uncoordinated balls in all directions, each playing by their own, mostly invented, new rules of Aboriginality.

But the crowd, recognising match-fixing when they saw it, shuffled out, except for the hard-core 'proud' fans who were paid by 'Indigenous Tennis Australia' to attend, clutching their Reconciliation Action Plans, and unquestioningly going along with the charade of the fake Aboriginal player. And so, this is where we find ourselves in modern Australia today - a genuine people of goodwill in a land infiltrated by an activist class of match-fixers, rent-seekers and their attendant city-based virtue-signalers.

How to use this book

This is a 'web-book'. It comes in two parts - this **hard-copy book** and an **online** repository of videos, photographs and copies of primary and secondary documents that can be accessed via the **QR-code** in Figure 1. Readers can use their iPhone, tablet or computer screen to access this material at the relevant pages as they read through the hard-copy book.

The web-book format allows the hard-copy book to be produced and distributed economically, to as many Australians as possible, but still allow immediate access to high-quality photographic, archival and audio-visual references that would be prohibitively expensive to produce in print form.

The sources are arranged in two ways - as footnotes (with the sequential numbering in each chapter only) and as citations (eg: [7.23]) where the first number refers to the chapter and the second to the sequential reference in that chapter. The citations occur at the relevant point in the text-body and are also collated at the end of each chapter, where they are linked via the QR-code to the full reference resource online.

We live in an 'Age of Assertions' - people just say and write things often without providing any real evidence for their claims. Additionally, footnotes and citations can sometimes be misleading - they may give a book the appearance of scholarship but, on checking, the reader finds they do not reflect what the author claimed. Bruce Pascoe's book, *Dark Emu*, has be-

Figure 1: QR-code For References for *Witness for the Prosecution*. Open this QR-code to access the references on your iPhone or tablet or log in via your computer at https://www.dark-emu-exposed.org/home/witness-for-the-prosecution-references

come notorious in this regard.[15]

Witness for the Prosecution aims to overcome any doubts in the minds of its readers by providing, instantly via the QR-code, links to the sources cited. Readers themselves can then verify the claims made in this book. When I first started posting critiques on the *Dark Emu Exposed* website, initially of Bruce Pascoe's assertions in his book *Dark Emu*, and then later his, and other 'fair-skinned' Australians' assertions that they were of Aboriginal descent, I did get a lot of criticism that I was wrong in my claims and that I wasn't qualified (i.e. I wasn't an academic, or Aboriginal, or an expert in any of these topics). I must be a racist, or a member of a Trump-like cult, my critics charged. But over time, all these criticisms have faded and the accusing emails have dwindled to essentially none as readers have come to appreciate the verifiable accuracy of the methodology described here.

Lastly, this web-book is another small example of the Internet Age disrupting the worlds of academia, legacy media and publishing. Modern 'print-on-demand' technology means readers can suggest amendments or corrections that can be quickly incorporated if appropriate prior to the next reprint. [See email contact on page (ii)]

---

[15]See Peter O'Brien, *Bitter Harvest: The illusion of Aboriginal agriculture in Bruce Pascoe's Dark Emu*, Quadrant Books, 2019.

Contents

Part I

Chapter 1

The FOI Revelations

We're not saying you can't talk about racial issues. What the judgment clearly said is it's how you handle it, you cannot be malicious. You must handle it based on truth and fact, not on fiction and racism.

Pat Eatock[1]

In December 2024,[2] I received an email with a 60-page attachment labeled, 'FOI Bundle (redacted)'. The contents included the original Australian Human Rights Commission (AHRC) complaint lodged by a Ms Pat Eatock against the journalist Andrew Bolt and his employer the *Herald and Weekly Times* (HWT).[3] The complaint read:

> I am complaining on my own behalf and on behalf of other Aboriginal persons who were likely to be offended, insulted and humiliated by Andrew Bolt's articles and blogs comments published by The Herald and Weekly Times on 15 April 2009, 16 April 2009 and 21 August 2009 (the Articles and Blogs).

---

[1] The thoughts of the successful Applicant in *Eatock v Bolt*[1.1]

[2] The dates of the revelations in this book are not necessarily chronological. The nature of research is such that information is often uncovered out of sequence.

[3] Holding Redlich Lawyers acted on behalf of Pat Eatock, the applicant. The file included all the correspondence, with some redaction, between the AHRC and the HWT, the second respondent, who also acted on behalf of the first respondent, their journalist Andrew Bolt. The redacted part of the file, five A4 pages out of the bundle's total of 60 pages, related to the confidential mediation session between the parties, which occurred over some 2 or 3 hours on 24 June 2010.[1.2]

Those who were likely to be offended, insulted and humili-
ated include those named in the Articles, including Graham
Atkinson, Dr Wayne Atkinson, Larissa Behrendt, Geoff Clark,
Bindi Cole, Leeanne Enoch, Anita Heiss, Mark McMillan and
Tara Winch Jones (those named in the Articles).

I am, and those named in the Articles are, and identify as,
Aboriginal persons on the basis of our descent, self-identification
and community recognition. The Articles and Blogs consti-
tute unlawful acts in contravention of the *Racial Discrimination Act 1975 (Cth)* (the Act), being conduct that was
reasonably likely, in all the circumstances to offend, insult or
humiliate those named in the Articles and Blogs, and other
Aboriginal persons who form part of the same group of persons as those named in the Articles and Blogs (the Group),
because of their race and/or colour (the Offensive Behaviour).

- signed *Pat Eatock*, 13/4/10

This was the AHRC complaint that would eventually morph
into the notorious *Eatock v Bolt* case. But why had the complaint been launched in the first place? Bolt had simply stated
the obvious: that the 'fair-skinned' Eatock appeared to be using her claimed minor thread of Aboriginal ancestry to obtain
benefits as a 'white Aborigine'. Bolt's description of Eatock
was perhaps full of 'incivility', and even offensive in Eatock's
mind, but in 'tabloid-speak' it cut to the heart of the matter in
a way instantly understood by Bolt's mainstream Australian
readership: Was a typical 'white' Australian like Pat Eatock
really entitled to receive tax-payer benefits that were intended
for genuine Aboriginal people in real need?

Reading the correspondence, one gets the impression that
the complainant was just going through the motions of the
AHRC process and had no intention of settling the matter
within the AHRC conciliation framework. It appeared as
though the real aim of Pat Eatock and her group of Aboriginal
co-applicants, the Eatock Nine (and perhaps the legal advocates behind her as well?) was to get to the Federal Court
as quickly as possible. This was even acknowledged in the
correspondence. Her lawyers had lodged the complaint on 14

April 2010 and yet, within one day, the AHRC's Principal Investigator/Concilliator, Adam Dunkel, was emailing the HWT advising that:

> the complainant is giving consideration to whether she wants the complaint terminated [within the AHRC] so that the Federal Court proceedings can be commenced. - [*emailed 15/4/2010*]

Why the rush? Could it be that the applicant's (and/or her advocate's) original plan was always to go for maximum public exposure and publicity in the Federal Court rather than to quietly settle the matter down at the rooms of the AHRC? Nevertheless, after a week the Managing Editor of the HWT himself responded:

> Good morning Adam [*email sent 23/4/2010*]
>
> Further to our telephone conversation, may I reiterate that we are willing to enter any conciliation process you may deem fit. We would attend with a positive attitude, believing we will need to put something on the table to address the concerns of complainants [Eatock, *et al*]. There are many forms this could take, including significant exposure in the [HWT] paper itself and online. We represent and publish a wide range of views from a variety of columnists and readers in what we believe is a healthy environment of discussion and debate. The right of reply is paramount in these matters. Having said that, it is not our intention to offend any individual or group. Our record in this regard is exemplary. I take your comment that the action is against the *Herald Sun* and Andrew Bolt as an individual and await your instructions as to how we deal with this when the time comes. My direct line and personal mobile are listed below should you wish to discuss this further. Yours sincerely.
>
> Alan Armsden, *Managing Editor, Herald & Weekly Times*

This offer was not accepted by the complainant. One therefore wonders whether free speech, and the offer of a public forum in the pages of the *Herald Sun*, were all that important to the complainant and/or her advocates. Or was it all about winning against Bolt the person, and humiliating him in the 'court of public opinion'? We may never know given that Pat Eatock passed away in 2015. Ultimately, however, the complainant finally agreed to at least attempt (or be *seen* to attempt?) a conciliation:

> Dunkel (AHRC) to Armsden (HWT) [*emailed 28/4/2010*]:
>
> I have spoken to the representative for the complainant and it appears that they are agreeable to proceeding to conciliation. Unfortunately due to a number of circumstances, I understand that they will not be available for a face to face conference in Melbourne until after 15 June 2010. Given the above, I have tentatively set down this matter for a conference in Melbourne on the morning of 24 June 2010.

Reading through the FOI bundle, one could see the unfortunate course this matter began to take as it slowly wound its way towards the eight-day, $1.5 million,[4] Federal Court case. Eatock (and/or her advocates) never had any intention of settling the complaint through an AHRC brokered conciliation. This case was always destined for a full public trial - to be used, as Simon Breheny astutely observed, 'as a battering ram because of the negative perception that would be created by a breach of the Racial Discrimination Act'.[5]

The last two of the emails tell the story:

> Dunkel (AHRC) to Armsden (HWT) [*emailed 29/6/2010*]:
>
> Thanks for attending the conference last week.[6] As you are aware, it appears appropriate for this complaint to be terminated ... The *Herald Sun* has elected not to provide a formal response to the allegations. In this instance, my recommendation will be for the complaint to [be] terminated on the ground that there is no reasonable prospect of the matter being settled by conciliation (as you know the complainant intends to make an application to the FCA regardless of the ground of termination)...

---

[4] Chris Merritt, 'A question of principle rather than money', *The Australian*, 2 Apr 2011.

[5] Simon Breheny, 'Repeal section 18C, the 'Andrew Bolt' law: it stifles free speech', *The Australian*, 5 Feb 2016.

[6] Attendees - Mr Adam Dunkel A/Principal Investigation & Conciliation Officer Presiding. For the Complainants - Mrs Pat Eatock, Mr Geoff Clarke, Ms Bindi Cole, Legal Counsel Mr Ron Merkel QC & Ms Phoebe Knowles, Solicitors Mr Joel Zyngier & Ms Georgina French and support person to Mrs Eatock, Ms Aislinn Martin and possibly others via tele-conference facilities. For the Respondent - HWT Managing Editor, Mr Alan Armsden, General Counsel Ms Louise le Grice [n.b. Andrew Bolt absent].

And:

> Response by Armsden (HWT) to Dunkel (AHRC) [*emailed 29/6/2010*]:
>
> I'm disappointed that we could not come to an arrangement but that's life ... May I thank you for your assistance and for the detailed and professional way in which you handled this matter.

Legal counsel for the HWT wrapped up the complaint negotiations with a final letter to the AHRC on 30 June 2010, which indicated the respondents [HWT] clearly believed the applicant Pat Eatock was intent on going to Federal Court regardless of the outcome of the AHRC conciliation process:

> Dear Adam,
>
> *Re: Eatock (The Complainant) v The Herald and Weekly Times Pty Ltd and Andrew Bolt (The Respondents)*
>
> ... I note that you intend to recommend that Ms Eatock's complaint be terminated on the ground that there is no reasonable prospect of it being settled by conciliation. The Respondents are disappointed that the complaint will be terminated on this basis.
>
> I note your request that we confirm that "the Herald Sun has elected not to provide a formal response to the allegations". The Respondents would have been content to make written submissions to the Commission, addressing our contention that the alleged unlawful discrimination is not unlawful discrimination in this instance. However, in light of the complainant's clear intention to make an application to the Federal Court regardless of the basis on which the complaint is terminated, it appears that any written submissions we may make to the Commission would be a waste of time for both the Commissioner and the Respondents.
>
> If you are aware of any additional considerations that may warrant the Respondents providing written submissions being made, please contact myself or Alan Armsden.
>
> Yours sincerely,
> Elizabeth Beal
> Legal Counsel - Editorial. [*Full letter here*[1.3]]

And so the case made its way from the AHRC to the Federal Court to become perhaps one of the greatest legal 'stitch-ups' in recent years. By the time the trial was ready to proceed, Pat Eatock was all 'lawyered up'. Her *pro bono* legal team for the prosecution was assembled and well prepped and consisted of **Mr Ron Merkel QC** appearing with **Mr Herman Borenstein SC** and supported by Ms CM Harris, Ms PC Knowles, and **Joel Zyngier**, solicitor with Holding Redlich.

But who did the HWT appoint to lead for the defense of themselves and Andrew Bolt? They chose **Mr Neil Young QC** who, as it turned out, lost the case that most media commentators and supporters of free speech had thought Bolt and the HWT could win. Even if Bolt was not liked by some of the media, there had always been an underlying assumption, by both those on the Right as well as on the Left, that one could always speak one's mind. As a nation, we had prided ourselves on the freedom to 'call a spade a spade'. But, as in many other areas of modern Australia, by the 21st century we had found out that we were living a life of delusion - Australia was not like it used to be. The country had changed, as the *Eatock v Bolt* case would show.

And so mainstream Australia also found itself in Federal Court at 10.16am on Monday 28th of March 2011 with Andrew Bolt, behind Neil Young QC, the man entrusted with defending Bolt's, and indirectly all of our, right to free speech. It should have been a winnable case for Young.

To find the answers as to why Young lost the case so resoundingly, and why things were stacked against Bolt from the day he entered the court, we need to go back in time, some thirteen years prior. In 1998, a legal case, *Shaw v Wolf*, set the methodology for what it means to be Aboriginal in a legal sense, particularly a 'fair-skinned' Aboriginal person of distant descent. And very interestingly, the judge presiding in that 1998 Federal Court case was none other than Pat Eatock's now lawyer, Ron Merkel himself.

For References link - see QR code on page (xv)

References

[1.1]   Karl Quinn. *Bolt unrepentant but slur victims hail victory, Sydney Morning Herald.* 29 Sept 2011.

[1.2]   Pat Eatock. *AHRC Complaint Form.* 13 Apr 2010.

[1.3]   Elizabeth Beal (HWT). *AHRC Termination Letter.* 30 June 2010.

Chapter 2

Merkel v Merkel - The Justice & The Advocate

Controversy and disagreement have never been very far from Australia's hate speech laws but no single case has captured public attention in the way Eatock v Bolt & Herald and Weekly Times [HWT] has.

In 2009 Andrew Bolt wrote two articles ... on the topic of skin colour and Aboriginality ... The articles named a number of individuals, many of whom are prominent and successful, and questioned their identification as Aboriginal.

In each case emphasis was placed on the (fair) colour of their skin and on Bolt's assessment of the 'quantum' of their Aboriginal ancestry. His central message was that it was scandalous that these individuals identified as Aboriginal and benefited from doing so (eg one person was described as having chosen, from a mixed heritage 'the one [racial] identity open to her that has political and career clout').

Katherine Gelber and Luke McNamara,
Australian academics, 2013[1]

---

[1]Gelber K. & McNamara L. 'Freedom of speech and racial vilification in Australia: "The Bolt case" in public discourse', *Australian Journal of Political Science*, 48.4 (2013), pp470–84. See [2.1].

2.1   Witness for the Defence

Debbie Oakford

Thirteen years before Andrew Bolt found himself dragged into court to defend what he meant by his use of the word 'Aboriginal', a woman had already been through the same harrowing experience. In late April 1998, Tasmanian Aboriginal woman, Ms Debbie Oakford found herself in Federal Court before **Justice Ron Merkel**. She was there as a respondent in the case of **Shaw v Wolf** because the petitioners, two prominent members of the Tasmanian Aboriginal community, had challenged her eligibility to stand as a candidate in the Hobart Aboriginal and Torres Strait Islander Commission (ATSIC) Regional Council elections. The challenge to Oakford's legitimacy was brought under the Aboriginal and Torres Strait Islander Commission Act 1989 ('the Act'). This states that, to be an eligible candidate for election, a person must be: *'of the Aboriginal **race** of Australia'*.[2] The petitioners argued that Oakford was not an Aboriginal person for the purposes of the Act, because she was not a descendant of the Aboriginal race.

In her defence, Oakford submitted what she thought was an accurate family tree that traced her believed Aboriginal ancestry:

> through her father's family back to Wottecowidyer, a daughter of the Aboriginal chief Mannalargenna; she also traces her mother's family back to Teekoolterme, another daughter of Mannalargenna.[2.2]

Unfortunately for Oakford, her family tree proved to be wrong. Evidence presented by Ms Robyn Eastley, the Senior Archivist in the Archives Office of Tasmania, 'indicated that ... Ms Oakford's version of her family tree may not be consistent with the historical records'. Further evidence, provided in affidavit by a Ms Sculthorpe and based on historical records, raised,

---

[2]Yes, it is still within living memory that an Australian Labor government would enact legislation based on 'race', and quite happily use that word too, without any sense of racist hypocrisy.

'a persuasive case against the family tree put forward by Ms Oakford'. In consequence, Merkel J, concluded:

> In my view, Ms Oakford's material is inadequate to support her assertion that she is descended from Thomas Thompson, the son of Wottecowidyer ... She has also produced no material to support the other aspects of the family tree in respect of which the petitioners' [Ms Sculthorpe] material raises significant doubt...

> As a result I am satisfied, applying the Briginshaw principle[3] that on the balance of probabilities the petitioners have established that Ms Oakford has no Aboriginal ancestry deriving from her father's ancestors.[2.2]

Merkel J also assessed the presented evidence for Oakford's claims on her mother's side and came to a similar conclusion.

Despite the court having accepted that Oakford genuinely self-identified as an Aboriginal person, and enjoyed some community recognition as such, it was not satisfied she had what former High Court Chief Justice Robert French has referred to as **'statutory Aboriginality'** - the 'legal dimension' of what it means to be Aboriginal. This arises from a need in some circumstances for 'defining in a legal sense' who is, and who isn't, Aboriginal, notwithstanding how uncomfortable, personal and indeed racist these inquiries might appear to be to some people.[2.3] Deliberations over a period of many decades concerning what constitutes 'statutory Aboriginality' has led us to where we are today, to the generally accepted *Three-part (tripartite)* 'working definition' of Aboriginality, viz: An Aboriginal or Torres Strait Islander is a person:

- of Aboriginal or Torres Strait Islander **descent**

- who **identifies** as an Aboriginal or Torres Strait Islander and

- is **accepted** as such by the **community** in which he [or she] lives.[2.4]

Unfortunately for Oakford, Merkel J decided that if it can be shown that a claimant's belief in their own Aboriginal ancestry

---

[3]See Chapter 11.3 for definition of the Briginshaw principle.

or descent, no matter how sincerely believed, is based on a mistaken reading of the historical and genealogical records, then that person's claim to Aboriginal descent will not stand up legally. Oakford had failed to convince Merkel J and she was deeply disappointed, as an ABC *Four Corners* program recorded at the time.[2.5]

But the applicants were not completely happy with Justice Merkel's final decision either. Despite dismissing Oakford's defense, Merkel J nonetheless found that the case against the other nine, perhaps equally mistaken, claimants failed because, in the example of Mr Courto for instance:

> I am not satisfied on the material before me that the petitioners have established, on the balance of probabilities, that Mr Courto does not have any Aboriginal ancestry.
>
> Neither the respondents nor the petitioners' account is supported by formal archival records. In the absence of any written historical records as to the parents of Eliza Dare, the only historical material before me is the acknowledged family rumour or account of the father of Eliza Palmer being an Aboriginal blacksmith. The petitioners' view that her father did not have any Aboriginal ancestry is also, essentially, a matter of hypothesis.
>
> ... there are other relatives who are of the opinion that Eliza Palmer's father was Aboriginal. The photograph of Eliza Palmer, which does show that she appears to be a woman of dark skin colour, may offer some support for that opinion.[2.2]

In other words, if no credible and convincing evidence is put forward to *dispute* a person's claim to Aboriginal descent, then their strongly believed family 'rumours' and/or family oral history, as well as historical photographs, will most likely suffice to convince a Ron Merkel-minded judge that their claimed Aboriginality is truthful. This understanding and legal guidance by Justice Merkel in deciding who is, and who isn't, Aboriginal, was to have significant repercussions some thirteen years later.[4]

---

[4]Taxpayers should note that this 1998 hearing was said to have taken 2 years, gen-

2.2 Witness for the Prosecution

Pat Eatock

Fast forward to the year 2011 and once again we find Ron
Merkel in a Federal Court, involved in a case that is all about
the meaning of the word 'Aboriginal'. But this time he is not
the judge - rather he is the advocate for the applicant in what
would become the notorious ***Eatock v Bolt*** case. At 2:20pm
on Monday 28 March 2011, Mr Ron Merkel QC stood in court
before His Honour, Justice Mordecai Bromberg and asked:

Mr Merkel: And your Honour, can I now read the witness
statement of Pat Eatock, which is Exhibit A8?[5]

His Honour: Yes.

Merkel: Pat's witness statement, she says:

> **I am an Aboriginal person with Aboriginal ances-
> try.** My grandmother, **Lucy Eatock**, was born in Carnarvon
> Gorge in central Queensland in 1874. This is an Aboriginal
> birthing place, an Aboriginal women's place, an Aboriginal
> commitment place. She was one of the Kirri people.
>
> My grandmother's mother was an Aboriginal woman called
> **Kitty**. My grandmother had a non-Aboriginal father. My
> grandmother's father was, I believe, **Adam Wakenshaw**, al-
> though she was raised by his older brother, **Alexander Wak-
> enshaw**. Adam Wakenshaw was a carter. Carters often had
> Aboriginal women as slave sex partners or assistants. My
> grandmother lived with my mother and our family from 1947
> until her death in 1950. I have photos of Lucy; she is clearly
> Aboriginal but not particularly dark.
>
> My grandmother's husband, my grandfather, was an Aborig-
> inal man, **Bill Eatock**. They married in 1894. **He looked
> very Aboriginal.** I have seen a photograph of Bill; **he had
> a very black face** and a long white beard. Bill was from the
> Woga Woga Waka Waka people from the Queensland coast

---

erating 1000 pages of affidavits, at a cost of some $1.2m [$2.5m in 2025 dollars] all
pretty much for nought given that ATSIC, and thus its voting system, was disbanded
a few years later. See - Michael Connor, 'Andrew Bolt on Trial', *Quadrant Online*,
1 May 2011.

[5]*Eatock v Bolt*, Trans. Proc., Fed. Court (Vic) O/N 160844, Mon 28 Mar 2011, Day
One, p51ff.

from Fraser Island to Moreton Bay. Lucy and Bill had nine children, two girls and seven boys, including my father...

My father, **Roderick Eatock**, was the second youngest of Lucy's nine children. He was born on the banks of the Darling River in 1909. I have lots of photos of my dad, and photos of some of his brothers. **He was dark**, much darker than his mum, Lucy. My mother was **Elizabeth Stephenson Anderson**. **She was born in 1909 in Scotland** and came to Australia in about 1928...(emphasis added.)

Surprisingly, when Mr NJ (Neil) Young QC, counsel for the respondent, Andrew Bolt, came to examine Pat Eatock and her witness statement, he appears to have accepted her claims about her Aboriginal ancestors at face value - no questions asked, beyond the following short exchange that offered a glimpse of an interesting line of inquiry:[6]

Mr Young: When was it that you and your sister Joan started to do research on your family history?

Pat Eatock: That's two questions.

Young: When was it that you, personally, started to do research on your family history?

Eatock: When I started university, and started studying history, I became very aware of the importance of history, and I did five years of history. And during that process, I studied things like African history and women's history. And during that, it became also personal history and Aboriginal history.

Young: Yes, I'm just looking for a date, Mrs Eatock. When did you - -?

Eatock: Well, I started university in 1973, so I suppose around about then.

Young: Yes. All right. And - - -?

Eatock: I did Australian history that year.

Young: Yes. And so it was in the years following 1973 that you started to research your family history, is that correct?

---

[6] *ibid.*, p70.

Eatock: Yes, I would say so.

Young: Yes. Now, you suggest that I asked two questions. When did your sister Joan become involved in that process of researching your family history?

Eatock: I'm not really sure.

Young: Well, she did become involved, did she not?

Eatock: She did, and she wrote a book on it.[2.6]

Young: And sometime after 1973, I take it?

Eatock: Yes.

Young: Now, you and your sister Joan have taken a view, or expressed a view in the family history about your family descent lines, have you not?

Eatock: I'm sorry, I cannot accept responsibility for anything that Joan wrote. We have – we had, while she was alive, we had disagreements about interpretation in very many parts of that book.

Young: Yes, all right. Well, let me ask you this: some of your relatives do not identify themselves as Aboriginal, as you do?

Eatock: That's right.

Young: They've made different decisions about their Aboriginal identity?

Eatock: That's right.

Young: Nothing further.

Young's approach to Eatock's evidence raises the valid questions as to why he had failed to see the path the cross-examination should have taken: Where were the corroborating written records that Pat had uncovered during her five years of history study to support her belief that ancestors Lucy, Kitty and William (Bill) were Aboriginal? Where was her evidence to support her libellous sex-slave and adoption accusations against her ancestors, Adam and Alexander?

But Mr Young did not see this. One can only wonder if this was an unintentional oversight or if he had a different reason for not pursuing that line of cross-examination. Coincidentally, it would now be another thirteen years before the public's mind would be once more be prompted to think about who is, and who isn't, Aboriginal in Australia in the eyes of the law. In 2024 the legacy of the late Pat Eatock and her testimony were once again to be cross-examined, but this time with the backing of professional genealogical and historical researchers - and a very annoyed ex-respondent from 2011, Andrew Bolt, who felt he had been 'stitched up.'

For References link - see QR code on page (xv)

References

[2.1]   Gelber K. & McNamara L. *"Freedom of speech and racial vilification in Australia: 'The Bolt case' in public discourse."* In: *Australian Journal of Political Science* 48.4 (2013), pp. 470–84.

[2.2]   *Shaw v Wolf FCA 389; 83 FCR 113.* 1998.

[2.3]   Justice Robert French. *"Aboriginal Identity–The Legal Dimension"*. In: *Australian Indigenous Law Review* 15.1 (2011), pp. 18–24.

[2.4]   John Gardiner-Garden. *The Definition of Aboriginalty.* Social Policy Group Information and Research Services, Aust. Parl., Dec 2000.

[2.5]   *ABC Four Corners - Blackfella Whitefella.* Youtube, 26 August 2002.

[2.6]   Joan E Eatock. *Delusions of Grandeur: A Family's Story of Love and Struggle.* jukurrpa books/Iad Press, 2003.

Further Reading

1. Connell, Rachel - *Who is an 'Aboriginal Person'?: Shaw v Wolf*, IndigLawB 49; (1998) 4(12) *Indigenous Law Bulletin*, p20ff.

2. De Plevitz, L. & Croft, L. *Aboriginality under the Microscope: The Biological Descent Test In Australian Law*, *QUT Law & Justice Journal*, Vol 3 No 1 (2003) p1-17.

Chapter 3

The Blackness of Pat Eatock's Politics

Occasionally cases come before court which show the law has been used as an instrument of injustice.
The present is such a case.

Former Justice Ron Merkel[1]

Outside the Federal Court in Melbourne on 28 September 2011, a large incongruous group of people had gathered – some cheered with happiness, raised their arms in a battle triumph and waved brightly coloured flags; others yelled and screamed insults at still others in dark suits and ties, who looked forlorn and bewildered at their unexpected loss in the court battle.[3.2]

To some, a great injustice had been righted by the presiding judge, Justice Bromberg - *Herald Sun* journalist Andrew Bolt had been humiliated and brought to heel for contravening the Commonwealth *Racial Discrimination Act 1975* by offending a woman, a 'white Aborigine' as Bolt had called her, who Bolt alleged had only *chosen* to identify as Aboriginal to advance her career. After her win, Pat Eatock exited the court

---
[1]Speaking in 2006 with regard to an immigration case.[3.1]

and gushed, "I'm telling you now, this is the highlight of my career, of my life."[3.3]

Others believed the opposite had occurred – a new injustice had been created and a legal precedent set to restrict the right to free speech for Australians in general and journalists in particular. "This is a terrible day for free speech in this country," Andrew Bolt told the assembled media.[3.3]

But there was another, very small, unnoticed group of observers who had been carefully following the case - amongst them lawyer Peter Faris QC [3.3]; *Quadrant Magazine's* Keith Windschuttle [3.4], Michael Connor [3.5], John Izzard [3.6], [3.7] and Steve Kates [3.8]. Together with Andrew Bolt[2] and myself today, this group feared the case would have profound implications for Australia over the coming decades, if not generations.

Thirteen years later, these fears appear to have been well founded. For Justice Bromberg the issue had not only been about whether or not Pat Eatock *the individual* was reasonably likely to have been offended but also whether *a group* - the new 'class of persons', described by Bromberg J[3] as **'fair-skinned' Aboriginals** or, as Bolt labelled them, **'white Aborigines'** - were reasonably likely to be offended.[4] Bromberg J, perhaps unwittingly, had formally recognised (some might say legally created or even invented) a whole new class of Australians before the law. These were Australians who claimed Aboriginal ancestry, often very minor or even non-existent, and who self-identified as Aboriginal, but who 'would be particularly sensitive to the fact that their appearance does not fit the stereotypical image of an Aboriginal person and would be the more offended' by challenges to the legitimacy of their identity.[5]

---

[2]See Bolt's view at the time: Andrew Bolt, 'Andrew Bolt: Damned as the Devil', *Quadrant Online*, 23 May 2016.

[3]'Bromberg J' is an abbreviation for 'Justice Bromberg'.

[4]*Eatock v Bolt* [2011] [3.9] at 270 & 288, and Kirby, N., [3.10], p30.

[5]Kirby, N.,[3.10], p30-1, and *Eatock v Bolt* [2011] [[3.9] at 290 & 291.

The advocacy of Ron Merkel QC and the judgement of Bromberg J would, in the opinion of these few insightful observers, spawn a new injustice that would go on to create dangerous divisions within our country based on race and skin colour. The way was now clear for any Australian, no matter how 'fair-skinned', to brazenly fake their Aboriginality without the fear of being challenged.[6]

Prior to 2011, the odd 'pretender' who appeared, self-identifying as a fake Aboriginal, was laughed out of their silliness, or humiliated by exposure. But after *Eatock v Bolt*, real Aboriginal people would once again experience what dispossession felt like as they watched their organisations and what little remained of their culture and history, steadily taken over by the new, self-identifying fake Aborigines, the new cultural colonisers.

The broader Australian community would not be immune either to these box-tickers,[7] with their fakery, pseudo-indigenous culturalism and ideological drive to reinterpret and even erase our nation's history.[8] After Bolt's loss, anyone, whether Aboriginal or not, who wanted to question a claimant's belief that they were Aboriginal, would think twice and probably keep their concerns to themselves – no-one would have the courage to call them out and ask for their proof, for fear of being sued, or branded as 'racist' [3.12], 'scum' or 'an evil person', as Bolt had been called outside the court on that judgement day in 2011.[3.5]

But how did we, as a country, get to this point, staring down an ugly road to a future society based on legal and court-enforced racial and skin-colour divisions? This is where the story gets interesting, very interesting, because in fact the prime applicant in enforcing this new apartheid-style racism,

---

[6]See a video summary by Andrew Bolt on the now extensive problem of the 'fakes'.[3.11]

[7]See Chapter 11.1 for definitions.

[8]See Moore, T., & Pybus, C., 'Myth-making Isn't the Right Way to 'Indigenise' Our Universities', *Quillette*, 26 June 2022.

Pat Eatock, was herself what is now commonly referred to as a fake Aborigine. According to genealogical records, all of Pat Eatock's ancestors were of Scottish descent except one - her biological great-grandfather, **Richard Rose**, who was actually a 'man of colour' from the island of Bequia in St Vincent and the Grenadines in the West Indies. Richard Rose was born a slave in 1831, the son of **William Rose**, a planter with some 166 'negroes' on his Union Estate plantation. One of the estate's slaves, the domestic worker, **Harriet**, was most likely Richard's mother.

On William Rose's death in 1839, his illegitimate eight-year-old son Richard was recognised in the will and left some funds for his future care. Later, Richard became a registered seaman, found his way to Queensland where he worked as a miner and had a brief relationship with a married Scottish woman, **Catherine Eatock (*nee* Davidson)**, which produced a child, **William Rose**. Richard Rose separated from Catherine before William was born, resulting in William's birth surname being changed to Eatock to match his mother's married surname (discussed in detail in Chapters 4 and 5).

Thus, the modern Eatock family line is actually descended from William Rose (later Eatock) who was a Queensland stockman as the family claimed, but he was not an 'Aboriginal' one, as they believed. When Ron Merkel QC read out to the court his client's witness statement, a statement that Pat Eatock had signed and swore an affirmation to [3.13], he was unwittingly misleading the court:

> My grandmother's husband, my grandfather, was an Aboriginal man, Bill [William] Eatock. They married in 1894 [sic 1895]. He looked very Aboriginal. I have seen a photograph of Bill; **he had a very black face** and a long white beard.[3.14]

Pat was undoubtedly correct that William probably had a 'black face' - his grandmother after all had been an African or West Indian negro slave - but Pat had just assumed that 'blackness' in Australia was solely derived from being an authentic Aboriginal. It was almost as if Pat had thought to herself, "My grandfather was black and looked 'very Aboriginal', so *he must have been* Aboriginal."

And thus the irony and injustice of the *Eatock v Bolt* case is revealed: Pat Eatock successfully sued Andrew Bolt because he dared to look at her 'fair skin' and made assumptions about her ancestry, and then went on to speak and write about her not being an Aboriginal in a real, meaningful way. Rather, he saw her as a white Australian woman of mainly Scottish ancestry who was relying upon a small percentage of claimed Aboriginality to 'thrive as an Aboriginal bureaucrat, activist and academic.'

But Pat Eatock did exactly the same thing when she looked at the dark skin of her grandfather and made an assumption about his ancestry. She only saw him as a black Aboriginal man rather than the Australian stockman of mainly Scottish with some West Indian heritage that he really was. She was allowed to continue to write and speak mistakenly about being an Aboriginal woman with no fear because she was now one of the protected, new class of 'fair-skinned' Aboriginal people.

The court had vindicated Eatock but condemned Bolt for both doing exactly the same thing - looking at a person's appearance and skin colour and making assumptions and forming an opinion about their degree of Aboriginal ancestry and how society thus treated them. In reality, Bolt got his facts essentially correct and Eatock was wildly mistaken as to her own ancestry. But more worryingly, Ron Merkel QC and Justice Bromberg believed her, and agreed with her, and thereby created a legal precedent that, on the face of it, would protect all future fake Aborigines from legitimate scrutiny. I believe this has led to a great injustice, not only to Bolt, but also to the rest of Australia, particularly to the genuine Aboriginal Australians who now find the fakes infiltrating and influencing increasingly larger segments of their lives and culture. By censoring Bolt, Bromberg J has thwarted the real value that free speech plays in a liberal, democratic and egalitarian society like Australia's - citizens need to be able to freely speak their minds, without fear or favour, so ideas and proposals can be debated, assessed and selected to enable societal progress, or rejected, or modified, as the case may be.

This case was clearly a 'stitch-up' of Andrew Bolt, given that the main applicant was a fake and all the legal intellects down in the Federal Court should have known that she was.[3.15] However, as with all things legal, often nothing is quite as it seems, especially with landmark cases such as this. The real consequences can take years to develop and can often surprise. Appealing or reopening this case today by an aggrieved Bolt is not an option.[9] Nevertheless, the surprise is that despite the legal loss, Bolt might still be vindicated, courtesy of none other that Justice Bromberg himself, with a little help from University of Melbourne Law Professor Adrienne Stone. More on this later in Chapter 9.

In the next chapter, evidence is presented to support the claim that the late Pat Eatock was mistaken to believe that her grandparents, William and Lucy Eatock were Aboriginal. She, along with the historians and the Federal Court of Australia were all wrong, very wrong, indeed.

---

[9]See Chapter 9.5. History records that the HWT decided quite quickly not to appeal the ruling - (See - 'No appeal in Andrew Bolt case', *Herald Sun*, 20 October 2011.) - thereby cementing in the minds of many members of the public that Bolt was guilty as charged. After the loss, I understand that Bolt turned down the HWT's offer to appeal - the stress and damage had been too great for him to contemplate repeating the process for another year or two. He also felt he had needed to win the case first up 'in the court of public opinion' - a win on appeal was useless to him, the damage to his reputation was already done. (Bolt, *pers. comm.*)

For References link - see QR code on page (xv)

References

[3.1] Ron Merkel. *The Law Report, ABC Radio.* 23 May 2006.

[3.2] Photographs. *Outside court after the Eatock v Bolt decision.* 28 Sept 2011.

[3.3] ABC TV. *Bolt brands racial discrimination ruling anti free speech.* 2011.

[3.4] Keith Windschuttle. "The Trial of Andrew Bolt (II): Real Aborigines versus Phoneys". In: *Quadrant* (1 Dec 2010).

[3.5] Michael Connor. "The White Aborigines Trial". In: *Quadrant* (1 Nov 2011).

[3.6] John Izzard. "The Trial of Andrew Bolt (I): Designer Ethnicity anti-free speech". In: *Quadrant* (1 Dec 2010).

[3.7] John Izzard. "The Trial of Andrew Bolt". In: *Quadrant* (5 Oct 2010).

[3.8] Steven Kates. "Andrew Bolt and the Orwellian State". In: *Quadrant* (21 Jun 2011).

[3.9] *Eatock v Bolt, FCA 1103.* 2011.

[3.10] Nicolas Kirby. *Media responsibility under the Racial Discrimination Act.* Bar News. Winter 2012, p30-2.

[3.11] SkyNews. *Andrew Bolt calls out those who 'claim' Aboriginal heritage without evidence.* Aug 2024.

[3.12] Katherine Murphy. "Andrew Bolt declared a racist on his own show by Craig Emerson". In: *Guardian Online* (17 Aug 2014).

[3.13] *Eatock v Bolt, Trans. Proc., Federal Court (Vic), Bromberg J, Pat Eatock and Andrew Bolt and Another, O/N 160844, Mon 28 March 2011, Day One, p60.*

[3.14] *Eatock v Bolt, Trans. Proc., Federal Court (Vic), Bromberg J, Pat Eatock and Andrew Bolt and Another, O/N 160844, Mon 28 March 2011, Day One, p51ff.*

[3.15] SkyNews. *Sky News host Andrew Bolt claims he was "stitched up".* 13 Sept 2024.

Chapter 4

Pat Eatock's Mistaken Aboriginality

Quite often...I found cases that would come before me where the actual outcome was something no-one ever intended.

Former Justice Ron Merkel[1]

She's basically being told – the public is basically being told: this woman is a fake.

Ron Merkel QC[2]

Using information from the Eatock family, coupled with publicly available genealogical records, newspaper reports, and other archival sources,[3] the apparent Family Tree of Pat Eatock was constructed by genealogical researchers. One branch of this tree, outlining Pat Eatock's relationship to her grandparents William and Lucy Eatock, is shown in Figure 4.1.[4]

---

[1]Speaking with regard to immigration cases.[4.1]

[2]Referring to Bolt's articles about his client Pat Eatock during submissions in *Eatock v Bolt*, Trans. Proc., Fed. Court (Vic) O/N 160844, Mon 4 Apr 2011, p497.

[3]Including Australian Institute of Aboriginal and Torres Strait Islander Studies [AIATSIS] Canberra; various slave plantation databases in the West Indies & the UK; Qld Government Gazettes and Mining Records; Australian Security Intelligence Organisation [ASIO]; National Archives of Australia [NAA]; various databases in Scotland and the genealogical websites, *Ancestry.com* and *Findmypast.com*.

[4]The full Family Tree is detailed here -[4.2]

William Eatock (Rose)

This branch of the Eatock Family Tree shows Pat Eatock's paternal grandfather, William Eatock (birth name Rose) was *not* Aboriginal but was in fact of both Scottish and African or West Indian slave ancestry. No Aboriginal ancestry was found in the William Eatock (Rose) branch of the Family Tree (subject to the usual *Disclaimer*[5]).

Lucy Eatock was not Aboriginal either, both her parents being born in Scotland. Her branch of the Eatock Family Tree is shown in Figure 4.2 and discussed below.

The primary document that all other past researchers have relied upon when investigating the Eatock Family Tree is the marriage record of William Eatock and Lucy Harriet Wakenshaw[4.3]. The details of this marriage record appear in the *Australian Dictionary of Biography* (ADB) entry on Lucy Harriet Eatock [1874-1950].[4.4] Many other Eatock family members include these same details in their published family trees on *Ancestry.com*.[4.5]

This marriage record provided the names of who William *believed* his parents were - 'Thomas [*sic*] Eatock' and 'Catherine Davidson'. However, no record has been found of a *Thomas* Eatock marrying a Catherine Davidson - instead there is a record of her marrying a *Timothy* Eatock, in Gympie, Queensland in 1868. This indicates that William Eatock, in his own marriage record, mistakenly recorded his father's[6] first name as 'Thomas' when it should have been 'Timothy'. This suggests he never really knew who his father was. Timothy Eatock appears to have separated from Catherine and their first son Donald, even before William was born (further discussed in the following chapters).

Timothy Eatock and Catherine Davidson said on their own marriage record that they were born overseas - in England

---

[5]See page (ii) at the front of this book.
[6]Who William *believed* his father was.

In the West Indies

William Rose [Planter]	m.-	**Harriet Williams [Slave]**
Owner of Union Estate	not married;	Domestic on the Union
plantation, Bequia, St Vincent &	*Slave owner & slave*	Estate plantation,
Grenadines, **West Indies**		Bequia, St Vincent &
b. unknown – d. 1839		Grenadines, **West Indies**
(*Of Scottish ancestry*)		b. ca1805 Africa or West
(*Pat's 2x Great-grandfather*)		Indies
		(*Pat's 2x Great-grandmother*)

In Australia

Richard Rose	m. –	**Catherine Davidson**
b. 1831 Kingston, St Vincent,	not married	b. 1840 Edinburgh,
West Indies – d. unknown		**Scotland** – d. unknown
(*Pat's Great-grandfather*)		(*Pat's Great-grandmother*)

William Eatock (*birth name* **Rose**)	m. 18 November 1895	**Lucy Harriet**
b. 19 August 1869 Gympie,	Springsure, Queensland	**Wakenshaw**
Queensland – d. 21 May 1943		b. 7 June 1874
Prahran, Victoria		Springsure, Queensland
(*Pat's grandfather*)		– d. 12 February 1950
		Brisbane, Queensland
		(*Pat's grandmother*)
		See Figure 4.2

Roderick Eatock	m. 1932 Glebe, NSW	**Elizabeth Stevenson**
b. 5 July 1909 Brewarrina, NSW –		**Stuart-Anderson**
d. 18 June 1987 Sydney, NSW		b. 20 May 1909 Ayr,
(*Pat's father*)		Ayreshire, **Scotland** – d.
		10 October 1979
		Brisbane, Queensland
		(*Pat's mother*)

June Patricia "Pat" Eatock	m. 1957 Sydney, NSW	**Ronald Adam Eatock**
b. 14 December 1937 Redcliffe,		(*Pat's husband and first*
Queensland – d. 17 March 2015		*cousin – son of*
		Roderick's brother,
		Richard Eatock)

Figure 4.1: The branch of the apparent Eatock Family Tree showing Pat Eatock's line to her grandparents, William Eatock and Lucy Harriet Wakenshaw, and then on to William's Scottish & West Indian ancestors. Download detailed Family Tree at [4.2](subject to the *Disclaimer* on page (ii).)

and Scotland respectively.[4.6] All the other family researchers on *Ancestry.com* finalise their family trees at this point. They all believe that the apical ancestors of this family tree branch are Timothy Eatock, born in England and Catherine Davidson born in Scotland (See [4.5]). No other family members appear to claim any Aboriginality in this branch of their family trees - Pat and Joan Eatock were the only family members of their generation, to my knowledge, to claim Aboriginality.

Before considering the new research which indicates the Eatock family, as well as all other *Ancestry.com* researchers, were mistaken to believe that the Englishman, Timothy Eatock, was the biological father of William Eatock, it is instructional to provide the background on how two family descendants, the late Pat Eatock and her late sister, Joan de Cressac (*nee* Eatock), successfully fabricated the family's oral history to 'fake' their own Aboriginality.

I suspect that during their family history research, Pat and Joan came to a dilemma - they could find no documentary proof that their father Roderick Eatock and his parents (their grandparents) William and Lucy Eatock were Aboriginal. However, deep down they knew these three must have been Aboriginal because, as Pat said, they each had 'a very black face', and 'clearly looked Aboriginal.' So, to overcome this lack of documentary proof, a family oral history was largely invented by Pat and Joan. This was published by Joan as a family history book, *Delusions of Grandeur* in 2003.[7]

This fabrication was so effective that it apparently fooled some of Australia's finest legal minds at the Federal Court in 2011. While they were alive, developing their family story together, Pat and Joan could not always agree on the exact

---

[7] Joan Eatock, *Delusions of Grandeur: A Family's Story of Love and Struggle.* jukurrpa books/IAD Press, 2003. IAD press is 'Australia's oldest Aboriginal book publisher'. It will 'publish the work of Aboriginal writers and artists' and is 'committed to representing an authentic Aboriginal perspective'. Nevertheless, fake Aboriginal author Joan Eatock still has her book listed with the IAD online bookshop.

details of the family's oral history.[8] This is not surprising when family members set out to fake an imaginary family ancestry. However, they appeared to be both of one mind when it came to their grandparents, William and Lucy Eatock, being Aboriginal. It is only speculation but one could imagine Pat creatively discussing late at night with her sister: "Come on Joan, they really were Aboriginal because, *we really need them* to be Aboriginal. I've got my new career, now that people know I'm Aboriginal, and the Lefties love me. I'm getting a lot of support from these communist uni-people who love hearing about grandma Lucy and her tough Aboriginal life fighting with the Commies for worker's rights. Plus you've always wanted to be a family historian and go on the radio and write that book about our family - no one will ever listen to you, or publish your book, unless you say we are an Aboriginal family [see footnote 7]. No one is interested in us if we are just like them - we need an identity that is in demand so that when they look at us, they will respect us as being special and listen to what we have to say."[9]

If it took some family tall stories, a manipulation of the archival records and a few outright fabrications, then so be it. Pat Eatock perhaps saw an opportunity to escape her disappointing marriage and a poor working class life as a suburban mum, often on the edge of a breakdown.[10] All she had to do

---

[8]See p36-7.

[9]This is conjecture on my part. However, after speaking to close Eatock family members, corresponding by email with others and listening to the extensive recordings of family discussions held in the AIATSIS archives, plus relying on Pat and Joan's own public statements [4.7],[4.8],[4.9], in my opinion, some type of collaborative Aboriginal myth-making by Pat and Joan must have occurred. The records show that their mother and siblings understood there was no Aboriginality at all in the family's ancestry. This caused a major rift between Pat and Joan on the one hand and their mother and other siblings on the other.

[10]In a 1987 newspaper feature, Pat indicated just how difficult her life was at that time: "This feeling of powerlessness is all too familiar. In 1971 I was a suburban housewife, the mother of five children, the youngest 7 and severely retarded and epileptic ... [I] lived the previous seven years on the brink of a total breakdown, I signed myself into a mental institution ... [This time] was the beginning of my conscious desire for real control of my life. I had been married for 15 years. The fifth child was placed in an institution ... Married life was soured even before the handicapped child, whose illness created a social and economic barrier to our ending

was declare her Aboriginality and allow herself to be swept up in the excitement of the new Aboriginal activism of the Left, with its Tent Embassy, the proclaimed righteous cause for Land Rights, Aboriginal sovereignty, political justice and a new truth-telling regime aimed at righting the self-perceived racism and past injustices of Australia's colonial history. The only problem was that none of what Pat and Joan claimed about their professed Aboriginality was true. But then, Pat was not the first person in the 1970s to let a few facts about one's lack of Aboriginality get in the way of seeking a better future as an 'Aboriginal' activist. (See Eatock's close political colleague, Roberta 'Bobbi' Sykes.[11][4.10])

4.1 Pat and Joan's Fabrications

The Aboriginal Intruder

Pat and Joan Eatock were the only family members to actively claim Aboriginality for William and Lucy, and thus for themselves. Even though the editors at the *Australian Dictionary of Biography* (ADB) agreed that William was Aboriginal, they diplomatically declined to go further and claim that Lucy was Aboriginal also. The ADB entry also hints as to why Lucy's grandchildren (Pat and Joan) might have been eager to claim Aboriginality:

> When, in **a time of reawakened pride for indigenous Australians,** Lucy's grandchildren and great-grandchildren reclaimed their Aboriginality, they also suggested that Lucy's mother had been Kitty, an Aboriginal woman employed by

the marriage. The marriage disintegrated with frighteningly violent scenes. Being of mixed racial origins, my identity resolved and focused on my Aboriginality more and more throughout the years. Childhood and marriage (to a first cousin on the Aboriginal side of the family) led to an incredibly isolated existence providing no real protection against continuing racist barbs. However during 1971 I was increasingly active in the Aboriginal Land Rights movement, visiting a number of Aboriginal reserves throughout NSW. In 1972 I attended the National Land Rights Conference in Alice Springs. In April 1972, I took the baby and left my home in Sydney ... arriving in Canberra, the first 'refugee from suburbia' that the Canberra Women's Liberation Group had to deal with." - *The Age*, 6 Mar 1987, p14.

[11] *Wikipedia: Roberta Sykes.*

the Wakenshaws. **Neither Lucy nor any of her children** [which includes Roderick, Pat and Joan's father] **is known to have made such an assertion.** (emphasis added.)[4.4]

No other family trees on *Ancestry.com* claim Aboriginality in this branch of the Eatock family line. In particular, none claim that William Eatock, Pat's grandfather, was Aboriginal.[4.5] This lack of Aboriginality in William Eatock is supported by a 1906 robbery report in the *Queensland Times*, when he was an employee of Cobb & Co.:

Winton, June 11.

At the Police Court, to-day, **William Newman, an aboriginal**, was charged with entering a dwelling-house for an unlawful purpose, and also with illegally using a horse, the property of Cobb and Co. Evidence showed that the accused entered a tent at the Alice tank, on the Longreach-road, occupied by **Mrs. [Lucy] Eatock**, wife of a groom [William Eatock] there, during the night. The woman, who was awakened by the **blackfellow** accidentally kicking a kerosine tin, seized a pair of scissors, and the black, thinking it was a revolver, fled, taking one of Cobb's horses. On [William] Eatock's return the latter went in pursuit, and captured the aboriginal, and tied him up till the police came. Accused was sentenced to six months' imprisonment on each charge, the sentences to be cumulative. (emphasis added.)[12]

This report raises an interesting point - if Pat Eatock was correct that her grandparents were Aboriginal, why wasn't that noted in this article? The only person reported as being 'aboriginal' or a 'blackfellow' in this incident was the intruder, William Newman. Interestingly, as the research into the claims of Aboriginality in the Eatock family progressed, it became apparent that both Pat and her sister Joan were embellishing, if not outright fabricating, some parts of the family's history. For example, the following account published in Joan's book of the 'aboriginal intruder' story above is markedly different to that of the newspaper's. Joan's book version reads:

At night she would often read by the hurricane lamp until the

---

[12] *Queensland Times, News*, Thur 14 Jun 1906, p10.

dawn. Reading kept her sane. There wasn't a tree in sight, just a shimmering plain, which under the blazing sun looked like a huge sheet of water. After a time it became known to the local Aborigines that the whites had left The Tank and they began to visit the strangers that had taken over. They never stayed long, as they resented strange, uninvited Aboriginal people as much as they did white invaders. They would stay around long enough to accept what tucker this woman of both races in white men's clothing would give, then disappear into the desert. Lucy's habit of sitting and reading far into the night intrigued the local Aboriginal people. Her lamp light shone from the windows and through the cracks around the doors long past the time for sleeping. Knowing her and her children to be alone, they wondered why the woman was continually sending light out into the darkness. One night a young male, who as yet had not completed his initiation and therefore had not been accepted as a husband by the women of his community, crept near to the hut. Quietly he waited until at last the light went out and all was silent. Lucy woke as he was about to slip into her bed, her screams of fright sending him running off into the darkness. Not daring to close her eyes, Lucy sat at the table with a rifle on her knees for the rest of the night, and for many nights after she slept with the loaded gun close at hand.[13]

Joan's version illustrates a common ploy of 'fakes' - they include Aboriginal cultural markers or tropes that the reader should be aware of, so as to give legitimacy to the hoax. This lulls the reader into thinking, "Oh yes, Joan must be a real Aboriginal and telling the truth - she recognises all the right cultural mores: 'the Aboriginal intruder is a young male who as yet had not completed his initiation'; 'the local Aborigines are wary of the new Aborigines, William and Lucy'; the local Aborigines are 'humbugging fringe dwellers living on hand-outs of food and clothing'. Never mind that the intruder was reported during another incident as, 'a neatly dressed young aboriginal giving the name of William Newman'; and the incident with Lucy was nothing more than a case of petty theft. Interestingly the Aboriginal Newman was described in this

---

[13] Joan E Eatock, *Delusions of Grandeur*, p15.

second newspaper article as a 'a colored coon' which, as racist as that sounds to us today, does indicate that William and Lucy were not considered 'coloured', 'coons' nor Aboriginal by the newspaper reporters, as they were not referred to in these terms. Also it appears that Joan has taken some aspects of this second article, where the Aboriginal William Newman was convicted of slipping into a woman's bedroom, and falsely woven these details into the report of Mrs [Lucy] Eatock being robbed in the first newspaper article.[14]

Similarly, if William and Lucy were Aboriginal, why were they listed on the Queensland Electoral Roll in 1903 and 1908? [4.12] Queensland at that time had some of Australia's most restrictive laws regarding Aboriginal voting, freedom of movement and labour, custody of children and control over personal property.[4.13] William and Lucy did not seem to have any of these rights restricted in their case at all, which is further evidence that they were not considered Aboriginal.

Lucy Eatock (*nee* Wakenshaw)

Neither the late Pat Eatock [1937-2015], nor her late sister Joan [1936-c2006], ever cited or published any corroborating documentary evidence to support their claims that William and Lucy were Aboriginal. Instead, they self-proclaimed their Aboriginal ancestry by asserting that they had undertaken historical research themselves as well as relying upon their own memories and the so-called oral history of the family.

When Ron Merkel QC stood up in Federal Court and read out his client's affirmed witness statement, he gave the appearance of believing in what he was presenting and, because of his eminence, the court understandably concluded that he was endorsing Pat's assertions about her grandparents as being truthful. But anyone applying even a little critical thinking could see that Pat's claims just sounded like 'Grandma's fam-

---

[14]'A Colored Coon in Court', *The Evening Telegraph, Charters Towers Qld*, 8 Feb 1908, p1. [4.11]

ily rumours'. For example, Ron Merkel QC told the court on Pat's behalf that:

> I am an Aboriginal person with Aboriginal ancestry. My grandmother, Lucy Eatock, was born in Carnarvon Gorge in central Queensland in 1874. This is an Aboriginal birthing place, an Aboriginal women's place, an Aboriginal commitment place. She was one of the Kirri people.

During the trial, no one tendered, or even asked to be tendered, Lucy Eatock's birth record to corroborate Pat's claim. If they had, they would have seen that it did not state she was an Aboriginal from the 'Kirri tribe' (no record of a tribe with that exact name exists in Tindale's compendium [4.14]), nor did it state that she was born in Carnarvon Gorge, 172 kilometres south of her actual birth place, Springsure.[4.15] Instead, it records that she was born at the Wakenshaw's family home, *Fulham*, which had been built by her bushman father, Alexander, when he settled in Springsure in 1870. Lucy's delivery was recorded as being by the town's *accoucheur* (obstetrician) Dr Joseph Callaghan, who in 1874 had been the second appointed surgeon at Springsure's new hospital. The assisting nurse (midwife) was noted as Ann Keaogh. The tall story about Pat's grandmother Lucy being born in Carnarvon Gorge, that Ron Merkel QC related to the court as he read her witness statement, clearly did not match the documentary evidence.[4.16]

At the time, Ron Merkel QC made no comment as to the veracity of his client's claims and pushed on delivering Pat's affirmed witness statement before Justice Bromberg:

> My grandmother's mother was an Aboriginal woman called Kitty. My grandmother had a non-Aboriginal father. My grandmother's father was, I believe, **Adam Wakenshaw**, although she was raised by his older brother, Alexander Wakenshaw. Adam Wakenshaw was a carter. Carters often had Aboriginal women as slave sex partners or assistants. My grandmother lived with my mother and our family from 1947 until her death in 1950. I have photos of Lucy; she is clearly Aboriginal but not particularly dark.

Alexander Wakenshaw	m. – 10 April 1857 Collingwood, Victoria	**Jane (Jean) Lindsay Cousins**
b. 1832 Coldstream, Berwickshire, **Scotland** – d. 23 June 1913 Springsure, Queensland *(Pat's Great-grandfather)*		b. 1835 Kinross, Kinross- shire, **Scotland** – d. 2 September 1907 Springsure, Queensland *(Pat's Great-grandmother)*
Lucy Harriet Wakenshaw	m. 18 November 1895 Springsure, Queensland	**William Eatock (Rose)**
b. 7 June 1874 Springsure, Queensland – d. 12 February 1950 Brisbane, Queensland *(Pat's grandmother)*		b. 19 August 1869 Gympie, Queensland – d. 21 May 1943 Prahran, Victoria *(Pat's grandfather)* **See Figure 4.1**
Roderick Eatock	m. 1932 Glebe, NSW	**Elizabeth Stevenson Stuart-Anderson**
b. 5 July 1909 Brewarrina, NSW – d. 18 June 1987 Sydney, NSW *(Pat's father)*		b. 20 May 1909 Ayr, Ayreshire, **Scotland** – d. 10 October 1979 Brisbane, Queensland *(Pat's mother)*
June Patricia "Pat" Eatock	m. 1957 Sydney, NSW	**Ronald Adam Eatock**
b. 14 December 1937 Redcliffe, Queensland – d. 17 March 2015		*(Pat's husband and first cousin – son of Roderick's brother, Richard Eatock)*

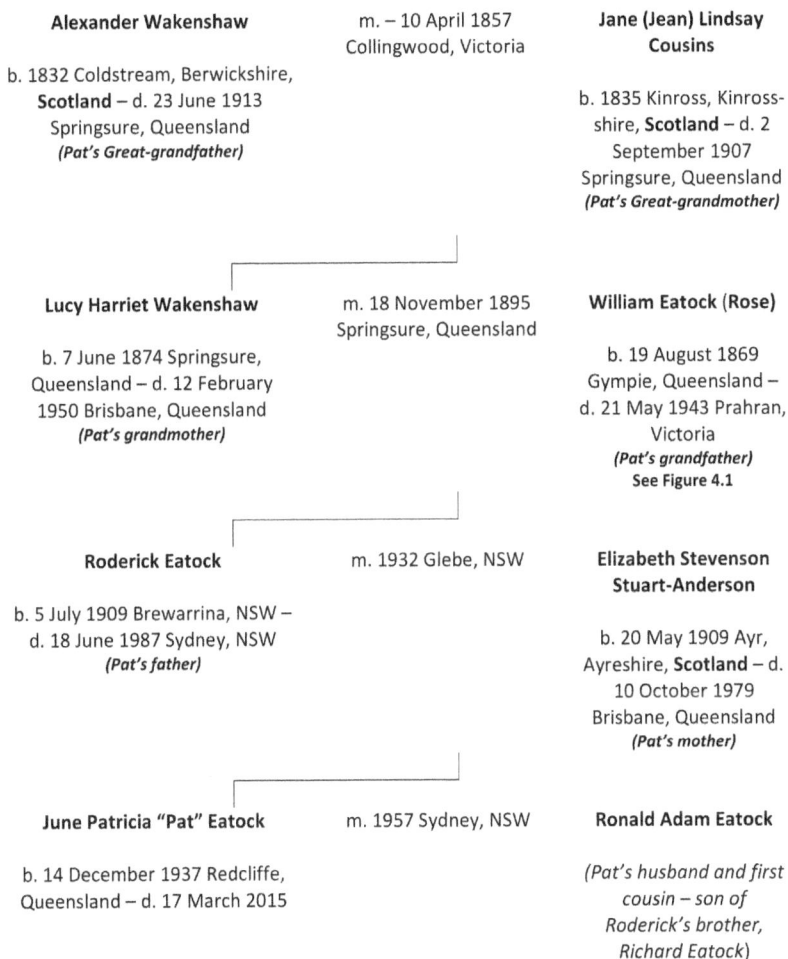

Figure 4.2: A branch of the apparent Eatock Family Tree showing Pat Eatock's line to her grandparents, William Eatock and Lucy Harriet Wakenshaw and then on to Lucy's Scottish parents. Download the detailed Family Tree at [4.2](subject to the *Disclaimer* on page (ii).)

One wonders whether Ron Merkel QC was conscious of the libellous nature of these assertions, as he slanderously transmitted them to the court, for slanderous indeed they were. As the birth record confirms, Alexander Wakenshaw was legally recorded as the father of Pat's grandmother, Lucy. She was born on 7 June 1874, so if Alexander's brother, Adam Wakenshaw, had really been Lucy's biological father, as Pat alleged, he would have had to have cohabited with Kitty in the Carnarvon Gorge/Springsure area some 40 weeks earlier, around 1 September 1873.

Unfortunately for Pat's tall tale, Adam was a well-respected and busy farmer with his own large family and had always lived in the Euroa region of Victoria, some 1,800 kilometres south of Springsure.[4.17] And more importantly, as documentary proof that Adam could not have fathered a child around 1 September 1873 in Springsure, a notice in Victoria's *North Eastern Ensign* newspaper recorded that Adam Wakenshaw was to be at a farmer's meeting he had called at Duck Ponds in Victoria on 3 September 1873.[4.18] Adam could not have been at two places, 1,800 kilometres apart, at the one time. He physically could not have been in the Springsure area fathering a child with his alleged slave sex partner Kitty while chairing a schoolhouse meeting in Duck Ponds, Victoria.

The sad irony one often sees in the process of exposing fakes is how desperate they are to abandon and to even hate their own European heritage in exchange for some self-appointed life as a fake Aborigine, putting on a coloured T-shirt and trying to live in a culture they will never understand, nor gain any real acceptance within. Pat Eatock would have done better justice to herself and her family if she had studied and embraced her own Scottish heritage, perhaps heeding the warning of her real tribal elder **Sir Walter Scott**:[15]

> *O what a tangled web we weave*
> *When first we practice to deceive*

---

[15]Sir Walter Scott, *Marmion* (canto 6, stanza 17), 1908.

Without providing any further detail or documentary proof, Pat Eatock had simply asserted that, "My grandmother's mother was an Aboriginal woman called Kitty", despite Lucy's birth record legally confirming her mother to be, '**Jane Lindsay Cousins**' (Alexander Wakenshaw's wife).[4.16] Further into her witness statement she claimed:

> I have photos of Lucy; she is clearly Aboriginal but not particularly dark.

An inspection of three available photographs, said to be of Lucy Eatock, would not, to many people's mind, reflect a 'clearly Aboriginal' appearance. Rather, Lucy clearly had similarities in facial structure and appearance to her solid, Scottish birth record mother, Jane Wakenshaw (*nee* Cousins), as one would expect.[4.19]

The late Joan Eatock, Pat's sister, had her own theories about Lucy's Aboriginality too, although she was much more vague about where it had originated from. In her somewhat aptly named book, *Delusions of Grandeur*, Joan just states that Lucy was a 'half-caste', but does not provide any evidence to support her claim. Joan however does introduce an Aboriginal woman named Kitty into the household, as Pat did in her court witness statement, but she does not say how Kitty relates to Lucy's assumed Aboriginality. Perhaps she was letting her readers connect the imaginary and scandalous dots themselves?

The fact that the sisters had 'disagreements about interpretation' of the family's oral history was revealed by Pat under cross-examination by Bolt's counsel, Mr Young:[16]

Young: Now, you and your sister Joan have taken a view, or expressed a view in the family history about your family descent lines, have you not?

Eatock: I'm sorry, I cannot accept responsibility for

---

[16] *Eatock v Bolt*, Trans. Proc., Fed. Court (Vic) O/N 160844, Mon 28 Mar 2011, Day One, p70.

anything that Joan wrote. We have – we had, while she was alive, we had disagreements about interpretation in very many parts of that book.

Young: Yes, all right. Well, let me ask you this: some of your relatives do not identify themselves as Aboriginal, as you do?

Eatock: That's right.

Young: They've made different decisions about their Aboriginal identity?

Eatock: That's right.

The Real Story from the Joan Eatock Archives

Archival material held at the Australian Institute of Aboriginal and Torres Strait Islander Studies (AIATSIS) in Canberra was found to shed further light on Joan's interpretation of Lucy's ancestry, and it is a very dim light indeed that inspires no confidence whatsoever in what Pat or Joan have asserted. The archive holds the research and transcription notes from a series of interviews that the ABC podcaster **Lea Redfern** held in 1999 with people connected to the Eatock family.[17] Redfern used their input to produce an *ABC Radio* podcast for the 1999 *Hindsight* program, *Lucy's Legacy*. In one of the archival interview transcripts, Redfern records (reproduced below in Redfern's annotations with some abridgment and editing of grammar and spelling) Joan's candid comments that confirm she had no real evidence to support her claims about the birth of her grandmother - "I just don't know" is her final conclusion:

Joan Eatock: ... it was only occasionally she'd come across this [racism] all of a sudden and the more she was with her husband, she'd find that the more she was dragged in to [*sic*] being a Koorie - even though (laughs) [one] couldn't deny it

---

[17]AIATSIS Call number MS 4304 - Research papers of Joan E Eatock.

but the thing was that she had never - you don't ask yourself in the mirror and think, "Ooh I'm a Koorie, I'm an Aboriginal person" - you see yourself ... you just see yourself - and she was shocked, you know, when she came across racism, and the more she was with her husband [William (Bill) Eatock], who I think - by the colour of their sons - was a bit darker than what she was ...

... she [Lucy] didn't look to be accepted in the Aboriginal community, she looked to be accepted in the European Community which was the sad part of the whole family.

Lucy grew up in Springsure Queensland. She was the eighth child - according to the birth certificate too - and I'm putting question marks there and its nothing I know, so I can't really say. It's a question mark - Ahhh to, um, Jane Lindsay Cousins and Alexander Wakenshaw ...

Interviewer [Lea Redfern]: Now, you put question marks around the birth certificate, can you tell me why?

Eatock: Because the resemblance between the photos I've seen of her isn't there - there isn't that much resemblance - and I just don't know how. She's an Aboriginal woman - Jane Lindsay Cousins may have been an Aboriginal woman - it could have been that way. I can't find Jane Lindsay Cousins coming to Australia on any boat record, I can't, I haven't tried to get her birth certificate from Scotland where she is supposed to have come from ... [*but Dark Emu Exposed researchers have now found Jane Lindsay Cousins recorded on the Census' in Scotland in 1841, '51 & '61 and her arrival in Brisbane on the boat,* Jessie Munn, *1862.* [4.20]].

... Jane Lindsay Cousins, she could have been Aboriginal but they [other extended family members] deny it, and I'm not gunna [*sic*] argue with them. If she wasn't an aboriginal woman she wasn't my grandmother's mother - it's just that simple, but if she was an Aboriginal woman, she could have been, I don't know. I don't trust just bits of paper that somebodies [*sic*] written - that's not to my [*sic*] proving anything when I know the woman.

Interviewer: So, if Jane wasn't your grandmother's mother, who do you think was?

Eatock: - well it could have been Kitty. Kitty was the housekeeper and in my aunt's memoirs she said a lot about Kitty and I remember her talking about Kitty, but not anything specific, but as soon as I saw Kitty it triggered some memories - my thoughts - that I had heard about Kitty, but I don't know how many people talk so much about the house-keeper, the kitchen girl or the young Aboriginal girl who was there.

Interviewer: So what do you think happened in that family?

Eatock: - well if Jane Lindsay - if - this is all supposition, but if Jane was a white woman, then I think she just had enough of having children and she shut the door on her husband, and when he went elsewhere, she probably just agreed to put - because he put her name on the birth certificate not her - he did a month after the baby was born and she might have just agreed to put her name down and fostered the child because obviously she was a nice woman ... I don't know where the truth comes from - all I know is that they produced a very strong, very handsome, Aboriginal woman [Lucy] and how she was produced, I just don't know.

Reading these notes by Redfern, one can see that Joan refuses to accept the birth certificate evidence that Jane Lindsay Cousins was Lucy's mother - 'I don't trust just bits of paper that somebodies [*sic*] written,' she tells Redfern. Instead, she falls back on that old favourite of amateur family historians 'oh, the photo of Lucy's mum just doesn't show any resemblance to Lucy so she can't have been her mum.' Joan wants, indeed *needs*, Lucy to be Aboriginal and she ignores any evidence to the contrary.

Lea Redfern also interviewed **Hall Greenland** in 1999

during her research into Lucy Eatock. Greenland wrote the ADB entry on Lucy (Harriet) Eatock, where he diplomatically pointed out that it was only:

> Lucy's grandchildren and great-grandchildren [who] reclaimed their Aboriginality [and only they] suggested that Lucy's mother had been Kitty, an Aboriginal woman employed by the Wakenshaws. Neither Lucy nor any of her children [eg. Roderick, Pat and Joan's father] is known to have made such an assertion. The grandchildren [Pat & Joan] had made these suggestions about Lucy's Aboriginality in the new 'time of reawakened pride for indigenous Australians.[4.4]

During her interview of Greenland, Redfern probed the family's attitude to their Aboriginality:

Interviewer: [Did] you talk [about the] family's attitude to their Aboriginality?

Greenland: Wasn't talked about ... only post Lucy's death in 1950s ... that people started to talk ... some of the Eatocks decided to claim [Aboriginality] ... others decided they were now part of white society and they've never mentioned it again and may or may not become annoyed if people did raise it ...

But then Greenland just goes on, with no evidence or documentary proof of his own, to parrot the hearsay of Pat and Joan when he tells his interviewer that:

> And I think Lucy was the result of, and I think there must have been a bit of this, a liaison between a white father and Kitty the housekeeper, the Aboriginal housekeeper.

The most troubling aspect of this family oral history is the lack of evidence about the central character, the so-called Kitty. No one has provided any evidence, photograph, diary entry or other documented proof for the existence of this woman, who is said to have been a family employee in the 1870s-80s. Joan Eatock is expecting her readers to believe what she says about Kitty based on an aunt's unpublished memoirs and Joan's own 'triggered' memories after she says she saw a photograph of

Kitty - an unpublished photograph as Joan did not deem it worthy of inclusion with the other family photographs in her book. And all this speculation was being formulated as Joan wrote her book, some 120 years after Kitty was supposed to have lived with the Wakenshaws. It all just sounds like a made up story to fit Pat and Joan's narrative that they, alone amongst all of Lucy's grandchildren, were Aboriginal.

But then a hint of who the mysterious Kitty might have been was found in the archives.

Lucy's Letter

In August 1925, a 'letter to the editor' appeared in Sydney's *Labor Daily*. It came from LH Eatock, who was none other than Pat and Joan's grandmother, Lucy (Harriet) Eatock, herself.

> KANAKA HISTORY,
>
> Sir, — Re the alleged enslaving of the Kanaka. I am a native of Springsure (not Springshore), and I know of no inhuman treatment of Kanakas. About 1884 a few were brought from the Islands, amongst them being four for Mr. Henry Richards, three men and one woman. One of the men went mad and murdered his two mates. My mother took the woman, and she was a very slow worker, but very kind and good to us children. She lived only a few years ... I am certain that no Kanakas were treated as slaves round Springsure.— Yours, etc.,
>
> L. H. EATOCK. Bankstown [Sydney][18]

Could this South Sea Islander woman, a Tongan named Lizzie or Tacrow (from the inquest notes) have been the faint family oral history memory that ultimately became, 120 years later, the 'Kitty' of Pat and Joan? Grandma Lucy Eatock had been moved enough in 1925 to write 'to the editor' about a black housekeeper of her childhood, of 40 years prior. By the late 1940s, Lucy was living with her then 10-year-old or so grandchildren, Pat and Joan, re-telling the family stories of

---

[18]L H Eatock, 'Kanaka History', *The Labor Daily*, Sydney, 11 Aug 1925, p4.

the past. Was this particular story of the black housekeeper, from the childhood memories of Pat and Joan, reimagined to become 'Kitty, the Aboriginal'? The modified story of Kitty could thus be retold, as Hall Greenland implied, at a 'time of reawakened pride for indigenous Australians' and provide the link to 'blackness' that Pat and Joan needed as reawakened Aboriginal women.

Lucy would have been about seven when the horrific killings of the Kanaka men - the Marmadilla Tragedy - was reported in the press in 1881.[4.21] It is quite possible that the sole survivor of the group, the black Kanaka 'gin' (from the press reports), was taken in by the Wakenshaws and looked after Lucy.

Many observers would see the Presbyterian Wakenshaws as being very compassionate people by taking in a 'black' Kanaka survivor from a mass killing. Somehow, when one reads the published life of Alexander Wakenshaw[4.22] - his successful rise from poor immigrant, to bushman and farmer and family man on the Queensland frontier, and ultimately to a respected civic and church figure in Springsure - and then compares that to the so-called achievements of his granddaughters, Pat and Joan Eatock, with their lives of relative poverty and libellous, unfounded accusations against Alexander's family, one just feels so disappointed that the family's proud colonial heritage ended up being trashed like this by its descendants.

We will probably never know for certain who this imaginary Aboriginal Kitty was, or even if she existed at all, but the following story is a good example of just how far Joan Eatock would go in reimagining the family's past.

Joan's Imaginary Cattle Brand

Joan Eatock's *Delusions of Grandeur* is riddled with tall stories based on embellished or even false tales, whose sole aim is to subtly guide the reader into believing the family has an oppressed Aboriginal ancestry. In one tale, Joan wrote:

> Lucy had written away and registered a cattle brand in the family name. A simple 'WE', the brand was fashioned out of two pieces of metal, four inches in length by one-and-a-half inches in width and about an inch deep. When not in use the two pieces would fit together simply by reversing the W into the E and pushing them together. Their branding iron became as inconspicuous as a tobacco tin and as easily carried around in a pocket. When in use, the brand would be slipped onto a split green twig taken from a nearby tree and held over a fire. It was a very slow way of branding, but very safe. Bill knew that it would go badly with him if he, or any Aborigine, was caught with a branding iron. If disturbed in the act, the two metal pieces could be doused in water, pushed together and thrown in the long grass to be retrieved later. The intruder would find Bill sitting, playing with a green stick, by a fire. So what if the temperature was up close to a century, the bosses never queried the stupidity of anything a black did. The owners of the vast properties rounded up stock and branded the young calves only once a year. A cattle duffer would slip in and drive off a dozen or so of these unbranded calves and as soon as possible legalise their ownership by putting their own brand on them. The prime beef was then driven south to market. Bill would never do this while other work was to be found. - (*ibid.*, p13-4.)

Joan wants the reader to believe that William and Lucy were two oppressed Aborigines, living on the margins of a white society that denied them their fair share of the pastoral boom. She implies William had to use the subterfuge of getting his wife to apply for a registered cattle brand that he could only use in secret. This is completely wrong. Both William and Lucy were quite entitled to apply for a brand legally under Queensland's Brands Act 1872, which is exactly what they both independently did.

A year prior to his marriage to Lucy, William already had his own 3-digit stock brand registered - a notice had appeared in a *Supplement to the Queensland Government Gazette* to advise he had been granted a 'change of residence' of where the brand was to be used. Not to be outdone by her husband, Lucy obtained a brand in her own name by transferring (buying?) one from a Ned Collins in the year 1901, as reported in the *Queensland Government Gazette*.[4.23]

This is perplexing for Joan Eatock's readers - if William and Lucy were oppressed Aborigines, how were they legally allowed to register their own stock brands? What was the real story in the 1890s-1900s - were Aborigines allowed to own brands or not? Or maybe William and Lucy were just not Aboriginal after all?

Another fundamental error Joan made in this fabricated story about her ancestor's hidden 'WE' cattle-brand is that, under Queensland law, all brands had to be of three digits: either, two letters plus one numeral; or two signs and one numeral. William and Lucy's legally registered brands were both of three digits. It was not possible, as Joan claims, that 'Lucy had written away and registered a cattle brand ... a simple "WE".' An application for the 2-digit 'WE' would have been rejected and any cattle with a 2-digit brand would have been seen as being clearly unregistered and rejected at market. The truth is that Bill and Lucy did not fabricate some illegal brand, but rather they complied with the law.[19]

Joan Plays the 'Race Card'

Joan Eatock weaves a speculative black/white narrative, for which she offers no corroborating evidence, regarding how Lucy and Bill married in Springsure. She then distorts the truth regarding what happened in their lives a decade later at the time of the birth of Roderick, their seventh child. This culminated, she says, in Bill's decision to leave Lucy and their new home in Brewarrina:

> It was here [in a boxing tent in Springsure] that she first laid eyes on Bill, or William, as she preferred to call him. This

---

[19]William's brand was "J6E" and Lucy's "ONQ".[4.23]

man took her breath away with his natural grace, near perfect physique and dark skin. They married [in 1895] despite the anger of the other members of the family and the rows that were sure to follow. Lucy was six months pregnant with her first child before her wedding to 'the best man around'. Had it simply been a physical attraction, or was it also an act of defiance? Lucy felt a stab of pain as she remembered how the older girls in the family had put pressure on the young newlyweds to leave town. Their family were respected members of the white community and, but for the occasional slight, she had been accepted despite her origins. Lucy's obvious Aboriginal appearance saved Bill. If his attentions had been given to a white girl, his fate would have been much different.

But that was long ago. Now Lucy had seven children to care for and she was determined to do her best by all of them. Roderick's birth would be the last contact he would have with his father for many years...

It had become obvious to Lucy that while Bill and their dark-skinned older boys were around she would not be accepted in Brewarrina. It was almost a relief to her when soon after Roderick's birth, Bill feeling too restricted at the meat-works set off to find work up country, taking with him the three eldest boys, Don, George and Alex. And so there was to be no-one to teach Roderick about men's business ... Bill had only done as Indigenous custom had expected of him. He removed the young males from the influence and care of women. Boys who had reached a certain standard of development (this was not age related) would be taken and educated in the knowledge and skills of men's business. Mixing his customs with the necessities of the white man's world, Bill took the boys into the bush to work with horses and at times travel with boxing troupes. Lucy knew that Bill Eatock didn't consider his leaving to be a desertion of his family. He had been brought up in a mixture of cultures so that no one social norm prevailed. She would never stop loving him, for wasn't he still 'the best man around'?

An educated woman, Lucy was well known throughout the bush for her skills. She was hopeful ... she would be able to find work as a housekeeper on a property ... Her family had managed better than many of their Aboriginal brothers and sisters, but now, with the departure of Bill and the older boys, Lucy would have to forge a new life for them ... At one stage Lucy found work as a housekeeper on a station homestead

called **Yambacoona**. [I]n 1912, Lucy found she had another
baby to care for when Noel was born. The circumstances
surrounding **Noel's birth were quite mysterious.** Lucy
had packed the family up and headed back to Sydney and
her friend Mrs Henderson. Leaving all the children in her
care, and with only Cath [her daughter] for company, Lucy
then visited some of her mother's relations in Euroa, Victoria.
A few months later they returned with the new baby. For
the next thirteen years, Lucy worked long hours as a cook or
housekeeper on various places west of Sydney. To say that her
children led lives lifted straight from an Australian version of
a Dickens novel might give the reader some idea of the depth
of their despair. The children were frequently boarded with
strangers in private homes and boarding houses. They lived
on leftovers and were made to contribute to their keep by
doing chores. (emphasis added.)[20]

The fantasy Joan wants her readers to believe is again based
around the usual racial tropes: supposedly white racist attitudes in Brewarrina, where Joan claims Lucy's 'dark-skinned
older boys' were not accepted, coupled with the assertion that
'Aboriginal' boys needing to go through their traditional initiation rites, are the reasons why Bill took the boys and left
Lucy in Brewarrina. The reality is a lot more mundane. Joan's
grandmother Lucy had an affair while working at Yambacoona
Station, by which she got pregnant with her last child Noel
(b.1912 - d.unknown). When Bill found out he left her and
filed for divorce. Not the most ideal outcome for the sake of
the children, but perhaps understandable from Bill's point of
view. The divorce petition, lodged in 1915, details the sad circumstances.[4.24] The unfortunate consequences - Bill wander-
ing the country, pursued for maintenance payments until his
death in Prahran, Melbourne in 1943 - follow a typical working class trajectory from the early 20th century.[4.25] Nothing
particularly Aboriginal about these social conditions at all -
just another tall story from Joan seeking to fake her family's
Aboriginality by libelling her own white Australian family and
its society.

---

[20] Joan E Eatock, *Delusions of Grandeur*, p10-11 & p26-7.

When one reads of the family divisions caused by Joan's book of fantasy, as well as by Pat and her false claims to Aboriginality [4.26], and watches Pat's videos[4.27],[4.28],[4.29] where she relates the story of her attempt at fame and fortune as a communist, radical feminist and Aboriginal activist, only to end up with the broken-down life of penury that she described in court,[21] one can't help but feel very, very sad that the court judgment of Justice Bromberg is only going foster more of this racial disharmony in families as more fakes are encouraged.

In this chapter the focus was on providing examples where Pat and Joan fabricated much of their family's oral history in their effort to show that Lucy Eatock was Aboriginal. The evidence clearly shows that Lucy Eatock (*nee* Wakenshhaw) was not Aboriginal - both her parents had been born in Scotland, and nowhere in the archives was it found that she was ever referred to as being Aboriginal.

In the next chapter, evidence will be provided that William Eatock, Lucy's husband and grandfather to Pat and Joan, was not Aboriginal either, as the sisters claimed.

For References link - see QR code on page (xv)

References

[4.1]   Ron Merkel. *The Law Report, ABC Radio.* 23 May 2006.

[4.2]   *Apparent Full Eatock Family Tree.* 19 Aug 2024.

[4.3]   *1895 Marriage Record for William (Bill) Eatock and Lucy Harriet Wakenshaw.* QLDBDM 1895/C/1891, 18 Nov 1895.

[4.4]   Hall Greenland. *Australian Dictionary of Biography - Lucy Harriet Eatock.* 2005.

[4.5]   Ancestry.com. *Family Trees from other Eatock Family Members.* 2024.

[4.6]   *Evidence Catherine Davidson was born in Scotland.* 2024.

[4.7]   Youtube. *Pat Eatock as a black activist feminist.* 1990s?

[4.8]   Joan Eatock. *Joan Eatock Book Launch Flyer.* jukurrpa books, Indigenous publishers, Alice Springs, 2003.

---

[21] *Eatock v Bolt*, Trans. Proc., Fed. Court (Vic) O/N 160844, Mon 28 Mar 2011, Day One, p60.

[4.9]   Lea Redfern. *Lucy Eatock, Legacy and Family, on ABC Radio, Hindsight Program Promo.* 27 June 1999.

[4.10] ABC. *Roberta 'Bobbi' Sykes honoured in Sydney.* 2010.

[4.11] The Evening Telegraph (Charters Towers Qld). *A Colored Coon in Court.* Trove, 8 Feb 1908 p.1.

[4.12] Electoral Rolls. *1903-1980 Queensland, Eatock - Lucy & William, 1903ff.*

[4.13] Qld Parliament. *Indigenous Suffrage Timeline Factsheet Queensland.* accessed: July 2015.

[4.14] Norman Tindale. *Aboriginal Tribes of Australia.* ANU, 1974.

[4.15] Google Maps. *Springsure - Carnarvon Gorge Map.* 2024.

[4.16] *Birth Record for Lucy Harriet Wakenshaw.* QLDBDM 1874/C/3610, 1874.

[4.17] *Research Notes on Adam Wakenshaw (1837-1904).* 2024.

[4.18] Notice. *Adam Wakenshaw jnr Farmer's Meeting Duck Ponds. The North Eastern Ensign,* Benalla, Vic., 22 Aug 1873, p3.

[4.19] Photographs. *Of Lucy Eatock (3) and mother Jane Wakenshaw (1).* Source: family members on *Ancestry.com.*

[4.20] *Research Notes on Jane Lindsay Wakenshaw (nee Cousins) (1835-1907).* 25 Aug 2024.

[4.21] Morning Bulletin Rockhampton Qld. *The Marmadilla Tragedy.* 29 Oct 1881, p2.

[4.22] *Research Notes on Alexander Wakenshaw (1832-1913).* 25 Aug 2024.

[4.23] *Research Notes on William and Lucy Eatock's registered stockbrands.* 25 Aug 2024.

[4.24] *Divorce and Matrimonial Cause Case Papers-Records NSW, Petition by William Eatock for Divorce from his Wife Lucy on the Account of Adultery, No. 616 of 1915, NRS-13495.* 1915.

[4.25] *Research Notes on the later life of William and Lucy Eatock.* 25 Aug 2024.

[4.26] Pat and Cathy Eatock. Michelle Arrow (Ed). *The Personal is Political, in Women and Whitlam, Revisiting the Revolution.* Newsouth, April 2023.

[4.27] Youtube. *Pat Eatock with a Version of her Declaring her Aboriginality.* ca1990s?

[4.28] Youtube. *Pat Eatock speaks of her early political life of as a black, feminist, activist.* ca1990s?

[4.29] Youtube. *Pat Eatock being interviewed about her political life and her father, Roderick Eatock.* 1977.

Chapter 5

Merkel's Magic Wand - Turning Whites into Blacks

The greatest dangers to Indigenous Australians lurk in insidious encroachment by men of zeal, well-meaning, but without understanding.

Former Justice Ron Merkel[1]

Looking for William Eatock

By the time *Eatock v Bolt* went to trial in 2011, there were already a number of published references regarding the ancestry of William Eatock, Pat Eatock's paternal grandfather. Firstly, in 1999, *ABC Radio* had broadcast a podcast, *Lucy's Legacy*, which is believed to have mentioned, in passing, William's life while focusing on the program's main subject, his wife Lucy Harriet Eatock.[2][5.3]

As discussed in Chapter 4, the podcast's producer, **Lea**

---

[1]From a speech in 2012[5.1] where Merkel paraphrased a 1928 comment by US Justice Brandeis.[5.2]

[2]The podcast appears to be no longer available publicly.

Redfern interviewed historian **Hall Greenland** as part of her research. The rough transcription notes of these interviews can today be found in the Canberra AIATSIS archives as a part of the Joan E Eatock collection.[3] As Greenland told Redfern during their interview:

Greenland: ... all of my research points to the very obvious fact that their [*sic* there] was Aboriginality. That Bill [William] Eatock was probably orphaned during the Frontier Wars in Queensland, that he was adopted by a [*sic*] Scottish parents. He had a white older brother and a white younger brother both of whom have birth certificates that have been traced and Bill's [certificate] wasn't ... [*discussed further below.*]

Interviewer: Why do you think that Lucy and her children didn't talk about their Aboriginality?

Greenland: Wow that is a good question. I think they didn't talk about it because, for two reasons: one they didn't know ... there was racial prejudice so they didn't want to invoke that ... shame [of] the lesser race [and then the] second reason, [a] good reason, everybody [was] supposed to have overcome [by the] second half of century - people started facing up and talking about it, but [back] then people didn't talk about it. [E]specially, if you lived in white society. They lived in an urban setting - they were workers - regardless of racial and cultural origins ... in that generation people wanted to be Australians ... melting pot people.

Greenland correctly pointed out that William's mother, Catherine Davidson, did have two other sons, both 'white' - **Donald Eatock** born in 1866, three years before William, and **James Eatock** born in 1871 (two years after William) but who died within a month. The researchers were unable to find any other children recorded as being born to Catherine beyond these three - the two 'white' sons and then William.[5.4]

---

[3] AIATSIS MS 4304.

Greenland was correct, at the time of his interview in 1999, that no birth record c1869 in the name of a William Eatock had ever been found in the archives. This is still the case today. All the other commentators have therefore relied upon William Eatock's own marriage record, and his mother's marriage records, and the birth records of her two 'white' sons, to show that the Englishman, Timothy Eatock, [b. c1828 - d. unknown] was allegedly William's father. There is no dispute, except of course by his grandchildren - Pat and Joan Eatock - who needed William to have had an Aboriginal mother and/or father to support their narrative and claims for Aboriginality.

Unlike the amateur storyteller that Joan Eatock turned out to be, Greenland at least studied history at University,[4] but the methodology he alludes to, in determining why he thought William was Aboriginal, is a novel approach to doing history to say the least. He observed that Catherine Eatock had two 'white' sons with, he believed, Timothy Eatock, and their births were recorded. Catherine's other son William had no birth record and Greenland seizes on this as an opportunity to further the so-called 'Frontier War' theory. This theory was gaining much momentum by the late 1990s in which its adherents claimed the Queensland pastoral frontier had been a place of brutal and constant warfare between the Aborigines and the settlers and pastoralists. The theorists claimed it had led to widespread killings, and even massacres, of Aboriginal people such that numerous Aboriginal children emerged during this period as orphans, or were simply adopted or stolen to be enslaved as house-gins or stock-boys. Even Pat Eatock in her court witness statement promoted the theory by falsely claiming that her great-grandfather's brother, Adam Wakenshaw, had kept an Aboriginal woman as a 'slave sex partner'.[5]

In line with this theory, Greenland, with no real evidence, unabashedly speculated that the reason why no one has lo-

---

[4] *Wikipedia: Hall Greenland.*

[5] *Eatock v Bolt*, Trans. Proc., Federal Court (Vic), Bromberg J, Pat Eatock and Andrew Bolt and Another, O/N 160844, Mon 28 March 2011, Day One, p60.

cated a birth record for William Eatock, the 'black' boy, is because, as he told Redfern, he was, "probably orphaned during the Frontier Wars in Queensland [and] that he was adopted by a [sic] Scottish parents". Greenland then went on to write the 2005 ADB entry for Lucy Harriet Eatock, where he recorded her husband William as being 'an Aboriginal stockman'. He cites no specific documentary evidence to support the claim of Aboriginality for William. The editorial staff at the ADB approved his methodology when they peer-reviewed Greenland's submission and then allowed it to be published.[6]

This is not the correct way to do historical research. Historians who just join a series of dots in the historical record, hoping they are related, and make the observations fit their own pet-theory, are ultimately going to get found out, even if it is twenty years later, as this book will show.

The Methodology of Eatock's Genealogy

As the editor of the *Dark Emu Exposed* website I have received a number of appreciative comments from family history enthusiasts. They are fascinated by the methodology that accompanies many of the genealogical problems that are solved on the website and William Eatock's genealogy turned out to be just as fascinating. The methodology used illustrates the correct way to do historiography - thinking within the context of the times plus joining isolated historical observations with documentary, or other corroborating proof and evidence, rather than just relying on speculation or the parroting of the current orthodox narrative.

When our head genealogist arrived at the same contrary point in the Eatock family tree as everyone else had - on the one hand finding William at the top of his branch, but without a birth certificate; knowing that on his marriage record

---

[6]Greenland succumbed to 'presentism', that 'tendency in much Australian historical writing for authors to make judgments about the past that are really formulated out of their concern to advance a particular political agenda in the present.' John A Moses, *The Fallacy of Presentism in History, Quadrant online*, 18 Jan 2022.

his father and mother were recorded as Timothy [Thomas] Eatock and Catherine Davidson (born in England and Scotland respectively), but then, on the other hand, finding that academics, historians[7] and Federal Court jurists all believed William was somehow Aboriginal - she thought something was not right. Rather than just give up and fall into one of the two conflicting camps, she decided to make a cup of tea and think, and apply the historical method.

William probably wasn't just of English and Scottish heritage, she thought. No one had ever presented a photograph of him, but the family photographs that were available of two of his sons, Roderick (who was Pat and Joan's father) and Alex, clearly indicated there were some non-European, perhaps even Aboriginal, facial features and darker skin tones.[5.6] The family knew themselves there was some 'colour' in their ancestry, but it probably didn't really matter much to their daily lives until Pat and Joan's generation when, in the 1960s, skin colour started to take on a much more political and profitable dimension. Pat and Joan's mistake was that they just assumed, because they were in Australia, their father's obvious 'colour' was of Aboriginal origin when, as will be shown, it wasn't.

So Where Did the Family 'Blackness' Come From?

Our genealogist first explored the ancestry of Timothy Eatock and Catherine Davidson back in the United Kingdom. Did either of them have a 'coloured' family member that resulted in 'blackness' being brought into the Eatock family line when Timothy or Catherine emigrated to colonial Australia? After much research, no 'coloured' connections could be found. Then the research refocused on William's mother, Catherine Davidson. The records indicate she was not a 'settled' person. In 1866, at age 26, she had her first child out of wedlock, Donald, two years prior to marrying the boy's supposed father, Timothy Eatock. But then they appear to have separated and

---

[7]Peter Read, Hall Greenland, Angela Woollacott - see [5.5]

were recorded as living in different towns.[5.7]

Life could be tough for a single mother in colonial times and Catherine appears to have taken up with another man, or men, having two more children in the process, William and James. She gave the boys the surname Eatock because that was still her legally married name. In 1873, when she was in her early thirties, she married for a second time to a Thomas O'Neill. She probably became a bigamist with this second marriage, as no record has been found indicating she had divorced Timothy Eatock before marrying O'Neill.[5.8]

There is some indication that Catherine might have still been using the Eatock surname in 1874, even after marrying O'Neill, as a 'dead letter' record to that name has been found.[5.9] Thomas O'Neill died in 1879 and Catherine too seems to have disappeared from the records around this time.

Catherine's unsettled, perhaps even loose, character suggests there was a real possibility she might have had one or more children out of wedlock. She might have used her maiden name to record that child's birth. She might even have taken another man's surname unofficially. What this means is that the surname Eatock might not have been used to record her son William at his birth. This might explain why no birth certificate for a 'William Eatock' has ever been found.

The genealogists therefore began to search under the subject's maiden name, viz: 'women named Catherine Davidson, who recorded a birth in Queensland, within a 2 to 5 year buffer either side of 1869' (William's recorded date of birth from his marriage certificate - but he may have been wrong about his age). This search resulted in quite a few mothers named 'Catherine Davidson' being located - the respective fathers' names that were retrieved included a 'Thomas Gould', a 'Charles Ernest Koppe', a 'James McIntosh', amongst others. Each search result had to be individually checked and then, as the checking progressed, the word bingo! reverberated through the *Dark Emu Exposed* offices - for there he was; a child named

William in the 1869 *Birth Records Book* for the Wide Bay District (includes Gympie) in the Colony of Queensland kept by Registrar John Harry Stevens.[5.10]

The book recorded that a **Richard Rose** had fathered a child named William, on 19th August 1869, in the town of Gympie in Queensland. In the 'Mother' column was neatly written '*Catherine formerly Davidson*' Age: *27 years* [i.e. born c1842], Birthplace: *Edinburgh, Scotland.* [5.10] This was 'our' Catherine Eatock, *nee* Davidson, as her details matched the records of her early years in Scotland, as well as the details recorded for her marriages and on the birth records of her two other sons.

The records continued to support the idea that Catherine led a very unsettled or even a loose life:

a) On her marriage certificate to Timothy Eatock she recorded herself as a 'widow', but there is no record of her ever having been married before;

b) On her son William's birth record she told the registrar that she and the boy's father, Richard Rose, were married on '7 August 1867 [in] Sydney New South Wales'. This is not true. A search of the NSW marriage records revealed nothing. Was she trying to make William's birth look legitimate by making up a fake marriage in another colony that would have been harder for the registrar to check?

c) She had married Timothy Eatock on 24 August 1868, one year prior to giving birth to William on 19 August 1869, who was conceived with another man, Richard Rose. Catherine was thus having an affair with Richard just three months after her wedding day with Timothy. It is not surprising then the records indicate that Timothy and Catherine had separated and were living 230 kilometres apart shortly after getting married.[5.7]

Also noticeable is that the 'Informant' column on William's birth record says, '*Certified in writing by Catherine Rose mother Gympie'*. Catherine was calling herself and her child Rose, even though she never married Richard Rose. This is why no one had ever located a birth certificate for a William Eatock - there isn't one, because Eatock was his *adopted* name given to him after his birth. His name at birth was Rose, that of his biological father, Richard Rose.

Even more tantalising however, are the details recorded for William's father: *Richard Rose*; Profession: *Miner*; Age: *38 years* [i.e. born c1831]; **Birthplace: *Kingsto[w]n, St Vincent, West Indies***. Could this be the real source of the 'blackness' in the Eatock family line - the West Indies? At the risk of being accused of 'racial profiling', a close study of the Eatock family photographs does, in this new light, suggest that Pat and Joan's father, Roderick, might well have had West Indian rather than Aboriginal features.[5.6]

The genealogical research continued for the name of a 'Richard Rose' in Queensland and once again an important piece of evidence was found: on 11 December 1889 a **Richard Rose** had married an **Elizabeth Maria Wooding** in Charters Towers, Queensland. This was 'our' Richard Rose because the groom's details matched those of the Richard Rose on William Rose's birth record: Richard Rose, *Bachelor*; Aged: *57* [i.e. born c1832, 'same' as c1831 on his son William's birth record]; Profession: *Miner* [same as son's birth record]; Birthplace: *West Indies* [same as William's birth record]. The correlations were too close for it not to be the same Richard Rose.[5.11]

With the discovery of this marriage record however, the family history of Pat Eatock became a whole lot more interesting - much more interesting than even Pat herself could have imagined. For in the far right columns of the marriage record book appeared the names of Richard Rose's parents - William Rose and Harriet Williams - and his father's Profession - that of 'Planter'.[5.12]

It is worth pausing for a moment to consider what these new revelations might mean. Firstly, Richard Rose might have been the 'white' son of a West Indian planter, who came to Queensland seeking his fortune - his father William Rose and his mother Harriet (Rose) *nee* Williams on his marriage record both say, Scottish. If this was the case, he would have brought no 'colour' with him, so we are none the wiser as to where the Eatocks' self-perceived 'blackness' may have originated from.

Alternatively Richard Rose might have been the result of a union between his 'white' planter father, William Rose, and one of the female domestics or slaves on the plantation, Harriet Williams, who most certainly would have been 'black'. Richard was born in c1832, just before British slavery was formerly abolished in the empire, so he could well have been a slave himself. Was this the source of the 'blackness' in the Eatock family line?

Our genealogists were getting excited - were they about to open a secret door onto a whole new fascinating genealogical vista that no one in Australia had previously been aware of, not even the Eatocks'? Was the discovery of the real source of the Eatocks' 'blackness' - derived as it was from a West Indian slave - about to turn the judgment in the *Eatock v Bolt* case on its head?

But before the project took on the huge expense in time and money that delving into the genealogical records of the West Indies would entail, it was deemed prudent for the researchers to make absolutely sure this Richard Rose was the father of the boy William Rose. And they also had to be one hundred percent certain that William Rose really was William Eatock. And once again, as they say in Greece, 'the Gods were smiling', and the proof miraculously materialised.

Were William Rose and William Eatock the Same Person?

On the 28th of June 1870, a miner walked into the Gympie Mining Warden's office and lodged an application to transfer his mining lease on the goldfields. His name was **Richard Rose** and he had held a quartz mining claim on the New Monckland Reef No.1A North in Gympie since 9 March 1868. He now said he wanted to transfer his claim into the name of a four-year-old boy, a boy called **Donald Eatock**.[5.13] Donald Eatock had been born in 1866 and was the first son of Catherine Davidson. By endorsing this transfer, Richard Rose was essentially giving control of the mining lease to Catherine, the mother and legal guardian of young Donald.

But why would Richard Rose transfer this asset to the control of Catherine Davidson, who, within three months of acquiring it, subsequently transferred (sold?) it to a Riley Duckworth on 19 September 1870?[5.13] Readers will know why - because Richard Rose and Catherine Davidson had been in a previous relationship. Although they never married, Richard was the father to Catherine's younger boy, the one-year-old William Rose and, by this act of transfer, Richard was publicly acknowledging this relationship, as well as at least some responsibility to the future welfare of both Catherine and his son William. Donald, the four-year-old, was chosen as the recipient, rather than William, perhaps because William was still only a vulnerable baby, less than a year old.

This mining lease connection is documentary evidence there was a personal link between Richard Rose (a miner in Gympie, born in the West Indies) and the Eatock family - in this case Donald Eatock whose mother Catherine Eatock *nee* Davidson was also the mother to a boy born William Rose in Gympie, with a birth record to prove it. Ultimately, William Rose would acquire his mother's married name and would go on to become the Eatock family's apical ancestor, William Eatock.

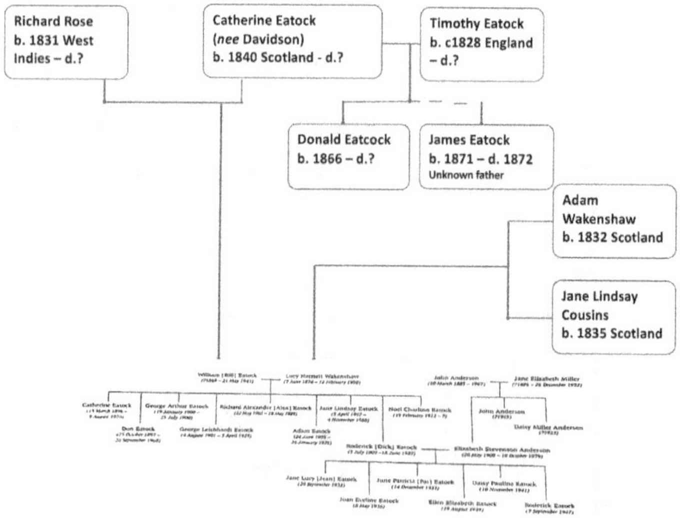

Figure 5.1: The original Family Tree published in Joan Eatock's book has William (Bill) Eatock and his wife Lucy Harriet Wakenshaw as the apical 'Aboriginal' grandparents of Pat and Joan Eatock [Lower section in graphic]. The new genealogical evidence confirms the parents of both William and Lucy were all born overseas (Scotland and West Indies). Thus William and Lucy could not have been Aboriginal (subject to the *Disclaimer* on page (ii).) See QR code [5.14] for a higher resolution image of Figure 5.1

5.1   *Eatock v Bolt* - A Miscarriage of Justice

The chain of documents presented so far confirms that William Eatock was really born William Rose and was of West Indian and Scottish descent, not Aboriginal - and we were the first to locate his birth record to prove it.[5.10]

This conclusion would normally justify the completion of the research project at this point, it now having been shown that the parents of William Eatock had both been born overseas, so William could not have been Aboriginal. The consequence of this must therefore be that the *Eatock v Bolt* case was a miscarriage of justice given that Pat Eatock had no standing in launching proceedings in the first place. She was not an 'Aboriginal person' by Justice Bromberg's own definition - she had no Aboriginal descent. Additionally, Pat Eatock's non-Aboriginal genealogy has now been proven to the point of satisfaction of the Briginshaw principle, a point that even her own counsel, Ron Merkel QC would concede (See Chapters 2.1 and 11.3).

The final, apparent family tree for Pat Eatock can now be presented two ways - as a modification to the Eatock Family Tree, as published by Joan Eatock in her book *Delusions of Grandeur* (Figure 5.1), and in a standard simple layout (Figure 5.2). The detailed apparent Eatock Family Tree can be downloaded by the QR code at [5.15].

But what would still be fascinating to know would be the answer to the question: Where is the evidence that Richard Rose was a 'man of colour'? This required the genealogists to open that secret door that led to the archives of the slave plantations of St Vincent and the Grenadines in the West Indies, and so they went through...

A Sliding Doors Moment

In a hot, humid office on the island of St Vincent in the West Indies, the Registrar, John Beresford, was certifying a copy of

Pat Eatock
b. Redcliffe Qld
1937 - 2015

Roderick Eatock
b. Brewarrina
NSW
1909 - 1987

Elizabeth Stevenson
Stuart Anderson
b. Scotland
1909 - 1979

William Eatock
(born Rose)
b. Gympie Qld
1869 - 1943

Lucy Wakenshaw
b. Springsure Qld
1874 - 1950

Richard Rose
b. West Indies
1831- ?

Catherine Davidson
[Eatock]
b. Scotland
ca1841 - ?

Alexander Wakenshaw
b. Scotland
1832-1913

Jane Cousins
b. Scotland
1845/6-1907

William Rose [planter]
b. West Indies
? - 1839

Harriet [Williams, slave]
b. West Indies or Africa
ca1805

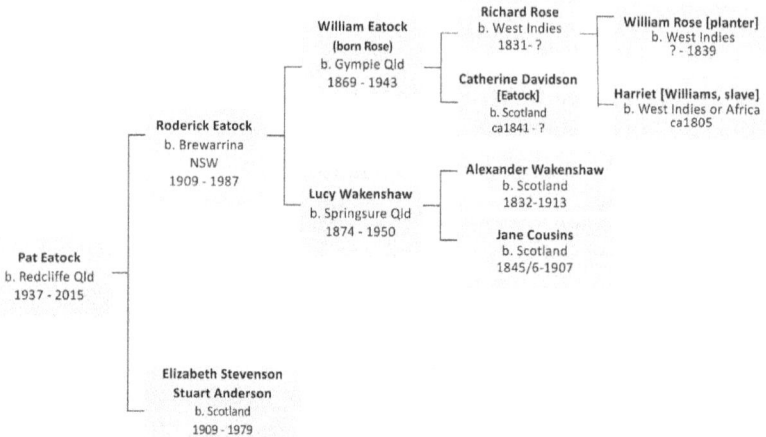

Figure 5.2: A summary of Pat Eatock's apparent Family Tree showing that all her ancestors came from only Scotland or the West Indies. The detailed apparent Family Tree is available for download [5.15](subject to the *Disclaimer* on page (ii).)

the last Will and Testament of a local planter, **William Rose**. It was the 21st of November 1838 and a 'Sliding Doors moment'[8] was in play that would ultimately influence Australian socio-political policy in the early 21st century along with the legacy of an Australian journalist, Andrew Bolt, although of course no one in Beresford's office knew, or even cared, at the time.

Beresford had been a busy man since the Slavery Abolition Act had been passed in Britain in 1833. The slave-plantation system in the islands of St Vincent and the Grenadines[5.16] was being overturned and the planters were frantically getting their estates, paperwork and wills adjusted to cope with the impending changes to their old social and economic order. One of Bereford's clients, William Rose, who owned the Union Estate on the small island of Bequia (pron. *bek-way*) had already received his 3,882 pound stirling compensation

---

[8] *Wikipedia: Sliding doors.*

package, two years prior in 1836, in exchange for the liberation of his 166 'negro' slaves.[5.17] The Will of William Rose provided the details of the impending Sliding Doors moment; for while some planters had taken their compensation money and run, leaving their slaves to fend for themselves, and other more unscrupulous types had taken their compensation, but then still on-sold their slaves to planters outside the British islands where slavery was still legally practiced, [5.18] those specific slaves on William Rose's estate that he had fathered with slave women - all seven of them - were provided for when his Will was proved in 1840, a year after his death.

His eight-year-old son, **Richard Rose**, was one of those seven child beneficiaries. It is fascinating to speculate that if William hadn't left him the modest funds in his Will that appeared to have allowed Richard to escape the islands, become a seaman and make his way to a 'new' New World on the Queensland goldfields, then Richard would not have had a son, William Eatock, and 'blackness' would not have entered Pat Eatock's family line. Pat would then not have mistakenly, or perhaps deliberately, self-identified as a 'black woman', and an Aboriginal activist black woman in particular. Journalist Andrew Bolt would then not have been dragged into court, to be defeated by Pat, an 'angry and upset'[9] woman who was allowed to bring her complaint because Justice Bromberg had created a new class category for her to do so, that of the 'fair-skinned' Aboriginal person. Simply put, no inheritance for Richard Rose in the West Indies, no *Eatock v Bolt* in Australia.[10]

But as the executor read the Will, it became apparent that William had not slipped through the 'sliding door' that would have left his slave-children out of his Will - instead William had decided to leave them funds for their care and education:

---

[9] *Eatock v Bolt*, Trans. Proc., Fed. Court (Vic) O/N 160844, Mon 28 Mar 2011, Day One, p58.

[10] Indeed, did this trial only ever proceed because of the unique qualities, abilities and career history of the lead applicant - the witness for the prosecution - Pat Eatock? (see Chapter 8.2.3).

I, William Rose of Bequia within the Government of Saint Vincent ... bestow and bequeath my house ... in Kingstown and all my plate linen and furniture of every description unto Charlotte Jardine [his wife] ... and after her decease to my three children Elizabeth, Grace and Georgiana [three of his legitimate and white children] to be equally divided ...

I give my house in the town of Bequia unto my children Carrington, John and Mary [three of his illegitimate, 'coloured' children]...

I give devise and bequeath all my other real and Personal Estate of what nature ... Unto William Rose Scott, William M'Donald, Adam Stelly and Charles Shephard of Saint Vincent Esquires ... in trust for the following purposes -

first to pay all my just debts and funeral expenses and the charges of proving my Will;

also to sell and dispose of my estate in Bequia with all convenient speed and to secure the sum of four thousand four hundred pounds Sterling in good security in the names of my said trustees for the benefit of my eleven children;

and to pay to care of my four children Jane, Elizabeth, Grace & Georgiana [the 'white' issue from his wife] the sum of six hundred pounds sterling;

and the sum of three hundred pounds sterling to care of my seven children Carrington, John, Mary, Elenora, Duke, **Richard** and Favorita [the 'coloured' issue from his slave women] as they respectively attain the age of twenty-one years or days of marriage and in the meantime the interest to be applied to their maintenance and education and the share of any child dying under age and unmarried to be divided among the survivors ... etc, etc

    - **extracts of the Last Will and Testament of William Rose Jnr.** [d. 1839][11]

And so history turns - a simple, just decision to help an illegitimate slave-boy ultimately leads to a great injustice nearly two centuries later, on a continent far away, that will have adverse repercussions for a journalist, his society's free speech, and for generations of real Aboriginal people.

---

[11]See complete original Will[5.19] and a part transcription.[5.20]

The Gympie Miner & the Coloured Slave of Bequia

Despite all the evidence presented so far, some readers might still be thinking, "Where is the evidence that *really proves* the Australian Richard Rose was this particular Richard Rose, the slave-child beneficiary of William Rose's Will? Sure, they have the same surname, but where is the evidence linking them?"

It is true that, except for the 1889 marriage record of Richard, no additional corroborating document could be found that *definitively* linked Richard Rose, the son of William Rose of the Union Estate plantation on Bequia, St Vincent to Richard Rose the miner of Gympie, Queensland. For example, no record showing his departure from the West Indies and his arrival in Australia, nor any supporting diary entry, letter, newspaper report or other correspondence to, or from, the West Indies has been found to date.

However, the circumstantial evidence is very extensive, so extensive that the genealogists are confident he is one and the same person. To support their belief, the genealogists provided the following evidence:

a) The traditional way the Scots often named their sons followed a simple set of rules:

> 1st son named after father's father
>
> 2nd son named after mother's father
>
> 3rd son named after father.

It might not *prove* anything but Richard Rose's father's name was William Rose (of St Vincent in West Indies) who was also of Scottish decent. Thus, it would have been traditional for Richard to name his first son by Catherine, William, after his (the baby's) father's father, which is what occurred. This is just a very small piece of circumstantial evidence, but nice to have.

b) The Richard Rose from Gympie stated on two records that he was born in 'Kingsto[w]n, St Vincent, West Indies' (on his son's 1869 birth certificate [5.10]) - or that he was born in the 'West Indies' (on his 1889 marriage record to Elizabeth Wooding[5.21]).

c) The island community of St Vincent and the Grenadines was quite small in the 1800s, so a search of all the slave and plantation records that were owned by a planter named 'Rose', although time consuming, soon resulted in a short list of candidates named 'Rose'.[5.22] The name 'William Rose' occurred in the list several times and cross-checking with the database at the Centre for the Study of the Legacies of British Slavery[5.23] narrowed the candidates down to only two planters - **William Rose Snr.** [d. c1817] and his son **William Rose Jnr.** [d. c1839]. William Rose Snr. had established the Union Estate on the island of Bequia c1781.[5.18] When he died in 1817, the estate was inherited by his son, William Rose Jnr., who himself died around 1839.[5.18] No other planters named William Rose in St Vincent were found in the archives. Richard Rose, who said he was born in 'Kingsto[w]n, St Vincent, West Indies', and whose father he said was a 'planter' named 'William Rose', was almost certainly the son of one of these two men. Because Richard was born c1832, his claimed father must have been William Rose Jnr., as the senior Rose had died in 1817.

d) Richard Rose, the Gympie miner, was recorded as being born around 1831 or 1832 (based on his marriage record and his son William's birth record respectively). The Registry of Slaves on the Union Estate of William Rose, which lists the names, ages and occupations of the slaves held by William Rose in 1834 is available. It records a 'Richard' as being a child-slave whose age is 'Under 6 years' (See near the bottom of first column.[5.24] This correlates, as the Richard Rose from Gympie would have been two or three years old in 1834.

e) Richard Rose from Gympie stated on his marriage record that his father was a 'planter' called William Rose and that his mother was named Harriet Williams.[5.12] The slave list from William Rose's Union Estate contained the name of a 29-year-old domestic slave called 'Harriet', but she was listed by her first name only, so we do not know for certain if her surname was 'Williams' (See second column near bottom.[5.25]) However, by the following circumstantial evidence and reasoning it is more than likely that she was Harriet Williams, mother of Richard Rose.

A careful analysis of these two pages of the slaves list reveals that:

a) Most of the slaves six years and older have an occupation attached to their name - labourer, vine gang, carpenter, sailor, etc. This implies they were slaves working in the fields or workshops on the estate. A few, including Harriet, are listed as being a 'Domestic', implying they worked in the household. Harriet would therefore perhaps have been in a position within the household where William Rose could more easily maintain an intimate relationship with her. To further support this idea, another set of researchers following the family genealogy of another of William's illegitimate slave-children Favorita (see below), state she 'was born about 1835 on the Union Estate' and that her mother was 'Margaret, a Slave.'[5.18]

The name of a 27-year-old 'Domestic' named 'Margaret' is also listed near Harriet's entry on the Registry of Slaves on the Union Estate.

b) There are a number of slaves that have no occupation listed - **Duke** (aged 7), Alexander (6), **John** (6), **Carrington** (9), Manny (10), Anne (11), and all the children under six years including **Richard** and **Mary.** The names in bold also appear in William Rose's Will as being part of his group of seven children (presumably the illegitimate issue from his relationships with slave women) namely **Carrington, John, Mary,** Elenora, **Duke, Richard** and Favorita. This suggests that these children were not put to labour, but were perhaps schooled.

c) The name 'Richard Rose' could not be found in the extensive passenger list records for immigrants who arrived in Australia between 1850 and 1870. It is therefore more likely that Richard arrived as a crew member on a ship. Unfortunately, crew lists for vessels arriving and departing Australia were rarely kept or archived and no documentary evidence could be found to confirm Richard arrived as a seaman. Nevertheless, an entry for a Richard Rose has been found in the 1855 British Merchant Seamen records which states that his age was '24' and that he was born at 'St Vincent'. This supports the notion that Richard arrived in Australia as a crew member on a ship rather than as a passenger. This Richard Rose, the seaman, is more than likely 'our' Richard Rose given it is highly unlikely that the small community of Kingstown would produce two locally born men, both called Richard Rose, both born c1831/2 and both becoming British merchant seamen. Additional corroborating evidence was found that appears to show that one of Richard's brothers (half- or full-) **Duke Rose**, also became a British merchant seaman.[5.26] The age of the slave named 'Duke' in the Union Estate slave-list was recorded as '7 years old' in 1834, which puts his birth date at c1827.[5.27] This matches (in genealogically acceptable terms) the birth year of the 'Duke' in the seaman's record (1828). This supports the notion that they are one and the same person named 'Duke'.

d) Very noteworthy is the British Merchant Seaman entry for Duke Rose, which is more detailed than the one for his likely half- or full-brother, Richard. The entry describes Duke's **'Complexion' as: 'Boy of Color'**[*sic*]. This is the closest mention so far that any of the seven children of William Rose - including Duke and Richard - were 'coloured'. It is evidence to support the observation of Pat Eatock that her ancestors had 'black faces'.

So Pat Eatock was most likely correct when she claimed her grandfather 'had a very black face'. However, he had inherited it not from an Aboriginal parent as Pat mistakenly believed, but rather from his father Richard Rose, a part-negro slave from the West Indies, Pat Eatock's biological great-grandfather. Rather than imagining her ancestors living in a simple 'gunya'[[5.28] see at 00:35] out on the Queensland frontier, Pat actually should have rather seen her 'roots' as having been more realistically depicted as in a typical family portrait from the 18th-century Casta School of colonial paintings of slave societies - white planter father, black domestic mother and illegitimate, half-caste boy.[5.29]

And so the research rested until, quite unexpectedly, another hidden door in the family history of the Eatocks suddenly opened.

5.2   DNA - The Corroborating Evidence

In April 2025, within a few days of each other, two emails arrived in the *Dark Emu Exposed* inbox:

> Hi, if you would like DNA proof of Pat Eatock's non-aboriginal blood line, I would be happy to chat with you. - *signed* [name supplied]

and:

> Hi, I am Pat Eatock's [relationship supplied] ... I have very recently done an ancestry DNA test and was surprised to find a small amount of DNA showing African origins, among other expected results. Looking at my most closely matching Eatocks they too seem to have some African origin. Naturally I was intrigued by this and after some searching came across your articles on Pat Eatock, in particular the family history of William Eatock (Rose). This would seem to fit with the DNA results I received. Thought you may be interested in this if you have not had access to any other Eatock DNA test results. If you would like further information please contact me. - *signed* [name supplied]

Of course the opportunity to speak was taken and a long conversation with each ensued over the telephone and by further emails. What had been puzzling both these informants was that they were 'white' Australians of Scottish descent, yet their DNA test results revealed they had 3% and 7% West African ancestry respectively (See Figure 5.3 [5.30]).

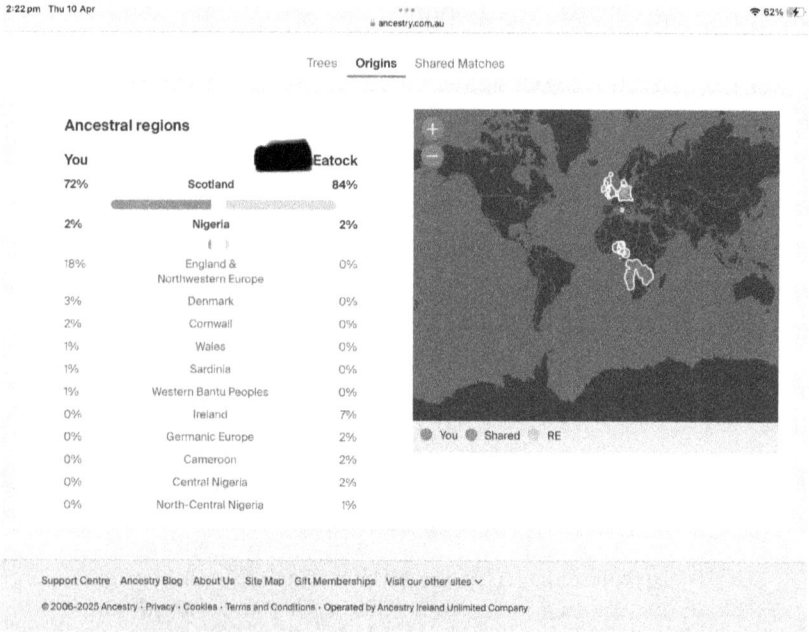

Trees **Origins** Shared Matches

Ancestral regions

You		Eatock
72%	Scotland	84%
2%	Nigeria	2%
18%	England & Northwestern Europe	0%
3%	Denmark	0%
2%	Cornwall	0%
1%	Wales	0%
1%	Sardinia	0%
1%	Western Bantu Peoples	0%
0%	Ireland	7%
0%	Germanic Europe	2%
0%	Cameroon	2%
0%	Central Nigeria	2%
0%	North-Central Nigeria	1%

● You ● Shared ○ RE

Figure 5.3: The DNA results for two family members closely related to Pat Eatock - One labeled 'You' [the person who supplied the graphic] and their Eatock relative [first name redacted]. See [5.30] for a download of the graphic.

These two family members told me they knew of Pat and Joan's claims about the family being of Aboriginal ancestry, but they, like most of the family (if not all), had discounted their claims.

This DNA information nicely corroborates the independent genealogical work and allows me to say confidently, "Case Closed - Pat Eatock was not Aboriginal - she was a fake."

And so concludes Part I in the reassessment of the notorious *Bolt v Eatock* court case.[12]

---

[12]The research notes for the Eatock family genealogy can be downloaded here: [5.31]

For References link - see QR code on page (xv)

References

[5.1] Ron Merkel QC. *Human Rights Oration.* 11 Dec 2012.

[5.2] *Olmstead v. United States, 277 U.S. 438 (1928).*

[5.3] Lea Redfern. *Lucy Eatock, Legacy and Family, on ABC Radio, Hindsight Program Promo.* 27 June 1999.

[5.4] *Research Notes on Catherine Davidson's Marriages and Sons.* 25 Aug 2024.

[5.5] *Historians who vouched for Pat Eatock's Aboriginality.*

[5.6] Photographs. *Eatock family photograph selection. Sources: Ancestry.com and Delusions of Grandeur.*

[5.7] *Records indicating Timothy and Catherine Eatock had separated by 1869 prior to William Rose's Birth.*

[5.8] *Marriage record for Catherine Davidson and Timothy O'Niell - Entry No. 127/307.* QLDBDM 1873/C/127, 21 Nov 1873.

[5.9] *Record indicating that Catherine Eatock was still using her 'Eatock' married name as late as 1874.*

[5.10] *Birth record file for William Rose (later Eatock).* QLDBDM 1869/C/1969. 19 Aug 1869.

[5.11] *Marriage Record file for Richard Rose and Elizabeth Wooding - Entry No. 1186/1506.* QLDBDM 1889/C/1136, 11 Dec 1889.

[5.12] *Excerpt of Marriage Record file for Richard Rose and Elizabeth Wooding showing groom's father as a 'Planter' - Entry No. 1186/1506.* QLDBDM 1889/C/1136, 11 Dec 1889.

[5.13] *Full book and excerpts from Mining Lease Register showing Richard Rose's transfer to Donald Eatock p151 - Entry Claim No 1935.* Gympie Mining Claims 1868-1901 (Queensland Archives), 1870.

[5.14] *Figure 5.1 Modified Joan Eatock's Family Tree.*

[5.15] *Apparent Full Eatock Family Tree.* 19 Aug 2024.

[5.16] Google Maps. *Map of St Vincent and the Grenadines showing small island of Bequia, the location of the William Rose Union Estate.*

[5.17] Centre for the Study of the Legacies of British Slavery. *St Vincent 693 Union Estate Claim Details.* 26 Feb 1836.

[5.18] Archives. *Biographical sketch of Edward K. Biddy and his family.* 26 Feb 1836.

[5.19] William Rose. *Last Will and Testament of William Rose, Planter.* PROB 11/1912/294, Proved on 1 June 1840.

[5.20] *Transcription of Will and Last Testament of William Rose Planter.* PROB 11/1912/294, Proved on 1 June 1840.

[5.21] *Marriage Record notes for Richard Rose and Elizabeth Wooding.* QLDBDM 1889/C/1136, 11 Dec 1889.

[5.22] *List of Slave-owning Planters recorded in St Vincent, all with the Surname 'Rose'.* Source - *Former British Colonial Dependencies, Slave Registers, 1813-1834 on Ancestry.com.*

[5.23] Centre for the Studies of the Legacies of British Slavery. *List of Slave-owning Planters Named 'William Rose'.*

[5.24] *'Richard, an Under 6yrs old slave' listed on the Registry of Slaves May 31st 1834 on the Union Estate of Wlliam Rose. Ancestry.com,* 31 May 1834.

[5.25] *'Harriet, a 29yr old domestic slave' listed on the Registry of Slaves on the Union Estate of William Rose. Ancestry.com,* 31 May 1834.

[5.26] *Duke Rose in British Seamens Registry 1846-8. Findmypast,* 18 June 1846.

[5.27] *'Duke, a 7yr old slave, 'free' of occupation so possibly 'schooled', on the Registry of Slaves on the Union Estate of William Rose. Ancestry.com,* 31 May 1834.

[5.28] Youtube. *Pat Eatock with a Version of her Declaring her Aboriginality.* No date -(ca1990s?)

[5.29] *Imaginary portrait of Pat Eatock's ancestral 'black' family , after the Casta School.)*

[5.30] Eatock Family. *DNA Scans for some members of the Eatock family.*

[5.31] Dark Emu Exposed. *Research Notes For Eatock Genealogy.*

Part II

Chapter 6

The Aftermath of *Eatock v Bolt*

"words on paper have consequences"

Justice Robert French AC[1]

Justice French's words came from a 2011 paper in which he lamented:

> Legal discourse in the courts is probably the least promising field in which to explore the concepts of [Aboriginal] identity. It projects interrelated individual and communal realities on to a pointillist landscape of disputes and 'matters'.

However, he also noted:

> Nevertheless, issues of identity and the related concept of 'recognition' have played a significant part in legislation and litigation involving Indigenous people in Australia.[2]

French neatly summed up where we find ourselves today as a society, as exemplified by the *Eatock v Bolt* case - battling out disagreements about fundamental rights, responsibilities, recognition and indeed definitions of Aboriginal people as a

---

[1]Former Chief Justice of the High Court of Australia.

[2]Robert French, 'Aboriginal Identity–The Legal Dimension', *Aust. Indigenous Law Rev.*, 15.1, (2011), p22.

group, while having to deal simultaneously with fiercely contested 'issues of identity' - who is and who isn't Aboriginal - at a personal level in stressful scenes in court, the 'least promising' of places.

His observation that 'words on paper have consequences' is at the heart of the debacle that this unpleasant court case turned out to be. On the one hand, Andrew Bolt's 'words on paper' were claimed by academic and commentator Professor Marcia Langton AO, to potentially have serious consequences for 'fair-skinned' Aboriginal people by 'putting the[ir] lives and physical well being in danger from the mentally unwell' amongst Bolt's fans and readership. Additionally, Langton claimed she was concerned 'for the safety and well being of the Aboriginal people he attacks'.[3]

But Bolt did not get off scot free either. His words on (news)paper had serious consequences for himself - the stress and expense of a two-year litigation, the humiliation of the defeat, and the subsequent curbing of the free speech that he needed to ply his craft as a fast-paced, satirical, witty and sometimes outrageous social commentator and journalist. Some might say the cost to Bolt was just that - a self-inflicted cost to one man only, whereas the harm he was alleged to have perpetrated was against all the many thousands of 'fair-skinned' Aboriginal people. But Bolt's supporters could

---

[3] [6.1] Like many of her contradictory public announcements, Langton's technique appears to be to throw a 'slur' at her target, in this case Bolt and his 'mentally unwell' readership, and then avoid condemnation by walking back on it somewhat and implying that she was only concerned for the victims. This is a technique she also used at a forum in Western Australia during the 2023 Voice referendum, where her words came across to many observers as, 'If you vote No, you are a racist'. As the storm of criticism unfolded she then spent the next week walking back from her comments, all the while gaining free publicity, as she perhaps had intended. In Bolt's case she added the apparently heartfelt proviso: "Some [of Bolt's targets] are my friends and colleagues, and many I have never met. They [do] not deserve the horrendous treatment that he metes out to them in his column and blog. I am astonished that the media and the Australian public allow this to continue. He believes that he is not racist, and I believe that he is sincere in this belief. Nevertheless, I am particularly concerned about the harm that his attacks do to these young people, the impact on their self esteem, and the harm to other young Aboriginal people. I am concerned because of the very high rates of suicide among our youth and I believe that this kind of abuse contributes indirectly to this outcome."

rightly reply that, no, the cost was actually against all Australians in having their free speech restricted. Additionally their taxes were going up to fund raced-based policies and benefits that were intended only for Aborigines in real need, but now were inflated by the 'trend' in the increasing numbers of 'fair-skinned' claimants. These 'white Aborigines', as Bolt called them, often suspiciously looked like highly educated and affluent city people far from being in any real need. Worse still, many of them looked and sounded like fakes, with no provable Aboriginal ancestry at all. As importantly, many Aboriginal organisations have also pointed out that real Aboriginal people are now having to deal with 'fair-skinned' cultural interlopers hell-bent on pushing them aside for priority access to the Indigenous-only positions in academia, the arts, government and business, or the race-based programs and benefits currently offered by our society.

This is the nub of the argument which Bolt, perhaps in what some people took admittedly as a 'humiliating, offensive and insulting' way, was trying to get our society to address - the need to resolve the disagreements over the few 'words on paper' consisting of, 'who counts as Aboriginal today'?[4]

6.1   A Contest of the Meaning of Words

Who is an Aborigine? A traditionally-minded, ordinary Australian like Andrew Bolt appears to have taken a 'conservative' meaning - in the sense of maintaining the previously understood meaning - of what the words 'Aboriginal person' meant. To Bolt, along with perhaps the majority of the public, a person of clearly Aboriginal appearance, character, cultural and social habits, often speaking an Aboriginal language and with parents and grandparents who considered themselves Aboriginal, *was* Aboriginal, no questions asked. There was no need

---

[4]Bronwyn Carlson, *The Politics of Identity: Who counts as Aboriginal today?* AIATSIS, 2016.

for an apartheid-style classification system, which our government's borderline racist 'three-part rule' threatens to be.

These people and their own community knew they were Aboriginal and didn't need any fancy lawyers to argue their case. And just as importantly, the rest of Australia naturally knew they were Aboriginal too - Australians didn't need to be dragged into court and lectured on how a newly invented band of 'fair-skinned' applicants *really were* Aboriginal because they, as they often falsely told us, had 'self-identified as such since childhood'.

Bolt and the Australian public weren't saying that Justice Bromberg's 'fair-skinned Aboriginal people' couldn't in their own private, family and community lives self-identify as Aboriginal if they wanted to. Rather Australians were saying they weren't going to go along with the idea that they *had to* agree with the delusional claims of these white Aborigines when it came to accessing the scarce tax-payer funds that were intended for genuine Aboriginal people in real need. The fundamentals of the dispute were civic, political and economic, not racial.

Australians weren't stupid - they could now see that with Justice Bromberg's help some white people would try to redefine, and indeed expand, the meaning of the word 'Aboriginal' so as to gain recognition for themselves. This expansion of the meaning of Aboriginal was simply an example of that old ideological technique used by the Communists who were convinced 'that you could change reality by changing words'.[5]

The activist and communist Pat Eatock[6.2] believed that all she had to do to change the reality of her life as a white, working-class, suburban, Aussie mum was to proclaim in an interview, "I *am* Aboriginal"[6.3] and she would thus become one. Eatock's elaboration as a self-identifying Aborigine went even further, as noted by one observer at the trial:

---

[5]Scruton, R. *Fools, Frauds and Firebrands*, Bloomsbury Continuum, 2015, p8.

> The black, China-made, cotton T-shirts, with messages of
> land rights spelt out in yellow and red, are not ordinary
> clothes. [These are] the 'skin' of the white Aborigines. These
> clothes are racial identifiers. In a country where it is now
> unacceptable to associate black skin and Aboriginality, white
> people dress in these clothes to signal and assert their own
> Aboriginality. If that seems fanciful it is exactly what Pat
> Eatock claimed in her written trial submission: "As my health
> has deteriorated, I have become more accustomed to wearing
> clothes that clearly announce my involvement with Aboriginal
> issues, usually black trousers with T-shirts and with Aborigi-
> nal flag and appropriate slogans. I have been known to draw
> attention to these shirts as 'my skin'. They certain [sic] allow
> my Aboriginality to be very visible to all.[6]

Bolt's 'white Aborigines' wanted to use their new definition
of who is an Aboriginal to develop political, economic and
social policies that benefited their own class of people, but
invariably would greatly affect *all of us*. Bolt was acting as
the mouthpiece for the inherent commonsense of mainstream
Australia when he challenged these self-appointed intellectual
and legal gate-keepers, hell-bent on redefining just who is, and
who isn't, Aboriginal in modern Australia.

The fact of the matter is that, as the inter-marriage and
assimilation of Australians of Aboriginal descent continues,
the differences between non-Aboriginal and 'fair-skinned' Aboriginal Australians becomes ever smaller. Australian society
entered into a very dangerous place when Justice Bromberg
sanctioned the creation of this new, legal class of 'fair-skinned'
Aboriginal people whose Aboriginal ancestry could legally be
so distantly small, or even non-existent as in the case of Pat
Eatock. These new 'white Aborigines' had grown up with the
rest of us in our mainstream Australian culture, lived next
door to us on our street, went to our schools and married our
brothers and sisters, but now they wanted to tell the rest of
Australia that they were somehow 'racially special' and we
needed to give them special, state-funded benefits, jobs and

---

[6]Michael Connor, 'The White Aborigines Trial', *Quadrant Online*, 1 Nov 2011.

voting rights. Australians were told they needed to recognise and pay respects to them and their Elders as they demanded their Voice be listened to preferentially when implementing race-based public policy, even though that policy would affect all of us equally as Australians.

Bolt's point was that just because someone had a distant great-great-grandma who may have been part-Aboriginal, that doesn't necessarily make them Aboriginal in a real, meaningful way and we don't need to defer preferentially to their political, social and economic wishes. In particular, Bolt warned we should be mindful of the opportunists willing to leverage their claims of a faint, or even non-existent, Aboriginality for their own personal gain over the needs of real Aboriginal people in regional and remote Australia. Bolt had the courage to demand his right to his opinion and the free speech he thought necessary to critique this new class of 'white Aborigines', even if it potentially would 'humiliate, offend or insult' them.

Our society needs commentators like Bolt to freely speak their minds without fear or favour in the same way we need people like the 'white Aborigines' to feel free to offer up their ideas for improving society.

But unfortunately, the free speech necessary to discuss the increasing numbers of 'white Aborigines' and the fakes, and their growing opportunism and divisive influence, took a further major hit in Australia on 28 September 2011, with Bolt's court loss.

I say free speech took a *further* major hit because our society had been there before, way back in 1978. The same questions that Bolt raised in 2011 were brought up back then and beaten down before they could be adequately discussed. And what a loss it has been for a productive discourse on race relations over those decades, culminating in the very divisive, failed Voice Referendum of 2023. For, back in 1978, in Hobart, Tasmania, a real life example was unfolding of Australians *choosing* to be, as Bolt warned, members of the 'white Aborigines – people who out of their multi-stranded but largely European genealogy, decide to identify with the thinnest of all those strands, and the one that has contributed least to their looks. Yes, the Aboriginal one.'[7] The 'trend' that Bolt was warning Australia about really began in 1978, in Tasmania, a trend Bromberg J commented on: "Mr Bolt's motivation was to draw attention to a 'trend' which emphasised racial differences, rather than common humanity"[8]

6.1.1   The Tasmanian Aborigines are Extinct

In 1978, the film *The Last Tasmanian* was released, causing much controversy and being responsible for one of the earliest losses of free speech in the discussion of Aboriginality. The main aim of the movie, by film-maker Tom Haydon, was 'highlighting the level of violence unleashed against the Aborigines by British colonialists in the nineteenth century'.[9] A film synopsis was provided in a study guide for the film:

> *The Last Tasmanian*[10] tells the story of the swiftest and most destructive genocide on record. The Tasmanians were a distinct people, isolated from Australia and the rest of the world for 12,000 years. In 1803, British colonisation began and in 1876, Truganini died. She was the last full-blood and tribal Tasmanian Aboriginal. Within her one lifetime, a whole society and culture were removed from the face of the earth.[6.5]

Leaving to one side as to whether it is valid to use the word 'genocide' in describing the demise of the Tasmanian Aborig-

---

[7] Andrew Bolt, 'White fellas in the black', *Herald Sun*, 21 August 2009.

[8] "Mr Bolt's evidence was that he wrote each of the Articles in order to draw attention to what he believes to be a 'discernible trend' in Australia, whereby persons of mixed genealogy, where that genealogy includes Aboriginality, identify as Aboriginal persons, where they could instead identify with another race or other races, or assert no racial identity at all. Mr Bolt said that he believed that this 'trend' was an undesirable social phenomenon, because it emphasises racial differences, rather than common humanity."- Bromberg J in *Eatock v Bolt* [2011] at 23.

[9] Johnson, M. & McFarlane, I., *Van Diemen's Land - An Aboriginal History*, 2015, p362.

[10] RONIN Films, 1978. The film was also featured in the *The Sunday Times Magazine* in the UK to coincide with its screening on the BBC in May 1978. (See magazine here: [6.4])

ines,[11] the concept of 'extinction' created a controversy, albeit one that the film makers claimed was 'essentially a semantic one.' The film used the term 'Tasmanian Aborigines' just as other historians and commentators have used it, to apply to the *first people* who occupied the island and created there a distinctive society and culture. The extinction that occurred after British colonisation not only meant that no 'full-blood' Aborigines existed in Tasmania after Truganini's death,[12] it also meant that 'the society with its languages, its culture, the way it thought and everything else' came to an end with her death in 1876.[13] Essentially nothing of the genuine traditional tribal life has survived - language, religion, stories, song, dance, connection to country and so on, are all gone.

The *descendants* of these 'Tasmanian Aborigines', are just that - *descendants*. They evolved a new variety of society and culture largely on the Bass Strait island of Cape Barren. This island was not occupied by the original Tasmanian Aborigines and its traditions owed more to the sealer fore-fathers than the Tasmanian Aboriginal fore-mothers. The primary focus of the film was on the fully tribal, and traditional-living, Aborigines of the 18th and 19th centuries, from whom those wanting to identify today as 'Tasmanian Aboriginal' are *only descended*. This logic is the same as when the film describes the earlier, prehistoric people of Tasmania as 'Ancestors'.[14]

As the film's maker, Tom Haydon, explained on the ABC

---

[11] There is a vigorous historical debate as to whether the extinction of the Tasmanian Aborigines was formally a 'genocide', as in the sense that it was a 'deliberate killing of a large number of people from a particular nation or ethnic group with the aim of destroying that nation or group' [*Oxford Dict.*]; or an 'extermination of a national or racial group as a planned move' [*Macquarie Dict.*]. It wasn't, but the end result (due to conflict, disease, loss of hunting lands, low fertility and assimilation) is that, within 70 years of settlement, the Tasmanian Aborigines *were* extinct - the same outcome as that of a planned genocide. (Semantically analogous to a man recklessly driving a car who kills a pedestrian - he didn't *intend* to do it, so it was accidental manslaughter, not premeditated murder, even though the outcome is the same: an extinct victim.)

[12] Others nominate the names of some Aboriginal women still living on other islands.

[13] Monday Conference transcript: *The Last Tasmanian* by Moore, Robert, 1932-1979, producer. AIATSIS Call Number RP00865, Item: 0027597, p3.

[14] *The Last Tasmanian Study Guide*, 1978, p9. See QR Code [6.5].

TV program *Monday Conference* in September 1978:[15]

> I think it is worth, before we start, making clear that a lot
> of the problem we have has to do with words. Whichever
> way you look at the stumbling [in the way in which we talk]
> about 'full-blood' and all that kind of thing, we do seem to
> constantly need some way of distinguishing the Tasmanian
> Aborigines, who Mike [Mansell] calls tribal and were here in
> this island for ... about 12,000 years, and those people, a
> lot of whom are here in the cinema tonight and who Mike
> represents, who [also] call themselves Tasmanian Aborigines
> today. [W]e do need to find some way of distinguishing these
> two kinds of people for everyday language.[16]

What Tom Haydon is articulating here is what many Bolt-
minded Australians think - why does a 'fair [skinned] Michael
Mansell, the Tasmanian firebrand, [who] clearly has more European than Aboriginal ancestry ... not also identify with
his obvious European background?'[17] How can Mansell stand
there and tell Australia he wants to be considered a 'Tasmanian Aborigine', the same as a Truganini or a William Lanne,
when clearly he is *only a descendant* or *part*-Tasmanian Aborigine? Haydon continued:

> In the film we are talking, essentially, about the people who
> had one of the most remarkable existences in terms of being
> a separate people quite isolated from the rest of the world
> for 12,000 years, who had a very distinctive culture and were
> different from the Australian Aborigines because they had
> been separated from them for 12,000 years. And it's that
> society with its languages, its culture, the way it thought and
> everything else which we are saying in the film came to an
> end with the death of Truganini in 1876.
>
> I think it's tremendous that people today want to resurrect
> and use the name Tasmanian Aborigines. To start with it
> was a British-given name, Tasmanian Aborigines. It doesn't
> in fact relate to the names of the tribes who were here[18]... I

---

[15] Monday Conference transcript, *op. cit.,* p3.

[16] Monday Conference transcript, *op. cit.,* p3.

[17] Andrew Bolt, 'It's so hip to be black', *Herald Sun,* 15 April 2009.

[18] As the inheritors of the British society that established itself in Tasmania, with its
science and culture, *we* as modern Australians *own* the words 'Tasmanian Aborigines. *We* have the exclusive rights to define what those words mean.

think that in everyday conversation, even amongst Aborigines
and Aboriginal writers, other terms are sometimes used like
descendants ... and terms like part-Aboriginal and so on.

If we're talking about, do I recognise Mike Mansell, and the
community [he] represents ... as descendants of the tribal
Aborigines who [were] here, yes I do. If you are asking me,
do I recognise him as a descendant of one the community of
sealers who established themselves on the islands in the Bass
Strait and who were responsible, amongst other things, for
some of the most barbarous acts against the Aborigines in
this island, I also recognise him as that. [However] I am not
prepared to simply see all people in this country of Australia,
both Australian Aborigines and Tasmanian Aborigines, as the
people I would think of as Aborigines just because they claim
to be so.[19]

Mansell wasn't impressed. Mansell was what Professor Elizabeth Rata (see Chapter 9), would describe as a member of an
'emergent ethnic elite' pursuing a strategy to 'entrench ethnicity as a political category and, with that entrenchment, to
cement their own privileged positions'. This strategy involves
the 'cultural production' of a 'neo-tribal' ideology, which en-
ables the elite to make a spurious claim for continuity with an
'authentic tribal past'. As a result, the elite would claim economic resources and political partnership as *their inheritance*
of that tribal past. Rata's work implies that if Mansell was
to achieve his aim of being *the* recognised spokesperson of the
Tasmanian Aborigines, *he needed to be one of them*. People
with views like Haydon and Bolt would be expected to be a
block to his strategy,[20] because they wanted a more nuanced
vocabulary to characterize people like Mansell - he was *only*
a descendant, a part-Aborigine, and he also should be held to
account for some of the barbarous acts that *his* white, Euro-

---

[19]Monday Conference transcript, *op. cit.*, p3-4.

[20]And what a successful strategy it has been with 'the House of Mansell' and the
Tasmanian Aboriginal Council (TAC) receiving some $120 million in tax-payer funds
over a ten-year period[6.6], plus other outcomes: Aboriginal land returns in 1995,
1999, 2005; Return of ancestral remains from overseas and Australian institutions;
Aboriginal cultural fishing rights; Financial compensation to the Stolen Generations;
Land purchases for community ownership; Establishment of Aboriginal health and
community services; Revival of Tasmanian Aboriginal language.[6.7]

pean ancestors committed against the Tasmanian Aborigines.

This critical point was clearly identified by a University of Tasmania Master's student, Dennis Daniels in his thesis:

> The term Aboriginal descendant seemed to many, including the government, satisfactory enough. But it was [Michael] Mansell who first saw the problem this posed in terms of unifying the community and the Aboriginal cause. One could be a descendant, even taking out any benefits which might be provided, without being committed to each other or the struggle. "The identity issue is crucial," he said. "Flinders and Cape Barren don't help. Flinders blacks want to assimilate, and as for Cape Barren, they want to be called Islanders - how cute."
>
> It was Mansell who decided all Tasmanian descendants should call themselves Aborigines. "It is our white blood," he said, "which is used to call us descendants - half-castes, descendants, part-Aborigines are all white man's terms. If we want to call ourselves Aborigines, lets do it and be proud." In [her book] *Pride over Prejudice*, Ida West recognised Mansell's contribution to the identity question; "I would like to thank Mr Mick Mansell, for he called us Aborigines instead of using those words, half caste, quarter-caste. Terrible words."
>
> However, some leaders recognised the problem this caused for light-skinned members of their community, and sought to encourage them. "By identifying," said Rodney Gibbons, "they are standing up for something they can hide if they want to and showing they are prepared to take all the ridicule."
>
> One Aborigine told me that she had never heard the word Aborigine applied to her community until she was visited by a group from [Mansell's] TAC. When told she was an Aborigine it took away all the hurt associated with words such as half-caste and part Aborigine.
>
> On the other hand, another told me he refused to let his children call themselves anything but descendants, since they had never lived as Aborigines.[21]

At the conference, Mansell countered Haydon's commentary with:

---

[21]See QR code [[6.8], p35.]

I think Mr Haydon, you're assuming that to be Aboriginal you merely have to walk around the street and say, "I'm an Aboriginal". Now you are way off beam...[22] The first thing, you have to be descended from people who've been here for thousands of years, so there are genes attached to the argument. You have to be part of the existing Aboriginal culture as it is today, and then it is also a feeling, a feeling of being Aboriginal, how we perceive ourselves in relation to the rest of society and how that society sees us.

Crucially, Haydon then responded as a Bolt-minded critic might:

Well, I think that's the question ... I mean the question is have you always felt that way? [or in Bolt-speak, "have you made a more recent *choice* to identify as a Tasmanian Aboriginal?"] I know that Dr Lyndall Ryan is here tonight, who has done a lot of research on the question of the descendants in the Bass Strait islands and ... she particularly calls these peoples Islanders [which] historically [has been] used on and off over the last hundred years for the people from Bass Strait, also the word Straitspeople or Straitsmen ... It is only in perhaps the last ten years or so, in many people's view, that they have started to think of themselves here in Tasmania as Aborigines.

Mansell and Haydon then debated back and forth to no real avail in changing each other's mind. Haydon stressed his point that, 'we had a people with a very distinctive culture and society of their own which was eliminated ... not just as a

---

[22]How wrong Mansell turned out to be. Fifty years after his comment, the streets are now full of people walking around falsely claiming, "I'm an Aboriginal". Bolt's trend took off in Tasmania under Mansell's watch and political activism: In the 1967 census, 67 Tasmanians identified as Aboriginal; in 1972 (670); 1976 (2942); 1981 (2636); 1986 (6721); 1991 (8819). 'Genealogist' Bill Mollison indicated there were 3000 in 1974.[6.8] Today Mansell is reaping the Aboriginal new identifier seeds he sowed: "Michael Mansell says it's 'unbelievable' that the state's Indigenous population has increased by 6000 in the five years between censuses and attributes those figures to 'poor whites' claiming ancestry for benefits and prestige [from 23,572 in 2016 to 2021 approximately 30,000 in 2021, and thus now comprising 5 per cent of the state's population]" - (*from:* Alex Treacy, 'Aboriginal population Tasmania: Rise due to 'white identity seekers", *The Mercury*, 30 June 2022.) The use of the word 'genocide' might be appropriate if one accepts that the Tasmanian Aborigines of old became extinct with the passing of Truganini in 1876 due to deliberate British policies aimed at their extinction, but is the concept of 'genocide' valid if the numbers of people who call themselves 'Tasmanian Aboriginal' today is 5 to 10 times higher than when the British settled in 1803?

people but their culture as well' and people today who 'call themselves Aborigines are a people who carry the genes of those people but who in their language, their society, in their culture, carry the culture of the invaders'.[23] Mansell however, stuck to his position that if you have some of the 'genes' of the Tasmanian Aborigines, and you are 'part of the existing Aboriginal culture as it is today', and you have 'a feeling of being Aboriginal',[24] then you *are* a Tasmanian Aboriginal - the same as Truganini and William Lanne were.

But then a really interesting thing happened. A young woman in the audience who had appeared in the film was brought into the conversation, expressing an agency that confirms Bolt's observation about the *choosing* of a particular strand of one's ancestry. Her name was **Mrs Annette Mansell**, President of the Cape Barren Island Community,[25] and the compere asked, "Mrs Mansell, why in the film [do] you draw the distinction between being the descendant of Aborigines, and being an Aborigine yourself, and you go to some pains to make that distinction?"

> Well I don't believe that I am an Aboriginal. My father is a white man so therefore I must respect him and I bring myself down to a descendant and I'm proud to say that I am a descendant of an Aboriginal (loud interjections of disagreement by audience members).[26]

Those September 1978 audience interjections to Annette Mansell's position were the first hints of the controversy that was to develop over the next six months. On New Year's Day in 1979, in a *Filmnews* review, archaeologist **Anne Bickford** launched a scathing attack on the film, and particularly on the choices the two Cape Barren Islanders had taken in the way they identified:

---

[23] Monday Conference transcript, *op. cit.*, p6.
[24] *ibid.*, p4.
[25] Tom Haydon says she is no close relation to Michael Mansell.
[26] See a film clip here of Annette Mansell at 06:40.[6.9]

The man [**Melvyn Everett**] and woman [**Annette Mansell**] interviewed in the film may say they don't consider themselves to be Aborigines, denying their Aboriginality. Identity as an Aboriginal in a racist society is not a matter of free choice. Part-Aborigines are not a people 'in between' who can choose to be white or Aboriginal. White society associates part-Aborigines with full-blood Aborigines. So part-Aborigines, even though they may share more aspects of white than traditional culture, unable to enter white society, are pushed to one side — to identify as Aboriginal, or to be people in limbo.[[6.10], p11.][27]

Tom Haydon hit back in his response to Bickford on April Fool's Day 1979, in the same *Filmnews* magazine:

Bickford says a monstrous thing about these two people. She says they cannot deny they are Aborigines. She has the astounding sentence in her article: "Identity as an Aboriginal in a racist society is not a matter of free choice". Yet, just before this she quotes the Australian Government's definition of an Aboriginal: that an Aboriginal is a person of Aboriginal descent who identifies as an Aboriginal. Bickford and others frequently use this phrase "who identifies" as neat support for those Aboriginal descendants who do call themselves "Aborigines". But Bickford won't permit it to be used the other way around. She is saying Annette Mansell is not free not to identify. I find this compulsion repugnant to any notion of personal freedom. If anyone is being racist, she is. I am reminded of those 'Jew hunters' in 1930s Germany, who would flush out a person's Jewish ancestry, and dub him a Jew, regardless of whether he wanted to be one, or not.[28]

---

[27] Bickford's views of small-minded totalitarianism blind her to another, and the preferred, option which Bolt tried to guide us towards: "Let's go beyond racial pride. Beyond black and white. Let's be proud only of being human beings set on this land together, determined to find what unites us and not to invent such racist and trivial excuses to divide. Deal?" - Andrew Bolt, 'It's so hip to be black', *Herald Sun*, 15 April 2009.

[28] *reductio ad Hitlerum* works both ways (see Chapter 8.2.1) - Michael Mansell is said to be a descendant of Thomas (John) Beeton, 'from a Jewish family of jewellers in London' (see Lucy Beeton in ADB & Michael Mansell in *Wikipedia*). Perhaps Mansell, of all people, should be more circumspect in promoting a political ideology which links one's genes to one's political and social position within a society, like he demands for his Aboriginal self. Mansell believes he can go back to the Aboriginal wife of Beeton the Jew, and accept he has inherited certain political and cultural rights from her genes, but he then completely ignores what her British, Jewish husband has passed on to him. Fortunately, Mansell lives in modern Australia and not 1930s Germany where his genes would have carried a death sentence. Societies

Haydon believed Annette was 'simply talking common-sense'. She knew she was a 'descendant' of whites as well as Aborigines and she inherited some of the 'white discrimination against Aborigines but none of this makes her feel or think she is an Aborigine'. Haydon emphasised that she sees a big difference between herself and 'the old fellas' - the Tasmanian Aborigines:

> Here were [the Cape Barren Island] people who, for several generations had to live in one part of the one Island, isolated from the rest of Australia, economically restricted to a simple life style. They bear comparison with the Pitcairners and the people of Tristan da Cunha. Annette Mansell [was] trying to explain the meaning of her experience. She is saying that because so little survives of the Tasmanian Aboriginal culture, she cannot feel herself to be a Tasmanian Aborigine. The other descendant who speaks in the film, Melvyn Everett, gives his reason very concisely: "We can't speak the language[29] ... therefore why should we be called Aborigines. No one can prove it." [6.12]

Haydon explained that 'at the heart of the testimony by Annette and Melvyn lies an essential historical statement: The Tasmanian Aborigines, as a distinct human society with their own culture, are no longer with us'. Nor were they simply a regional division of the Australian Aborigines. Haydon explained it needed to be appreciated that:

> twelve thousand years ago, the Tasmanian Aborigines were cut off from the Australian mainland by the rising sea; the same rising sea which, about the same time, severed America from Asia at the Bering Strait. The Tasmanians have as much claim to being recognized as a separate people as have the American Indians [as being distinct from the Siberians and Asians.]

Today Mansell and Bickford would not dare to lump the Tor-

---

and ideologies which insist on the use of genes to grant or withhold citizen rights rarely turn out well in the long term. Australia has been there before, but we educated ourselves and *progressed* out of it. Mansell appears to want society to mentally *regress* back to some sort of 'Black Australia Policy' situation.

[29] Linguist Peter Sutton found remnants of south western English dialects on Cape Barren Island in 1969 - many of the sealers came from the West Country. See extract of his report here: AIATSIS 242533-1001/MS 378.[6.11]

res Strait Islanders in with the Australian Aborigines, as just
another regional division. Yet that is exactly what they are
trying to do with the Tasmanian Aborigines, who were unique,
distinct and are no more. Unless we are being asked to suspend our common sense, the people known as the Tasmanian
Aborigines cannot now be subsumed into just being a part of a
present-day Pan-Aboriginal Australia movement.[30] Their *descendants* can be if they wish, but it would be authoritarian to
force any Australian carrying some small part of Tasmanian
Aboriginal ancestry *to have to* identify as Australian Aboriginal as Bickford is suggesting. The very notion that Tasmania
in human terms belongs to Australia is only the result of 19th-
century European politics.

The Totalitarianism of Small Minds

O con noi o contro di noi

You're either with us or against us

Benito Mussolini

As Professor Rata's research indicated, an 'emergent ethnic
elite' needed to be able to establish a 'continuity with an authentic tribal past' and Tom Haydon's film just cut that life-
line off for the aspiring Tasmanians. How could the TAC and
the elites get acceptance as real 'Tasmanian Aborigines' if the
public ended up believing Haydon that they were extinct?

The spirited, if delusional, debate in *Filmnews* from Bickford was one thing, but would it be enough to cancel the
film, and more importantly destroy any community acceptance of its message? Thus, the attacks on the free speech
of the film-maker were ramped up[31] and escalated to what

---

[30]This leads to an interesting thought: if any Tasmanian Aborigines were alive today,
a national Indigenous body might justifiably be named: *The Aboriginal, Tasmanian
and Torres Strait Islander Commission* (ATTSIC)

[31]Haydon wrote: 'Anne Bickford called the film "racist" and anti-Aboriginal ... even
before she'd even seen it. Some might have heard her at the Australian Film Con-

could be seen as bullying. To do this, a seasoned fake Aboriginal was brought in who apparently had no hesitation in spraying racist or 'problematic' commentary at an otherwise well-accepted movie (it would end up being sold for television in 22 countries). **Roberta 'Bobbi' Sykes**, a fake Aboriginal, who the elites still refuse to call out,[32] continued the apparent bullying by writing a very critical review of Haydon's film. She also added to the verbal bullying[33] Annette Mansell had first begun to experience with the interjections from the audience of *Monday Conference*. Sykes, ever the political activist, firstly tells the film's archeaologist and presenter, Dr Rhys Jones, that his decades of experience and scholarship are worth nought compared to her opinions: "Unfortunately, Rhys Jones is so incorrect that even a mainland Black such as myself can see the flaws". The chutzpah of a fake like Sykes is breath-taking.[34] And then, with the confidence and arrogance that only a fake Aborigine could muster, she warns Annette Mansell that, "I am sorry for Annette Mansell who

---

ference in Sydney, June last year [1978]. The intended screening was canceled, but Bickford attacked nonetheless'.[[6.12], p12.]

[32] Professor Marcia Langton's University of Melbourne still promotes Roberta 'Bobbi' Sykes as a legitimate *indigenous* Black activist and still has a scholarship for Indigenous students awarded in her name. Ingeniously, the university describes her as a small 'i' indigenous: "Roberta Sykes graduated from Harvard in 1984 as the first **indigenous** Australian to graduate from an American university". The university appears not to have the integrity or courage to admit that Sykes promoted herself widely when she was alive as Aboriginal, despite having no Aboriginal ancestry at all. She was not a capital 'I' Indigenous Australian, but just a locally born, small 'i' indigenous one, like the majority of other Australians. Colloquially her award is known as, **Roberta's 'Tar-Brush' Scholarship**: some 'white Aborigine' winners are miraculously turned into accepted 'black' Indigenous academics and then fed into Indigenous-only slots in academia - see the fake Aborigine, **Professor Kerrie Doyle**, who claims to be the first Aboriginal graduate of Oxford University after winning one of Roberta's 'Tar-Brush' Scholarships.[6.13]

[33] In a 1972 interview, Bobbi Sykes claimed: "My mother made me marry a white man when I was a kid and now I hate them. I don't believe in them." Her favorite label for people she has not liked [was], "uptown nigger". Another favourite sneer is the "black bourgeoisie". (*Identity Magazine*, Nov 1972, p33.[6.14])

[34] "While Dr Sykes was careful to define herself by colour rather than as being indigenous, she was widely believed to have been part-Aboriginal until her white mother disclosed that Dr Sykes's father was an African-American serviceman. The revelation led to controversy in indigenous circles, with Dr Sykes widely criticised, among others, by lawyer Pat O'Shane ... for adopting the Aboriginal snake motif as her own when she entitled her three-part, prize-winning autobiography *Snake Dreaming*" - *from:* Obituary, 'A bright, passionate chameleon', *The Australian*, 17 Nov 2010.

will probably come to regret her unpoliticized comments and her self-denial". So much for the sisterhood sticking together to validate each other's agency. No, Sykes's version of her own racism says that, "if you do not think the way that *I say* a part-Aborigine should think, then you are in self-denial. There is no room for your own agency or personal freedom if it is against how my political ideology says you should behave. It is OK for a fake like me to *choose* to be an Aboriginal, but how dare a part-Aboriginal like you *choose not* to identify as Aboriginal!"[35]

This attitude apparently continues in modern-day Tasmanian Aboriginal politics with its echoes of Mussolini's mantra - if you are not for us, you are against us.[36] Haydon takes up the story of what happened next:

> Bickford will not heed Annette's own reasoning. She makes the gratuitous suggestion that Annette denies she's an Aborigine because she wants to avoid persecution of her children.[37]

> The really shocking fact is that since Annette made her statement in the film, there has been persecution of herself and family, but not from whites. She has suffered physical attack on her home, and threats of worse, which has led her and her kids to leave Cape Barren Island. Michael Mansell (no close relation), the leader of the Tasmanian Aborigines party-line, has openly abused her in print, and there has been exploita-

---

[35] As another observer noted: "It was Bobbi Sykes' lack of association with, and understanding of, Aborigines that has been the cause of so much of her disappointment at failing to identify with the mainstream of black thinking in Australia. [Like a number of fakes] she has often adopted the attitude that the *Aboriginal people should be pleased to have her* now that *she has decided to be one of them.* But unfortunately for Bobbi Sykes, the Aboriginal people have not been at all impressed with her sudden conversion to Aboriginality." (*Identity Magazine*, Nov 1972, p32.[6.14])

[36] Another case of *reductio ad Hitlerum* working both ways (see Chapter 8.2.1).

[37] Bickford wrote: "There are many reasons why people of Aboriginal descent deny their Aboriginality. Australia is a racist country. Oppressed people [are] constantly under threat, and excluded from society not because of some undesirable quality of their own but, because of discrimination, many deny their Aboriginality in an attempt to be accepted for themselves, not rejected for their colour. It is not uncommon for women to deny their Aboriginality in order to protect their children from the persecution they themselves have suffered. Perhaps this is why Annette Mansell, interviewed in the film, doesn't wish to be seen as an Aboriginal. In Tasmania, the Aboriginal survivors have a double burden of oppression to bear." [[6.10], p6.]

tion of longstanding family feuds to 'send her to Coventry'. Annette is now in Burnie, and her appearance on the *Monday Conference* shows she has every intention of sticking to her guns and fighting back.

So in 1978, Annette Mansell and Melvyn Everett had the fortitude to *choose* to deny they were Aboriginal, as Haydon explained:

> Why does Bickford not listen to Annette's own reasons for denying she's an Aborigine? Annette explains in the film: "There are no Aboriginals. There's not much in any of us ... There's no tradition in Tasmania with the Aboriginals. I don't think you'll find any half castes, quarter castes or any castes in Tasmania that could talk the Aboriginal language, in Tasmania that is."

She is saying that because so little survives of the Tasmanian Aboriginal culture, she cannot feel herself to be a Tasmanian Aborigine. The other descendant who speaks in the film, Melvyn Everett, gives his reason very concisely:

> We can't speak the language ... therefore why should we be called Aborigines. No one can prove it.

Mansell and Everett express the common sense of ordinary people - one's identity is not just genetic, it is also largely cultural - the language and traditions of one's family and society.[38] Without the language, culture and tradition of a medieval Norseman, one is not a Viking by just possessing 1% Viking DNA.[39] At the heart of the testimony by Annette and Melvyn lies an essential historical statement: the Tasmanian Aborigines, as a distinct human society with their own culture, are no longer with us.[40]

But by 1995 Annette Mansell was making choices again. It was reported that, 'Annette Mansell is currently Manager

---

[38] This is of course what is being used on the mainland to validate being an Aborigine - re-enacting (inventing) 'culture' to prove 'Aboriginality'.

[39] See Chapter 7.4.2

[40] Tom Haydon, 'A Witness to History', *Filmnews*, 1 April 1979, p12ff.

of Tasmanian Aboriginal Centre in Burnie'.[41] So here was real proof of Bolt's 'trend' that some Australians of mixed Aboriginal ancestry can, and do, choose to identify with one or another of strands that are available to them. Annette Mansell had appeared on film, adamant that she was *choosing not* to identify as Aboriginal in her younger years, but then later in life, she was just as adamant when *choosing to* revert to her maiden name and identify as Annette Peardon, **a Tasmanian Aboriginal** activist at the TAC.[6.15]

As Bolt had observed in other cases, Annette seemed to be reaching into her bag of multi-ancestries and choosing one to identify with, the Aboriginal one.

6.1.2 Parlevar Truganini v Mansell the 'Hybrid'

Activists pushing the views of Michael Mansell had tried to bully the Tom Haydon supporters into believing the first peoples of Tasmania had not become extinct with the passing of Truganini. Mansell had achieved some success in changing consciousness - the number of people identifying as Tasmanian Aborigines had grown from 671 in the 1971 census to 2,942 in 1976 and academics such as Dr Lyndall Ryan had begun to publish in support of his modernisation of the definition Tasmanian Aboriginal.[42]

But the general public, as well as the government and parts of the judiciary, were still wedded to the traditional understanding of the facts of Tasmania's Aboriginal history, as Mansell was to discover.

The Parlevar and the Statutory Aborigines

In 1978 the committee of a critical state government report on the future of Aboriginal affairs in Tasmania canvassed a number of possible definitions for Tasmania's Aboriginal people:

---

[41][6.8] p25.
[42]Ryan, L., *The Aboriginal Tasmanians,* 1981, p253-5.

"I would sooner be called an Aborigine than a half-caste."
Ida West, Hobart Aboriginal matriarch 1 Sept 1978;

"... the documented fact that Truganini died in 1876 has been used to dismiss any argument that the Cape Barren islanders are survivors of the Tasmanian ..." - **Dr Lyndall Ryan**

"This hybrid people, the progeny largely (but not entirely) of Tasmanian Aboriginal women and European men ..." - **NJB Plomley**[43]

In the end the committee came to a what they believed was a sensible compromise suitable for a modern Tasmania:

> For the purposes of this report the words Aborigine or Aboriginal is used to describe a living person of Aboriginal descent according to the usual usage of the Commonwealth Department of Aboriginal Affairs, that is 'an Aboriginal is a person of Aboriginal descent who identifies himself as such and who is recognised by the Aboriginal community as being an Aboriginal' [i.e. Statutory Aboriginality by the three-part rule].

> In order to avoid confusion between past and present people, the former full-blooded tribes people of Tasmania will be referred to by their own most common generic term of *Parlevar*.[44]

> The words Aborigine or Aboriginal will therefore be used to describe the existing Aboriginal population of Tasmania who identify as such, and who have been previously generally referred to by a number of terms including Bass Strait Islander, Cape Barren Islander, Islander, Straitsman, Hybrid, Part-Aboriginal, Half-Caste, or Aboriginal Descendent [*sic*].

> Within the terms of the usual usages of the words Aborigine or Aboriginal, the Australian Bureau of Statistics 1976 Census of population and housing (28/8/78) reveals an Aboriginal (or Torres Strait Islander) population in Tasmania of 2,942 people who have rights as such under Commonwealth Law.

On the face of it this does seem sensible, but like many political compromises in life, the parties holding the two opposing views

---

[43] Report of the Aboriginal Affairs Study Group of Tasmania, Parliamentary Papers, 1978, p7.[6.16]

[44] 'The root of this word, which means 'human being', in the same sense as the word Maori, was used by the original tribes of Tasmania in the south, east, north and north-west of the island'.(*ibid.*, p8.) (See *A word List of the Tasmanian Aboriginal Languages* by NJB Plomley & Tasmanian Government 1976, p316.)

were unlikely to be fully satisfied. The committee was saying
that 'any claim that there are no aborigines in Tasmania is
false - there were nearly 3000 of them that claimed to meet the
current Commonwealth definition'. A Tom Haydon-minded
person would agree with the Commonwealth's qualifier that
they were of (Tasmanian) Aboriginal descent, which is true.

The committee also noted that, 'the last full blooded aborigine Truganini died in 1876', and she and her past people,
'the former full blooded tribes of Tasmania will thus be referred
to as Parlevar.' Clearly the committee recognised that modern Tasmanian Aborigines were *different* to Truganini and the
'old people', the Parlevar. They even stated that ,"this original race [Parlevar] died out during the nineteenth century."[45]
A Tom Haydon-minded person would be pleased with these
definitions.

However, the Michael Mansell-minded Aboriginal activists
were not, as the next round of 'legal discourse in the courts,
the least promising field in which to explore the concepts of
[Aboriginal] identity' would show.

6.1.3   The Tasmanian Dams Case

Just after the lunch recess on Friday 3 June 1983, Murray
Gleeson QC rose to his feet in the High Court. He was acting
for the Tasmanian government who had wanted to dam the
Franklin River. The Commonwealth was opposed, one reason
in their statement of claim being that the dam area was of
'particular significance to people of the Aboriginal race'. It
was the fourth day of the trial where the meaning of an Aboriginal person was to be critical to the outcome of the case,
and Gleeson was sent in to argue for the Tasmanian government.

The question Gleeson said, agreeing with the commonwealth, was whether the site was 'of particular significance to

---

[45] *op.cit.*, p17.

the people of the Aboriginal race'. It would have been better
if Gleeson had stopped there, but he didn't, noted one observer.[46] He pressed on:

> Now, the word "Aboriginal" is a word whose meaning varies
> according to the context in which it appears. It is used in
> relation to the Red Indians in the United States of America
> and to the Maoris in New Zealand. It is undefined in the
> World Heritage Properties Conservation Act of 1983 but we
> would submit that it means people who belong to the same
> race as the persons who inhabited Australia at the time of
> white settlement ... Now, the facts seem to indicate that the
> Tasmanian Aborigines were a distinct race of people from the
> race of people who occupied the mainland of the continent
> at the time of white settlement, and the facts also seem to
> indicate that the former race is now extinct.
>
> I simply say that, to indicate that, it is not entirely easy to
> understand precisely how the protection and conservation of
> these caves is of particular significance to the people of the
> Aboriginal race.

Michael Black QC, who appeared as counsel for the Wilderness
Society, is recorded as saying:

> Once he said that, you could almost feel the atmosphere freeze
> ... It warmed up afterwards because people in Tasmania who
> had Aboriginal ancestry, they got terribly upset about it.

Yet, Gleeson was only doing what he thought was his job. His
thinking reflected what had been taught in schools for the past
100 years - that a woman called Truganini, who died in 1876,
had been 'the last Tasmanian Aborigine' - but, as he was to
find out, this was far removed from more recent thinking.

The TAC had instructed barrister Stephen Walmsley to
appear on their behalf to counter Gleeson's statements. Before
the hearing resumed on Day 6 (Tuesday 7 June), the TAC's
Michael Mansell led a small contingent of demonstrators outside the court and claimed to represent 4000 Tasmanians with
Aboriginal blood: "It's a demonstration of our existence," said

---

[46]This section is a paraphrase from Michael Pelly, *Murray Gleeson – The Smiler*,
Federation Press, 2014, p112-5.

Mansell. He said it was a common misconception that Tasmanian Aboriginals were extinct just because Truganini had been the last full-blood Tasmanian Aboriginal - many had left the state and returned later while others had children with white settlers. Mansell continued:

> They think that by propagating the myth that we don't exist they can relieve the High Court of any responsibility to us or our interests. If we're sitting on the steps of the High Court they can hardly continue to claim that we don't exist.[47]

After Tasmania and the states finished their submissions, Walmsley got to his feet and, in addressing the court, played the 'victim card of hurt feelings':[48]

Walmsley: Your Honours, leave is sought to intervene on a limited basis ... Last Friday, at page 361 of the transcript, Mr Gleeson ... referred to the existence of the Tasmanian Aborigines as a race. And at that page it was suggested by him that the facts seem to indicate that that race was extinct. Now, the suggestion that the Aboriginal race of Tasmania was extinct was ... one which was very hurtful to the Tasmanian Aboriginals and the hurt is evidenced by the affidavit evidence which has been filed, in particular the affidavit of Heather Sculthorpe and it is referred to as well by Michael Mansell in his affidavit.

Chief Justice Harry Gibbs: Do I understand you to say that the sole purpose of your intervention is directed towards combating this suggestion that the Aboriginal natives of Tasmania are extinct? ... we know that it is certainly disputed that the Aboriginal natives of Tasmania are extinct.

Walmsley: Yes, and that the caves have particular significance to them.

Ellicott QC [Acting for Tasmania with Gleeson] rose to his

---

[47]Stephen Mills, 'Tasmanian Aborigines plan to demonstrate their existence', *The Age*, 7 June 1983.[6.17]

[48]'Tasmanian Dams Case', Transcript of Proceedings at Canberra on Wed 8 June 1983, AT 10.03 AM, p517.

feet as soon as Walmsley finished.

Gibbs: Yes, Mr Ellicott?

Ellicott: Your Honours, as a statement has been made that, what Mr Gleeson was intending to say was intended to be hurtful to anybody, might I just say that those comments were not intended to be — (*interrupted*)

Gibbs: I do not think Mr Walmsley said it was intended to be hurtful, he said, "It was hurtful".

Ellicott: Well, I just wanted to make it clear they were not intended to be hurtful.

Gibbs: I am quite sure no one thought Mr Gleeson was intending to be hurtful.

In the end, there was no specific mention of Gleeson's 'extinct' argument in the judgement but it was clearly rejected by those in the majority.[49] They said the dam site had sufficient 'particular' significance to Aboriginal people to justify special laws. Those in dissent said the decision to protect the site was significant for all mankind not just the Aboriginals, so it could not be a special law.

The court may have accepted that Gleeson didn't intend to be hurtful, but his comments left him and the Tasmanian Government open to attack from activists and politicians such as Federal Minister for Aboriginal Affairs, Clyde Holding:

> It is one thing to perpetuate the lie that there are no Aborigines, but it is bordering on contempt to assert the lie as a meaningful legal submission before the High Court as the Tasmanian Government did last week.[50]

Gleeson had touched a raw nerve with those who had Aboriginal antecedents, particularly the 'emerging ethnic elites' who needed to establish, no matter how spurious, their claim for continuity with an 'authentic' tribal past. If Mansell could not

---

[49] The case was decided 4 to 3.

[50] Amanda Buckley, 'No Tasmanian Aborigines? It's a lie says minister', *The Age*, 8 June 1983.[6.18]

convince that *he* was the inheritor of that past, then he and the TAC had no political future.

Although the TAC strategy of 'bullying by demonstration' was an effective way of publicly shaming those like Gleeson who perpetuated the so-called 'extinction myth', the change in public consciousness is still far from complete. The fact of extinction is still widely believed today, otherwise a recent 2021 Tasmanian Government report on Truth-telling would not have devoted so many paragraphs trying to dispel it in the public's mind. It is obvious from the report that a goal of the authors is to bully the public by repetition into discarding their belief in extinction and to accept the 'white Aborigines' of Tasmania as authentic Parlavar with a rightful claim on Tasmania's tribal past:[51]

> The Truth-Telling Commission should ... create a permanent and official historical record of the past, which includes clarifying the historical record, quashing the extinction myth and recording and explaining the resilience and survival of the Aboriginal people;[52]
>
> Timeline: 1876 - Truganini dies, sparking a myth about the extinction of Tasmanian Aboriginal people;[53]
>
> Timeline 1983 - Tasmanian Dam Case – the Tasmanian Government claims that the kuti kina Cave [*sic*] could not be of special significance to Aboriginal people because Tasmanian Aborigines were extinct;[54]
>
> Education in schools and tertiary institutions was also seen as a way of disseminating the truth, including revising history books to address the falsity of the extinction myth;[55]
>
> Healing was frequently mentioned as an outcome of truth-telling. Some saw it as an essential step in working through inter-generational trauma; others saw it as a means of demonstrating [their] pride ... for others it was seen as a means of tackling the extinction myth. Some people expressed hope

---

[51]Professor Kate Warner, *et al*, *Pathway to Truth-Telling and Treaty Report to Premier Peter Gutwein*, Nov 2021.
[52]*ibid.*, p8.
[53]*ibid.*, p15.
[54]*ibid.*, p16.
[55]*ibid.*, p33.

that quashing the extinction myth would also have a positive impact on how Tasmanian Aboriginal people are perceived by mainland Aboriginal communities – that Tasmanian Aboriginal people would 'be taken seriously' and that pale-skinned Aboriginal people would not be faced with scepticism in the face of their claims of Aboriginality;[56]

Anthropologist Christopher Berk writing of the value of palawa kani [the concocted new language] argues, 'palawa kani is a cultural artefact ... As such, it is 'a vehicle through which Tasmanian Aboriginal extinction and non-existence can be challenged and effectively erased'.[57]

As many of us reflect on our own Tasmanian education, we recognise the false history presented to us as children – particularly that the Aboriginal people of Tasmania became extinct in 1876 with the death of Truganini. We can readily grasp the fundamental importance of education as a vehicle to ensure that all Tasmanian students learn the truth of our history of colonial invasion and violent dispossession of land without negotiated agreement; the rounding up of remaining Aboriginal bands and their exile to Flinders Island; the resilience and survival of Tasmania's Aboriginal people despite the apocalypse to which they were subjected; the richness of culture, language, spirituality, and the deep, deep connection to Country that results from an abundant life in this beautiful place since time immemorial ...

Any pathway to truth-telling and treaty must include a commitment to ensure that Tasmanian students are taught truths about our own history.[58]

Like Bolt, many Australians 'refuse to surrender [their] reason and pretend white is really black, just to aid some [Tasmanian's] self-actualisation therapy'[59] that the original Tasmanian Aborigines are not extinct. The science *is* settled and anthropologically, as a people, the original Tasmanian Aborigines really are extinct, although they are still very much alive and with us ideologically and politically.

---

[56] *ibid.*, p37.
[57] *ibid.*, p90.
[58] *ibid.*, p93.
[59] Andrew Bolt, 'White fellas in the black', *Herald Sun*, 21 August 2009.

6.1.4   It's So Hip to Be Black-face

> *No doubt he has Aboriginal ancestry, but why does he not also*
> *identify with his obvious European background ... a question*
> *for even our most famous Aboriginal leaders ... Fair Michael*
> *Mansell, the Tasmanian firebrand, clearly has more European*
> *than Aboriginal ancestry ... I'm saying only that this self-*
> *identification as Aboriginal strikes me as self-obsessed, and*
> *driven more by politics than by any racial reality.*

Andrew Bolt[60]

Jim Everett, a founding colleague of Michael Mansell's TAC,[61]
would also appear to be a case in point of Bolt's critique.
Everett claims[62] to be:

> a plangermairreenner [Aboriginal] man of the First Nations
> of north-east Tasmania. I am not Australia's imagined Abo-
> rigine, nor do I identify as an Australian citizen...

> my matriarchal grandmother [*sic*] is wapperty [= Wabbitti =
> Wobberetee] of the plangermairreenner, and my patriarchal
> grandfather [*sic*] is manalargenna of the leetermairremener.
> My mother is Ena Everett (née Maynard), and my father is
> Keith Everett.

> I am known as Jim Everett-puralia meenamatta ... I don't
> identify as an Australian citizen because Aboriginal people
> haven't made any agreements with Australia to be citizens.

> The Australian governments, right back to the colonial gov-
> ernments, have never asked us to be citizens: They never
> made any agreements with us to be citizens. We had no for-
> mal documentation or ceremonies to mark such an occasion.

However, what Jim Everett is engaging in here is 'selective
remembrance' - he has not disclosed that, by necessity, he is
also a direct descendant of the infamous sealer **James Ev-**

---

[60] Andrew Bolt, 'It's so hip to be black', *Herald Sun*, 15 April, 2009.

[61] "As the newly appointed secretary of the Tasmanian Aboriginal Centre [TAC], Jim
Everett was catapulted into national controversy by Michael Mansell's trip to Libya
in April this year. A close associate of Mansell, Jim welcomed the opportunity to
put his case for Aboriginal sovereignty." (Cassandra Pybus, 'Ancient links give poet
fight', *The Age*, 26 Dec 1987.)

[62] *There Is No Other World: Country and Politics* - a Keynote Presentation to the
ASAL 2022 Conference Keith "Jim" Everett puralia-meenamatta", 26 Oct 2022.

erett, whose surname he still carries. The Aborigines Protector, George Augustus Robinson, records James Everett as being the abductor of the Aboriginal woman, Worethmaleyerpodeyer (Piper River, b. c1811), who he is alleged to have later murdered because 'she did not clean the mutton birds to please him'. Jim is as much a British descendant from his great-grandfather James as he is an Aboriginal descendant from his great-grandmother **Betsy Miti**, who was half-Aboriginal and half-Maori.[6.19]

This is the problem that Andrew Bolt was alluding to in the 2009 newspaper articles that saw him 'stitched up' in the Federal Court. Instead of looking at their identity as a mixed-ethnic whole, like most of Australians do, many Aboriginal activists seem to be obsessed with only selecting one part of their mixed ancestry, that which they perceive will give them political and financial clout - the Aboriginal one.

As Bolt, perhaps offensively to some, but certainly effectively, told his readership:

> that's modern race politics at our universities and anywhere else where grants and privileges are now doled out. Hear that scuffling at the trough? That's the sound of black people being elbowed out by white people shouting, "but I'm Aboriginal too." They are the 'white Aborigines' - people who out of their multi-stranded but largely European genealogy decided to identify with the thinnest of all those strands ... the Aboriginal one.[63]

The point of all this is to demonstrate that Jim Everett has reached deep into his mixed bag of ancestries and solely chosen his Aboriginal strand as the way to identify himself. There is nothing wrong with this from a cultural, social, family or community point of view. He has the perfect right to self-identify any way that he wants to, and it is no business of anyone else.

---

[63] Andrew Bolt, 'White fellas in the black', *Herald Sun*, 21 Aug 2009.

However, the moment Everett steps into the public square and demands special political and economic rights because of his ancestry, this is a direct challenge to Australia's system of equality before the law.[64] His proposals are a great danger to democracy. As Australian citizens and taxpayers, we have a right to critique, disagree with, and push back against his claims which are based on racism - the dividing of us by race. This is not just a political observation against Everett on my part. Jim himself is quite open about the professional, taxpayer-funded route he took with his career as a 'professional Aborigine', in Bolt's terminology:

> Eventually, I got a job as the first State Liaison Officer for Aboriginal Affairs; the first state-government specified position for an Aboriginal person. Just prior to that, I had five months working for the Tasmanian Aboriginal Centre as a legal aid officer, and that was a big thing for me, to work with people like Michael Mansell, Heather Sculthorpe, and many others, including Pierre Slicer, who later became a justice of the Supreme Court here in Hobart. And they were the political thinkers that I grew up with. Very quickly, I learnt politics. And I was writing political papers, almost from the word go in 1980. I became involved in these politics, and I have been ever since.[65]

In reality, Jim's claims appear to be a spurious attempt to create an 'authentic tribal past'. Apparently, Jim wants Australians to believe he is the same as a Truganini, a William Lanne or a Woorrady, one of the old people, the Parlevar. Although he has said he believes that Aboriginality is not a matter of genetics or skin colour - "Our black is inside us," he says, "nurtured and defended"[66] - that is not how he seems to act. Rather, as will be shown, his actions confirm what Bolt was saying - that there is a relationship between one's ancestry and how one looks.

---

[64] As now seen in Victoria with the new Statewide Treaty 2025 legislation - See Janet Albrechtsen, 'The hustle for special rights is a hoax', *The Australian*, 12 Nov 2025.

[65] Everett, J., 'There Is No Other World: Country and Politics', a Keynote Presentation to the ASAL 2022 Conference, 26 October 2022.

[66] Cassandra Pybus, 'Ancient links give poet fight', *The Age*, 26 Dec 1987.

There is an old saying that is useful when trying to determine someone's real political stance - 'don't listen to what he says, but look at what he does'. In Jim Everett's case, the fact that he seems to be a supporter of 'black-face' pretty much says it all. As the Aboriginal cultural consultant to the 2018 film, *The Nightingale*, Jim advised the local Tasmanian Aboriginal community and the film's producers that bringing in black Aboriginal actors from the Northern Territory was the way to go:

> In fact, they could see the sense of it because we [in Tasmania] have no trained actors who are 23 who have got really, really dark skin. So they understood the common sense of that and they had no problems at all.[6.19]

Ultimately, the leading role as the Tasmanian Aboriginal character in the film went to the very 'black-skinned' Baykali Ganambarr from Elcho Island, off the coast of the Northern Territory:

> One day I was just chilling, minding my own business and the next thing you know someone on Facebook tagged me on a post: "Need an Aboriginal actor with no acting experience". I was just like, might as well just give it a try. I auditioned and after I got the role, the first thing I did was call my sister. I was like, "Hey, sis, I got a lead role in a feature film".[6.20]

This begs the question, if distant ancestry and skin colour are so unimportant to one's acceptance as a Tasmanian Aborigine, why didn't any of the thousands of Tasmanian Aborigines living in Tasmania today get this role for an actor with no experience?

Everett himself was also quite happy to appear in the 1992 film, *Black Man's Houses*[67] doing his own 'black-face'. He needed to do this so he would look like a tribal Tasmanian Aborigine and be validated as one of the Parlevar.[6.19] If skin colour is not a factor in being an authentic Tasmanian Aborigine, then why did Jim Everett feel the need to do 'black face' to gain acceptance?

---

[67]Ronin Films, 1992.

Once again, this obsession with racial difference that becomes so strong in a man like Jim Everett that he is driven to blacken his face to fit the stereotype, only serves as real evidence that we should have heeded Bolt's warning, from way back in 2009:

> Let's go beyond racial pride. Beyond black and white. Let's be proud only of being human beings set on this land together, determined to find what unites us and not to invent such racist and trivial excuses to divide. Deal?[68]

6.2   An Alternative View - Was Bolt Wrong?

Of course as we know there's an extraordinary ability of people to take offense when it suits them and to indicate that this offence has occurred even before they fully felt it. Being offended is a dramatic capacity of human beings. It's a histrionic ability - you begin by pretending you're offended, you get a response, then you feel you are really offended and eventually you've worked yourself up into a state of anger which you cannot control.

Roger Scruton[69]

University of Melbourne academic and commentator, **Professor Marcia Langton AO**, is generally recognised as the public nemesis of Andrew Bolt's views. They have clashed numerous times over the past decade or more, with both Langton and the Australian Broadcasting Corporation (ABC) (where her comments are frequently aired) having to apologise for allegedly describing Bolt as a 'racist' for his views on a past occasion.[6.22] It is therefore instructional to consider Langton's comments as the other side of the debate on Bolt's opinions regarding the definition of Aboriginality in general, and the *Eatock v Bolt* court case in particular.

---

[68]Andrew Bolt, 'It's so hip to be black', *Herald Sun*, 15 April, 2009.

[69]Roger Scruton, 'How Socialism got Repackaged into Human Rights', Institute of Public Affairs lecture, 2019. See [6.21] at 08:00.

Surprisingly, they appear to agree on several major points, but Langton fails to provide a coherent rebuttal of Bolt's main point - that Australians who are clearly of so little Aboriginal descent should not be making claims on the taxpayer and the state for benefits that the majority of Australians agree should only be going to genuine Aboriginal people in real need. Bolt says the current system is open to abuse, especially by fakes with no Aboriginal ancestry at all. Langton has never accepted that fakes are a major problem. She instead takes the position that it is offensive, harmful and racist to *even query, or ask for proof of* a 'fair-skinned' Australian's claim to self-identify as Aboriginal (see Langton's film-clips here[6.23] & [6.24]).

In 2014, Langton was quoted as saying that:

> I believe that [Bolt's] obsessive writing about the colour of the skin of particular Aboriginal people is malicious and cowardly ... He believes that he is not racist, and I believe that he is sincere in this belief. Nevertheless, I am particularly concerned about the harm that his attacks do to these young ['fair-skinned Aboriginal'] people, the impact on their self esteem, and the harm to other young Aboriginal people. I am concerned because of the very high rates of suicide among our youth and I believe that this kind of abuse contributes indirectly to this outcome.

> [H]is practice, often, is to publicly name a young fair-skinned Aboriginal person ... and draw attention to their 'light skin' or appearance, and then draw an inference that the fact that this person identifies as Aboriginal is somehow fraudulent, or that this person has somehow gained an unfair advantage (such as entry to university) by identifying.

> The inference is that someone who doesn't fit a 'racial' stereotype and who identifies as Aboriginal is necessarily fraudulent. At no time has he provided evidence to support these implied accusations, and the reader is left with the impression that every 'fair-skinned' person is fraudulently claiming benefits that the 'taxpayer' must pay for.

> Bolt argues that there is only one 'race' and yet it is only 'fair-skinned' Aboriginal people who are subjected to his taunts, and not, for instance, Dutch Australians or Italian Australians,

who might benefit from say the fact of the existence of SBS.[70]

I believe that Bolt believes something similar to me ... but
instead of separating the issues, he continues to imply that
any Aboriginal person who does fit a 'racial' stereotype and
who claims to be Aboriginal, does so for the imagined financial
and other benefits that he says are accorded to them.

Further, rather than saying that any benefits ought to be on
the basis of need, his repeated (and I believe, obsessive) published comments and articles on this matter present a series of
imputations that as a whole can be interpreted as a complete
rejection of the right of people descended from an Aboriginal
person to identify as Aboriginal.[6.1]

Langton completely misses Bolt's main argument, which is
that the Australian taxpayer provides resources to assist Aboriginal people in need to integrate into mainstream Australian
society, whether it be by educational or vocational scholarships
and grants, funding for Aboriginal-specific cultural, health or
housing programs, or Indigenous business support, amongst
many other programs, worth some $30 billion per year.[71] When
the public see an Australian step forward, self-identify as Aboriginal and then claim one or more of these taxpayer-funded
benefits, they rightly expect, as Bolt suggests, some audit of
the *bona fides* of that claimant. This is especially true when it
is not immediately apparent they are in fact Aboriginal. Australians are not mugs - they don't subscribe to the notion that
just because someone's great-great-grandfather was Scandina-
vian they can therefore culturally identify as a Viking.[72]

But that is the type of 'self-making'[6.28] that Langton
wants Australians to accept. Her policy would allow any 'white'
Australian to reach back several generations and find one 'convenient ancestor' to claim as being Aboriginal, with no proof
required. All the modern, self-making, 'white' descendant

---

[70]*Special Broadcasting Service*, the predominately taxpayer-funded, 'ethnic-themed'
television and news service.

[71]$6 billion directly & $24 billion indirectly.[6.25]

[72]See Daniel Strand and Anna Kallen, 'I am a Viking! DNA, popular culture and the
construction of geneticized identity', *New Genetics and Society*, Jan 2021, 40(1),
p1-21,[6.26] & film clip here.[6.27]

needs to do is pluck up some courage, self-identify and claim
that his or her family and/or local community now recognises
them as Aboriginal and hey presto, we now have a new proud
(insert tribal name here) Aboriginal Australian ready to sign
a 'to the best of my knowledge' Statutory Declaration.[73] and
start collecting the benefits.

To delegitimise this common sense appraisal of what is
happening on a wide scale in Australia (see following sections),
Langton counters by gaslighting Bolt's opinions - she suggests
his aggressive scepticism of the 'white Aborigines' will lead to
Langton being 'concerned because of the very high rates of
suicide among our youth and I believe that this kind of abuse
contributes indirectly to this outcome'. But she is merely giving license to a technique that is routinely adopted by the
guilty or the exponents of victimhood to avoid scrutiny, viz:
"If you audit or criticize me, or my claims, you will 'trigger'
me and lead me to do 'self-harm' or 'suicide', so you had better
back off."

But this is a concern that we as a society already have to
deal with when it comes to assessing, for example, the claims
and *bona fides* of asylum seekers. On a regular basis, asylum
seekers who arrive illegally on our shores have been very sadly
committing suicide in the Australian community, or while de-
tained in on-shore or off-shore detention centres, due to the
intense questioning of their identity during the asylum-visa
application process. For example, refugee Mano Yogalingam,
aged 23, died by self-immolating in Melbourne in August 2024,
after more than a decade spent on a stalled bridging visa application whilst in Australia.[6.31] He was being asked to prove
who he was - his identity, his ethnicity and his asylum-seeking

---

[73]e.g. "I honestly believe I'm Aboriginal because my grandma told me" or, "We always
knew we had a bit of colour in the family but no one wanted to talk about it because
of the racism in the 1950s" or, "My nana was a Stolen Generations woman, so all
her records were lost". Some fakes don't even need to risk perjuring themselves
by signing a Statutory Declaration[6.29] given that some institutions accept the
'details of two culturally appropriate referees who can vouch for the applicant's
claim to Indigeneity'. See an example of the two referee method used by Bronwyn
Carlson in her application form for the 2013 AIATSIS Stanner Award.[6.30]

claims - before he could be granted the benefits of Australian residency. This is a very tragic outcome, but we as a society demand these requirements, which are supported by both Labor and Liberal governments. In fact, Australia even allows or indeed encourages the use of DNA testing as a way for immigrants to 'prove' their ancestral and familial claims.[6.32] Absolutely no one wants tragic outcomes like Yogalingam's, but as a society we cannot be held to ransom by threats of self-harm by the perceived victims themselves, much less by 'concerns' of their third-party advocates such as refugee-lawyers or, as in the case of questions of Aboriginality, Professor Langton.

The answer to very vexed questions such as these is not to capitulate to moral blackmail by the claimants and alleged victims. To maintain a functioning modern society, Australia cannot give in to the wholesale demands for 'self-determination' and 'self-identification' by groups such as 'fair-skinned' Aborigines, who may or may not be fakes, asylum-seekers and indeed any person who wants a driver's licence, passport, or a job as a doctor in a hospital, without the proof that confirms they are who they say they are.

Another argument used by Professor Langton is an illogical one. She claimed that Bolt should, by his anti-'fair-skinned' Aborigines logic, also object to, 'Dutch Australians or Italian Australians, who might benefit from say the fact of the existence of SBS'.

But Bolt, like his readership, can clearly see that any Australian, of any race, ethnic group or ancestry can turn on the television and 'receive the benefit' of watching a program of Dutch or Italian content. They do not need to submit proof that they are of Dutch or Italian heritage to gain access, unlike for the benefits available specifically and exclusively on the basis of the Aboriginal race that Langton supports. Bolt therefore is not 'singling out "fair skinned" Aboriginal people' on 'the issue of race [which] could be construed as racist'. Rather, he is the complete opposite of a real racist - he, as a 'white man' himself, has spent years and countless newspaper articles and television programs calling out 'white people' for faking their Aboriginality, or for being of such distant Aboriginal descent that they are not Aboriginal in any meaningful way. Based on his public record over decades Bolt is the antithesis of a racist.

Langton also undermines her own critique of Bolt when she admits, 'I believe that Bolt believes something similar to me' because, in a lecture published in 2013, Langton essentially agreed with Bolt's 'cynical and sceptical' view about the claims of Aboriginality of some when she wrote:

> What Andrew Bolt cannot suspect is that many Aboriginal people, including me, are just as cynical and sceptical about all the claims made to 'Aboriginality' or, to use the even more modern and meaningless phrase, 'Indigeneity', by people raised in relative comfort in the suburbs. They cannot be described as disadvantaged, unless you take seriously the racist proposition that one is automatically disadvantaged by having an Aboriginal ancestor and a trace of Aboriginal 'racial' characteristics. Yet they are eligible for special Aboriginal non-government scholarships and, yes, as Bolt argued, although in a highly defamatory way about the particular individuals he targeted, special consideration for enrollment in universities. I have served on scholarship selection committees, and I contend that economic disadvantage must be one of the grounds for selection, and not simply identifying as indigenous. It is nonsense to hand out scholarships funded by philanthropic efforts to people who are not economically disadvantaged. Being descended from an Aboriginal or Torres Strait Islander person who lived before British annexation of our lands is not sufficient reason by itself to hand out money to people who make a claim to being indigenous. This attitude of entitlement is poisoning Aboriginal society just as much as it is poisoning Australian attitudes to indigenous people.[[6.33], p7.]

Langton's only real critique of these views of Bolt's was that he presented them in 'a highly defamatory way' - that is, she agreed with his content but, like Justice Bromberg might have put it, she didn't like his 'manner' or 'tone'.[74] Additionally, with what we now know about Eatock's fake Aboriginality, Bolt's commentary was very unlikely to be defamatory - his honest opinion about Eatock, given in good faith and in the public interest, was substantially true. So yes, perhaps Bolt's journalistic style can be 'humiliating, offensive and insulting' to those who have incurred his literary attention, but that is the price that any of us need to consider before we step into the public square and claim, without any real proof, a special racial identity and then put our hand out for a benefit from the taxpayer based on that identity at the expense of the real people in need for whom the benefit is intended.

At this point it is instructive to consider the impact of the word 'choice' as it appeared in *Eatock v Bolt* and within the context of Justice French's discussion of 'statutory Aborginality'. For to exercise one's personal agency or choice to identify as Aboriginal is at the heart of the conflicting views as to who is, and who isn't, considered Aboriginal in our society today.

To provide an understanding of what racial choice might look like in modern Australia, consider the case of Professor Langton's academic colleague, former University of Canberra Chancellor, **Professor Tom Calma AO** and Langton's co-author of the *Calma-Langton Indigenous Voice Co-Design Report 2021.*

---

[74] *Eatock v Bolt* [2011] at 296, 412 to 416, 425 & 462.[6.34]

For References link - see QR code on page (xv)

References

[6.1]   Prof. Marcia Langton AO. *NACCHO Aboriginal health and racism: Marcia Langton the nature of my QandA apology to Andrew Bolt.* 2014.

[6.2]   Diane Fieldes. *Obituary: Pat Eatock. In RedFlag.* 22 March 2015.

[6.3]   Youtube. *Pat Eatock with a Version of her Declaring her Aboriginality.* No date -(ca1990s?)

[6.4]   The Sunday Times Magazine. *The Last Tasmanian,* 21 May 1978.

[6.5]   Ronin Films. *The Last Tasmanian Study guide.* 1978.

[6.6]   Dark Emu Exposed website. *House of Mansell.*

[6.7]   TAC. *Achievements of the TAC.* 2024.

[6.8]   Dennis W Daniels. *The Assertion of Tasmanian Aboriginality - From the 1967 referendum to Mabo. Master Thesis.* University of Tasmania, December 1995.

[6.9]   Ronin Films. *The Last Tasmanian film clip.* 1978.

[6.10] Anne Bickford. *The Last Tasmanian: Superb documentary or Racist Fantasy? Filmnews.* 1 Jan 1979, p11-14.

[6.11] Peter Sutton. "Cape Barren English". In: *AIATSIS Archives.* Code 242533-1001.Call Number MS 378 (1969), p. 23.

[6.12] Tom Haydon. *A Witness to History. Filmnews.* 1 Apr 1979, p12-14.

[6.13] Dark Emu Exposed webposts. *Kerrie Doyle.*

[6.14] Identity Magazine. *Roberta Sykes Quotes.* 1972.

[6.15] Youtube. *Annette Peardon-Mansell choosing, or not, her Aboriginality.* 1978-2025.

[6.16] Tas. Parliamentary Papers. *Report of the Aboriginal Affairs study Group of Tasmania.* 1978.

[6.17] Stephen Mills. *Tasmanian Aborigines plan to demonstrate their existence, The Age.* 7 June 1983.

[6.18] Amanda Buckley. *No Tasmanian Aborigines? It's a lie says minister. The Age.* 8 June 1983.

[6.19] Dark Emu Exposed website. *The Two Faces of Jimmy Everett.* 2025.

[6.20] Nate Jones. *The Nightingale's Baykali Ganambarr Wants to Bring More Aboriginal Culture to the Big Screen, Vulture Magazine.* 8 Aug 2019.

[6.21] Roger Scruton. *How Socialism got Repackaged into Human Rights.* 16 Sept 2019.

[6.22] Alexandra Back. *The ABC apologises to commentator Andrew Bolt*. *SMH*. 18 March 2014.

[6.23] Prof. Marcia Langton AO. *A Defence of Bruce Pascoe's Aboriginality - on Youtube*. 2021.

[6.24] Prof. Marcia Langton AO. *A Defence of the Aboriginality of Lisa Jackson Pulver - on Youtube at 03:15*. 2023.

[6.25] The Conversation. *FactCheck Q&A: Is $30 billion spent every year on 500,000 Indigenous people in Australia?* 5 Sept 2016.

[6.26] Strand & Kallen. "I am a Viking! DNA, popular culture and the construction of geneticized identity". In: *New Genetics and Society* 40.4 (2021), pp. 520–540.

[6.27] History Channel. *Vikings*. 2024.

[6.28] M. Elliott. "The Inconvenient Ancestor: Slavery and Selective Remembrance on Genealogy Television". In: *Studies in Popular Culture* 39.2 (2017), pp. 73–90.

[6.29] ABC Q&A. *Peter Malinauskas Premier of SA redefines Aboriginality with Senator Jacinta Nampijinpa Price*. 2023.

[6.30] Bronwyn Carlson. *AIATSIS Application Form for 2013 Stanner Award*. 2013.

[6.31] The Guardian Online. *The asylum seeker who saw no way out of Australia's 'cobweb of cruelty'*. 30 Aug 2024.

[6.32] Australian Government. *Information about DNA testing for visa and citizenship applicants*. October 2020.

[6.33] Prof. Marcia Langton AO. *Indigenous Exceptionalism and the Constitutional 'Race Power'*. 2013.

[6.34] *Eatock v Bolt [2011] FCA 1103*. Sept. 28, 2011.

Chapter 7

Choices, Choices

Despite genealogy's history as a form of status-seeking for the aspiring elite ... [it has also] been propelled by the individual pursuit of 'self-understanding' and efforts at 'self-making'. As a cultural practice, genealogy thus exists at an intersection of history and identity, as individuals look to discover unknown information from their family histories as a way of shaping their contemporary identities. Genealogy is indeed a 'way of writing history' but its historical narratives are highly personalized and intended to shape the way subjects see themselves and are 'counted by others'.

Matthew Elliot[1]

7.1 Selective Remembrance & Self-Making

Choosing Race or Ethnicity as Required?

One of the reasons why Justice Bromberg found against Andrew Bolt was that his newspaper articles implied that the 'white Aborigines' [Bolt's term] or 'fair-skinned Aboriginal persons' [Bromberg's classification] *chose* to be Aboriginal at the expense of their other clearly dominant European ancestry.

---

[1]Associate Professor of English at Emmanuel College Boston, USA. From *The Inconvenient Ancestor*, See QR Code [7.1] p74.

Justice Bromberg concluded that:

> in relation to most of the individuals concerned, the facts
> asserted in the Newspaper Articles, that the people dealt with
> chose to identify as Aboriginal, have been substantially proven
> to be untrue.[2]

The fact that Bolt is a popular commentator suggests that
mainstream thinking in Australia might not be in agreement
with the progressive-thinking Justice Bromberg on this point.
Many Australians are acutely aware of Bolt's 'trend' - an increasing number of 'fair-skinned' people *are* popping up and
appear to be *choosing* to identify as Aboriginal - and something doesn't look quite right about some of these claims.
Australians have every right to be concerned about the consequences of the apparent legal ability to *choose* a particular strand of one's multi-race or multi-ethnic ancestry so as
to become a member the new class of Australians known as
'fair-skinned Aboriginal people.'[3] It is naive for anyone to
think that the issue is now simply resolved by the judgment in
Eatock v Bolt. Until recently, nobody except Bolt was saying
much about it, but now even 'progressive' organisations such
as SBS are airing programs on the 'trend'.[4]

This chapter will use a few examples of Australians who
have publicly presented their family histories as a way of invit-
ing us, as Elliot describes in the quotation above, into their
world of 'self-understanding' and their efforts at 'self-making'.
These are well-known public figures who have publicised 'in-

---

[2] *Eatock v Bolt* [2011] FCA 1103 at 378; and [7.2]

[3] Bromberg J at 40: 'The group of people critiqued and the alleged choice of identity
made by them is described [by Bolt] as: "[a] booming new class of victim you'd
never have imagined we'd have to support with special prizes and jobs. They are
'white Aborigines' – people who, out of their multi-stranded but largely European
genealogy, decide to identify with the thinnest of all those strands, and the one that's
contributed least to their looks. Yes, the Aboriginal one now so fashionable among
artists and academics"; [And at 41] '...reader[s are led] to understand that Mr Bolt
was asserting that the people in the 'trend' had made a deliberate choice to identify
as Aboriginal people include: "...people, who, out of their multi-stranded but largely
European genealogy, decide to identify with the thinnest of all those strands."; See
[7.3]

[4] See Karla Grant, 'Indigenous Identity. Why are more people identifying as First
Nations, who decides and what's at stake?', *SBS Insight*, No. 34, 2022. See [7.4]

formation from their family histories as a way of shaping their contemporary identities ... and intended to shape the way [they] see themselves and are counted by others'. The goal of this chapter is to further explore the issues raised between the *Bolt-minded* and *Bromberg-minded* sides of the debate, namely, should we be using the law to divide Australians into 'classes' based on their historical and genealogical identities - their 'race' no less?

7.2 Professor Tom Calma's Self-Making

Professor Tom Calma AO is a well-known and respected Australian academic and public servant. He was formerly the chancellor of the University of Canberra and has spent a career as an Aboriginal Australian human rights and social justice campaigner. He has been involved in a large way in the Stolen Generations, Reconciliation and Close the Gap movements. He publicly self-identifies as an:

> Aboriginal Elder from the Kungarakan tribal group and a member of the Iwaidja tribal group whose traditional lands are south west of Darwin and on the Cobourg Peninsula in the Northern Territory of Australia, respectively.[7.5]

Notwithstanding clearly looking like an Aboriginal man and being considered as such by others, on the 26th of January 2023, Professor Calma reached into his bag of mixed family genealogies and revealed to the world that he also considered himself, on this particular day, to be Dutch.

For on this Australia Day in 2023, The Dutch Australian Cultural Centre (DACC)[5] wanted to congratulate Calma for being chosen as Senior Australian of the Year, and also to point out and recognise Calma for having a Dutch grandfather. When the Ambassador of the Embassy of the Kingdom of the Netherlands, Mrs Marion Derckx, congratulated Pro-

---

[5]The DACC was 'founded in 1983 to provide a central organisation to preserve the rich Dutch history in Australia'. (See: www.dutchaustralianculturalcentre.com.au)

fessor Calma on his award, she also revealed that Tom was, 'also proud to share that his heritage is 75% Indigenous and 25% Dutch.' She also proudly related how **Edwin Verburg**, Tom's mother's father, had been a pioneering Dutch engineer and agriculturist in the Northern Territory who 'with a few blacks to help him ... constructed a grand little weir in the Adelaide River' that later was upgraded to a bridge that still carries his name today.[7.6] This illustrates nicely that Calma himself is quite comfortable to have his ancestry described in terms of a 'blood quantum'.

Perhaps that perfectly illustrates Andrew Bolt's point and reflects badly on Professor Langton's and Justice Bromberg's confused understanding as to what Bolt was really articulating in his articles. It is that we all have choices to decide how we see ourselves, our identity, and which parts we want to emphasize in making each of us who we want to be. As the above opening quotation by Matthew Elliot observed, there is a rising trend for many in our community to engage in self-understanding and self-making as a way of shaping their contemporary identities. By way of writing history, people can create historical narratives that are highly personalized and intended to shape the way subjects see themselves and how they are 'counted by others.' Yet sometimes those choices and attempts at self-making look confusing, even delusional, as well as self-serving or political, and the law's response to defend or enforce those choices looks hypocritical and unjust.

Bolt was crucified by the law for suggesting that Pat Eatock, a 'fair-skinned' woman of predominately Scottish descent, had reached into her bag of family genealogies and *chose* to pull out her minority Aboriginal ancestry so as to obtain a series of public benefits. In contrast, the Dutch Ambassador was celebrated for encouraging Tom Calma, a 'dark-skinned' Aboriginal man, to do exactly the same thing in a 'reversal of colour' - reaching into his own bag of family genealogies and *choosing* to identify as a Dutchman on Australia Day in 2023 so as to receive the benefit of recognition from a Dutch cultural group. If Calma moved to Amsterdam, claimed that he was Dutch, and applied for a job legally reserved for people of Dutch ancestry, would he get the job, no questions asked? Probably not.

In our private lives no one really cares, or even should care, how we identify. But if we are a public figure like Calma, or the recipient of public largesse, like Bolt's 'white Aborigines', we have extra responsibilities to society - to those funding us, to those who genuinely qualify, and to those who are in real need and for whom the benefits are really intended. How this looks to others then becomes important - we need to be *seen* to be doing the right thing - and our actions should be open to critique where discrimination, hypocrisy or even fraud appear to be lurking. Bolt's popularity is that he articulates for his readership this hypocrisy, which many Australians can clearly see.

The Hereditary Aristocracy of Professor Calma

The topic of ancestral choice can be explored more deeply by delving further into the family genealogy of Professor Calma. Calma is recognised as someone who very publicly appears to rely explicitly upon his Aboriginality to reinforce his qualifications, lived experience and suitability to be chosen for various taxpayer-funded government positions. His ancestry will thus provide an excellent proxy for the topics discussed here - ancestral claims, choice, identity and the benefits or costs that flow from those choices.

These all have a direct bearing on Aboriginal truth-telling, political self-determination, justice, recognition and the reconciliation agendas that Calma himself has championed over the past decades. Longer term, the progression of these agendas will have a profound effect on Australia because the logical political goal of this process is the UN-sponsored, self-determination of Australia's Aboriginal and Torres Strait Islander peoples as a 'First Nations' polity. This will necessarily mean dividing Australians by race and will lead ultimately to the breaking up of Australia's current single polity of equal citizens.[6] In place of today's single sovereign state of the Commonwealth of Australia, a new additional internationally recognised political and social hierarchy - an Aboriginal 'state' within a state - will be developed. This is an important goal of the advocates of this process.

On one level, this First Nations 'State' will resemble an aristocracy given it will be based on one's birthright as a descendant member of the first peoples of this land and one's ancestral connections to kin and so-called 'Country'. On another level, it will be hereditary in the sense that any rights accrued to these 'first peoples' will be passed on to their children, they too being classed as Aboriginal by descent. And finally it will racist, just like South Africa's failed apartheid system was, because it will require a legal system that recognises statutory Aboriginality, which is an acceptance of 'separateness' (apartheid in Afrikaans) that will formally divide Australians based on race.[7]

This new, aspirational Aboriginal aristocracy has already begun speaking in words that reflect a system of titles and

---

[6]This is the ultimate aim of the United Nations Declaration on the Rights of Indigenous Peoples (UNDRIP) agenda which the activists and many of Australia's intellectuals and institutions are constantly, but very quietly at this stage, pushing for. Australia endorsed UNDRIP in 2009 and in international forums has committed to take actions to implement the Declaration. No Australian government has as yet, due to the inevitable legislative difficulties and the UNDRIP's unpopularity, taken steps to implement the UNDRIP into law, policy and practice.[7.7] An important goal in UNDRIP's implementation was the proposed Voice, whose 2023 referendum was resoundingly defeated by the Australian public.

[7]If this sounds far-fetched, just consider how South Africa's Apartheid system started, in many ways by people of political goodwill. According to Brian Lapping in his book, Apartheid - A History[7.8], South Africans were, "not uniquely evil or racist or authoritarian people. They did not go suddenly wrong in 1948, when the National Party came to power and imposed a rigid form of racial segregation; they went wrong because every previous step along the fatal road had seemed to work. When they launched into full-blown apartheid it seemed to nearly all of them the only way forward." Then watch the film clip of Dr Hendrik Verwoerd, South African Premier in 1948, and Australia's Prime Minister, Anthony Albanese in 2023, explaining Apartheid and The Uluru Statement respectively - and then try to explain how, as naive politicians, their reassuring words don't actually both sound the same? [7.9]

connections to particular bits of land or estates, just like their European counterparts, the landed gentry of old.[8] These new aristocrats aim to develop new laws and organisations to *demand* 'recognition, deference, and respect' from the rest of us, the 'plebs' who make up the non-Aboriginal classes. They will also claim support from government grants, and land-holdings (Native Title rights, and the national parks[7.10] and Crown land now being handed over from the state to Indigenous corporations) which will fund a vast, rent-seeking aristocratic lifestyle. The construction of the foundations for this new aristocracy are already well underway in Australia, as evidenced by the additional 'voices' being sought in parliament (e.g. the national Uluru Statement) or by treaty (Victoria's First People Assembly) or by a legislated pathway direct to parliament and government (South Australia's *First Nations Voice Act 2023*).

This is what Aboriginal self-determination really means - a splitting of Australia and Australians into two separate polities based on race. Australia will have adopted a version of apartheid, or separateness, for its Aboriginal and Torres Strait Islander races. Former Prime Minister Bob Hawke's commitment "In Australia, there is no hierarchy of descents, there must be no privilege of origin" will have come to nought.[9]

---

[8]e.g. "Proud Yuin man and Elder, Uncle Bruce, from Yuin Country"; "Senator Malarndirri McCarthy is a Yanyuwa woman from the Gulf country in the Northern Territory."

[9]*Fuller excerpt:* "Indeed, in today's Australia, our very diversity is an ever growing source of the richness, vitality and strength of our community. It is true that all these things I have mentioned go to shape the Australian character and define the Australian identity. Yet beyond them, there remains one vital factor in the answer to the question; who is an Australian? And that factor is: a commitment to Australia and its future. It is that common commitment which binds the Australian-born of the seventh or eighth generation and all those of their fellow Australians born in any of the 130 countries from which our people are drawn. **In Australia, there is no hierarchy of descents, there must be no privilege of origin**. The commitment is all. The commitment to Australia is the one thing needful to be a true Australian. Today, at this historic place and at this historic hour, let us renew that commitment, our commitment to Australia and Australia's cause the cause of freedom, fairness, justice and peace." Prime Minister Bob Hawke, 'Australia Day Speech', *Sydney Opera House*, 1988.[7.11]

It is important to note that Professor Calma is not being used as an example for any other reason than he is a respected public servant, funded by taxpayers and he himself appears to have made very specific and public *choices* about which parts of his own family's history and ancestry he chooses to identify himself with, and use as his contemporary public persona. In the terminology of Matthew Elliot,[10] Calma's 'contemporary identity' has been 'highly personalized and intended to shape the way [he sees himself] and [is] counted by others.' He has spoken proudly and fondly about those chosen parts of his ancestry, for which he has publicly provided considerable detail, and how they influenced his own public and political life.[11] Furthermore, his ancestral claims were verifiable from the details publicly provided by Calma himself, coupled with the publicly available genealogical and archival records. This made his apparent Family Tree relatively straightforward to construct.

Selective Remembrance by Professor Calma

Professor Calma's 'self-making' involves his choosing of particular ancestors and also only certain particular events in the lives of those ancestors to support his modern-day political claims. This is what sociologist Eviatar Zerubavel has called 'selective remembrance'.

> Such acts of selective remembrance are inevitable when faced with the sheer number of possible paths one may take into the maze of any ancestry. Because everyone's biological ancestors double each generation heading backwards into the past, roots-seekers face many choices, whether conscious or not, about where to focus their genealogical research and stake their ancestral claims.[12]

Calma identifies as an Aboriginal man, of the **Kungarakan** tribal group on his mother's side and the **Iwaidja** on his fa-

---

[10] See chapter opening quotation above.
[11] *SBS Living Black*: 'Tom Calma - A Lifetime Of Service', No. 16, 2022.[7.12]
[12] [7.1] p76.

ther's side.[7.12] Occasionally, an additional more distant Aboriginal tribe on his father's side, the **Woolwonga**, will be acknowledged.[7.13] Calma only ever publicly identifies as Aboriginal, except for the one instance mentioned above when he acknowledged his 25% Dutch heritage.

Calma is engaging in selective remembrance, for it transpires that his Aboriginal ancestry appears to be less than a majority in his personal ancestry (it is estimated at 44%). His apparent Family Tree (Figure 7.1) indicates that his family ancestry is probably *more than half non-Aboriginal*, consisting of a combination of Dutch (25%), English (est. 19%) and Filipino (est. 12%). Indeed, his own surname is a Filipino one and a direct hand-down from his paternal great-grandfather, **Fortunato Calma**, who was born in the Philippine Islands in 1875. Fortunato arrived in Australia in 1898, staying three years on Thursday Island, then moving to Palmerston (Darwin) where in 1910 he married **May Crawford**, a part-English and part-Woolwonga Aboriginal girl.[7.14] Professor Calma has spoken frequently and publicly about the life of his Aboriginal great-grandmother, May Crawford, but not about her Filipino husband, his great-grandfather, Fortunato. His selective remembrance ignores his Filipino roots. This is disappointing given the important and proud role Filipinos played in the colonisation of northern Australia.

Andrew Bolt in his articles had summed it up well for his readership, who were wedded to the political idea that, as Australians, we are all now equal citizens and our society finally had within its grasp the political and legal reality of racial equality:

> I'm saying only that this self-identification as Aboriginal strikes me as self-obsessed and ... divisive, feeding a new movement to stress pointless or even invented racial differences we once swore to overcome. What happened to wanting us all to become colour blind?[13]

---

[13] Andrew Bolt, 'It's so hip to be black', *Herald Sun*, 15 Apr 2009.

Fortunato CALMA	m. 16 July 1910	**May CRAWFORD**
b. 27 Feb 1875 Argao, Cebu,	Palmerston (Darwin),	b. ca1892 Victoria River,
Philippine Islands – d. 14	Northern Territory	NT – d. 21 Sept 1929
October 1947 Darwin, NT		Darwin, NT
100% Filipino		*50% Aboriginal –*
(*Tom's Great-grandfather*)		*Woolwonga*
		50% English
		(*Tom's Great-grandmother*)

Juana (Johanna) Frenanda	m. not married	**Reuben John COOPER**
CALMA		b. 6 Feb 1898 Wandi, NT
b. ca1908 Darwin, NT – d. 5		– d. 25 Sept 1942
April 1954 Darwin, NT		Oenpelli Mission, NT
25% Aboriginal -		*50% Aboriginal Iwaidja*
Woolwonga		*50% English*
50% Filipino		(*Tom's Grandfather*)
25% English		
(*Tom's Grandmother*)		

Thomas CALMA Snr	m. 1952	**Ada VERBERG**
b. 21 May 1924 Darwin, NT	Northern Territory	b. 11 Nov 1931 Darwin,
– d. 29 Sept 1979 Darwin,		NT – d. 30 Sept 2021
NT		Fannie Bay, NT
37.5% Aboriginal –		*50% Aboriginal -*
Woolwonga & Iwaidja		*Kungarakan tribe*
25% Filipino		*50% Dutch*
37.5% English		(*Tom's Mother*)
(*Tom's Father*)		

Professor Thomas (Tom)	*44% Aboriginal –*	
Edwin CALMA	*Woolwonga, Iwaidja &*	
b. 1953 Adelaide River, NT	*- Kungarakan*	
	12% Filipino	
	19% English	
	25% Dutch	

Figure 7.1: A branch in the apparent Family Tree of Professor Tom Calma AO indicating his ancestral Filipino ancestry up to his great-grandfather Fortunato Calma whose surname Tom still carries. Ancestry percentages (%) are only approximate estimates. Full apparent Family Tree for download.[7.15] (Subject to the standard *Disclaimer* on front page (ii).)

And of course, Bolt suffered the legal consequences by those forces intent on establishing selective remembrance as an acceptable and unchallengeable political tool in their campaign to divide Australia by race. Racial equality is slipping from our grasp under the onslaught of movements promoted by people like Professor Calma, such as the divisive Voice referendum and the Uluru Statement, which then fuels others to promote even more divisive policies such as the banning of 'white people' from access to some national parks.[7.10]

In the following sections evidence will be provided to show that Calma's use of selective remembrance is actually *anti*-truth-telling, very divisive and will actually undo reconciliation, which has already largely occurred in Australia.[14]

The *Anti*-Truth-Telling of Professor Calma

During a lunch interview with the *Australian Financial Review* (AFR) in 2023, Professor Calma showed how he uses selective remembrance of his family's history to create his preferred political version of Australia's history - a guilt-laden denigration of race relations in Australia. This is very unfair given that he and his ancestors have done pretty well out of Australia by making the most of the opportunities afforded to them. Calma tells the reporter 'there's nothing vindictive about this

---

[14]Political & social 'reconciliation' has already been achieved in the minds of many Australians with the passing of the 1967 referendum, Aboriginal land rights legislation (from the 1970s up to *Mabo*) and the passing of anti-discrimination laws. Aboriginal Australians now have *exactly the same opportunities* as any other Australian. It is the Aboriginal activist-minded people in Australia, like Calma, who apparently cannot accept that the *'reconciliation' outcome* has been achieved, because they seem to need to maintain the *'reconciliation' process* as a way of validating their own continued political and professional existence. Calma's own definition has largely been met: "In a ... reconciled Australia the length and quality of a person's life will not be determined by their racial background. Our vision of reconciliation is based and measured on five dimensions: historical acceptance; race relations; equality and equity; institutional integrity and unity."[7.16] To paraphrase Senator Jacinta Nampijinpa Price's comments, her ideas represent the best response: reconciliation is what you make it - ditch your victimhood, take up the opportunities offered by our society, and move on. We have reconciled our shared past - Aboriginal, convict, settler, and recent migrant alike. That is why migrants flock here to be part of one of the world's greatest democratic experiments where inter-marriage between 'white-fellows' and 'black-fellows' is the norm.[7.17]

[critique of Australia]' but that would seem to indicate that
he thinks it might sound that way. In his interview resentment rather than gratitude over Australia's history seems to
be Calma's dominant theme:

> Tom Calma has moved appointments to make Lunch with
> the AFR happen today. We meet on the UC campus, where
> the Kungarakan elder and Iwaidja man serves as chancellor
> ... Calma explains his parents met at Coomalie Creek, on the
> family's traditional lands ... His father was an Iwaidja man,
> from the Coburg Peninsula, but like many Aboriginal Aus-
> tralians, his family was dispossessed of their land. He worked
> his way up from being a truck driver, to a work supervisor,
> eventually becoming a technical officer with the federal gov-
> ernment. "He was probably one of the highest-ranking Abo-
> riginal public servants..."

> "My mother was a homemaker and worked on the farm. Her
> mother, my grandmother, a lady named Anmilil, had her
> three youngest children forcibly removed. Mum and her sister
> were lucky, because when they were taking children my grand-
> father sent them to St Gabriel's boarding school in Charters
> Towers, in Queensland. Rather than being taken away, he
> actually sent them away. That was the legacy that we be-
> came very aware of as young children. All the way through
> my growing up we were aware of the practice, because we had
> on both sides of the family children who were removed."

> The experience of his forebears was front of mind when Calma
> delivered a formal response to Kevin Rudd's 2008 national
> apology to the Stolen Generation. Speaking at Parliament
> House, Calma told the story of his great-grandmother on his
> father's side, who was taken from her family. Her name ap-
> pears on a December 1899 document titled List of half-castes
> in the NT. The report says the girl's mother refused to part
> with her, evidence Calma cites to rebut people who claim
> Aboriginal children weren't taken away, but were handed over
> willingly by their parents.

> Despite the pain, he used the speech to call for a process of na-
> tional healing to begin that day. "That's what truth telling is
> a little bit about, it is making sure that things that are history
> are actually known to everybody. There's nothing vindictive
> about this, about people understanding who we are as a na-
> tion, and that we have to really take the opportunity to form

a new nation. We have to shed ourselves of the past, when we were colonised and to recognise that with colonisation, not only in Australia but globally, there are a lot of significant detrimental impacts on Indigenous peoples."[15]

Calma tells the AFR that his father (Tom Calma Snr.) was an [Aboriginal] 'Iwaidja man, from the Coburg Peninsula, but like many Aboriginal Australians, his family was dispossessed of their land'. What Calma doesn't tell the reporter is that the records indicate that his own grandfather and great-grandfather were the ones undertaking the dispossession, if indeed that is the right word to describe colonisation and settlement.[16] According to a book published by **Joy Cardona**, *The Buffalo Shooter*, both herself and Tom Calma were grandchildren of the 'half-caste' buffalo shooter **Reuben Cooper** (1898-1942).[17] Reuben's father had been a white-man, the legendary

---

[15]Tom McIlroy, 'There's nothing vindictive about the Voice' says Tom Calma.', *Australian Financial Review*, 28 April 2023.

[16]The so-called dispossessed Aborigine often expressed their own agency and welcomed the new settlers and their modern world with a willingness to receive which was driven by desires that more often exceeded the losses they may have felt as the frontier moved across Australia. As anthropologist WEH Stanner observed: "The arrival of Europeans here and there in the region of which I speak — a vast region, never fully explored or occupied by the newcomers - was sufficient to unsettle Aborigines still long distances away. The repercussions spread, evidently with great rapidity, along the network of structural interconnections. Eventually, for every Aboriginal who, so to speak, had Europeans thrust upon him, at least one other had sought them out. More would have gone to European centres sooner had it not been that their way was often barred by hostile Aborigines. As late as the early 1930s I was able to see for myself the battles between the encroaching myalls and weakening, now-sedentary groups who had monopolised European sources of supply and work. The encroachers used every claim of right they had - kinship, affinity, friendship, namesake-relationship, trade partnership — to get and keep a toehold." (*Continuity and Change among the Aborigines*, Presidential Address to Section F (Anthropology) ANZAAS, Adelaide, 1958.) And: 'Aborigines told the anthropologist WEH Stanner that their, "appetites for tobacco and to a lesser extent for tea became so intense that nether man nor woman could bear to be without" and as a result, "individuals, families and parties of friends simply went away to places where the avidly desired things could be obtained." - quoted in Partington, G., *Making Sense of History*, Xlibris LLC, 2013, p83. And historian Henry Reynolds agreed, "European goods like steel axes and knives; pieces of iron, tins, cloth and glass were all eagerly sought and used by the Aboriginal tribes even before contact had been made with settlers ... Western food, tobacco and alcohol also exerted a tremendous attraction." - quoted in, Partington, G., *ibid.*, p83.

[17]Joy Cardona's family history book was a finalist in the NT Literary Awards 2009. She is much respected and carried the Olympic Torch in 2000. A 'loving' family photograph with Tom Calma in 2010[7.18] suggests that no family rift occurred when Cardona claimed that, "Reuben was not faithful to [wife] Sally ... he had

Joe Cooper (1860-1936), and his mother an Iwaidja woman named **Alice** (b.unknown - 1929). Joe had married her by Aboriginal custom in about 1890 and then formally, after their continued devotion to each other, in Darwin in 1917.[[7.22] p110.]

Calma uses selective remembrance to very publicly *choose* to 'proudly' claim himself Iwaidja via his father's side of the family right up to his apical ancestor Alice, his great-grandmother, a 'full-blood' Iwaidja woman. However, he fails to apply the same logic and reveal publicly his equal ancestry to her husband and his great-grandfather, the 'coloniser' and 'dispossessor' of English heritage, Joe Cooper (See the Cooper branch of his apparent Family Tree in Figure 7.2).

During Bolt's trial, Justice Bromberg admonished him for leading his readers:

> to understand that Mr Bolt was asserting that the people in the 'trend' had made a deliberate choice to identify as Aboriginal people ... people, who, out of their multi-stranded but largely European genealogy, decide to identify with the thinnest of all those strands.[18]

Yet isn't Calma doing exactly what Bolt had claimed? Calma's, choice may be of a strand that is thicker than that of one of Bolt's typical 'white Aborigines', but it is nevertheless still a choice that is intended to create a personal and often a political persona that he is *only* Aboriginal. Calma can thus claim continuity with an authentic tribal past,[19] that of the historically dispossessed Iwaidja peoples. The fact that his own white ancestors were some of the ones doing the so-called dispossessing is not mentioned by Calma. Much academic and popular in-

---

children to other women [including] Sally's sister ... He then had a child ... with a Tiwi Island lady called Murrawee and another child, **Tom Calma [Snr.], with Juana Calma**".[7.19]. The families' association is confirmed in a 1935 report of a Mr Martin Calma delivering stores for Mr Reuben Cooper.[7.20] Martin was Juana Calma's brother (His parents were the same as Juana's viz: Fortunato and May (from *Findmypast.com*)) However, no birth record could be located for Tom Calma Snr.; his RAAF record says his father was 'unknown'.[7.21]

[18] *Eatock v Bolt* [2011] at 41.

[19] See Chapter 9.3.1 for more on connecting with an authentic tribal past.

George COOPER
b. 1832 Norfolk, **England** – d. 6 September 1911 Cummins, SA
(Tom Calma's 2x Great-grandfather)

m. 11 August 1853
Adelaide, South Australia

Harriett Peverett PLACE
b. 27 September 1835 Stow, Bardolph, Norfolk, **England** – d. 21 July 1871 Rochester, South Australia
(Tom Calma's 2x Great-grandmother)

Robert Joel (Joe) COOPER
b. 29 February 1860 Fairview, South Australia – d. 7 August 1936 Darwin, Northern Territory
100% English ancestry
Buffalo "King of Melville Is"
(*Tom Calma's Great-grandfather*)

m. c. 1890
By Aboriginal Custom
Northern Territory

Alice Rose
b. unknown – d. 27 August 1929 Port Essington, Cobourg Peninsula, Northern Territory
100% Aboriginal Iwaidja from Port Essington
(*Tom Calma's Great-grandmother*)

Reuben John COOPER
b. 6 February 1898 Wandi, Northern Territory – d. 25 September 1942 Oenpelli Mission, Northern Territory
50% Aboriginal Iwaidja from Port Essington
50% English
(*Tom Calma's Grandfather*)

m. didn't marry

Juana (Johanna) Frenanda CALMA
b. c. 1908 Darwin, Northern Territory – d. 5 April 1954 Darwin, Northern Territory
25% Aboriginal - Woolwonga
50% Filipino
25% English
(*Tom Calma's Grandmother*)

Thomas CALMA snr
b. 21 May 1924 Darwin, Northern Territory – d. 29 September 1979 Darwin, NT
37.5% Aboriginal – Woolwonga & Iwaidja
25% Filipino
37.5% English
(*Tom Calma's Father*)

m. 1952
Northern Territory

Ada VERBERG
b. 11 November 1931 Darwin, Northern Territory – d. 30 September 2021 Fannie Bay, NT
50% Aboriginal - Kungarakan tribe
50% Dutch
(*Tom Calma's Mother*)

Thomas (Tom) Edwin CALMA
b. 1953 Adelaide River, Northern Territory
44% Aboriginal – Kungarakan, Woolwonga & Iwaidja
12% Filipino
19% English
25% Dutch

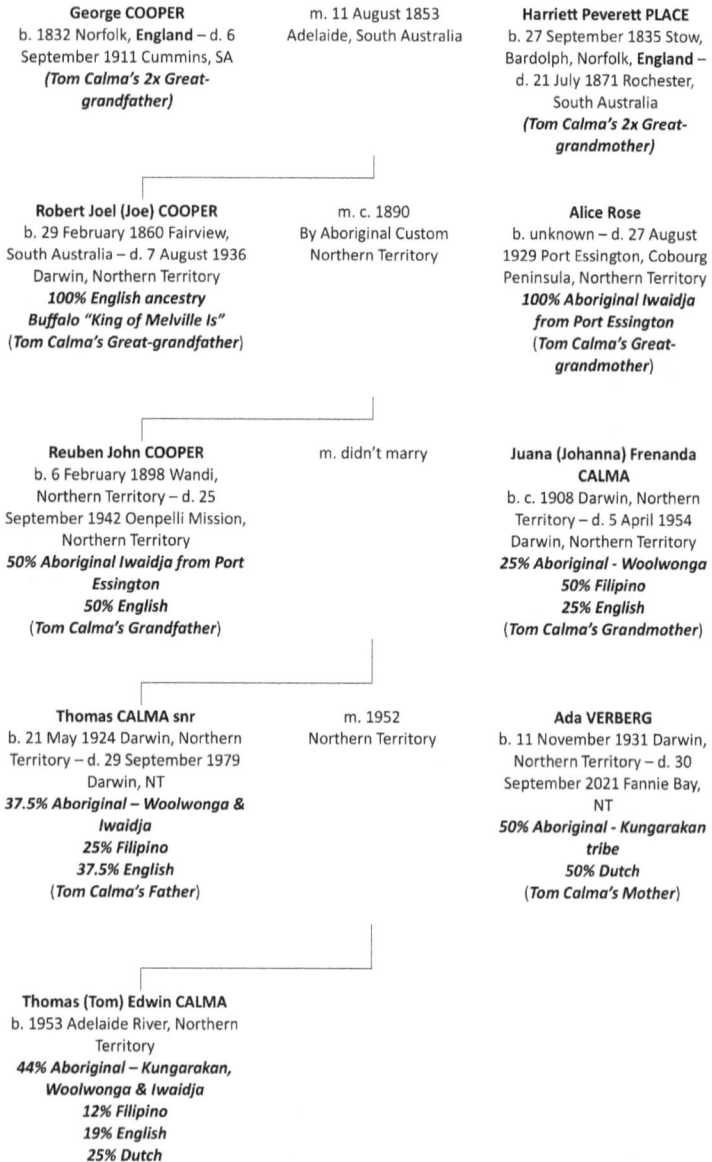

Figure 7.2: A branch of Tom Calma's apparent Family Tree showing his ancestral links to both the Cooper family and the Iwaidja Aborigines. Ancestry percentages (%) are only approximate estimates. The full appaent Family Tree is available for download[7.15] (Subject to standard *Disclaimer* on page (ii))

terest has been shown in the lives of the white and 'half-caste' colonising ancestors in Calma's family. For example, it has been claimed that author **Xavier Herbert's** character in his epic 1938 novel *Capricornia*, **Norman Shillingsworth**, was apparently modeled on **Reuben Cooper** (Professor Calma's 'half-caste' grandfather), a buffalo shooter and Aboriginal rights advocate, who is said to have been the footballer who 'created [and] originated Aussie Rules [football] in the Northern Territory'.[7.23] He was the 'son of legendary Joe Cooper, the white 'King' of Melville Island.'[7.24]

Similarly, Calma's great-grandfather **Joe Cooper** (1860-1936), the white 'King', was a figure of notoriety and a typical derring-do 'son of the empire' who had been born to English colonists in South Australia. The details of his life, and that of his son Reuben, are proudly recorded in the *Northern Territory Dictionary of Biography*:

> In 1894, Joe Cooper, accompanied by EO Robinson [the pastoral lessee of Melville Island] **kidnapped four Aboriginal Tiwi** from Melville Island and returned with them to the Port Essington area, where reciprocal Tiwi/Iwaidja language training was undertaken. In 1895 Cooper, as Robinson's manager, returned to Melville Island with his **four 'hostages'** and a party of Iwaidja Aborigines and set up a camp to shoot buffalo. His wife Alice, [Professor Calma's great-grandmother] an Iwaidja woman ... accompanied him on all his expeditions, and their son **Reuben John** [Calma's grandfather] was born in 1898 while they were at Pine Creek. For 10 years from 1905 the family [Joe, Alice, Reuben...] lived on Melville Island with a party of about twenty Iwaidja, and it was probably during this time, supported by stories of his first foray, that the legends of 'King Joe' [Professor Calma's great-grandfather], started to grow amongst the white population. He was the first European settler on the island since Fort Dundas had been abandoned in 1828, others having been deterred by the reputedly fierce and aggressive Tiwi. He overcame their aggression by the expedient of learning their language and treating them fairly and with kindness. He considered that he was on good terms with the Aborigines, who knew him as 'Jokupa', but nevertheless, he rarely left his camp

unarmed. In 1911 **he was appointed Honorary Sub-Protector of Aborigines**[20] on the island ... He hosted a visit by **Hermann Klaatsch**, the German physical anthropologist, in 1906 'who gained a reputation in his time as an Aboriginal "grave-robber" – reportedly he had 'dug up a grave at night time and reported that his assistant had later been killed because of it'. He 'was also chased away from the Normanton area by people calling him "devil devil" because of his grave robbing activities.' (*Wikipedia*). In 1914 **Cooper resigned as Honorary Sub-Protector** and, by late that year, when his son Reuben returned from college in Adelaide, many of the mainland blacks had been removed from the island. Stories abound with reasons for this action by the authorities — from complaints by one Sam Green, a saw-miller on the island, about Cooper's cruelty to the islanders and the overbearing attitude of his band of Iwaidja, through **indiscriminate shootings** of Tiwi by the Iwaidja, to Cooper's own statement in a letter to Baldwin Spencer in December 1915 to the effect that the authorities were complaining to him about the Tiwi, while the Tiwi were complaining to him about the government in Darwin. Although he was largely exonerated in the subsequent enquiry, the Melville Island lease having changed hands and all the mainland Aborigines having been removed, Cooper and his remaining family left the island in 1916.(emphasis added.)[21]

This short history of Calma's white great-grandfather and his 'half-caste' grandfather nicely illustrates the point that we are all in this together as Australians. Calma wants us to believe that he really was being honest when he told the AFR reporter, "That's what truth-telling is a little bit about. It is making sure that things that are history are actually known to everybody ... We have to ... recognise that with colonisation, not only in Australia but globally, there are a lot of significant detrimental impacts on Indigenous peoples."

If that is true, then a good place to start might be to begin the truth-telling process within his own family history. Imagine Calma applying his demonstrated excellent commu-

---

[20] The modern-day political implications of that are remarkable - Professor Calma's ancestor was officially appointed to a role as a Protector of Aborigines.

[21] Excerpt from *Northern Territory Dictionary of Biography*.[7.22]

nication skills by publicly enacting a *Makarrata* for his own family. To promote further reconciliation in this country, he could start by guiding us through his own family's 'coming together after a struggle, facing the facts of wrongs and living again in peace'.[22]

Calma's father's family certainly has all the elements to be able to demonstrate a successful *Makarrata*. Despite the turmoil caused by the kidnappings, killings and disruption of the Iwaidja and Tiwi carried out by his own great-grandfather, 'King' Joe Cooper, the family went on to successfully intermarry with the Iwaidja, producing football heroes such as 'half-caste' son Reuben; one of the Northern Territories' top Aboriginal public servants in Calma's father (Tom Snr.); and the productive and resilient Filipinos who gave the Professor his surname. Indeed, his ancestor Fortunato Calma consciously decided to *return* to Australia from an overseas visit despite the discrimination of the White Australia Policy in force at the time which required him to apply for an exemption certificate before he could travel. If the 'colonising white Australians' were such bad people, why did Calma's non-white ancestors willingly marry into them and continue to live in Australia despite the onerous documentation and restrictions required?[23]

Despite the jovial and reasonably-minded exterior, Professor Tom Calma AO is a deeply political man. He has a very strong professional aim to achieve political self-determination for an Aboriginal polity in Australia.[24] Although he himself

---

[22]Definition of the Yolngu word, *Makarrata,* from the NT Government Department of Territory Families, Housing and Communities website.

[23]For example, Fortunato Calma was registered as a 'half-caste', along with his daughter Juana Stew and her children, during the 1945 wartime evacuation of Balaklava township in the NT[7.25]; and he required a Certificate of Exemption from Dictation Test to visit the Philippines and return to Australia in 1926.[7.26]

[24]I (Roger Karge, author) have met Calma only once, at the Indigenous Voice Consultation at Melbourne's Convention Centre on 14 April 2021. In the audience of approximately 50, I alone stood up and announced, in the interest of debate, I would 'play devil's advocate' by asking questions that contradicted the aims of the Calma-Langton Report, which Calma was presenting that day.[7.27] Calma was professional and gave me plenty of opportunity to ask questions of himself and his co-panelists,

appears to have carefully *chosen* and crafted a public persona that neglects the inconvenient aspects of some of his own family's Elders, he doesn't hesitate to attack inconvenient aspects of Australian and British figures, who many other Australians consider their Elders. Perhaps Calma does this as a way of smearing and delegitimising the history of The Australian Project.[25]

One statement he makes in his lunchtime interview with the AFR is telling:

> we have to really take the opportunity to form a new nation.
> We have to shed ourselves of the past, when we were colonised
> and to recognise that with colonisation, not only in Australia

---

Fr. Frank Brennan and Prof. Maggie Walter. Questions such as, "Why do the Aboriginal people of, for example Aurukun, say they need a Voice to Parliament to give them a say in decisions affecting their health, education and living conditions[7.28], when it was reported that the Aurukun locals were sitting on a $120m trust fund that made them, 'The richest poor people on Earth'?(see QR Code [7.28-B]). Why didn't they spend their own money on fixing their sewer systems and sending their kids to boarding school for a better education? They hardly needed an additional Voice to do that", I asked. Calma replied to the effect that, "Why should they use their own trust-fund money from mining royalties to pay for things that other city-based Australians get the government to pay for?" And so the cycle of lack of action, blame-shifting and remote-community disadvantage repeats itself, I thought. During a session break, Calma came to where I was sitting, pulled up a chair and sat down, then leaned back with his legs extended and his hands behind his head, and asked calmly who I was and where I was from. What organisation had sent me, he inquired? Within a minute of me telling him my name and that I was just a Melbourne local very interested in, but opposed to, the Voice, he just said OK, got up and walked away. He had no interest in my opinion, nor wanted to really discuss or debate his report. In my view, he was thus revealed as just another ambitious political activist, steeped in socialism and more interested in identifying and fighting opponents and leveraging the plight of poorer Aboriginal communities for political gain than lifting them up from disadvantage and onto a successful life-path that he himself had enjoyed as an assimilated Australian.

[25]The term 'The Australian Project' encompasses the history of Australia since 1770/1778 - its discovery by Cook and Australia's settlement as a British penal colony on a solid base of Enlightenment values and British institutions. Simply put, until recent times Australia was arguably unique in human history by being a 'mass civilzation' - an increasingly democratic polity of aspirational working peoples with a small administrative class of officials and politicians but with no aristocracy, long-term dominant elite class nor a history of chattel slavery. The question, "Is the world a better place because of Australia and the Australians" must be answered in the affirmative. This fact is apparently deeply troubling to intellectuals steeped in anti-British, anti-colonial and pro-Marxist ideologies. Envy of the success of Australia without recourse to their ideological control is what has, since the 1970s, driven many of them to attack and attempt to delegitimise white Australians and their Project. The now rising Aboriginal activist class has contained many of these critics.

but globally, there are a lot of significant detrimental impacts on Indigenous peoples.

Calma clearly believes that the Australia of today, fundamentally based as it is on British colonisation, is illegitimate. He is channeling the standard Marxist and UN mantra when he proclaims, "We have to form a new nation", but who does he exactly mean by "we"? Millions of Australians, and likely his own Cooper descendant's, are very comfortable recognising that 'we were colonised' and have no desire, even if his delusional plea was possible, to 'shed ourselves of the past'. It is very surprising to many Australians that a person with such an apparent anti-Australian sentiment would be given such prominent government-funded positions, as Calma has had, to voice such negative views about Australia. When pushed on the question, "Is the world a better place because of Australia and the Australians" - Yes or No - how would Calma actually respond?

A further example of the ideological disdain Calma seems to have for the British legacies of The Australian Project is his open condemnation of the memory of Winston Churchill. He expressed this in his 2022 Churchill Essay: *An Indigenous Perspective on Winston Churchill, the British Empire's Political Legitimacy and the Unfinished Business of Australian Governance.*[7.29] Calma heavily criticises Churchill for being an 'advocate of the British Empire's political legitimacy' and the adverse implications that had for 'Aboriginal and Torres Strait Islander self-governance' today.

Yet, as indicated in the previous section, Calma's own ancestors, the Coopers, were as much 'derring-do' colonialists as Churchill ever was. The Coopers and Churchill were products of their time, around the end of the 19th century, so it is anachronistic for Calma to pen an essay today that smears Churchill as an advocate of the British Empire. Back then, everyone including his own ancestors, was an advocate for the success of British colonialism.

To attack Churchill and the British empire's legacy is rather delusional given that prior to the Nationality and Citizenship Act 1948 (*Cth*) all Australian citizens were in effect British subjects. Australians saw themselves as British with varying degrees of local 'character' such as being currency lads and lasses, native born or colonials. Britain's interests were Australia's interests. Even Calma's own Aboriginal father, Tom Calma Snr., understood the need for Australians to defend the legacies of Britain, and its former colony Australia, when he swore an oath of allegiance to 'His Majesty, our Sovereign Lord King', upon joining the Australian Air Force in 1944.[7.30] Why would Tom Calma denigrate his own father's sense of loyalty? Is Tom Junior really being genuine when he tells his audience, "I would like to pay my respects to my Aboriginal Elders, past and present"?

Calma then further illustrates his ideological position by using a classic phrase of a Marxist manifesto - 'I unreservedly condemn' - when he chooses to identify solely as an 'Indigenous person' and further condemns Churchill and the British for colonisation:

> As an Indigenous person whose ancestors suffered atrocities in the name of the British Empire Churchill whole-heartedly supported, I unreservedly condemn his racist and imperialist attitudes. Indeed, I have dedicated my life to healing and resolving the unfinished business of British colonisation and its contemporary legacies including dispossession of lands and waters, inter-generationally transmitted trauma and poverty, present day racism, social exclusion and social determinants of physical and mental health conditions among Indigenous peoples in Australia.

Yet Calma does not mention the 'racist and imperialist attitudes' of *his own ancestors*, the Coopers, during their so-called dispossession of the lands of the Tiwi and Iwaidja. He may be concerned about the 'mental health' issues for Aboriginal people arising from the legacy of colonisation, but what about his own personal mental health? How does he reconcile, in moments of quiet reflection, the potentially 'schizophrenic' consequences of his own ancestors being such successful colonisers? For Tom Calma is as much a 'son of empire' as Churchill, and the very non-Aboriginal Australians he seeks to admonish today. Nor does he acknowledge the Aboriginal people who supported the Empire and Churchill's leadership by fighting for the British during the World Wars.

More surprisingly, for a public servant extolling Australians to come together and reconcile peacefully and claiming "there's nothing vindictive about this", his essay then goes on to to praise the confrontational and vindictive strategies of the corrupt Black Lives Matter movement:

> In my opinion, the Black Lives Matter protesters spraying 'racist' in red paint on Churchill's statue in Parliament Square, London (among other calls for statues to fall) had the potential to open up a much broader debate about Churchill and other historical figures, but that opportunity was largely subsumed into yet another front of the 'culture war': this time being whether such statues should be torn down or not ... It is for the above reasons that I also am happy to support the Winston Churchill Memorial Trust (the Trust) as Patron. First, knowing that the Trust is clear eyed about Churchill's racist and imperialist attitudes and statements and has publicly rejected this part of his legacy. But, second, I support the Trust as an active promoter of Indigenous scholarship including that which is concerned with promoting legitimate Indigenous governance in Australia through power sharing by governments and in the context of the child protection, education and justice systems. Indeed, there have been 57 Indigenous scholarly recipients of Trust support since 1967.

Calma's essay, up on the *Winston Churchill Trust* website for all to see, [7.29] confirms that the Marxist-inspired 'march through the institutions' is almost complete. Churchill must be turning in his grave after reading Calma's essay and seeing his memorial trust being hijacked by proponents of Calma's ideology of 'Indigenous governance' (i.e. The Voice) and apartheid-style ideas such as a separate Indigenous justice system, ideas which have fortunately been roundly rejected by Australians, so far.[7.31]

However, possibly the most worrying aspect of Calma's essay was what Andrew Bolt was trying to warn us about in his articles when he wrote:

> self-identification as Aboriginal strikes me as self-obsessed, and driven more by politics than by any racial reality. It's also divisive, feeding a new movement to stress pointless or even invented racial differences we once swore to overcome and 'the white Aborigine - or political Aborigine ... such as Pat Eatock ... [who] only started to identify as Aboriginal when she was 19, after attending a political rally, so little did any racial difference matter to her before her awakening to far-Left causes. But she thrived as an Aboriginal bureaucrat, activist and academic.'[26]

For it appears that Calma himself might be mentoring a 'white Aboriginal' academic who is not only anti-colonial and anti-Australia, but is also a fake. In 2013, Calma was part of the presentation team that awarded the prestigious Stanner Award for Indigenous scholars to **Bronwyn Carlson**.[7.32] She went on to be made a Fellow of the Winston Churchill Trust which described her as being:

> deeply committed to truth-telling about Australia's colonial history and the ongoing impact on Aboriginal and Torres Strait Islander people and communities.

> As an Aboriginal scholar and public intellectual Bronwyn devotes her time to engaging in research that is of interest and benefit to Aboriginal and Torres Strait Islander people and providing information and resources for all people to have a deeper understanding of history.[7.33]

However, Carlson appears to be mistaken about her claimed Aboriginal ancestry. Recent genealogical research indicates that all of Carlson's ancestors were from England, Ireland and Scotland, with an individual ancestor from each of Gibraltar/Spain, Sweden or Norway, and perhaps British India. No evidence of any Aboriginality could be found in her family's genealogical records (see Chapter 7.5.2 for details).

Nevertheless, as Calma noted in his essay, one of the real

---

[26]Andrew Bolt, 'White is the new black', *Herald Sun*, 15-16 April 2009.

purposes of the Trust Fellowships is to:

> support the Trust as an active promoter of Indigenous schol-
> arship including that which is concerned with promoting le-
> gitimate Indigenous governance in Australia through power
> sharing by governments ... Indigenous peoples, in exercising
> their right to self-determination, have the right to autonomy
> or self-government in matters relating to their internal and
> local affairs, as well as ways and means for financing their
> autonomous functions ... Indigenous peoples have the right
> to maintain and strengthen their distinct political, legal, eco-
> nomic, social and cultural institutions, while retaining their
> right to participate fully, if they so choose, in the political,
> economic, social and cultural life of the State.

When Calma speaks of 'Indigenous governance through power
sharing' this comes across as code for an undemocratic and
blatant 'power grab'.[27] It is very disappointing and even something of a shock for a veteran public servant of the calibre of
Professor Tom Calma to be seen to be so closely associated
with a 'fake' Aboriginal academic and such blatant Marxist
political ideology as he expresses in his essay.

This begs the question: If an Aboriginal intellectual as
prominent as Professor Calma can't spot a fake, like Bronwyn Carlson, what future is there for transparency and integrity within all our institutions as they attempt to insert
more Aboriginal people into their organisations as the 'Aboriginalisation' of Australia proceeds?[28]

Black and White Inter-marriage

Australia's overall success in race relations is best summed up
by the ultimate test of reconciliation - who would you marry?
How much more reconciled can you be as a person if you are

---

[27] A point that No Voice campaigner, Warren Mundine noted during the 2023 referendum: 'The Voice is a political ploy to grab power - not just from the Australian
nation, but also from Traditional Owners. We know from the Calma-Langton report, that the Voice is intended to be a vast new expensive bureaucracy interposed
at every level of government decision making.'- Patrick Staveley, *Sky News Australia
online*, 26 Sept 2023.

[28] See: Alex McDermott, 'Schooled in harsh narrative of strife and resentment', *The
Australian*, 11 Sept 2025 and [7.34]

willing to inter-marry with someone of an historically antagonistic race, faith or ethnic nationality?

Comparing the family portrait of English-Australian Joe Cooper, his Iwaidja wife Alice and their two children circa 1914-16, with a family photograph of Cooper's great-grandson, Professor Tom Calma and his family in 2023 says it all. Both were mixed, inter-racial marriages.[See here [7.35]]

Unfortunately, the only people still constantly raising the issue of reconciliation, of which they never actually define what its final achievement might look like, are the political activists employed within the reconciliation industry itself. Tom Calma needs to cease his divisive, selective remembrance and his promotion of the never-ending political reconciliation *process* and instead understand that his own family photo albums are evidence of the successful reconciliation *outcomes* that our country has already achieved.[29]

To seal a valuable and lasting legacy for his decades of public service, Tom Calma is in the perfect position to be the founding patron of 'Inter-Marriage Day', a day to celebrate marriages between Indigenous and non-Indigenous Australians. This is an idea first raised by the chairman of Close the Gap Research, Gary Johns:

> the dominant relationship between non-Aboriginal and Aboriginal people is inter-marriage. We are reconciled - people love each other. Race is not an issue here. We're getting on so why don't we celebrate that? Why don't we celebrate the bringing together, the coming together of men and women, getting married, partnering and bringing up wonderful children. All of that's been forgotten, for God's sake - we've got to bring that back into the discussion.[7.37]

---

[29]Calma's claim that the nation is not reconciled is at odds with large sections of mainstream Australia. For example, when ABC Radio asked song-writer Dobe Newton about his band's version of the song, 'I Am Australian', he replied: "The whole impetus of the song was to celebrate the fact of what a wonderful job we had done of creating a safe and inclusive multi-cultural society." Newton's conclusion does not suggest 'we' are an un-reconciled nation. (*I Am Australian* has now been added to the National Film and Sound Archives' Sounds of Australia, a collection of recordings with cultural and historical significance.)[7.36]

Professor Calma's Lost Generation: Great-grandmother May Crawford

On Wednesday the 13th of February, 2008, Professor Tom Calma, as the Aboriginal and Torres Strait Islander Social Justice Commissioner, stood in the Member's Hall, Parliament House, Canberra and addressed his audience of politicians, bureaucrats and distinguished guests:[30]

> I have been asked by the National Sorry Day Committee and the Stolen Generations Alliance; the two national bodies that represent the Stolen Generations and their families, to respond to the Parliament's Apology and to talk briefly about the importance of today's events...

> Today is an historic day. It's the day our leaders – across the political spectrum – have chosen dignity, hope and respect as the guiding principles for the relationship with our first nations' peoples. Through one direct act, Parliament has acknowledged the existence and the impacts of the past policies and practices of forcibly removing Indigenous children from their families...

During his speech, Calma found a place to include a bit of history about his own family:

> Let me tell you what this apology means to me. For many years, my family has been searching in vain to find information about my great-grandmother, May, who was taken at the turn of the 20th Century. Recently, *Link Up* in Darwin located some information in the archives. In a document titled, 'List of Half-castes in the NT', dated 2 December 1899, a government official named George Thompson wrote the following about my great-grandmother:

>> Half-caste May is a well grown girl, is living with her mother in the black's camp at Woolwonga, her mother will not part with her, she mixes up a great deal with the Chinamen, she only has a *narga* on.

---

[30] In attendance were: "The Prime Minister, the Hon Kevin Rudd; Opposition Leader, Brendan Nelson; the Minister for Indigenous Affairs, the Hon Jenny Macklin; former Prime Ministers, Professor Bruce Wilson representing the late Sir Ronald Wilson, Stolen Generations patrons Dr Lowitja O'Donoghue and Bobby Randall, NSDC Chair Helen Moran and SGA Chair Christine King, Ministers; Members of Parliament; Senators, members of the stolen generations and your families; my Indigenous brothers and sisters; and distinguished guests from around Australia and overseas".

My great-grandmother's ordeal was not uncommon and nor was the chilling account - 'her mother will not part with her'. This is not a black armband issue; and it's not an issue of guilt. It never was. It is about belonging. The introductory words of the 1997 Bringing Them Home report remind us of this. It reads:

> the past is very much with us today, in the continuing devastation of the lives of Indigenous Australians. That devastation cannot be addressed unless the whole community listens with an open heart and mind to the stories of what has happened in the past and, having listened and understood, commits itself to reconciliation.

By acknowledging and paying respect, Parliament has now laid the foundations for healing to take place and for a reconciled Australia in which everyone belongs. For today is not just about the Stolen Generations - it is about every Australian. Today's actions enable every single one of us to move forward together – with joint aspirations and a national story that contains a shared past and future. It is a matter of great sadness that the experiences of the Stolen Generations have been used as a source of division among the Australian community since the release of the Bringing Them Home Report. There are many individuals who have made their name as 'Stolen Generations deniers and rebuffers'.[7.38]

Professor Calma's comments appear to be confirm Bolt's observation that there is a 'trend' of Australians choosing only certain strands of their ancestry and certain events within those strands for political ends. For when Calma told his distinguished audience about his great-grandmother May, he failed to put her details into context. He omitted the fact that Thompson's report, a 'List of Half-castes in the NT', was actually commissioned in late 1899 by Police Inspector **Paul Foelsche**. He had given instructions to Mounted Constable George H. Thompson to 'report on the conditions of Aborigines and their relations to other nations'. He was to ascertain the names of all non-Aboriginal persons who were cohabiting with Aboriginal women, with special note taken of cases where such females appeared to be children - his report was to be

Edward James Frederick CRAWFORD
b. 1809 Banbury, Oxfordshire, **England** – d. 8
May 1880 Gippsland, Victoria
(Tom Calma's 3x Great-grandfather)

m. 31 July 1841
Sydney, NSW

Frances Mitchell
b. 10 June 1819 Liverpool, **England** – d. 1
April 1877 Sale, Gippsland, Victoria
(Tom Calma's 3x Great-grandmother)

Lindsay CRAWFORD
b. 9 April 1852 North Adelaide, South
Australia – d. 20 March 1901 Nr Newcastle
Waters, NT
100% English ancestry
(Tom Calma's 2x Great-grandfather)

m. didn't marry

Jennie (or Maggie?)
b. unknown – d. unknown
100% Aboriginal – Woolwonga
(Tom Calma's 2x Great-grandmother)

May CRAWFORD
b. c. 1892 Victoria River, Northern Territory –
d. 21 September 1929 Darwin, NT
50% Aboriginal – Woolwonga
50% English
(Tom Calma's Great-grandmother)

m. 16 July 1910
Palmerston
(Darwin),
Northern Territory

Fortunato CALMA
b. 27 February 1875 Argao, Cebu, **Philippine
Islands** – d. 14 October 1947 Darwin, NT
100% Filipino
(Tom Calma's Great-grandfatherr)

Juana (Johanna) Frenanda CALMA
b. c. 1908 Darwin, Northern
Territory – d. 5 April 1954 Darwin,
NT
25% Aboriginal - Woolwonga
50% Filipino
25% English
(Tom Calma's Grandmother)

m. didn't marry

Reuben John COOPER
b. 6 February 1898 Wandi,
Northern Territory – d. 25
September 1942 Oenpelli
Mission, NT
50% Aboriginal Iwaidja
50% English
(Tom Calma's Grandfather)

Thomas CALMA snr
b. 21 May 1924 Darwin, Northern Territory – d. 29
September 1979 Darwin, NT
37.5% Aboriginal – Woolwonga & Iwaidja
25% Filipino
37.5% English
(Tom Calma's Father)

m. 1952
Northern Territory

Ada VERBERG
b. 11 November 1931 Darwin,
Northern Territory – d. 30
September 2021 Fannie Bay, NT
*50% Aboriginal - Kungarakan
tribe*
50% Dutch
(Tom Calma's Mother)

Professor Thomas (Tom) Edwin CALMA
b. 1953 Adelaide River, Northern Territory
*44% Aboriginal – Kungarakan, Woolwonga &
Iwaidja*
12% Filipino
19% English
25% Dutch

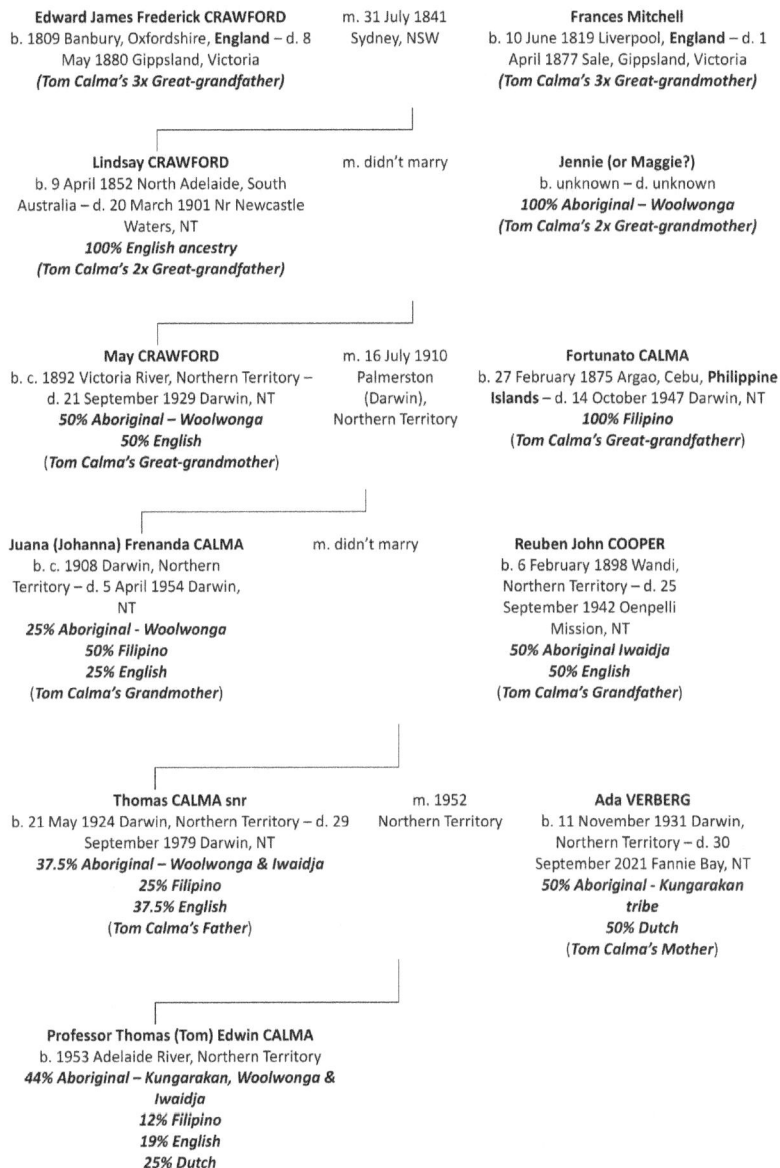

Figure 7.3: The Crawford branch of Tom Calma's apparent Family Tree.
Ancestry percentages (%) are only approximate estimates. Full Family
Tree available for download here - [7.15] (Subject to the *Disclaimer* on
page (ii).)

of all 'half-caste' children, comprising their names, sex[31], approximate age, name of mother, mother's tribe and reported father.[32] Thompson, accompanied by Police Tracker Paddy, commenced his survey in Pine Creek on October 18th, 1899, visiting mining camps and other settlements situated between Katherine and Darwin. The arduous task was completed in just under three months, on January 9th, 1900.

Calma fails to acknowledge the socially progressive mentality behind a report such as this. Here was a police inspector in 1899, out in the middle of nowhere on the frontier, who believed his duty was to report on the welfare of some of the most marginalised people in his jurisdiction - Aboriginal women and their children living in camps, amongst the rough and crude frontiersmen. (See [7.39] for photographs of the conditions some children faced.)

Calma doesn't seem to pause to reflect on where else in the world such humanitarian thoughts were being put into action at that time. He is critical of white colonial Australia, but where are the examples of similar welfare reports being written by concerned Aboriginal men or women? There aren't any, nor are there any written by Calma's own Aboriginal or Filipino ancestors, because welfare officialdom is a British social construct. The very idea of concern for the welfare of third parties - people other than one's own direct family, kin or tribe - is outside an Aboriginal society's ability to comprehend.

Reading other entries in Constable Thompson's report only confirms the wide range of conditions experienced by the half-caste children, ranging from being well treated, well fed and clothed and usefully employed to those in dire straits at risk of serious abuse, prostitution and neglect. There is no indication that any of these children were actually removed,

---

[31] Thompson's original report used the word 'sex' but the modern archivist has substituted the word 'gender' - see QR Code [7.41].

[32] *Thompson's List of "Half Castes" in the Northern Territory 1899-1900*. NT Archives Service, Government Resident of the NT, NTRS 790, *Inwards Correspondence, 1870-1912*, Bundle 10441. See full report with QR Code [7.41].

even though in several cases the children were in obvious danger and/or neglect. And the fact that many of these Aboriginal children *were not removed* if they were well looked after and employed indicates that the 'forcible removal' of children *just because they were Aboriginal* is a myth. Also interesting to note is that in nearly three months of field work, Thompson located only 49 half-caste children worthy of documentation, only a few of whom *may* have been ultimately forcibly removed. Certainly he may have missed some and others may have been hidden from him, but such a low number does suggest that the pool of children that *might* be forcibly removed is hardly as huge as we are lead to believe nowadays.[33]

Other examples from Constable Thompson's report include:

> Half cast [*sic*] **Binney** (aged 16) is employed by Mrs Henderson at the Telegraph Station. She is thoroughly domesticated, proficient in household duties, well fed, clothed and looked after. She has every appearance of being a half cast Chinese girl. (Mother, Minagilly (dead) of Woramonga tribe. Father, Not known. Supposed to be a Chinaman – was cook a the Powell Creek Telegraph Station.)

> Half cast **Sam Croacker** (aged 9) is employed by Mr T Pearce, publican of the Katherine. He works about the place, is a good horse man & very useful, well fed, clothed & looked after. (Mother, Annie of a Katherine tribe. Father, Sam Croacker (European).)

> Half cast **Nellie** (aged 15) is a servant for Mr Schunke of the Playford Hotel. She is well fed & clothed. But I have no hesitation in saying that she is an arrant prostitute, and the temptation is very great for her while living at an hotel. Most of the Bushmen boarding at the Hotel at different times tell it openly, that they have connections with her. She has been known to follow a man (whose name is known) into the W.C. & catch him by the private parts. (Mother, Polly (dead), Agagowilla tribe. Father, Andy Hunter.)

---

[33] A commonly believed myth is that, 'It is estimated that at least 100,000 Indigenous children were taken from their families during the period the mid-nineteenth century up until the 1970s', as claimed in *National Inquiry into the Separation of Aboriginal and Torres Strait Islander Children from Their Families, Bringing Them Home*, April 1997. The reality is that the records show only some 8,250 children were separated from their families for all reasons. See [7.40].

> Half cast **Annie** (aged 4) is living with the black[s] in the camp at Union, appears to be poorly fed & clothed. (Mother, Judy (dead), Eureka tribe. Father, P Heyden (dead).)[34]

Other report entries indicate that a child's father might initiate the removal of a child from the mother's care so as to be sent off to an institution for an education:

> Half Cast [*sic*] **Joe** (aged 6) is a well grown boy, appears to be well fed, clothed & looked after. Before the Daly River mission Station closed his father J Wallace offered the boy to Father O'Brien, Wallace said he would not object to him being educated, but would object to him being placed under the care of some people. If the children where sent to be educated, he would send the mother back to her own Country.

> **Victoria** (aged 18mths), sister to Joe above, is a perfectly white child, with very fair hair, well grown for her age, appears to be well fed, clothed & looked after. Her father J Wallace also offered Victoria to Father O'Brien just before the Daly Mission closed, Wallace would not object to her being educated, but would object to her being placed with some people. If the children where sent to be educated he would send the mother back to her own Country.

In the last two cases, if the father had agreed to send his two children off to be educated, then most likely their mother, Fannie, a half-caste Marha woman, would have been separated from her children and sent back to 'her own Country.' This may have been tragic for the mother if she disagreed and, on the face of it, may have fitted the description of a 'forcible removal' as one of Calma's so-called 'Stolen Generations'. But from the father's equally valid point of view he would not have seen it as 'forcible' - perhaps a very difficult decision to make, but still a conscious, valid decision in what he thought were the best interests of his child.

And this is exactly what one of Calma's grandfathers did. In the lunchtime interview with the AFR, Calma selec-

---

[34] Original handwritten field report by Mounted Constable 3rd Class George H Thompson 1899, plus a typed transcript. Source: NT Archives Service, NTRS 790, *Government Resident of the Northern Territory, Inwards Correspondence*, 1870-1912, Bundle 10441. See full report [7.41]

tively relates that another of his grandfathers removed (perhaps forcibly) Calma's mother and her sister from their Aboriginal mother, Anmilil. Calma accepts that when his own grandfather, the Dutchman Edwin Verburg did the removing, that was acceptable - the girls were 'lucky' to be sent to St Gabriel's boarding school, Calma told the AFR reporter. Yet he then admonishes Australia when others are found to have been involved in removing children into care. He wants Australia to apologise for something his own white ancestor was also involved in.

Calma, in the interests of 'healing', should be honest and admit that his own family was on both sides of this history. In his Apology speech he related how his great-grandmother **May Crawford** was his family connection to the Stolen Generations. He fails to mention however, the other details listed in Thompson's 'List of Half-castes' report - May's father was **Lindsay Crawford**, Calma's 2x great-grandfather. Calma lacks statesmanship by failing to admit that his own ancestor, Crawford, must carry a large part of the responsibility for his daughter and her mother ending up in the camp and on Thompson's list. Has Calma ever questioned if his ancestor could have done more to support his own child, May, and her Aboriginal mother, Jennie?

Instead, Calma only confirms Bolt's assertion that many modern-day 'professional Aborigines'[35] simply 'choose' to select only one strand of their ancestry when it comes to their involvement in the so-called Stolen Generations.

A real statesman would rise above this divisiveness and endeavour to bring Australians together to heal by admitting their own complicity on both sides of the argument.

---

[35] Andrew Bolt, 'White is the new black', *Herald Sun*, 15-16 April 2009.

Fortunato Calma

As Professor Calma gave his oration in the Members Hall in Parliament, selectively relating the moving story about his great-grandmother May Crawford, there were many Australians listening who were not convinced the nation was guilty of the wholesale forcible removal or 'stealing' of children *just because they were Aboriginal*.[36]

Calma claims his, 'great-grandmother May ... was taken at the turn of the 20th Century', but the report only says that Constable Thompson noted, 'her mother *will not part with her.*' There is no evidence that she was *actually* taken at all.

When commentators such as Andrew Bolt try to point this out[7.43] and ask for the proof and the names of children who were taken simply because of the their Aboriginality, Calma slurs them as 'Stolen Generations deniers and rebuffers'. However, as one researches the archives, some interesting facts begin to emerge about Calma's own family that may explain his hostility to the views of people like Bolt. Calma *chooses* often to not give agency to the decisions of his own ancestors. Rather, he seems to only apportion blame to others, and ultimately to modern Australians, for the injustices of the past. Another entry in Constable Thompson's *NT Half-Caste Report* is telling:

> **Lilly**, Female aged 14 years; Mother, Minnie and Father, G McKeddie. Half Cast Lilly is living with a Manila man named Antonio at the old ice house on the beach, she appears to be well fed & clothed.

---

[36]The primary Term of Reference for the inquiry that led to the *Bringing Them Home Report* was: 'trace the past laws, practices and policies which resulted in the separation of Aboriginal and Torres Strait Islander children from their families by compulsion, duress or undue influence, and the effects of those laws, practices and policies.' Controversially, because it wasn't true, the report also stated that, 'In contrast with the removal of non-Indigenous children, proof of "neglect" was not always required before an Indigenous child could be removed. Their Aboriginality would suffice.' All the examples of child removals in the records have been shown to have been for a primary welfare reason - death of parents, abandonment, neglect, abuse, health reasons and even at the request of the child - not just because they were part-Aboriginal. Full-blood Aboriginal children were expressly excluded from the program, except in rare, exceptional circumstances. ([7.42] p9.)

Calma quoted Thompson's report that his own great-grandmother, May, 'mixes up a great deal with the Chinamen, she only has a *narga* [loin cloth] on.' Was Constable Thompson implying that May, who was less than ten years old at the time, was sexually involved with those who he called Chinamen (which probably included Filipinos, like the Antonio above). For it seems that Calma's own Filipino great-grandfather Fortunato Calma may have been 'cruising' the Aboriginal camps, like Antonio, looking for a wife, who he ultimately found in May Crawford. They were married in St. Mary's Church Palmerston (Darwin) on 16 July 1910. He was 38 years old, she was thought to be 19 to 21.[7.44] (See the Crawford branch of the Calma Family Tree in Figure 7.3)

Once again, Calma confirms Bolt's observation that there is a 'trend' for Australians to selectively 'choose' the stories related to their thread of Aboriginal ancestry while ignoring, in Calma's case, the equally important story of his Filipino thread of ancestry.

Lindsay Crawford

The man recorded in Thompson's report as being the father of May, **Lindsay Crawford**, has apparently never been acknowledged by Calma as his 2x great-grandfather; and, one suspects, for good reason. For, although Crawford was quite famous in the history of the Northern Territory as a well-known and much respected pioneer, today, in modern Australia at the cocktail parties attended by Professor Calma, a celebration of Lindsay Crawford's life would be considered 'problematic'. Crawford's time on the Northern Territory frontier in the late 19th century included some twelve years as manager of the Victoria River Downs station, where he was 'subject to frequent attacks by the Aborigines'.[37] He was 'repeatedly warned by the natives that they intended to kill him if the opportunity

---

[37]Entry for 'Lindsay Crawford', *Northern Territory Dictionary of Biography*, 2008, p118.

offered.'[38] In one particular instance, Calma's ancestor led a party to investigate the murder of a Mr WS Scott at Willeroo Station by the Victoria River blacks. Crawford arrived at the scene to find the buildings looted and 'everything broken and scattered in all directions. No natives were visible when Crawford arrived but later he discovered thirty or forty camped in the horse paddock. Crawford and party charged their camp and found in it Scott's saddle and bridle and other articles.'[39] It was not recorded if any of the blacks were killed by Lindsay Crawford when the 'party charged their camp.'

The taxpayer-funded *Colonial Frontier Massacres Map* of the late Professor Lyndall Ryan at University of Newcastle is much more explicit and gives Lindsay Crawford a very bad rap:

> Following the killing of GS [*sic*] Scott, manager of Willeroo station in October 1892, two posses were formed to **avenge his death.** The first was led by station owner **Lindsay Crawford** who rode to Willleroo Station and when he realised that Aboriginal people had taken guns and ammunition from the store he and the party 'charged' the Aboriginal camp and retrieved some of the weapons. However he gave no indication of the number of Aboriginal people killed.
>
> A decade later Hely Hutchinson, who passed through Willeroo ... in 1905, and who met many of the early residents, wrote that [Lindsay] Crawford had 'found the myalls gloriously drunk and capering about the house like a mob of black devils'. **Crawford then avenged Scott's death,** in a **terrible manner,** and the **'gruelling'** he gave the myalls on that occasion is still spoken of by the niggers in those parts as the Israelites of old told to their children the horror of the wrath of the Lord, when he sent plague, pestilence and famine into their lands as a correction for their misdeeds... **He and his half-caste dealt out white man's justice with their Winchesters,** and when the police arrived from Pine Creek, a couple of days later, they found plenty of employment **burying the sons of darkness.**[7.45](emphasis added.)

---

[38] 'Obituary for Lindsay Crawford', *Northern Territory Times and Gazette*, Friday 22 March 1901, p3.

[39] *Northern Territory Times and Gazette*, Friday 4 November 1892, p3.

No wonder Professor Calma has kept his ancestral links to Lindsay Crawford off the record, especially since some think the only survivor from this alleged massacre was a lone woman, named 'Jennie'. Jennie was the name recorded in Thompson's report of Professor Calma's 2x great-grandmother, the mother to May Crawford. This suggests that Calma's 2x great-grandfather, Lindsay Crawford, might have massacred the whole of the Woolwonga people, except for one woman, Jennie, with whom he then had a relationship (or perhaps raped or kept as a concubine) and then abandoned, along with their daughter May, in a native camp, their existence being recorded seven years later as Constable Thompson rode through.

According to the ABC this seems to be what happened, as reported when a plaque was unveiled by the then Minister for Indigenous Affairs, Senator Nigel Scullion, in sad recognition of the massacre that led to the extermination of the 'warlike' Woolwonga people in 1884. There was said to be one survivor, but 'exactly how the Aboriginal girl known as Jennie survived the massacre of her people ... is not known', the ABC noted. She was known to have survived because, 'about four years ago an 1899 census document was found showing at least one had survived. According to the List of Half Casts [sic] in the Northern Territory, Jennie of the Woolwonga tribe had a daughter, May, in 1889. May took the surname of her father, the station manager Lindsay Crawford.'[40]

This was one and the same May Crawford that Calma claimed was his great-grandmother, one of the so-called Stolen Generations. This means the ABC are corroborating that Jennie was Calma's 2x great-grandmother and Lindsay Crawford was his 2x great-grandfather. Calma himself has apparently selectively 'self-**un**remembered' his family connection to Lindsay Crawford, the white pioneer.[41]

---

[40] James Purtill, 'Forgotten Woolwonga tribe demand recognition 130 years after 'extermination", *ABC News*, 24 Sep 2014.

[41] He was born in 1852 in Adelaide, the son of EJF Crawford, the head of an old and

This research confirms that Calma's commentary about his own family is also part of the 'trend' identified by Bolt.[42] Calma seems to have made a choice to only identify with the Aboriginal strands in his Family Tree (Figure 7.3), completely omitting to publicly mention his equally significant British strands via Lindsay Crawford, or his Filipino strands via Fortunato Calma. Bolt may have been more blunt in his articles but his readers knew he had a point. They felt that modern Australia was being divided by the politics of the likes of Tom Calma, where the white Crawfords, the Coopers and the Constable Thompsons of our history were disparaged, even though Calma himself had a direct ancestral line to some of those same people and the policy decisions they were responsible for.

It appears that Bolt was correct, at least in the case of Tom Calma, when he observed, 'this self-identification as Aboriginal strikes me as self-obsessed, and driven more by politics than by any racial reality.'

If Fortunato Calma was alive today he would no doubt be proud to see not only Tom carrying his Filipino surname, but also that his great-grandson had been feted as a Senior Australian of the Year[7.46] and had appeared onstage in the United States with President Biden and Prime Minister Albanese.[7.47] But is the pride mutual? Unfortunately, no examples have been found where Professor Calma has publicly provided any endorsement of his Filipino great-grandfather and the success he gained with his new life in Australia. Fortunato's life is a wonderful story of a migrant's hard work and persistence, coupled with Australian opportunity and a reconciliation between races - facts which Calma does not seem at all keen to explore or publicise. How disappointing.

---

highly respected South Australian brewing family. His mother was a sister of George Fife Angas's partner, Flaxman, and thus was a member, through close association, of Adelaide's commercial establishment. (*Northern Territory Dictionary of Biography, op. cit.*)

[42] "Mr Bolt was asserting that the people in the 'trend' had made a deliberate choice to identify as Aboriginal people; people, who, out of their multi-stranded but largely European genealogy, decide to identify with the thinnest of all those strands" (Bromberg J, *Eatock v Bolt* at 41.)

7.3   The Choices of Kerryn Pholi

In 2012, a young Aboriginal woman told the world that she had, 'burned my proof of Aboriginality.' After a career spent in jobs reserved for Indigenous Australians, **Kerryn Pholi** had had enough of being a 'professional Aborigine':

> I am a person of Aboriginal descent. This is nothing special; all it means is that I could trace my ancestry back to a stone-age way of life more easily, with far fewer steps, than most readers...
>
> I used to identify as Aboriginal, and I have worked in 'identified' government positions only open to Aboriginal people.
>
> As a professional Aborigine, I could harangue a room full of people with real qualifications and decades of experience with whatever self-serving, uninformed drivel that happened to pop into my head. For this nonsense I would be rapturously applauded, never questioned, and paid well above my qualifications and experience...
>
> About 18 months ago I burned my 'proof of Aboriginality' documentation (a letter from the NSW Department of Education acknowledging that I was Aboriginal, on the basis that my local Aboriginal Lands Council at that time, circa 1990, had said so). I walked away from the Aboriginal industry for good.[43]

Pholi made a conscious *choice* to *not identify* as Aboriginal. She was still 'a person of Aboriginal descent' but she had decided to no longer practice selective remembrance by choosing the Aboriginal strand in her mixed heritage to solely define her identity and how others saw her.

Thus, with the strike of a match, she was no longer considered by society an 'identified Aboriginal', and no longer could she receive benefits as such.[44]

This illustrates the total immorality of a socio-political system that seeks to divide Australians on the basis of race.

---

[43] Excerpts from an *ABC News* online report, 27 September 2012, [7.48]

[44] Although Pholi was still of Aboriginal descent, she failed to comply with the other two parts of the three-part rule: self-identification and community recognition (via her now burnt Certificate of Aboriginality).

Pholi was still exactly the same person, the same Australian, but without her apartheid-style paperwork both Tom Calma and Marcia Langton would consider her an altogether different Australian - one with fewer political and historical rights should ever the recommendations of their Calma-Langton Report be successfully legislated or constitutionally enshrined.

Pholi's actions were proof that Andrew Bolt was right to recognise that some Australians were able to *choose* to identify as Aboriginal and thus obtain benefits as a result, or as in the case of Kerryn Pholi, lose them when they *chose* not to maintain an Aboriginal identity. Bolt understood how the real world worked. Yet here he was being convicted, within the rarefied atmosphere of Justice Bromberg's courtroom, for implying that Pat Eatock, a woman with no Aboriginal ancestry at all, had simply chosen to identify as such.

Clearly, if an 'Aborigine' like Pholi could express her agency to choose not to identify solely by one strand of her ancestry, then others could also just as validly *choose to* identify with the Aboriginal strand of their ancestry, no matter how thin that strand might be.

Bolt was in fact warning everyone they need to decide whether or not Australian citizens, and Australia's democratic and political institutions, are to be divided by race or ancestry, where group membership can be decided by a personal choice.

If Australia takes that path it will inevitably lead to considerable social conflict and inequity between those who *chose* to 'tick the box' of an identity to gain a benefit versus those who cannot, or who *chose not* to.

7.4   The Self-Making of Professor Megan Davis

Our grandfather Fred Davis was a proud Aboriginal man. My grandmother Elizabeth Ober was a South Sea Islander woman. She was taken and brought here from Vanuatu. They would basically kidnap people and brought them here to work in the sugar cane industry.

Lucy Davis, sister to Professor Megan Davis[45]

Part of my family came to Australia via the practice of 'black-birding' – that is, the kidnapping and enslaving of South Pacific Islanders to work on plantations, especially in Queensland.

Professor Megan Davis[46]

Megan Davis is said to have earned a law degree from the University of Queensland and, under the mentorship of Aboriginal advocate Jackie Huggins, she joined the Foundation for Aboriginal and Islander Research Action (FAIRA) in Brisbane, which led her to apply for a United Nations Fellowship.

Her application was successful and, at the age of 24, Davis was sent by Australia on a five-year program (1999-2004) to the UN in Geneva as an international lawyer. There she helped work on the UN Declaration on the Rights of Indigenous Peoples (UNDRIP). She developed a career by 'specializing in Indigenous peoples and the law, democracy, and the constitutional recognition of First Nations.' This included a position with the United Nations Permanent Forum on Indigenous Issues, based in New York (2011-2016).

In Australia, Davis was appointed to the 2011 'Australian Government Expert Panel on the Recognition of Aboriginal and Torres Strait Islander Peoples in the Constitution'. She was a member of the Referendum Council from 2015 to 2017 and instrumental in developing the Uluru Statement From the Heart, a manifesto for the self-determination of Indigenous

---

[45]Speaking on the ABC's *Australian Story*, 30 Jun 2023.[[7.49] at 02:20]

[46]Opinion, 'Five questions to Megan Davis: on Aboriginal self-determination', *The Guardian online*, 16 May 2014.

peoples in Australia. As the Co-Chair of the Uluru Dialogue – First Nations leaders leading the Uluru Statement work - she served on several referendum committees that advised on the failed 2023 Voice to Parliament referendum.[47]

This section shows how in many ways Professor Davis also appears to have made *choices* to construct a selective remembrance narrative of her life, similar to the way that Professor Calma did with his. It appears she has done this as a way of shaping how she *chooses* to see herself and how she wants to be 'counted by others'. She seems to be using family history research to claim ancestral validation for her modern identity.[48]

Interest in Davis and her family history was first piqued after the airing of an episode of the ABC's *Australian Story*, from which the above quotation by her sister Lucy was taken. The program was broadcast in the lead-up to the 2023 Voice referendum and it appeared the Davis sisters were perhaps creating kidnapping claims to elicit emotional sympathy and support from the ABC audience. The notion that their family was historically oppressed and disadvantaged appeared to be designed to encourage Australians to vote Yes in the referendum as a way of recompense for past injustices to Indigenous peoples like the Davises.

Choosing to be Descendant of a Kanaka 'Slave'

After the *Australian Story* program aired, a complaint was submitted by *Dark Emu Exposed* to the ABC on 9 July 2023 as follows:[49]

> In this ABC *Australian Story: Voice From the Heart — Megan Davis*, Lucy Davis makes the claim on behalf of the family's ancestry that:
>
> "My grandmother Elizabeth Ober was a South Sea Islander woman. She was taken and brought here from Vanuatu. They

---

[47] *Wikipedia: Megan Davis*

[48] As described by sociologist Eviatar Zerubavel - see page 119.[[7.1] p76.]

[49] Abridged version; See full complaint here - [7.50]

would basically kidnap people and brought them here to work in the sugar cane industry."

The claim that the family's grandmother Elizabeth Ober was taken [kidnapped] from Vanuatu and brought to Queensland is not true and as such is misinformation and misleading to viewers.

Elizabeth Ober was in fact born in Queensland on 1 November 1891 as recorded in the *Queensland Births, Deaths & Marriages Records*, QLDBDM 1891/C/8961.

She was not born in Vanuatu but instead grew up with her parents in Queensland until her marriage to John Malary on 22 February 1911 as confirmed in the *Queensland Births, Deaths & Marriages Records*, QLDBDM 1911/C/2220. Further information can be found here: ***www.dark-emu-exposed.org...***

In our opinion, this is just misinformation by the Davises and the ABC and a correction or retraction should be issued by the ABC.

To the ABC's credit, a prompt and detailed response[50] was received within three weeks from the Executive Producer of *Australian Story*, **Rebecca Latham**: :

Dear Roger

Thank you for your email about our story on Megan Davis.

At the time of the interview, Lucy Davis told us the information about her family history as she understood it. She didn't have access to her grandmother's birth certificate and wasn't aware of the information you have which says that her grandmother Elizabeth was born here in Australia.

This was not a deliberate effort by the producers to deceive viewers. At the time of our interview with the Davis sisters they believed it was their grandmother, rather than their great-grandparents, who had come from Vanuatu.

As you outline in your *'Dark Emu Exposed'* website, Megan and Lucy Davis's two great-grandparents were born in Vanuatu and came here in the late 19th century at a time when many South Sea islanders were bought here to work in the sugar cane industry.

This information is new to the Davis family ... we allowed the Davis sisters to tell their story as they see it...

---

[50]Full ABC response with further notes at [7.51]

We thank you for your feedback and your correction of the family's birth details and we hope you continue to watch our program.

Sincerely,

Rebecca Latham, Executive Producer Australian Story

Although Latham had acknowledged the error, the program (as of 3 June 2025 on *ABC iView*) is yet to be re-edited or tagged with a correction notice. One could reasonably ask, does the ABC really care about truth-telling?

This engagement with the Davis sisters via the ABC only confirms the dangers of allowing people of influence such as politicians, public servants or academics to use their own family's ancestry and 'selective remembrance' to influence their advocacy for public policies that potentially affect all Australians. It is astounding that Davis, a highly qualified constitutional lawyer and academic, hadn't done the research to confirm her grandmother's details prior to relying upon her family's genealogy to advocate for inserting race-preference clauses into our constitution. The ABC claimed the information was 'new to the Davis family'. This is despite Professor Davis assuring her ABC viewers that, 'this is our family file [of documents], so it's all of the material that we've got from the Queensland archives'. Davis should have found what was in plain sight in the archives - her grandmother had not been kidnapped but was born in Queensland, and her great-grandparents were two Ni-Vanuatu who had willingly signed on as indentured labourers to work in Queensland. Both of them enjoyed and valued their time in Queensland so much that after returning to their islands on the expiry of their first contracts, they re-signed new contracts and returned to Queensland within a year. Hardly the actions of 'slaves'.[51] (See Figure 7.4 for this branch of the alleged Davis Family Tree).

On returning to Queensland on her second contract, their

---

[51] As evidence that both willingly returned to Queensland, see documents for Billy Willighan, (Davis's great-grandfather) [7.52]; and Mrs Ober's (Wallangartie) obituary above (Davis's great-grandmother).

Booty	m. ?	**Wallangartie**
(aka Robert Ober)		**(aka Mary Marlo)**
b. 1852 Aoba Island, **New**		b. 1853 Malao, Sanma,
Hebrides (Vanuatu), South		**Vanuatu, South Sea Islands**
Sea Islands – d. 24 Nov 1933		– d. 25 May 1948, Pialba?
Point Vernon, Qld		Qld
(Davis's Great-grandfather)		*(Davis's Great-grandmother)*

Elizabeth Ober (Malary)	m.1 John Malary (*dec.*	**Fred Davis**
b. 1 Nov 1891 Queensland –	*1915*)	b. ca1893 Warra,
d. 16 January 1969 Urangan,	m.2 never married	Queensland – d. 29 January
Qld	Fred	1978 Urangan, Qld
Full 100% Ni-Vanuatu,		`Half' (50%) Aboriginal and
South Sea Islander heritage		50% South Sea Islander**
(Davis's grandmother)		*(Davis's grandfather)*

Alfred Victor Malary	m. ?	**Dawn Jeanette Burns**
(known as Davis)		b. ca1942 Brisbane, Qld
b. 5 Nov 1935 Hervey Bay,		**100% Australian/British**
Qld – d. 1997 Brisbane, Qld		*(Davis's mother)*
'Qtr' (25%) Aboriginal and		
75% South Sea Islander		
(Davis's father)		

Sisters Megan Davis & Lucy	Estimated to be of
Davis	**12% Aboriginality,**
	plus of **38% South**
Megan b.ca1976 Qld	**Sea Islander** and **50%**
	British ancestry by
	this alleged family
	tree

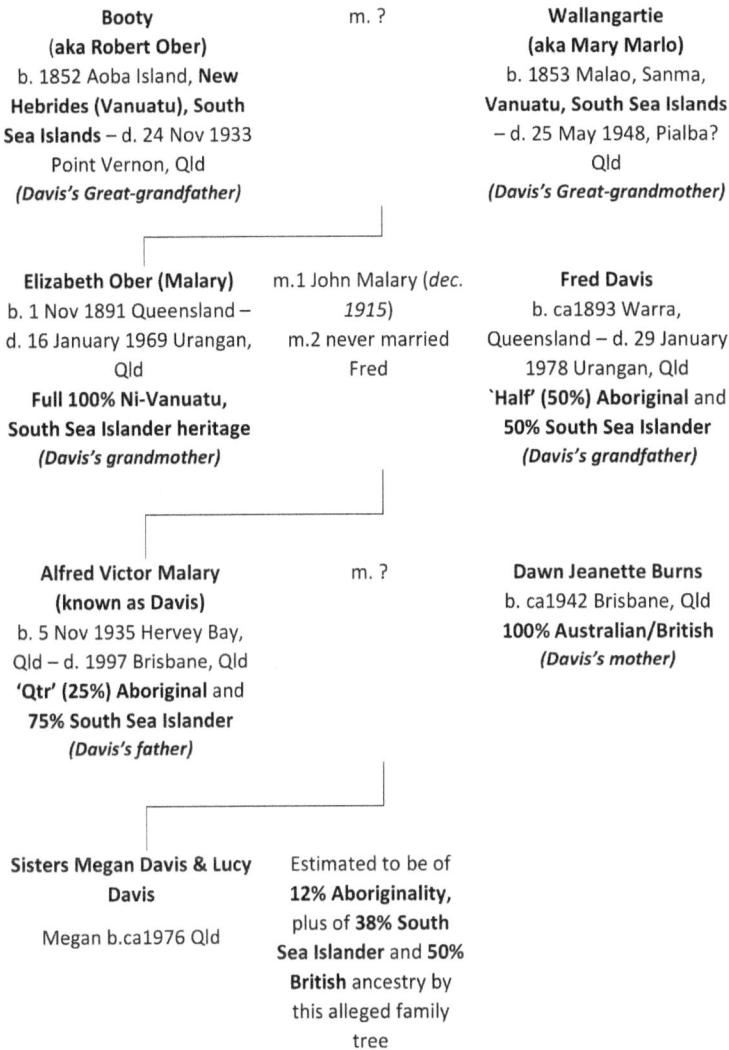

Figure 7.4: The branch of the apparent paternal Family Tree for sisters Megan and Lucy Davis, showing their Ni-Vanuatu ancestral links to grandmother Elizabeth Ober who was born in Queensland to Ni-Vanuatu migrant parents. Ancestry percentages (%) are only approximate estimates. Full paternal Family Tree available for download here - [7.53] (Subject to the *Disclaimer* on page (ii).)

great-grandmother, Mrs Mary Ober (Wallangartie), married,
their grandmother Elizabeth was born, and she successfully in-
tegrated into Australian society, as detailed in her 1948 obituary below. This completely contradicts the negative narrative
the modern-day Davis family seeks to promote:

LINK WITH EARLY DAY ISLAND LIFE

In the death of Mrs. Mary Ober, Urangan, on May 25, there
was severed another link with the old black-birding days,
when natives from the South Sea Islands were brought to
Queensland to work for the sugar industry...[52]

The late Mrs. Ober, who was in her 95th year, was born on Marlo
Island, in the New Hebrides, and was brought to Queensland as a
young girl in her teens.

She often spoke of her first position, in which she worked for white
people on Magnetic Island [off Townsville]. She could not understand one word of English, but **her mistress was very kind and
very patient**, and would repeat everything several times, until
Mary could say it after her. **She always spoke very highly
of those people**, for whom she worked [for] three years ... Mrs.
Ober [then] worked in Townsville, Cairns and Cooktown.

After her years of probation[53] were completed **she was free to
return to her island home**, but by that time she had become
accustomed to the ways of the white people and had overcome her
home sickness, but she had not heard from her home folk all those
years, and so she decided to return home. There was always much
feasting and jubilation when one of the long lost ones returned ...

---

[52]The term 'black-birding' did not just refer to kidnapping unsuspecting islanders for
shipment to Queensland as labourers. Rather the term covered the whole indentured
labour trade from outright kidnapping (only some 5% of recruits in Qld) to standard,
legal, labour contracts willingly signed by the recruits, who sometimes re-signed
two or more times - A typical newspaper report of 1892 headlined: THE NEW
"BLACK-BIRDING" REGULATIONS. *The Governor-in-Council approved of the
Kanaka recruiting regulations to-day. They provide that British subjects only shall
be employed in the labor trade ... Islanders under 16 are not to be recruited. There
is to be no attempt to retake unwilling islanders, nor to recruit islanders in the
employ of Europeans. Women are not to be recruited alone or without the chief's
consent. Recruiting is to be conducted by approved persons. No recruiting is to
take place on Sundays, and no recruit is to be engaged unless there are facilities
in Queensland for interpreting the agreement ... On their return the islanders are
to be landed at their own villages. A deceased islander's effects are to be handed
to his relations. There is to be a liberal allowance for clothing per schedule, and
hospitals in Queensland are to be established for housing sick islanders. - Bendigo
Independent,* Saturday 21 May 1892, p3.
[53]Under the terms of a standard indentured labour contract, which she would have
willingly entered into.

she remained on the islands for twelve months or so, and **then returned once more to Queensland on her own free will**. On her return to Queensland, Mrs. Ober worked ... on the Yerra Sugar Plantation. There she did all of the work from cutting, thrashing and planting cane, and working in the mills, to scrub cutting and clearing. It was at Yerra where she met her late husband. It was there they were married and raised their children ...

After years of faithful service to the country of her adoption, she was granted the monthly sum of £1 1s. 8p. per month, on which to clothe and feed herself. Her family tried often to get the old-age pension for her during those years, but it was not until three or four years ago that she was granted the full old-age pension. The late Mrs. Ober is survived by two daughters and one son. **Elizabeth (Mrs. Fred Davis - Megan Davis's grandmother)** ... also 17 grandchildren and 17 great-grand children...[54] (emphasis added.)

Choosing to Identify as a Cobble Cobble Aboriginal Woman

In the ABC's *Australian Story* program, Professor Davis was described as:

a Cobble Cobble woman, raised by a single mother of five in Housing Commission in Brisbane, she grew up to be a professor of law...[and] as a proud Cobble Cobble woman there was no other choice for her than to do something that was going to positively impact our people.

No evidence could be found that her mother ever described the family as being Cobble Cobble, nor that Davis's father or grandfather ever identified themselves as being Cobble Cobble. Indeed, as historian the late Keith Windschuttle has pointed out in a detailed study of Megan Davis's family, 'if you google "Cobble Cobble", the only results you receive are those of Megan Davis and her siblings'.[55]

Given there appears to be no ethnographic record of a tribe with this name ever having existed, Davis's self-making

---

[54]Obituary, *Maryborough Chronicle*, 9 June 1948, p3. See [7.54] for full research notes.
[55]Tindale's *Aboriginal tribes of Australia*, 1974 contains no reference to the Cobble Cobble tribe. The only mention of this name in any records is in reference to a cattle station, which later on appears to have changed its name to Warra Warra (now just Warra). See *Wikipedia - Warra Queensland*.

claims about which 'mob' she might belong to appear to be as inaccurate as Pat Eatock's were.

This is of concern to Australians because Davis has had, and will attempt to continue to have, an influential impact on the financial, social and political policies affecting not only Aboriginal Australians, but all other Australians as well. During the 2023 Voice referendum debates she attained a very high profile not only as an expert in constitutional law but also as an Aboriginal woman with, as she implied herself, the lived experience of her 'mob'. But which 'mob' is that exactly?

American academic Matthew Elliott[56] has studied celebrity family history television shows such as *Who Do You Think You Are?* In his paper, *The Inconvenient Ancestor*,[57] he provides a good explanation for the 'selective remembrance' of people like Davis and her sister, who are the 'celebrities' in this case. They have selectively taken that part of their family genealogy they wanted portrayed on the *Australian Story* program.

Elliot writes:

> genealogists never just discover ancestors; rather, they construct narratives that enable us to actually make them our ancestors ... Not only are ancestors selected ... for their story's potential emotional power [e.g. Elizabeth Ober the 'slave'], but they are presented to the subjects on screen without forewarning in order to prompt authentic emotional responses, whether excitement, anger, or sadness, all of which frequently result from these ancestral 'big reveals,' as such scenes have come to be known in reality television.

> For the most part, genealogy television serves ... as a form of affirmation. In fact, beyond using genealogy to make ancestors through 'selective remembrance' ... ancestors are often presented in ways that appear designed to reflect the celebrity subject [i.e. Davis], with a newly discovered ancestor functioning as a mirror of the genealogical subject or at least some dimension of his or her identity. This is done by highlighting connections and affinities between the ancestor and the

---

[56] Associate Professor of English at Emmanuel College, Boston, USA.

[57] Elliot, M., 'The Inconvenient Ancestor: Slavery and Selective Remembrance on Genealogy TV', *Studies in Popular Culture*, Spring 2017, Vol.39, No.2, pp73-90.

celebrity - that there is a distinctive family connection that bonds the subject to the ancestor, regardless of the historical or biological distance between them [e.g. Megan Davis calling herself a Cobble Cobble woman so as to reach back to Fred Davis the Aboriginal grandfather]. In this way, genealogy television uses what [has been called] the 'idiom of the family' to evade the many inevitable differences between the individual and the ancestor, as well as between the past and the present.

These differences of individuality are blurred and the gaps and ruptures of history are smoothed over as the newly discovered figures are declared part of the family, signaling a newly constructed collective identity, an 'imagined community' of kin. In turn, the vast majority of the show's guests, celebrities and otherwise, embrace the logic along with their new family, often echoing some version of the favorite refrain of the genre: **'I have found my people.'**[58] (emphasis added.)

Elliot's analysis would seem to explain Megan Davis's own personal discovery journey to find her people, the Cobble Cobble.

The Choices of Professor Megan Davis

> *In March, two months before the national constitutional convention at Uluru, the Nobel Prize–winning Saint Lucian writer **Derek Walcott** passed away. The singular poet's work defined **my adolescent search for identity** as I clumsily navigated the privileges and anguish of walking between **'two worlds'**. Walcott's epic poem 'Omeros' provided me with a luminous and challenging account of this antecedent struggle. His poetry made me feel not so alone in that dawning realisation of the dilemmas facing cultures like mine. In those exhausting weeks leading to Uluru, **Walcott's prose about the colonial experience** was often in my mind, and the themes of **'Omeros' – displacement, coexistence and redemption – resonate in the Uluru Statement from the Heart.***

Professor Megan Davis[59] (emphasis added.)

Before reading this piece of self-analysis by Davis, it was difficult to understand what forces and motivations had guided, perhaps even driven, her academic and political career. Why

---

[58] *op. cit.* Elliot, p77-8.
[59] Megan Davis,'To walk in two worlds', *The Monthly*, July 2017.

did she have such a serious professional commitment in lobbying for a division of Australians into two, race-based polities that would be enshrined within our founding document, the Australian Constitution?

Constitutional lawyers are typically quiet, scholarly types who only appear occasionally to address the media when the High Court makes what appears to the public to be an inexplicable decision.[60]

But Professor Davis was a different sort of constitutional lawyer, a very activist one, as she herself admitted in a podcast:

> My name is Professor Megan Davis. I'm Pro Vice-Chancellor Indigenous at the University of New South Wales ... I'm a Cobble Cobble woman from the Barrungam nation which is in southwest Queensland. So as an Aboriginal scholar, I have never been someone that is particularly fluent in theory ... I've always been a very practical scholar, meaning I always roll my sleeves up and get involved in law reform processes ... my job as a scholar is to take what I've learned and what I'm researching and apply it to the here and now.[7.55]

Her University of NSW biography completes the picture of a specialist in Aboriginal political activism. Professor Davis is:

> a renowned constitutional lawyer and public law expert, specialising on Indigenous peoples and the law, the constitutional recognition of First Nations and democracy ... [and] the leading Australian lawyer on constitutional recognition of First Nations peoples for two decades and designed the Referendum Council's deliberative process that led to the Uluru Statement from the Heart.[7.56]

---

[60] *Love/Thoms v Commonwealth*: 'A landmark High Court ruling has found indigenous people - even those born overseas - cannot be considered "aliens" under the Constitution and deported on character grounds ... Aboriginal people cannot be classified as "aliens", regardless of whether they held Australian citizenship or not ... Constitutional law expert Anne Twomey says the most contentious aspect of the judgment is whether it creates "special rights or privileges" for Aboriginal people and creates a race-based constitutional distinction ... the Constitution does not prohibit special treatment of a "race" and ... "equality is not about treating everyone the same". Professor Twomey predicts the issue will be a matter of ongoing debate.' - Olivia Caisley, *The Australian*, 11 Feb 2020.

In the *Australian Story* documentary, she described her teenage
fascination with the Australian Constitution, and its part in
the foundation of her career, when she realised that, "There is
something missing from it; and that is, the recognition of the
first peoples of this country." [7.57] Thus, a critical component
of Davis's legal and political persona, the way she sees herself
and how she wishes to be 'counted by others', is her Aboriginality - her membership of the 'first peoples'; it adds greatly to
her authenticity and credibility. However, it is rather surprising when other commentators point out that she and her life
experiences don't actually look all that 'Aboriginal' in a real,
meaningful way. Her apparent *choice* of her self-identification
was commented upon during the height of the Voice referendum debates by historian the late Keith Windschuttle. In a
2023 *Quadrant Magazine* article[61] he noted that:

> she was born in 1976[62] to a white mother who was a school
> teacher of English. Her father was an itinerant railway worker
> who was part-Aboriginal and part-Pacific Islander. She grew
> up as "a Queensland rail kid" moving with her father's em-
> ployment from Monto, where she was born, to Mulgildie, Ei-
> dsvold and Hervey Bay in eastern Queensland. Her parents
> separated when she was very young and her mother took her
> and her four siblings to Eagleby in Logan City, south of Bris-
> bane, where she brought them up as a single parent.

Windschuttle perceptively concluded:

> Davis's grandfather and his brother eventually left the Cher-
> bourg [Aboriginal] mission and went to live in Hervey Bay.
> The area must have given them well-paid employment because
> her grandfather was able to buy land at Hervey Bay and build
> a house. He met a Pacific Islander woman there (Elizabeth
> Ober) who gave birth to Davis's father. Davis tells journalists
> that she still keeps in contact with both parents. "I feel deeply
> connected to Hervey Bay; each Christmas I visit for a few
> weeks. It represents a continuity with my childhood, my dad
> and his land. I feel deeply connected to Eagleby and Logan
> too and get home as much as I can." However, neither Davis

---

[61]Windschuttle, K., 'White Man's Dreaming, *Quadrant Magazine*, 29 May 2023.
[62]1975 according to *Wikipedia: Megan Davis.*

nor her indigenous father grew up within anything that could be called an Aboriginal community. The 'continuity' she talks about with her dad and 'his land' is not a uniquely Aboriginal sentiment, since most normal Australians feel much the same about their own parents and the country towns or suburbs where they grew up. There is nothing particularly Aboriginal about it. Davis's connection to the [so-called] Cobble Cobble people is solely genetic. In her interviews with the press, she has described her real cultural heritage well. It was determined by her white mother's large home library, by her own childhood education in Queensland schools, and her tertiary education at the University of Queensland law school. In none of her interviews or numerous articles does she mention any cultural inheritance from contact with an Aboriginal community. She never spoke an Aboriginal language fluently and has never discussed any of the beliefs that sustained the Cobble Cobble people.[63]

Windschuttle then goes on to observe that Davis's remarkable career is a product entirely of the white culture and society 'that she and her fellow activists have spent their adult lives denouncing'. In other words, Davis 'never had a place within an Aboriginal community that might give her a special insider's view of their needs'. She is really no different to any of the white academics and policy makers currently employed in Aboriginal affairs but who Davis and the other activists now label as being the problem not the solution. Davis just comes across as an ambitious careerist trying to land an influential role within the Aboriginal policy bureaucracy by denouncing the current incumbents.

After reading Windschuttle's summary of Davis's life, and her apparent lack of any real cultural connection with a living Aboriginal community, it appears that the professor has simply done what Andrew Bolt had observed all those years before in Pat Eatock's case - she has just *chosen* that one 'strand' in her mixed Aboriginal, South Sea Islander, Scottish, English, Irish and indeed Australian ancestry to solely self-identify with today - as an Aboriginal Cobble Cobble woman. This wasn't

---

[63] If indeed a people of that tribal name ever actually existed. - See footnote 55.

always the case. In a *Guardian* interview in 2014 she presented her ancestry more broadly, like many 'mongrel' Aussies do, when she claimed, "My family is Aboriginal, South Pacific Islander and Australian." She then went further with the very illuminating claim that, "My mum's family is Australian; she eschews any claim to ancillary ancestry."[64]

This is where the 'penny dropped' for many observers. No longer would Australians feel obliged to always accept unquestioningly the social and political advice on Aboriginal affairs from the likes of Professor Davis because of her perceived greater authority as an 'Aboriginal' woman. In reality, she had not had the lived experience of being brought up in an Aboriginal household or community. In fact, her white, English-teacher, single mother, whose ancestors had come to Australia as convicts, settlers or immigrants from many parts of Britain,[65] thought exactly like many Australians - she identified as just an Australian and 'eschews any claim to ancillary ancestry.' As Windschuttle noted, Davis's 'connection to the Cobble Cobble people is solely genetic' via her part-Aboriginal grandfather.

Davis is entitled to have an opposing view to her mother by *choosing* to identify as Aboriginal despite the genealogical records indicating that she is only of about 12% Aboriginal ancestry.[66] However, many Australians now would be justified in feeling that a great moral and ethical burden has been lifted from them; as a people of goodwill they always felt some obligation to accede to the voices calling for social and political policy proposals that affected Aboriginal people, because those voices were *from* Aboriginal people themselves.

However, in the case of Professor Davis, perhaps they were misled. It would appear that the professor is simply another ethnically-mixed Aussie, like millions of other Aus-

---

[64]Opinion, 'Five questions to Megan Davis: on Aboriginal self-determination', *Guardian Online*, 16 May 2014.
[65]See apparent *Maternal* Family Tree here:[7.58]
[66]See apparent *Paternal* Family Tree here:[7.53]

tralians, each with their own multi-stranded ancestry. Previously, her *choice* in portraying herself *solely* as a member of the so-called Cobble Cobble people gave her an authenticity and credibility that made it difficult for critics to oppose her political and activist agenda for fear of being accused of being anti-Aboriginal, or indeed racist.

Anthropologist Peter Sutton was correct when he observed that inherent knowledge or scholarship does not derive from having Aboriginal ancestry alone, although in today's 'market' it is advantageous to believe that it does:

> there are people who believe that knowledge comes with your blood and from birth. That's obviously bullshit. So to claim Aboriginality, you know, is a big deal, and that's why it's humming at the moment. People were more relaxed about the issue when the payoff was not big. But now the payoff is big. You can get ahead in academia, the arts, the public service if you've got an Aboriginal identity.[7.59]

Returning to the quotation above by Davis, in which she credits the West Indian poet, **Derek Walcott**,[67] for assistance in:

> my adolescent search for identity as I clumsily navigated the privileges and anguish of walking between 'two worlds' ... His poetry made me feel not so alone in that dawning realisation of the dilemmas facing cultures like mine. In those exhausting weeks leading to Uluru, Walcott's prose about the colonial experience was often in my mind and the themes of 'Omeros' – displacement, coexistence and redemption – resonate in the Uluru Statement from the Heart.(See fn 59.)

Davis is confirming that she was influenced by Walcott's poetry so much during her impressionable adolescence that all she

---

[67] An excerpt from a paper by Raj Kumar Baral and Heena Shrestha, 'What is behind Myth and History in Derek Walcott's Omeros?', *Cogent Arts & Humanities*, (2020), 7: p1-18, serves as a summary of Walcott's poem. It is easy to see how a young advocate, perhaps like Megan Davis herself, could re-formulate (or indeed, perhaps just cut-and-paste) Walcott's ideas to suit an Aboriginal activist agenda in Australia. By just switching a few of Walcott's words - his references to 'West Indies', 'Africa', 'slaves', etc., to 'Australia', 'Aboriginal', 'Kanaka' or 'First Peoples', and adding 'missions' and 'Country' as appropriate, an ideological road map for a First Peoples reawakening in Australia could easily emerge. - see the excerpt here [7.60].

needed to do later in her career was to modify [perhaps just 'cut-and-paste'] his West Indian colonial experiences of 'displacement, coexistence and redemption' to successfully create a template for an Australian narrative of 'dispossession, reconciliation and treaty'. The result of this ideological journey became the political 'fix', of whom she was ultimately to become one of the main architects - the Uluru Statement from the Heart and its constitutional enshrinement. Being at the UN and familiar with Walcott's ideology, plus steadily making choices about how to project her own identity as an 'Indigenous' person, has perhaps shaped the Megan Davis of today - 'a globally recognised expert in Indigenous peoples legal rights ... and design[er] of the Referendum Council's deliberative process that led to the Uluru Statement from the Heart'.[7.56]

Her authenticity and credibility has certainly been enhanced by her choice to describe herself as 'a proud Cobble Cobble woman'.[7.61]. This professional persona is further enhanced by the intersectional 'cred' the family claims (mistakenly as it turned out) that they are burdened with a past that included Kanaka 'slavery'. Perhaps the ability to claim a legacy of slavery is an additional identity attribute that may be useful to offset the privilege that comes from being a successful, highly paid academic within the post-colonial, capitalist structure that is modern Australia.

Nevertheless, the point is that Megan Davis had the opportunity to *choose* to self-identify with any one or more of her valid ancestral options. She could have publicly self-identified as just an Australian like her mum (and like millions of other citizens); or she may have added a bit more by referring to her mother's British, English, Scottish or Irish ancestry, should she wish to be more specifically European; or she could have identified more publicly as South Sea Islander, based on her grand- and great-grandparents' ancestry. But instead, she *chose* to select her minor strand of about 12% Aboriginality to define her principle identity.

That Megan Davis was actually free to choose her identity was confirmed when some further family history unexpectedly appeared.

7.4.1 Same Ancestor, Difference Choices

In 2013, a short film was posted on Youtube of a lovely young Australian mother, who was relating the story of her family's connections with the Queensland sugar industry. Melanie Yasserie was of South Sea Islander descent and she had taken up an offer to learn more about her family's ancestry as part of a social history program.[68]

During the three-minute film clip, as Melanie outlined the details of each of the five generations of her family, she said something startlingly familiar - the researchers of this book had heard it before:

> We've always known that our family is from Urangan, Hervey Bay. Our great-grandfather **Frederick Davis**, he had settled there. He had bought land and was very active in the Hervey Bay Community. [[7.62], watch from 00:41]

It was familiar because in 2010 a younger Megan Davis had told an interviewer:

> We grew up mostly in Hervey Bay, where my grandfather, Fred Davis had bought land at Urangan.[69]

Piecing together this branch of the Fred Davis family tree indicated that one of his sons, Alfred, had given rise to Megan Davis's family line, and another of his sons, William, to Melanie Yasserie's family line (Figure 7.5). Megan Davis was in fact Melanie Yasserie's first cousin, once removed. They shared a common apical ancestor in the Aboriginal man, Fred[erick] Davis.

---

[68]State Library of Queensland, Griffith Uni and Ethnic Communities Council of Queensland (sponsors), 'The Australian South Sea Islander Multimedia Storytelling Workshop,' 25-27 June 2013.

[69]Jessica Trappel, 'An Interview with Megan Davis', *Indigenous Law Bulletin*, 7(19), 2010, p24.

Fred [Fredwich/Frederick] Davis b. ca1893 Warra, Qld – d. 29 January 1978 Urangan, Qld	m. never married	**Elizabeth Ober** b. 1 Nov 1891 Qld – d. 16 January 1969 Urangan, Qld
'Half' (50%) Aboriginal and **50% South Sea Islander** *(Prof. Megan Davis's grandfather & Melanie Yasserie's Great-grandfather)*		**Full 100% Ni-Vanuatu, South Sea Islander heritage**

Alfred Victor Malary (known as Davis) b. 5 Nov 1935 Hervey Bay, Qld – d. 1997 Brisbane, Qld	(brothers)	**William Futi Malary (known as Davis)** b. 7 Dec 1922 -13 Dec 1990 Qld
'Qtr' (25%) Aboriginal and **75% South Sea Islander** *(Prof. Megan Davis's father & Melanie Yasserie's great-uncle)*		**'Qtr' (25%) Aboriginal** and **75% South Sea Islander** *(Prof. Megan Davis's uncle & Melanie Yasserie's grandfather)*

Megan Davis Prof. Megan Davis is estimated to be of **12% Aboriginality,** plus of **38% South Sea Islander** and **50% British** ancestry (via mother) by this alleged family tree	**Melanie Yasserie's father or Mother**
	Melanie Yasserie **Identifies as South Sea Islander heritage**

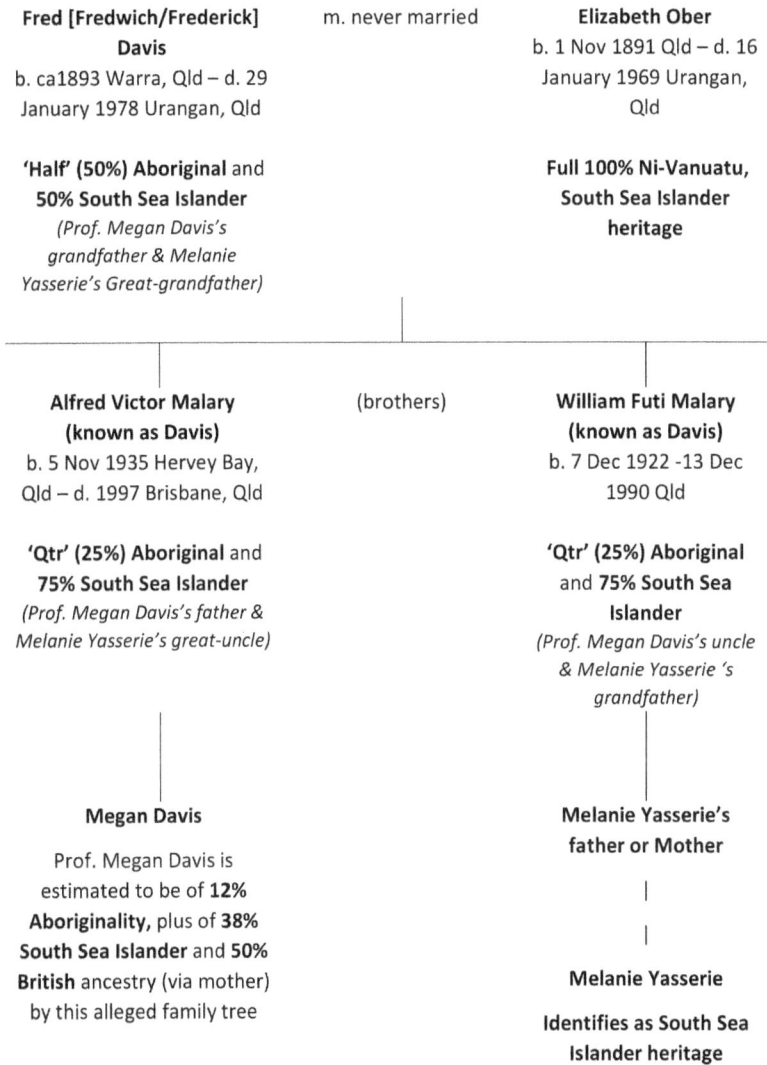

Figure 7.5: A branch of the apparent Family Tree for two brothers - **Alfred Victor Malary [Davis]** (his daughter was Megan Davis) and **William Futi Malary [Davis]** (his grand daughter was Melannie Yasserie). Both were sons of part-Aboriginal and part-South Sea Islander man, **Fredwich (Frederick/Fred) Davis.** Ancestry percentages (%) are only approximate estimates. (Subject to *Disclaimer* on page (ii).)

In the ABC's *Australian Story* program, Davis had offered a snippet of her grandfather's official file (see [7.63] for a screenshot), which indicated that he had been given an Exemption Certificate that allowed him to leave the control of the Aboriginal mission. This indicated the authorities considered he was 'not habitually associating with aboriginals' as defined under the Act.

The records show that he moved to Urangan in Hervey Bay, cleared a block of land to build his house, and raised a family with South Sea Islander woman, Elizabeth Ober. The house that Fred built became quite noteworthy when it was said to be 'the last of [its] Melanesian type in Australia', according to historian Peter Corris who visited it and its 85-year-old builder, Fred Davis, in 1977.[7.64]

The conclusion that can be drawn from these family histories is that everyone is free to express their own agency and 'choose' how they want to identify and, if they are so inclined, how they 'choose to be seen by others.' Fred Davis *chose* to 'no longer associate with aboriginals' and applied for an Exemption Certificate, which he obtained in 1926, allowing him to leave Cherbourg Aboriginal Mission and the stifling, but in many cases necessary, control of the Chief Aboriginal Protector. He *chose* to marry Elizabeth, a South Sea Islander, of the same heritage and culture as his father. He *chose* to move to Hervey Bay, build a Melanesian-style house and raise a large family. One of his sons, Arthur (Megan Davis's father), *chose* to marry a white, Australian girl of English heritage who gave Megan and her siblings an essentially typical Aussie upbringing, especially after their father left the family. On the other hand, one of Fred's other sons, William, *chose* to marry a South Sea Islander so that ultimately his granddaughter, Melanie Yasserie, inherited a family social life and culture that was much more South Sea Islander influenced than Megan's, although both were descendants of the *same* Aboriginal man, Fred Davis. To an impartial observer they were both

Australian citizens, Aussies, each of a mix of racial ancestries, neither more nor less deserving of special government measures than each other.

Yasserie identifies as a fifth generation Australian of South Sea Islander heritage. However, with the same apical ancestor as Yasserie (Fred Davis, the Aboriginal and South Sea Islander man), Megan Davis instead has *chosen* to solely identify with Fred's Aboriginal ancestral strand, and call herself a Cobble Cobble Aboriginal woman (despite her other 88% mixed ancestries). Both these women are correct and fully within their rights to choose how they identify themselves. Indeed, one part of the three-part rule for statutory Aboriginality in Australia is for people to 'self-identify' as Aboriginal - that is, **choose** to identify as such, or not as the case may be. All of this illustrates that Bolt was correct - some people can choose any one strand of often a number of ancestries by which to identify themselves. For Bolt to be sanctioned by Bromberg J for suggesting this possibility existed for the Eatock Nine - the 'white Aborigines' - was an injustice to Bolt.

However, more importantly this also supports Bolt's fear that using the law to assign certain rights and priviledges to Australians based on ancestry is a very bad idea. Specifically, if Professor Davis's Voice proposal had succeeded in the 2023 referendum, she and her family, identifying as Aborigines, would have been afforded certain political rights that Melanie Yasserie's family would not have enjoyed, given that they do not identify as Aboriginal.

How would that have been a good idea for the citizens of Australia? Is the history of Megan Davis's family all that different from that of Melanie Yasserie's? Does Megan suffer from failings in the Closing the Gap initiatives any more than Melanie does? As Windschuttle observed, the reality is that Professor Davis is a highly successful 'legal academic and bureaucrat who does not have, and never had, a place within an Aboriginal community that might give her a special insider's view of their needs. She is no better placed to understand Aboriginal problems, or to develop policies for Aboriginal people, than those white legal academics and bureaucrats employed in Aboriginal affairs but who she now labels the problem not the solution'.[70] Nor does she have any better insight into developing successful family policies for Aboriginal Australians than her successful first cousin once removed and mother of five, Melanie Yasserie.

7.4.2 Is This Professor Megan Davis's 'Viking' Moment?

In a 2018 trailer for the History Channel's series *Vikings*, a slightly overweight and boyish white middle-aged man opens the door to his suburban villa. He hurries towards the mailbox. Finding it empty, he appears disappointed. Over the following days, he repeats the process, becoming increasingly exasperated on finding the mailbox again empty. One day, however, it contains an envelope. Impatiently jerking it out, he sees that his genetic ancestry test results have finally arrived. They detail his ethnicity: '91.4% European, 5% Native American and 2% Non-specific East Asian.' As the man skims through the details of these figures, his eyes suddenly open wide. According to the test results, he is also '0.012% Viking.' With tears in his eyes, he falls to his knees and yells with excitement.

Next we see him standing outside his house dressed as a Viking warrior. To the sound of epic music, he raises his sword towards the skies and roars to the gods. Among genealogists and root-seeking individuals from Scandinavia, UK and USA, the desire to 'be a Viking' is a recurring phenomenon. On social media and online forums, people share news about their Viking ancestry, their connections, and their Viking DNA.[71]

To many Australians, the 'desire to be an Aboriginal' is a

---

[70] Keith Windschuttle, 'White Man's Dreaming', *Quadrant Magazine*, 29 May 2023.

[71] Paraphrased from Daniel Strand and Anna Kallen, 'I am a Viking! DNA, popular culture and the construction of geneticized identity', *New Genetics and Society*, Jan 2021, 40(1), p1-21.[7.65] & film clip here [7.66]

similar phenomenon, a 'trend', as Andrew Bolt put it. These
Australians, such as Professor Megan Davis focus on that one
strand of Aboriginal descent, no matter how thin that strand
might be, to define who they are, and how they wish to be
seen by others. Of course there is nothing wrong with that -
except when these Australians want their ancestry to have an
influence on their political or economic privileges.[72] This necessarily raises conflict with many other Australians who abhor
race-preferencing. Instead, they see Australia being first and
foremost a polity of citizens where one's ancestry or ethnicity should have no part in awarding special (either positive or
negative) privileges.

Finally, this conflict over choice - how one identifies - is
at the heart of many of the political schisms in modern Australia.[73] In *Eatock v Bolt*, Justice Bromberg essentially put
questioning a person's choice to identify as Aboriginal out of
bounds for discussion when he firstly found that one of Bolt's
newspaper articles described:

> a whole new fashion (or what Mr Bolt referred to as the
> 'trend') of which Mr Bolt is critical. The article asserts that
> the people who constitute the 'trend' have made a choice to
> identify as Aboriginal people ... [and] is likely to have been
> understood as largely answering the question posed by its
> sub-heading which asks - Why are so many people eager to
> proclaim their Aboriginality, despite it being such a small part
> of their heritage?[74]

His Honour then went on to disagree with Bolt that 'fair-
skinned' Aboriginal people like Pat Eatock had just chosen

---

[72] A counter-example illustrates this point perfectly: 'Dr Hannah McGlade, a Kurin
Minang [Western Australian] academic and member of the United Nations Permanent Forum on Indigenous Issues, told the National Indigenous Times: "Descent
alone is insufficient to claim Aboriginality in Australia. I was surprised to learn
from my father's DNA test that I may have remote Icelandic ancestry, that certainly does not make me Icelandic." (Totte, G., 'Anti-Voice campaigner condemned
for "blood will have to be measured" view on Aboriginal identity', *NIT*, 27 Jul
2023.)

[73] In addition, Diversity, Equity and Inclusion (DEI) policies are obviously being successful in disrupting and dividing modern Western capitalist societies as planned,
so the hard-Left Marxists will keep promoting DEI.

[74] *Eatock v Bolt* [2011] at 24-25.[7.67]

to identify as Aboriginal:

> Bolt also suggested in the first article that she identified as
> an Aboriginal for political motives after attending a political
> rally [when she was about 19-years-old.] That statement is
> untrue. [Instead] Ms Eatock recognised herself to be an Abo-
> riginal person from when she was eight years old whilst still
> at school and did not do so for political reasons.[75]

But is this the way it really is with all the 'fair-skinned' Australians who are now identifying as Aboriginal - those who
are part of Bolt's 'trend'? Do they always just know they
are Aboriginal from a very young age and are brought up as
Aboriginal, or do some make choices later in life, often in contrast to other family members, to self-identify and then seek
recognition as Aboriginal? We may never really know, because
Justice Bromberg is essentially saying that we cannot doubt
their claims. If Australians of very distant Aboriginal descent,
or even those who are total fakes like Pat Eatock, say they
have identified as Aboriginal from birth or from a very young
age, is Justice Bromberg telling other Australians that they
have to just 'suck it up' and believe them?

7.5   The Success of Pat Eatock's Fakery

People are only as good, or bad, as their incentives.

Anon

Show me the incentive, and I will show you the outcome.

Charlie Munger

Did She Embolden Others?

Prior to *Eatock v Bolt* in 2011, the odd case of a 'fake' Aborigine was generally in the form of a hoax – a non-Aboriginal
writer would adopt an Aboriginal persona and falsely claim the
authentic voice of someone with the 'lived experience' of being

---

[75]*Eatock v Bolt* [2011] at 382.[7.67]

of Aboriginal ancestry. During the 1980s and 1990s the literary market became increasingly hungry for authentic Aboriginal voices. Grants and employment opportunities were available to promote Aboriginal writers and academics. Publishers were keen to increase their portfolio of Aboriginal writers for inclusion in school reading lists, where large, profitable print runs were assured. The success of Sally Morgan's, *My Place*[76] – a story of a young Aboriginal girl growing up with a false heritage and not knowing where she came from – provided an incentive for other writers to examine their own ability to 'become' Aboriginal.[77] A number of new 'Aboriginal' writers and artists thus began to appear, confirming the old adage – 'show me the incentive, and I'll show you the outcome.'[78]

During the 1980s, Eric Willmot was a celebrated Aboriginal bureaucrat and writer. He had addressed the National Press Club in 1983, given the *Boyer Lectures* in 1986, and published an historical novel about the Aboriginal 'resistance fighter', Pemulwuy in 1987. This book was lauded as 'a landmark publication, a bestseller' and came with accolades from acclaimed author Thomas Keneally, political activist Charles Perkins (to whom Willmot dedicated the book), actor Jack Thompson and, even to this day, Wiradjuri man Stan Grant lauds it as, 'more than a novel, more than a story, it is the Big Bang: where the idea of Australia starts'.[79] Unfortunately, these literary titans had been fooled. Eric Willmot was a fake. His ruse was exposed when his family went public in late 1987.[80] The authorities moved silently to erase Willmot

---

[76] *My Place* sales were said to be over 600,000 by 2004. (Cited in Windschuttle, K. [2009]. *The Fabrication of Aboriginal History.* Vol 3. p305.)

[77] The claims Morgan made in her book were disputed by Judith Drake-Brockman, daughter of Alfred Howden Drake-Brockman. Judith's version of events is detailed in her book *Wongi Wongi*. In 2004, she suggested that Sally Morgan undergo a DNA test to prove her claims that Howden fathered Morgan's Aboriginal grandmother Daisy, then committed incest with Daisy and fathered Gladys, Sally Morgan's mother. Morgan declined to be tested. (*Wikipedia* and 'Fabricated abuse claims', *Sydney Morning Herald*, 21 Mar 2004.)

[78] Said to be a quote of the late Charlie Munger, Warren Buffett's astute US business partner.

[79] *Booktopia* review, *Pemulwuy, The Rainbow Warrior*, by Eric Willmot.

[80] Harvey, M., 'Black Blood row over family claim', *Brisbane Sunday Mail*, 18 Oct,

from his Aboriginal affairs portfolios, as well as his position as the Aboriginal representative on Prime Minister Bob Hawke's 1988 Bicentennial Committee.[81] That was how Australia was in those days – people who were found to be fake were exposed, and their 'Aboriginal' careers cancelled accordingly.

The same occurred in 1994 with the publication of *My Own Sweet Time*, a biography by supposed Pitjantjatjara Aboriginal woman, Wanda Koolmatrie, published by the Aboriginal publisher, Magabala Books. This double act of both writer and publisher being Aboriginal was clear and welcome evidence that the Aboriginal literary scene was coming of age. Koolmatrie described how she was taken from her mother in 1950 to be raised by white foster parents, thus becoming one of the so-called Stolen Generation. Her book received the Dobbie Literary Award and sales were brisk. However, it soon transpired that Koolmatrie's story was a hoax – 'she' was actually a 'he', and worse still, 'she' was not even Aboriginal. In fact, 'Wanda Koolmatrie' turned out to be a white Australian taxi driver named Leon Carmen. The whole affair erupted into a national scandal, with Carmen admitting he believed he would not have been able to break into the literary market had his book been published without this subterfuge.[82] In the 1990s the truth still mattered, and the literary career of Wanda Koolmatrie, aka Leon Carmen, imploded.

Another case of Aboriginal identity fraud in the 1990s was prosecuted with even more public vigour. The genuine Anmatyerre woman, Aboriginal artist Letty Scott Nupanunga, became incensed that a non-Aboriginal male artist, Sakshi Anmatyerre, had claimed the authority to paint particular Aboriginal designs, totems and motifs. She knew he was not of Aboriginal ancestry. Geoff Thompson, a reporter with the ABC's *7:30 Report* investigated the story and finally exposed

---

1987, p4.

[81] Parliament of Australia, *Australian Bicentennial Authority, Annual Report*, 2 Nov 1987, p2.

[82] Leon Carmen, 'Wanda and Me', *The Daily Telegraph*, 15 Mar 1997, p27.

Sakshi as being a fraud, proving in fact that he was of Indian heritage. Thompson subsequently won a Walkley Award for excellence in journalism for the story in 1998.[83]

These three examples demonstrate that genuine Aboriginality mattered in the 1990s. Aboriginal identity fraud, which was taken seriously by governments, the media and the public, was considered an affront to the sensibility of Australians, not to mention Aborigines themselves. The media had no qualms about openly discussing, challenging and indeed investigating the ancestry of prominent people claiming to be Aboriginal, over whom there was some considerable doubt. A mere decade later, however, something had changed.

7.5.1 The Statistics After *Eatock v Bolt*

In addition to the above three examples of prominent Aboriginal fakes, four more from the 1980s and 1990s have been identified - Roberta 'Bobbi' Sykes, B Wongar (aka Sreten Božić), Colin Johnson (aka Mudrooroo Narogin) and Pat Eatock. All were exposed at the time, except for Pat Eatock who was exposed posthumously (d. 2015) based on research carried out in 2024. As far as can be ascertained, no other prominent public figures are suspected of being fake during that period.[84]

However, in only one decade since Bolt lost his court case, evidence has been uncovered that indicates the number of prominent fakes has skyrocketed. This recent phenomenon is the basis of the proposition that Pat Eatock's win against Bolt emboldened others to fake their Aboriginality, knowing that not even a commentator as powerful as Andrew Bolt could succeed in calling them out and exposing them. Genealogical researchers have been able to discover the following thirteen alleged fakes[85] – people claiming Aboriginal descent when genealogical records indicate they may be mistaken, given they

---

[83]Goldsmith, B., 'A positive unsettlement: the story of Sakshi Anmatyerre', *Griffith Law Review*, 9 (2), 2000, p325.

[84]Other 'low-level' fakes, who were not in the public arena, have been ignored.

[85]see Chapter 11.1.5 for definition of a 'fake'.

have no apparent Aboriginal ancestors at all:

Six Professors at our universities: Bronwyn Carlson (Macquarie), Lisa Jackson Pulver (Sydney), Kerrie Doyle (UWS), Bruce Pascoe (Melbourne), Dennis Foley (Griffith) and Jaky Troy (Sydney).

Four politicians (all Labor): The Hon. Kyam Maher (SA Attorney-General) and his mother Viv Maher (unsuccessful SA State candidate), Dr Gordon Reid (Federal Member for Robertson) and Lauren O'Dwyer (unsuccessful Victorian State candidate).

Three from the arts: Adjunct Professor Margo Neale (ANU and National Museum of Australia), Adjunct Professor Wayne Quilliam (photographer and artist) and Eric Willmot (again – reprised in 2010 with his renewed claims in the film, *Pemulwuy* that he is Aboriginal).

This is a large number of alleged fakes that have been exposed in only five years of part-time research work. Additionally, a list has been compiled of some fifty other names of suspected fakes, who are yet to be fully investigated. These names have been supplied by concerned Aboriginal and Torres Strait Islanders. Just how many fakes are there in Australia? No one really knows for sure, but it's suspected that there are at least 100,000, and perhaps even as high as 300,000, as suggested by Sydney academic Suzanne Ingram.[86] Her research into those she calls 'box-tickers' or 'racial shifters' relates to those 'individuals who have changed their racial self-identification on the census form in recent years'. Ingram quotes work by Australian National University (ANU) researchers that found that in 2016, 40,000 people 'ticked-the-box'[87] for the first time, and in 2021 that number was around 92,300.[88] Other researchers have independently corroborated figures of these magnitudes.[89] The numbers in Figure 7.6

---

[86] See: *SBS Insight*, 'Indigenous Identity', No. 34, 2022.

[87] Refers to Australians who ticked the 'Yes' box to the question on the census form: 'Is the person of Aboriginal or Torres Strait Islander origin? - For people of both Aboriginal and Torres Strait Islander origin, mark both 'Yes' boxes'.(Source - ABS 2021 Census Form.)

[88] Ingram, S., 'Counting the cost of census box-tickers', *The Australian*, 16 Jul 2022.

[89] Taylor, A.,'The future growth and spatial shift of Australia's Aboriginal and Torres

Census Year	Total ATSI Population from Census	Australian Population Native-born [Total Population less number of Overseas-born Australians]	Native-born average annual population growth. (Note)	Total Resident Population of Australia.	ATSI Population as proportion of Total Resident Population.	ATSI Population as proportion of Native-born Population	ATSI average annual population growth. (Note)
	No.	No.	%	No.	%	%	%
1971	115,953	10,180,000	..	12,755,638	0.9	1.1	..
1976	160,915	10,830,000	1.2	13,548,448	1.2	1.4	6.8
1981	159,897	11,530,000	1.9	14,576,330	1.1	1.4	−0.1
1986	227,645	12,620,000	1.8	15,602,156	1.5	1.8	7.3
1991	265,378	13,320,000	1.1	16,849,496	1.6	2.0	3.1
1996	352,970	13,980,000	1.0	17,892,423	2.0	2.5	5.9
2001	460,140	14,820,000	1.1	19,386,461	2.4	3.1	5.3
2006	455,028	15,420,000	0.8	20,627,547	2.2	3.0	−0.1
2011	548,368	16,320,000	1.1	22,522,197	2.4	3.4	3.8
2016	649,171	17,280,000	1.1	24,385,064	2.6	3.7	3.4
2021	812,728	18,160,000	1.0	25,422,788	3.2	4.5	4.5
2024est	1,000,000+	18,670,000	0.9	27,204,809	3.6	5.3	7.6
	8-fold increase	*2-fold increase*	*decreasing*	*2-fold increase*	*4-fold increase*	*5-fold. increase*	*variable*

Figure 7.6: Aboriginal & Torres Strait Islander (ATSI) Population Increases Compared to Total Population for each Census Period. (*Source:* ABS) Notes:
– Average % increase per year over the 5 years. Apparent 'conflicting' ABS statistics reported elsewhere are due to variations in release dates and statistical refinements and adjustments.

clearly indicate there has been a much higher percentage population increase in the number of Australians identifying in the census as Aboriginal and/or Torres Strait Islanders (ATSI) – an eight-fold increase since 1971 – compared with the only roughly two-fold increase in Australia's native-born or total populations.

Interestingly, the wildly irregular changes up and down in the ATSI average annual growth rates (*far-right column*) indicate that non-demographic factors (i.e. other than natural birth increases or deaths) are at work. This suggests that in some years there is a rush, perhaps due to media publicity, for people to 'tick the box' and self-identify as an ATSI person.

Strait Islander population, 2016–2051', *Population Space Place*, 2021, 27: e2401.

Qualitatively, the increasing awareness of benefits and social prestige that has come from identifying as Aboriginal over the past forty years may be responsible for some of the non-demographic forces that have caused the larger than expected increases in the ATSI population. It is also possible, perhaps even likely, that Bolt's loss in court gave a signal to fakes, 'new identifiers' and 'box-tickers' that their mistaken or even fraudulent claims to Aboriginality would no longer be scrutinised by the media, hence their chance of exposure was low.[90]

The large growth in the number of new identifiers has not gone unnoticed in Aboriginal communities. Nathan Moran, the CEO of the Sydney-based Metropolitan Local Aboriginal Land Council, has estimated that over 40% of people who identify as Aboriginal were not born as Aboriginal, which he now says:

> is a very large problem ... in fact it's out of control the amount of people who are self-identifying, assuming roles and jobs in some cases going on to provide policy advice or to speak as authorities for Aboriginal people when they're not known to be Aboriginal and or known to have met the test of Aboriginality under Land Rights or Native Title.[7.70]

The 'trend' that Bolt observed, but was reprimanded in court for warning about, has come to pass a decade later. Surely by now, many institutions are aware of these potential problems and have instituted policies and practices to minimise the the number of fakes within their employ? Don't be so sure.

7.5.2   The University Response

By 2022, the mainstream media could no longer ignore the extent of Andrew Bolt's trend of white people coming forward and claiming to be Aboriginal. Although they would never acknowledge that Bolt had been a decade ahead of them all, reporters, such as the *Sydney Morning Herald's* Mary Ward,

---

[90]See discussions on ATSI population increases here [7.68]; [7.70] from 04:00; and [7.69])

finally weighed in with detailed articles that carried a Bolt-inspired headline:

> *Evidence that there is a Problem with Fair-skinned Aboriginal People who are in Fact Fakes*:
>
> The University of Sydney plans to crack down on students and staff self-identifying as Aboriginal or Torres Strait Islander without community recognition, as land councils raise concerns about people unduly claiming the status. Under the university's new Aboriginal and Torres Strait Islander Status Policy 2022 ... applicants for identity-dependent scholarships or staff positions can no longer sign a statutory declaration to confirm they are Indigenous. Instead, they must produce a confirmation of identity letter from a Local Aboriginal Land Council or other Indigenous community-controlled organisation, showing they meet the Commonwealth three-part identity test.[7.71]

Ward reported that Aboriginal land councils were so concerned that 'staff and students who do not meet the Commonwealth criteria are taking part in Indigenous programs' that one of them, the Metropolitan Local Aboriginal Land Council (MLALC) had 'complained to the Independent Commission Against Corruption (ICAC) about the number of students at the university identifying as Indigenous using statutory declarations'. CEO Nathan Moran said the current provisions were "embarrassing". "It's open fraud," he told the university.

However the new policy was 'criticised by students and academics, concerned the institution already struggles to attract Indigenous students. "This new policy is likely to disproportionately affect Indigenous people from the most disadvantaged backgrounds," a group of Indigenous students opposing the change said in a statement'.

Two academics quoted in Ward's article opposing the tightening of proof of identity checks were **Professor Jakelin Troy, a Ngarigu woman** and director of Aboriginal and Torres Strait Islander Research at the university, and **Aboriginal academic Professor Bronwyn Carlson**, author of the book *The Politics of Identity: Who Counts as Aboriginal Today?*, from Macquarie University, which recognises self-identification without further documentation for its Indigenous staff and students.

Troy noted that self-identification was accepted at many international research institutions. "I personally think universities shouldn't really be dictating to Aboriginal people about identity. I don't think anyone should be," she told Ward.

Similarly, Carlson voiced her concerns that scrapping statutory declarations was "a move that will create issues. It burdens our organisations with the responsibility to work with individuals who may have complex histories and are unable to provide written evidence of their family histories," she said. "Not all Aboriginal peoples have such documents at the ready."

Reading these defences from Professors Troy and Carlson, one is reminded of that infamous quote by Mandy Rice-Davies,[91] "Well, [s]he would say that, wouldn't [s]he?" For it appears that both Professors Troy and Carlson are mistaken to believe that they themselves are Aboriginal.

Challenging the Genuineness of the University Academics

- Professor Jakelin Troy

On the 15th of February 2023, Professor Troy was emailed a copy of her apparent maternal family tree, after she had produced a film claiming her maternal "great-grandmother, Olive" was a member of the "Aboriginal people in my family" [[7.72] at 02:40]. This family tree had been constructed by an experienced genealogist and researchers from *Dark Emu Exposed* who had used publicly available genealogical records, other archives, and information from family members related to Professor Troy. It was accompanied with a cover letter stating that:

> it very much appears, based on the publicly available records, that you are mistaken in your belief that you are of Aboriginal

---
[91] *Wikipedia: 'Mandy Rice-Davies applies'*

descent via your mother's side of the family. The research we
have undertaken appears to show, based on the publicly available records, that no ancestors in your mother's family tree
appear to be of Aboriginal descent, as you claim. All of your
mother's ancestors appear to originally have come from **Ireland, England or the USA**. We could identify no ancestors,
in your mother's family tree, who were of Aboriginal descent.
Subsequently, it would appear that there is no ancestry or genealogical evidence to support your biographical statement,
"I am Aboriginal Australian and my community is Ngarigu
of the Snowy Mountains in south eastern Australia".[92]

Professor Troy was invited to respond with any information
that suggested the researchers were wrong and she was offered
the opportunity to supply any amendments for consideration
prior to publication. No response was received.

- Professor Bronwyn Carlson

Likewise, following an interview on 702 ABC Sydney Radio,
where Professor Bronwyn Carlson claimed, "on my mother's
side, we are Aboriginal from South Australia,"[93] she too was
sent a similarly worded letter, including a maternal family tree
highlighting the fact that her ancestors on her mother's side
of the family all appeared to come from England, Ireland or
Scotland, and were not Aboriginal.

Carlson's response involved an exchange of emailed letters
from her lawyer's office[94] threatening legal action. After they
were provided further detailed evidence, her law office advised
to deal with Carlson directly, as they no longer represented
the professor in this matter.[7.74]

By late July 2024, Carlson's claimed Aboriginality had
come under some journalistic probing on *Sky News Australia's*
Bolt Report by a reinvigorated, but also a 're-toned'[95], An-

---

[92]See here [7.73]for Apparent *Maternal* Family Tree.

[93]702 ABC Sydney Radio, Tuesday 23 Feb 2016.

[94]Ji Robinson Stone, solicitor, *Illawarra Legal Centre*, 19 June 2024.

[95]See Chapter 9.2.2 on how Bolt had modified his 'tone' so as to comply with Justice Bromberg's ruling, without compromising his investigative journalism into the
claims of 'white Aborigines'.

drew Bolt.[7.75] And then something strange happened. With no public explanation, by 2 August 2024, the professor appeared to have renounced her on-line claims of Aboriginality. Her university staff web-page had changed - a new staff photograph was uploaded, there was no longer any claim that she was 'an Aboriginal woman' and any reference to her seminal textbook, *The Politics of Identity: Who counts as Aboriginal?* had disappeared.[96] Was this a public admission she had renounced her claim to be an 'Aboriginal' woman? Had Bronwyn Carlson decided to exercise her *choice* to not identify as 'Aboriginal' anymore? The public are none the wiser because neither Macquarie University nor Professor Carlson have made any public statements, nor contacted Bolt to explain the changes.[97]

These are the identity issues that so frustrate Aboriginal integrity campaigners, such as the MLALC's CEO Nathan Moran - the policy gate-keepers at the universities themselves appear to be mistaken about their own claimed Aboriginality. Or to put it more crudely, the university has installed fakes to vet the fakes.

It is therefore unsurprising that no real improvement in the integrity and transparency of the universities' Aboriginal student and staff appointment processes has occurred over the past two years. Indeed, as learnt from a *Daily Telegraph* article in October 2024, the push-back has begun formally, spearheaded by none other than those who had most to lose - the mistaken and fake 'fair-skinned' Aboriginal staff and students themselves.

---

[96] This book was based on a manuscript for which she won the 2013 *AIATSIS Stanner Prize*.[7.76]

[97] This is just one small, real example of a wider institutional problem in Australia: taxpayer-funded organisations deliberately failing to acknowledge, debate or admit failings. They will, as in this case, take steps that would seem to confirm that they realise they were wrong, but they don't have the ethical or moral strength to admit so in public.

The University Push-Back

> *If we want things to stay as they are,*
> *things will have to change.*

Giuseppe Tomasi di Lampedusa[98]

Two years after the University of Sydney announced changes to restrict the self-identifying system for its Indigenous students and staff, no action has been taken, largely because of complaints by many with a vested interest - those claiming to be Indigenous. As reported in October 2024 in *The Daily Telegraph*:

> The University of Sydney is allowing people to self-identify as Indigenous with a statutory declaration, despite planning to crack down on the practice two years ago. The leading institution, who benefit from millions of dollars in federal funding for Indigenous students, have failed to implement a policy which would have strengthened the Commonwealth's Indigenous three-part test.
>
> In October 2022, the university stated its intention to require staff and students to provide documentation from a local Aboriginal Land Council or First Nations' community organisation, confirming their ancestry had been officially verified. However, plans were scrapped after complaints the plan was unfair and even racist.[7.78]

The staff and students had played the 'victim card' with the university, which confirmed it had 'paused work on the policy review' following 'feedback from our staff and students ... about the stresses they were experiencing in the lead up to the Voice referendum'. The ability to 'claim First Nations heritage by signing a statutory declaration' was to be maintained.

Once again, Nathan Moran, CEO of the MLALC, publicly called out the current process as "bogus", saying "we have tried for many years now to have this addressed. A member of our Land Council raised the alarm on this back in 2015, when we were told there were many students at this university

---

[98]Giuseppe Tomasi di Lampedusa, *The Leopard*, Vintage Books, 2007, p19.[7.77]

falsely and fraudulently being inducted as Aboriginal." Moran was irate that, "when people are allowed to self-identify ... they can easily access funds, programs and initiatives that are meant to be for genuine Aboriginal people."

Honest Australians must be perplexed as to why students and staff would not proudly provide the convincing proof they are Aboriginal before accessing university funding reserved for Aboriginal staff and students. Those with a greater understanding of human nature know that people respond to incentives, especially monetary ones. As *The Daily Telegraph* story detailed, the University of Sydney qualified for $2.3 million in annual government funding for its 339 Indigenous enrolments and 105 course completions. Additionally, it was offering more than 70 scholarships for Aboriginal and Torres Strait Islander students, each worth up to $60,000 per year, and the university employs 110 Aboriginal or Torres Strait Islander staff. Indigeneity is big business at the University of Sydney. This funding provides the incentive that attracts customers (enrolments) who are willing to claim to be Indigenous.

And so nothing changes, despite public exposure of the mistaken, the fakes and the frauds by commentators such as Andrew Bolt[7.79]; despite articles in the *Sydney Morning Herald*, *The Australian* and *The Daily Telegraph*; and despite Aboriginal leaders like Nathan Moran, declaring:

> We have extensive proof of fraud ... People are just ticking a box to get benefits at school and in health. They are not meeting the definition of an Aboriginal person. In fact, they are born-again blacks.[7.70]

This is the Australia of the Vice Chancellors, which in the end turns out to be nothing like Tomasi's Sicily of the aristocrats. In Australia, if we want things to stay as they are, things will *not* have to change.

7.6   We Need to Talk About Anita

And he said unto them,
Render therefore unto Society
the things that be Civic,
and unto Oneself
the things that be Ethnic.

Paraphrase of Luke 20:25, King James Bible

Another applicant in court with Pat Eatock in the Bolt case
was Anita Heiss.[99] Andrew Bolt had included her as one of
his 'white Aborigines' in the offending articles in 2009:

> Meet now Associate Professor Anita Heiss, who says she's a
> "member of the Wiradjuri nation" ... Heiss's father was Aus-
> trian, and her mother only part-Aboriginal. What's more, she
> was raised in Sydney and educated at Saint Claire's Catholic
> College. She, too, could identify as a member of more than
> one race, if joining up to any at all was important. As it
> happens, her decision to identify as Aboriginal, joining four
> other "Austrian Aborigines" she knows, was lucky, given how
> it's helped her career. Heiss not only took out the Scanlon
> Prize for Indigenous Poetry, but won plum jobs reserved for
> Aborigines at Koori Radio, the Aboriginal and Torres Strait
> Islander Arts Board and Macquarie University's Warawara
> Department of Indigenous Studies.[100]

> I'm not saying [she] ... chose to be Aboriginal for anything
> but the most heartfelt and honest of reasons. I certainly don't
> accuse [her] ... of opportunism, even if full-blood Aborigines
> may wonder how such fair people can claim to be one of them
> and in some cases take black jobs. I'm saying only that this
> self-identification as Aboriginal strikes me as self-obsessed,
> and driven more by politics than by any racial reality. It's
> also divisive, feeding a new movement to stress pointless or
> even invented racial differences we once swore to overcome.
> What happened to wanting us all to become colour blind?[101]

---

[99]More symbolically than physically as she was not called as a witness and only
attended on Day 1.

[100]Heiss disputed this: "What Mr Bolt failed to mention is that I am an established
writer and highly qualified with a PhD in Media and Communication ... none of
the jobs he mentioned were actually 'reserved' or identified Aboriginal positions,
and the Koori Radio role was actually voluntary and unpaid." (Anita Heiss, 'Bolt
decision: Anita Heiss hopes for 'more responsible media", *Crikey*, 28 Sept 2011.)

[101]Andrew Bolt, 'It's so hip to be black', *Herald Sun*, 15 Apr 2009.

Reading what Australian National University (ANU) historian Frank Bongiorno, a Bolt critic, had written in a defence of Heiss, it is easy to appreciate why there was so much misunderstanding and conflict about Aboriginality and its apparent benefits. His critique illustrates these misunderstandings perfectly:

> That Heiss's life has been lived as part of the Aboriginal community could not be clearer. Her message is that there are many ways of being Aboriginal and her own – that of a middle-class, educated and professionally successful woman who lives in Sydney, loves shopping and drives a nice car – is as legitimate as any other. Aboriginal authenticity does not come from the darkness of one's skin, or from a desert lifestyle.[102]

But wasn't that exactly Bolt's point? Bolt's readership could see that Heiss was a modern Australian citizen, just like many others - "a middle-class, educated and professionally successful woman who lives in Sydney, loves shopping and drives a nice car" according to Bongiorno, and "an established writer and highly qualified with a PhD in Media [capable of getting] jobs [not] actually "reserved or identified [for] Aboriginal[s]" according to Heiss herself. Indeed, as Bolt might have concurred, what on earth does your race have to do with anything? You obviously are successful based on your own merits so why should your race and ethnicity ever be considered in the public funding of you professionally?

Bolt, Bongiorno and Heiss were having a fallout caused by Identity Politics. They were arguing at cross-purposes over the meaning of words and having a dispute over the economic, social and political influence of race and ethnicity in a society based on equal citizenship and equality before the law - Bob Hawke's Australia where 'there is no hierarchy of descents, there must be no privilege of origin.'

Heiss was an exemplar of all that was going wrong with race-relations in modern Australia. She honesty believed in the

---

[102]Frank Bongiorno, 'Getting under their skin traces the debate about blackness from Arthur Upfield to Andrew Bolt', *Inside Story*, 7 June 2012.

political self-determination of Aboriginal peoples and her right to leverage her ethnicity, race and ancestry into the political and economic spheres of the country. She could not see that for Australia to survive as a cohesive democracy the universal rule of law must be upheld in which all citizens are equal - none can be allowed to claim to be special because of their racial origins or ancestry. Instead, Heiss was asking Australians to 'walk with her' down a path to an Australia of either fragmented tribalism, or one of a moral and cultural totalitarism.[103] These are the only two outcomes possible when a society abandons the civic principles of liberal democracy for one based on race and ethnicity.

While Bolt was asking Heiss "what happened to wanting us all to become colour blind" and to stop for a moment and consider how her "self-identification as Aboriginal [was] divisive [and] feeding ... invented racial differences,"[104] she was off to Japan actually seeking more racial difference. As social commentator Michael Connor observed when reviewing the book of her travels:

> Surrounded by Japanese, Heiss wasn't happy, she felt unobserved and unappreciated by her hosts: "I wanted them to know that I was from Australia, that I was Aboriginal and not a westerner ... I wanted to scream, 'I'm the other! I'm the one the westerners write about!'"

> She went into a department store café and despised an Englishman who came in: "He spoke in a plum English accent and whined about his piece of cake." She ignores him, fears the Japanese will think they are alike: "I don't want to be alone in this place, but I don't want people to think I'm like you. You're the coloniser, and you complain too much. That's not me! I'm happy with any cake, especially the one I've got right now."[105]

Heiss's blindness is despairing. To Bolt-minded viewers (and

---

[103] The bitter tribalism of a failed African state, or the lethal stifling totalitarianism of Nazi Germany or modern communist China, or the tyranny of an Islamic republic.

[104] Andrew Bolt, 'It's so hip to be black', *Herald Sun*, 15 Apr 2009.

[105] Michael Connor, 'Passion and Illusions: Anita Heiss's Stories', *Quadrant Magazine*, 1 June 2012.

probably Frank Bongiorno as well) the problem Heiss had set for herself is immediately obvious. By asking, indeed demanding, everyone else sees the world as she does in 'Anitaland' - to be recognised as 'the other' and racialised as a 'proud Wiradjuri woman' - she wants to take everyone *backwards* to a time of overt, racial categorisation. Couldn't she see that she herself was becoming derogatory and perpetuating racial tropes? It was such an ideological cheap shot for her to describe the Englishman in stereotype - a whingeing Pom, a member of the arrogant upper classes, who spoke differently to Anita and, in earlier times, had roamed the world as an enslaving and looting coloniser. Had Heiss forgotten that she was a child of the colonising Austro-Hungarian empire herself,[106] and Japan's colonising zeal in WWII led to the death and enslavement of thousands of Australian and English men and women, including Aborigines. Yet here was Anita buying cake from them, two atomic bombs later, hoping to turn back the world to a time when race mattered all over again.

Heiss failed to understand why she felt 'unobserved and unappreciated' by the surrounding Japanese. It wasn't because of the English 'whitey' standing next to her - the Japanese saw him as different but respected him as someone they could deal with as an equal. Rather, it was because Japanese society was still largely stuck in the racialised world of colonial Japan - Anita was 'black' and thus she really was 'the other' - *inferior* and unapproachable - in the minds of many Japanese. If Heiss moved to Japan to live, she would likely face a discrimination the likes of which she had never felt in Australia.[7.80]

Bolt could see that the way Heiss pushed her 'self identification as Aboriginal', and leveraging that racial identity to make career and political claims on Australian secular society, would only re-ignite these 'invented racial differences we once swore to overcome'. Wasn't the Biblical advice, upon which Australia's liberal democratic society was built, worth

---

[106]Heiss's father was Austrian and migrated to Australia after WWII.

maintaining - to keep its material and political life separate from any spiritual and ethnic claims? Heiss appears to have no qualms about playing the race card - she honestly feels justified in muscling her way in to claim Aboriginal-only prizes for developing writers because she must believe that, well, 'I'm a proud Wiradjuri woman, so I'm entitled to them, regardless of my own current material and political status or needs. My race, my genes and my DNA give me the right to apply.'

Connor continues Anita's emotional journey as she leaves behind the Englishman with his cake and the surrounding Japanese:

> I got up quickly and headed to a familiar shop door across the street. Inside I felt happy, warm, at peace, at ease, at home, which some may think weird for a proud Wiradjuri woman, but I had just walked into Tiffany's.

Once again, Heiss appears to be tone-deaf to Bolt's main message, written in his inimitable way, that went to the heart of the matter - that successful, assimilated Aborigines like herself were peddlers of a form of:

> modern race politics ... where grants and privileges are now doled out. Hear that scuffling at the trough? That's the sound of black people being elbowed out by white people shouting , "but I'm Aboriginal too." [107]

Caroline Overington, writing in *The Australian*,[108] put it more politely; however, she comes to the same conclusion and advice as Bolt:

> Heiss's book, *Am I Black Enough For You?*[109] with its snappy title, misses the point: the issue isn't, and never was, whether somebody is "black enough", in Heiss's words, to be considered Aboriginal. The issue is whether those benefits designed to assist Aboriginal people out of their desperate poverty

---

[107] Andrew Bolt, 'White fellas in the black', *Herald Sun*, 21 Aug 2009.

[108] Caroline Overington, 'It's not about being black enough, it's about need', *The Australian*, 11 Apr 2012.

[109] Overington: "It's a provocative title, and I suppose it had to be: while the book would be part-memoir, it would also address Heiss's decision to take the News Limited columnist Andrew Bolt to court over columns he wrote for Melbourne's Herald Sun in 2009."

should be more sharply targeted at those with a genuine need
... In particular, there's an argument over whether everyone
who identifies as indigenous ought to be entitled to apply for
the various prizes, benefits, scholarships and grants that are
available to Aboriginal people, regardless of their personal circumstances.

Nevertheless, the modern Wiradjuri woman's already privileged middle-class life was boosted further by the $90,000 Aus-
tralia Council Aboriginal Arts grant[110] she received from the
taxpayer (not the publisher) to write her book. It came in
handy as she perused the shiny, glass cabinets at Tiffany's.[7.82]
For apparently Heiss has an extravagant hobby, as she told the
ABC's Benjamin Law:

> I'm collecting something from every Tiffany & Co around the
> world. I don't have kids, and I don't have a man, so I buy
> myself things I'd expect someone to give me for my birthday
> and Valentine's Day and Christmas. I'm the best Valentine
> I've ever had.[111]

Despite denying that she has accepted benefits 'reserved' for
Aboriginal applicants only, she in fact has also picked up $30,000
for the 2022 NSW Premier's Literary Awards Indigenous Writers' Prize, plus several Deadly Awards, [7.83] all of which are
race-based, being open to Aboriginal people only.

As Heiss marvelled at the trinkets and baubles at her favorite store, one can only wonder whether she had heeded
anything at all from the critiques of Bolt and Overington.
Did it even occur to her that, in the zero-sum game that
is the government budget, the cost of her Tiffany trinkets,
her three-month writing residency in Paris[7.84] and numerous other taxpayer-funded Aboriginal-only benefits, metaphorically meant another cold night on a concrete slab for Kate
Pitjara and her dozen family members outside Alice Springs,
due to the government's lack of money?[7.85]

---

[110]Caroline Overington, *ibid.*, - $123,000 in 2024 terms by RBA inflation calculator.
See also the justification from the Australia Council.[7.81]

[111]Benjamin Law, 'Indigenous author Anita Heiss: Speaking language is an act of
sovereignty', *The Age*, 6 Aug 2021.

For References link - see **QR** code on page (xv)

References

[7.1]   Matthew Elliott. "The Inconvenient Ancestor: Slavery and Selective Remembrance on Genealogy Television". In: *Studies in Popular Culture, Spring* 39.2 (2017), pp. 73–90.

[7.2]   The Age. *Andrew Bolt: Australia's least accurate columnist?* 2 Oct 2011.

[7.3]   *Eatock v Bolt, Judgement.* Sept. 28, 2011.

[7.4]   SBS. *Indigenous Identity. Why are more people identifying as First Nations, who decides and what's at stake? SBS Insight Program No. 34.* 2022.

[7.5]   ANZSOG. *Prof. Tom Calma AO Biography.* as of Oct 2024.

[7.6]   The Dutch Australian Cultural Centre. *Prof. Tom Calma's Dutch heritage.* 26 Jan 2023.

[7.7]   AHRC. *Implementing UNDRIP.* 2021.

[7.8]   Brian Lapping. *Apartheid - A History.* 1987.

[7.9]   Youtube. *Are the political foundations of the Voice the same as for apartheid?* 27 Sept 2013.

[7.10] News. *Bushwalker fined $300 for defying Mt Warning ban.* 7 Aug 2024.

[7.11] Bob Hawke PM. *Australia Day 1988 Speech - transcript excerpt.* 26 Jan 1988.

[7.12] SBS. *Tom Calma - A Lifetime Of Service. Living Black, Season 2022, Episode 16, SBSiView.*

[7.13] Reconcilliation Australia. *Tom Calma biography.* 2022.

[7.14] *Fortunato Calma - records and photographs.* 2024.

[7.15] *Tom Calma Apparent Family Tree.* 2024.

[7.16] Reconcilliation Australia. *What is Reconcilliation?* 2024.

[7.17] Youtube. *We are Reconcilled - Colonisation is complete, so get over it and move on: Senator Jacinta Nampijinpa Price, 2023.*

[7.18] Gaynor Lovett. *Territory Stories: Tom Calma and Joy Cardona.* accessed 18 Nov 2024.

[7.19] Joy Cardona. *The Buffalo Hunter, Northern Territory Literary Awards 2009.* accessed 18 Nov 2024.

[7.20] Northern Standard. *Lugger Badly Battered by Storm, p2.* 26 Mar 1935.

[7.21] *Tom Calma Snr - unknown father in RAAF records, NAA, p37.* July 1944.

[7.22] D. Carment. *NT Dictionary of Biography - Revised Edition. Excerpt entries for Joe Cooper and Reuben Cooper.* 2008.

[7.23] M. Stephen. *WWI and Sports in the Northern Territory: Celebrating a century of Football.* 15 July 2015.

[7.24] M.S. Feakins. *Behind the legend: A historical archaeology of the Australian buffalo hide industry, 1875-1958. PhD Thesis.* December 2019.

[7.25] *Balaklava NT Records.* 1945.

[7.26] *Exemption Certificate of Dictation for Fortunato Calma.* 1926.

[7.27] Tom Calma & Marcia Langton. *Indigenous Voice co-design process : final report to the Australian Government.* 2021.

[7.28] Liz Inglis. *The Voice to Parliament.* 5 Sept 2023.

[7.29] Tom Calma. *An Indigenous Perspective on Winston Churchill, the British Empire's Political Legitimacy and the Unfinished Business of Australian Governance.* ca2022.

[7.30] *Tom Calma Snr - Oath to King.* 1944.

[7.31] Dan Butler. *The Victorian government's response to the latest Yoorrook report has been slammed by legal advocates, SBS.* 3 Apr 2024.

[7.32] John Paul Janke. *Manuscript on Aboriginal Identity Wins 2013 Stanner Award.* 1 Aug 2013.

[7.33] *Churchill Fellowship 2023. Winston Churchill Trust.* 2023.

[7.34] University of Queensland. *Indigenising the Curriculum.* 2025.

[7.35] Photographs. *The Cooper (ca1914-16) and Calma (2023) family portraits showing inter-marriage.*

[7.36] ABC Radio. *How Dobe Newton and Bruce Woodley wrote - I Am Australian.* 14 Nov 2023.

[7.37] Bolt Report. *Gary Johns on DNA blood testing and intermarriage.* 24 July 2023.

[7.38] Tom Calma. *Let the healing begin-Response to government to the national apology to the Stolen Generations.* 13 Feb 2008.

[7.39] Photographs. *Aboriginal Camp Children.* 1920-40s.

[7.40] Keith Windschuttle. *The Fabrication of Aboriginal History Volume 3: The Stolen Generations 1881–2008.* 2009.

[7.41] George Thompson. *List of Half-Castes in NT.* 7 april 1900.

[7.42] Sir Ron Wilson and Mick Dodson. *Bringing Them Home Report.* 1997.

[7.43] Georgina Mitchell. *Andrew Bolt's claim Stolen Generations a 'myth' spurs Press Council complaint, SMH.* 2 Aug 2015.

[7.44] *File on May Crawford's Marriage, etc.* 2024.

[7.45] Prof. Lyndall Ryan. *Lindsay Crawford and the Willeroo Massacres on Colonial Massacre Map, University of Newcastle.* 1892.

[7.46] Australian of the Year Committee. *Professor Tom Calma AO Senior Australian of the Year.* 2023.

[7.47] The Australian. *Joe Biden and Indigenous leader Tom Calma put focus on First Nations business.* 26 Oct 2023.

[7.48] Kerryn Pholi. *Why I burned my 'Proof of Aboriginality'.* 27 September 2012.

[7.49] ABC. *Excerpt from Australian Story - Megan Davis.* 2023.

[7.50] *Full text of complaint to ABC.*

[7.51] ABC. *ABC Australian Story correspondence.*

[7.52] *Billy Willighan documents.*

[7.53] *Prof. Megan Davis's Apparent Paternal Family Tree.* 2024.

[7.54] *Prof. Megan Davis References 2.* 2025.

[7.55] UNSW. *Prof. Megan Davis podcast transcript.*

[7.56] UNSW. *Prof. Megan Davis Biography.*

[7.57] Youtube. *Prof. Megan Davis on teenage inspiration.*

[7.58] *Prof. Megan Davis's Apparent Maternal Family Tree.* 2024.

[7.59] ABC Documentary. *Peter Sutton on Aboriginaliy and knowledge. Excerpt from Dark Emu Documentary.*

[7.60] Baral and Shrestha. *Excerpt of a Review on Derek Walcott's Omeros.*

[7.61] Law Society NSW. *Professor Megan Davis biography.*

[7.62] Australian SSI Multimedia. *Family Heritage Story of Melanie Yasserie.* 2013.

[7.63] Megan Davis. *Screenshot of Fred Davis's Exemption Certificate.*

[7.64] Dark Emu Exposed website. *Fred Davis - His Agency and House.*

[7.65] A. Strand D. & Kallen. "I am a Viking! DNA, popular culture and the construction of geneticized identity". In: *New Genetics and Society* 40.4 (2021), pp. 520–540.

[7.66] History Channel. *Vikings.* 2024.

[7.67] *Eatock v Bolt [2011] FCA 1103.* Sept. 28, 2011.

[7.68] ABS Media Release. *Aboriginal and Torres Strait Islander population passes 1 million.* 24 July 2024.

[7.69] SBS Insight. *Community Leaders warn many who claim to be Indigenous could be 'fakes'.* 18 Oct 2022.

[7.70] The Bolt Report. *Nathan Moran on fake Aborigines.* 2 Sept 2024.

[7.71] Mary Ward. *Sydney Uni cracks down on staff, students 'self-identifying' as Indigenous. SMH.* 9 Oct 2022.

[7.72] Youtube. *Prof. Jakelin Troy Talks of her Great-Grandmother and Aboriginal Country.*

[7.73] *Professor Jakelin Troy's Apparent Maternal Family Tree.* 2025.

[7.74] Ji Robinson Stone. *Legal Letter from Bronwyn Carlson.* 19 June 2024.

[7.75] Andrew Bolt. *Andrew Bolt calls out those who 'claim' Aboriginal heritage without evidence.*

[7.76] Bronwyn Carlson. *The Politics of Identity Who counts as Aboriginal today? AIATSIS.* 2016.

[7.77] Dark Emu Exposed website. *Time to Dust Off Your Copy of The Leopard.* 1 Sept 2023.

[7.78] James Willis. *Sydney Uni fails plan to tighten 'bogus' Indigenous guidelines. Daily Telegraph.* 17 Oct 2024.

[7.79] The Bolt Report. *Youtubes on 'fakes'.*

[7.80] ABC News. *Japan's landmark racial discrimination case as foreigners fight back.*

[7.81] Lydia Miller. *Funding for Writers - Justifying Anita Heiss Grant.* 14 Apr 2012.

[7.82] Youtube. *Shopping Spree at Tiffanys Ginza.*

[7.83] NSW Govt. *NSW Premier's Literary Awards Indigenous Writers' Prize.* 2022.

[7.84] Creative Australia. *Paris Arts Residency.* 2020-2021.

[7.85] The Australian. *Kate Pitjara, one of about a dozen people living rough on the concrete slab a couple kilometres outside of Alice Springs.* 10 Mar 2023.

Chapter 8

Behind the Purple Curtain with Bromberg & Co.

Everyone knows that behind the decisions stand the Justices and behind the Justices there hangs a purple curtain. The question of real interest always has been: what is behind the curtain?

Commentators and Judges themselves [have come] to acknowledge frankly the uncomfortable fact that, in our common law system, Judges do make the law.

Justice Michael Kirby[1]

8.1 His Honour Justice Bromberg Presiding

In 1983 Justice Michael Kirby delivered a series of ABC Boyer Lectures entitled The Judges. In his fifth lecture he discussed 'Judges as Reformers':

---

[1]Australian Broadcasting Commission, *ABC Boyer Lectures*, 1983, p9 & p58.

The inclination to be bold, creative and reformist varies in society. The same variations are to be found in the judiciary. Some Judges in Australia ... remain terribly cautious. Others, whilst acknowledging a creative function, are keen to underline ... the limited opportunities and the care and caution that must be exercised when they stumble upon them.

But other Judges are plagued with fewer doubts. They see more openings. They perceive the urgent need for modernisation and reform in the law. They harken back to the great common law Judges of the past who, with determination and assurance, developed the common law from precedent to precedent. In Australia our exemplar in this respect [of 'judicial activism'] is Justice Murphy of the High Court. In Britain, Lord Denning was the boldest exponent of the reforming function of the Judge on the Bench.[2]

Kirby's reference to former Labor Senator, turned High Court Judge, Lionel Murphy, should give pause for thought as to whether Bolt's presiding Justice Bromberg might actually see himself as continuing in Murphy's legacy as a 'bold exponent of the reforming function'. Indeed, eyebrows were raised in some circles when Bromberg J was initially appointed as the judge in *Eatock v Bolt*, given his previous close ties with the Labor Party, whose policies were often on the receiving end of sharp critiques by the defendant in this case, Andrew Bolt.

Kirby also asked, "But might not this conception of the judicial functions [judicial activism] lead to uncertainty in the law?" He then quoted Denning:

I [Lord Denning] would agree it does, because in a sense I concentrate on the rights and wrongs of the individual before me, and if it does lead to uncertainty - so it does, but there's no certainty in the law. It's a complete will o' the wisp ... It really depends on the department of law in which you're dealing.

[W]hen it comes to **injuries to individuals** [or offense caused by racial discrimination] they aren't concerned with any particular strict rules of law. **They want justice** in the particular case - their compensation, it may be ... these [cases] are not capable of being guided by strict rules, and therefore in

---

[2] *ibid.*, p59.

all these cases **I strive to do justice,** knowing that the law
is necessarily uncertain in these areas. (emphasis added)[3]

Kirby continued:

> Judges also differ in their willingness to offer up litigants be-
> fore them as victims 'at the altar of regularity'. Some can do
> it without blinking an eyelid. Most, remembering their oath
> to do justice according to law, look hard amongst the prece-
> dents to see if there is not something that can be done. Lord
> Denning would search them high and low until he had found
> a satisfactory principle to justify the just and fair conclusion,
> as he saw it.[4]

In *Eatock v Bolt*, some might think that Australia had witnessed the conduct of a judge who perhaps had career aspirations as a 'new judicial Lionel Murphy', someone who maybe
conjectured about being an 'Antipodean Lord Denning'.

By his court's lack of any real inquiry as to whether or
not Pat Eatock's story was actually true - Bromberg J simply
accepted her word for it and that of counsel, with no judicial
prodding or questioning at all - and by the tone of his written
judgement, one gets the impression that he did not want to
offer up Pat Eatock as a 'victim at the altar of regularity'.
Instead, he spent 470 meandering paragraphs in a judgement
that 'would search [the precedents] high and low until he had
found a satisfactory principle to justify the just and fair conclusion, as he saw it'.

Justice Bromberg did find, using a 'Denning-like' mind,
the necessary precedents to save Pat Eatock from what an
impartial, non-activist judge would probably have realised the
law actually pointed towards - an acquittal of Bolt and the
Herald and Weekly Times. For not only was Pat Eatock's
unsubstantiated oral family history story as unbelievable as
it was untrue, it was also clear to all and sundry that Bolt's
articles were intended as a warning to society of the dangers of
promoting 'race-based' divisions within Australia. Specifically,

---

[3] *ibid.,* p59-60.
[4] *ibid.,* p61.

Bolt alerted his readership to the self-serving hypocrisy and injustice of allowing some activist Australians of very little or even no Aboriginal ancestry to have preferential access to services, employment, prizes, grants and reserved institutional positions funded by the taxpayer - and arguably all at the expense of genuine Aboriginal people in real need.

A non-activist judge or a judge who had a different view on where to draw the free speech line on the spectrum of possibilities[5] might have agreed with Bromberg J that Bolt had breached s 18C of the RDA, but may readily have found him protected by the exemptions offered in s 18D (b) & (c)(i) & (ii):

> RACIAL DISCRIMINATION ACT 1975 - s 18D Exemptions
>
> Section 18C does not render unlawful anything said or done reasonably and in good faith:
>
> (a) in the performance, exhibition or distribution of an artistic work; or
>
> (b) in the course of any statement, publication, discussion or debate made or held for any genuine academic, artistic or scientific purpose or any other genuine purpose in the public interest; or
>
> (c) in making or publishing:
>
> (i) a fair and accurate report of any event or matter of public interest; or
>
> (ii) a fair comment on any event or matter of public interest if the comment is an expression of a genuine belief held by the person making the comment.

However, Bromberg J concluded that Bolt's defence had failed:

> On the basis of those deficiencies [as listed] I am satisfied that the offensive imputation was not a fair comment and that s 18D(c)(ii) is not available to exempt the offensive conduct from being rendered unlawful.

It is a fair criticism of Justice Bromberg to suggest that he was being an activist and 'making the law'; other commentators too have raised similar points.

---

[5]See commentary by Andrew Dodd[8.1] and Dale Smith. [8.2]

The Partial, 'Hanging' Judge?

For example, *The Australian* reported that former Labor Party Senator, the late Kimberley Kitching, said she remembers:

> "being very surprised" when Federal Court judge Mordecai Bromberg decided to hear *Herald Sun* columnist Andrew Bolt's racial discrimination case, given his close relationship with the Labor Party. Speaking with Bolt on *The Bolt Report* ... Senator Kitching said she had known Justice Bromberg through the Labor Party ... he had run unsuccessfully for Labor preselection ... in 2001. "He was an active ALP person, he was active enough that he was in a faction, he ran for preselection," she said. "Obviously he would have had some views about you [Bolt], and perhaps he was not the best person to hear your case."
>
> Bolt asked Senator Kitching whether, as a lawyer, she was able to cast such aspersions on Justice Bromberg's impartiality as a judge "under our ridiculous laws against free speech". "I think that it's an expression I should be able to take," she said.
>
> Senator Kitching said she believed Justice Bromberg should have read section 18C more narrowly in Bolt's case.[6]

The 'Frolicking' Judge?

"When senior judges frolic with the law, citizens will, inevitably, distrust the law and the courts."

So concluded columnist Janet Albrechtsen, in an opinion piece on Justice Bromberg.[7] In her article, Albrechtsen followed up on Kimberley Kitching's observation that Bromberg had stood for preselection to the Labor party:

> Explaining his motivations to enter parliament, Bromberg said: "I'm certainly not doing this for the money. But I am committed to improving the Workplace Relations Act to make it fairer and more equitable and I think I can be more effective doing that in parliament." Alas, he had to settle for being a

---

[6] Rachel Baxendale, 'Andrew Bolt race-case judge had ALP links', *The Australian*, 16 Nov 2016.

[7] Janet Albrechtsen, 'When judges go on a legal frolic', *The Australian*, 11 Aug 2021.

judge. Analysis by the Menzies Research Centre of Bromberg on industrial matters suggests he sided with unions 91 per cent of the time.

Bromberg even admits he is 'committed to improving', in his eyes, an Act of Parliament, which suggests an activist mentality that perhaps crossed over into his role as a judge. Albrechtsen also noted that with regard industrial relations matters:

> Bromberg is prone to being overturned by our High Court to an extent that might be disconcerting to a judge of a less sanguine temperament. Since 2015, the High Court has tossed out five Federal Court decisions on industrial matters, all featuring Bromberg ... In a 7-nil decision, the court held that a casual employment contract between labour hire firm Work-Pac and Robert Rossato was exactly that. Six High Court judges told Bromberg he erred in trying to cast around for reasons to redefine, after the event, a casual employment contract as a permanent employment contract.

Albrechtsen admonishes Bromberg and his 'judicial misadventure', particularly where he thought 'it makes eminent legal sense for an employer and an employee not to know the nature of their contract until a creative judge tells them what it is'.[8] Albrechtsen's conclusion was that 'Federal Court legal adventurism imposed horrendous costs on the country' and 'when senior judges, like Bromberg, frolic with the law, citizens will, inevitably, distrust the law and the courts ... There must be a better way to deal with frolicking judges'.[9]

Interesting, one commentator, Sarah Goddard at the Australian National University, who one suspects is at the complete opposite end of the political spectrum as Albrechtsen, came to much the same conclusions regarding Bromberg's activism in court. In her 2013 Honour's Thesis, Goddard ap-

---

[8] Albrechtsen's insightful phrase is also eminently paraphrasable to this case: "some judges think it makes eminent legal sense for a journalist and his employer not to know the nature and extent of 'free speech' until a creative judge tells them what it is".

[9] Perhaps not unexpectedly, Albrechtsen's views on Justice Bromberg were strongly resisted by some. In a tit-for-tat response entitled, 'When Journalists go off on Frolic', Australian Judicial Officers Association President, Glenn Martin, came to the defence of Justice Bromberg's reputation.[8.3]

plied 'critical whiteness theory' to examine 'responses to the federal racial vilification law after *Eatock v Bolt*.'[10] She saw Bromberg's decision as being 'purposive':[11]

> When considered in light of the obstacles to bringing a vilification complaint ... Eatock is a welcome outcome. Bromberg J did not permit the respondent's procedural claims to obscure the merits of the case, and he showed a real desire to engage with the experience of those who brought the action. This suggests that Bromberg J eschewed 'technical and strict' interpretations in favour of a more 'purposive' and hence, 'complainant-supporting' approach. It takes, as Thornton suggests, 'a brave judge to pursue a purposive approach ... at the risk of being overruled by an appellate court.' Bromberg J's willingness to acknowledge vilification is also arguably unusual in a legal profession that has at times struggled to take vilification complaints seriously. Therefore, this case represents a momentary legal unsettling of otherwise impenetrable media discourses about the 'other'.

This quotation by Goddard is of interest because she confirms Albrechtsen's observation that Bromberg was a judge with an activist mentality. Although Goddard might not use Albrechtsen's term 'frolicking', she clearly concluded that Bromberg was a judge who would search high and low to find a 'complainant-supporting approach.'

---

[10] Goddard, S., 'Whiteness in the Press: A Critical Examination of Responses to the Federal Racial Vilification Law after Eatock v Bolt', *ANU College of Law Research Paper*, No. 14-05, 4 Nov 2013.

[11] The purposive approach to interpreting legislation looks beyond simply the words of the legislation - it tries to get to the intended purpose behind it. Critics of purposivism argue it fails to separate the powers between the legislator and the judiciary, as it allows more freedom in interpretation by way of extraneous materials in interpreting the law (*Wikipedia: purposive approach*); see also Justice Kirby: "In this last decade, there have been numerous cases in which members of this court ... have insisted that the proper approach to the construction of federal legislation is that which advances and does not frustrate or defeat the ascertained purpose of the legislature ... Even to the point of reading words into the legislation in proper cases, to carry into effect an apparent legislative purpose. This court should not return to the dark days of literalism." In effect, Kirby J is stating that today's preferred approach to interpreting legislation is that which promotes the purpose of the legislation, rather than one that does not. One can 'read words into' the legislation to ensure its apparent purpose is more easily recognised and promoted when making judgement. Kirby J's final words imply that the courts should adopt this more purposive approach for all judgments and the literal approach be forgotten.[8.4]

Just as interesting is that both Albrechtsen and Goddard understand the 'brave' nature of Justice Bromberg's 'complainant-supporting approach' and its high risk of being 'overruled by an appellate court.' Would Bolt have won his case on appeal? Perhaps very likely.

The 'Radical, Hard-Left, Activist' Judge?

Justice Bromberg is a 'radical, hard-Left, activist judge', according to *Sky News Australia* host and former Liberal senator Amanda Stoker. when describing his legal track record to her audience on 25 June 2023:

> This week ... [Labor's] Attorney General Mark Dreyfus appointed The Honorable Justice Mordecai Bromberg, known as Mordy Bromberg as president of the Australian Law Reform Commission for a five-year term. He is without a doubt the most radical, the most Hard-Left activist that the Federal Court bench has yet seen.

> This is the judge responsible for holding that there was a duty upon a minister, in making decisions about whether to approve mining projects, to take reasonable care to avoid causing personal injury or death to Australian children arising from the emission of carbon dioxide into the Earth's atmosphere. Thankfully this decision was overturned on appeal after what could only be described as a frolic of judicial activism, otherwise known as judges making law as they go along.[8.5]

Stoker went on to comment on the 'censorious, totalitarian Left' judgement by Justice Bromberg in *Eatock v Bolt*, citing the ABC's Jonathan Holmes in her commentary:

> Justice Bromberg is the same judge who decided that Andrew Bolt of this network was guilty of breaching section 18C of the Racial Discrimination Act in a decision that took a really restrictive approach to free speech.

> Now given you might consider my comments on this case colored by my employment, let's go instead to what the ABC's Jonathan Holmes from *Media Watch* had to say about it. He said Justice Bromberg's interpretation of the Racial Discrimination Act was, "profoundly disturbing" because it reinforced

concerns that section 18C creates, "one particular area of public life where speech is regulated by tests that simply don't apply anywhere else; and in which judges - never, for all of their pontifications, friends of free speech - get to do the regulating".

When even the ABC think you're leaning too far to the censorious totalitarian Left, well, that's really saying something. Justice Bromberg, to put it lightly, just does not have a good track record.

The Judge of 'Unintended Consequences'?

Quite often ... I found cases that would come before me where the actual outcome was something no-one ever intended.

Former Justice Ron Merkel[12]

If one accepts the above analyses of Kitching, Albrechtsen and Stoker, then, after reading *Witness for the Prosecution*, a reader could easily come to the conclusion that, with the passage of time, Justice Bromberg has made a critical error for the politics of the Progressive Left.

If indeed he had wanted to leave his mark as an activist judge of the hard-Left, biased against Bolt, and with a soft spot for the goals of the *pro bono* progressive legal team assembled before him as they defended a fake and 'white Aborigine', it now transpires that he has in fact provided a legal basis for Bolt today to actually pick off, on a regular basis, one fake Aborigine after another.

Instead of cancelling Bolt, Justice Bromberg has actually endorsed, perhaps even enshrined, him as Australia's foremost fake Aborigine debunker. It wasn't meant to be this way. The court 'stitch-up', as Bolt described his case, looked as if it initially worked; rumour has it that the celebrations back in chambers for the winning side were long, well lubricated and joyously smug - justice had been done, so they all thought.

---

[12]Speaking with regard to immigration cases, ABC Radio, 'The Law Report', 23 May 2006.[8.6]

However, in the fullness of time, the reality is that Justice Bromberg has provided commentators such as Andrew Bolt, and researchers like the *Dark Emu Exposed* team, with a new way through this legal minefield. As long as commentators and researchers adhere closely to the findings of Justice Bromberg, and the guidance of Law Professor Adrienne Stone,[13] they can legally challenge, question, comment on and expose where appropriate any claims of a 'fake' and/or 'white Aborigine'.

The hypocrisy and dangers of race-based ideology promoted by fake Aborigines and their facilitators in the universities, corporations, government and other institutions can in fact now be exposed, all thanks to His Honour, Justice Mordecai Bromberg.

8.2 Ron Merkel QC

The Prosecutor - Pat Eatock's *pro bono* Counsel.

Freedom of speech is indivisible,
unless we protect it for all,
we will have it for none.

Henry Kalven Jr.

It is technically impossible to write an anti-free speech code
that cannot be twisted against speech nobody means to bar.
It has been tried and tried and tried.

Eleanor Holmes Norton

The above two quotations, warning of the unintended consequences of writing codes to regulate free speech were cited approvingly by none other than Ron Merkel himself in a 1994 article he wrote for *Quadrant Magazine*.[14] Yet seventeen years later one of Australia's leading practitioners of free speech, An-

---

[13] *Eatock v Bolt* (2011) FCA 1103. Stone, A., "The Ironic Aftermath of Eatock v Bolt", *Melbourne University Law Review*, Vol. 38, 2015, p926-42.

[14] Ron Merkel, 'Does Australia Need a Racial Vilification Law?', *Quadrant Magazine*, November 1994, p19-20.

drew Bolt, found himself in the Federal Court face to face with the same Ron Merkel who now accused Bolt of using speech that was unacceptable and in need of both censor and censure.

Contrary to Kalven, Merkel now claimed free speech was in fact to be 'divisible'; his client, Pat Eatock, could exercise *her* free speech rights and claim, falsely as it turned out, that "I am an Aboriginal person with Aboriginal ancestry".[15] Yet, Merkel would vehemently oppose Bolt exercising *his* free speech rights in challenging her claims. And the judge also supported a 'division' of free speech. Bromberg J found that Bolt did have the right to challenge Pat Eatock's claims but it was *the way he did it* that got him into trouble - Bolt could have his 'speech' but it wasn't to be 'free' like Eatock's.[16]

By 2011, Merkel appeared to have changed his liberal-minded spots. The consequence of what he had warned about in 1994 in the Norton quote above, now came into full view - 'it is technically impossible to write an anti-free speech code that cannot be twisted against speech nobody means to bar'.

With Bolt in the witness box, Ron Merkel sent in Herman Borenstein SC [8.7] to do all the *twisting* required to effectively 'bar' Bolt's free speech, as recorded in the trial transcripts:

Mr Borenstein: Mr Bolt, I am putting to you that, in this blog, you have put forward a position and an explanation with examples relating to Mr McMillan [one of Bolt's 'white Aborigines'] as to why you believe it was a curious, let's say, situation that he, given his background, should have received this [Aboriginal-only] scholarship ... What I am putting to you is that, in the context of that discussion, it is entirely

---

[15] *Eatock v Bolt*, Trans. Proc., Fed. Court (Vic) O/N 160844, Mon 28 Mar 2011, Day One, p51.

[16] As Bromberg J found: "It is important that nothing in the orders I make should suggest that it is unlawful for a publication to deal with racial identification including challenging the genuineness of the identification of a group of people. I have not found Mr Bolt ... contravened s 18C simply because ... [he] dealt with subject matter of that kind ... [but] because of the **manner** in which that subject matter was dealt with." It was "the language, **tone** and structure [which contributed] to the unlawful manner in which the subject matter was dealt with." (*Eatock v Bolt* [2011] at 461-2.)

irrelevant, to make your point, to refer to him either being gay or non-gay?

Andrew Bolt: I don't share your implied assumption that being gay is an insult, okay. I don't. Maybe I am a different generation. It's about identity politics. And people familiar with my blog would have seen it as such.

Borenstein: You accept, do you not, Mr Bolt, that there are a large number of people in the community - some of them might even read the *Herald Sun* and some of them might even read your blog – who are homophobic? Do you accept that or not?

Bolt: There are some, and I have been repeatedly strong, publicly on radio, television and in print, condemning homophobia.

Borenstein: Okay. And so when you are writing a piece that is intended to express your view about the rights and wrongs of someone like Mr McMillan getting a scholarship, then you have to accept, do you not, that it can have nothing to do with that thesis what his sexual preference is?

Bolt: Can I repeat the answer I have given you three times already? Mr McMillan raised his anguish about his Aboriginality, his looks and sexuality all in the same piece talking about a confusion that he felt about his identity. And it is in the precise same context – precise – that I raise it. And that's why, because I take a different view, I am here defending my rights of free speech.

Borenstein: Well, can I suggest to you that the context is not the same. That the articles – the article which you are referring to is a discussion by Mr McMillan to – about his struggle with his identity?

Bolt: Yes.

Borenstein: Your article is about the phenomenon of people with a genealogical background which includes some non-Aboriginal elements to it, and being fair skinned, being acknowledged or recognised by various institutions as eligible for prizes that should go to Aboriginals who don't have that genealogical background. That's – in broad terms, that's what you're on about?

Bolt: I prefer the way I have said it several times.

Borenstein: Okay. But there's no - - -?

Bolt: Your summation is *always with a little twist*. I don't want to go passing (*sic*, parsing) phrases and all that. I have already answered that.

Borenstein: ... But what I am asking you is – not what I am suggesting to you is – it's no part of a consideration of that phenomenon whether the person in question is gay or not gay. Now, that's correct, isn't it?

Bolt: Again, *I will stick with my answer.* We're talking about identity politics in the broad. This is a subsection of them. The identifying as Aboriginal by people who have various options open to them, who maybe, in previous generations, would have made another choice, who, even today, have people in the same situation making different choices. They make this choice. And it's all about identity politics and you see it in the universities as well. This is, again, something I have written about [extensively]. You have picked out four articles. I am being tried for my bad opinions on those, but if you looked at the vast body of my work, you would see that these are issues I have been engaged with. A familiar – I am well known for engaging with it for a long time.

As Borenstein's grilling continued, so did his attempts at **'twisting'** Bolt's statements:

Borenstein: Now, again, this is an article which you've [Bolt] written, in which you make comment about Ms Enoch's [one of Bolt's 'white Aborigines'] appearance leading you to question her identification as Aboriginal?

Bolt: *There's a twist you've put on that.* What I'm saying is that her appearance suggests that, in her ancestry, her heritage, her upbringing, she has other influences and other genealogies and all that, that would enable her to choose, as others have, differently to how she has chosen.

Borenstein: And you deduce that from the fact that she has a paler complexion?

Bolt: That was the first indication of it, yes. Obviously. I mean, it's fairly obvious, but, you know, [I] made some other checks, and that comes clear.

Borenstein: And then you go on to say, and this is the last paragraph on the first page, you go on to say: "Exactly how Aboriginal is Enoch"?

Bolt: Yes.[17]

It is surprising how Ron Merkel's principled stand on the importance of free speech in 1994 could undergo such a complete turn-around by 2009. Had Bolt's opinions and speech really worsened and gone beyond an acceptable line in those years? Or was it, as historian Hall Greenland had observed with Pat Eatock's claim for Aboriginality, the new 'time of reawakened pride for Indigenous Australians' that had prompted Merkel's apparent conversion? Had Ron Merkel become a 'virtue-signaller' keen to join the tail end of the 'crusade' (after the 1967 referendum, *Mabo* and Land Rights successes) that wanted to still roam the land looking for a fight over the ever diminishing examples of so-called Aboriginal 'injustice' and racism?

One can only speculate but perhaps political scientist Kenneth Minogue's apt *St George* analogy explains the mindset of

---

[17] *Eatock v Bolt*, Trans. Proc., Fed. Court (Vic) O/N 160844, Day Three, 30 March 2011, p246-7.

a crusading liberal, as Merkel may well see himself:[18] [19]

> The story of liberalism, as liberals tell it, is rather like the
> legend of St George and the dragon. After many centuries
> of hopelessness and superstition, St George, in the guise of
> Rationality, appeared in the world somewhere about the six-
> teenth century. The first dragons upon whom he turned his
> lance were those of despotic kingship and religious intolerance.
> These battles won, he rested a time, until such questions as
> slavery, or prison conditions, or the state of the poor, began
> to command his attention. During the nineteenth century, his
> lance was never still, prodding this way and that against the
> inert scaliness of privilege, vested interest, or patrician inso-
> lence. But, unlike St George, he did not know when to retire.
> The more he succeeded, the more he became bewitched with
> the thought of a world free of dragons, and the less capable he
> became of ever returning to private life. He needed his drag-
> ons. He could only live by fighting for causes - the people, the
> poor, the exploited, the colonially oppressed, the underprivi-
> leged and the underdeveloped. As an ageing warrior, he grew
> breathless in his pursuit of smaller and smaller dragons - for
> the big dragons were now harder to come by.[20]

In Merkel's advocacy against Bolt and his articles, perhaps a
new Ron 'St George' Merkel had found in Bolt's speech something he felt could not allow to remain free but needed slaying.
'St Ron' had been called to protect his 'princesses', who he
himself described as the young 'fair-skinned' Aborigines who,
because of 'youth, inexperience or psychological vulnerability',
were vulnerable to attacks on them.[8.8] Moreover, 'St Ron'
mused, they "shouldn't have to be answerable to the world
around [them] for being a fairer, rather than a darker, skinned
Aboriginal person."[8.9]

---

[18] *Human Rights Commission* website: "Ron Merkel has devoted himself to access to
justice for people who are marginalised and disadvantaged, having a long and out-
standing commitment to the promotion and advancement of human rights as a legal
practitioner ... specialising in the areas of human rights ... the rights of Aboriginal
peoples, migration law, equal opportunity and anti-discrimination law ... with a particular focus on public interest and indigenous matters ... Ron is a Founding Member of the Victorian Aboriginal Legal Service." (https://humanrights.gov.au/about-
us/human-rights-awards-2025/hra-nominees/16528)

[19] As Merkel related to Michael Gordon, 'Lunch with Ron Merkel', *Sydney Morning
Herald*, 29 Aug 2014.

[20] Minogue, K.R., *The Liberal Mind,* Methuen & Co London, 1963, p1.

8.2.1   Ron Merkel QC Goes to Nuremberg

> *Having gone through the "evidence" he himself no doubt be-*
> *lieved, Merkel smeared me as Nazi-like for doubting people*
> *like Eatock, the lead plaintiff in this action on behalf of nine*
> *"fair-skinned Aboriginals" I'd written about. "This kind of*
> *thinking led to the Nuremberg race laws," he raved, even hint-*
> *ing I could inspire genocide: "The Holocaust in the 1940s*
> *started with words and finished with violence."*

Andrew Bolt[21]

There are said to be two main techniques that successful prosecutors focus on when cross-examining their quarry in the witness box - one is the crash or crash-through, 'take no prisoners',
approach favoured by the likes of the late Murray Gleeson, as
Justice Michael McHugh related:

> Murray ... had a great sense of where the weakness was in
> somebody's case and he would zero in on that ... and break
> through and smash it, and then say to the judge, "Well, I've
> destroyed his case. I must win." Whether he was for the
> appellant or the respondent he always had to attack.[22]

The other technique is more subtle and calculating. The prosecutor seeks to slowly poke and prod the defendant and wit-
nesses, looking for chinks in their story which can be prised
open, making them admit what the prosecution wants to hear;
or they relentlessly seek to *twist* questions and answers, all the
while slowly building their case against the defendant. These
prosecutors always have one close eye on the judge - they need
to make sure the judge is being guided along the path they
have clearly laid out, and on which they hope to lead His
Honour to their preferred conclusion - guilty!

Andrew Bolt was known as a tough nut, a thick-skinned,
experienced and intelligent street-fighter in the court of public
opinion. The crash-through prosecution approach of a Murray

---

[21]Andrew Bolt, 'New evidence exposes Pat Eatock's tall tale', *Herald Sun*, 11 Sept
   2024.
[22]Michael Pelly, *Murray Gleeson, The Smiler*, The Federation Press, 2014, p100.

Gleeson wasn't going to work with him. Bolt could give as good as he got, physically as well as literally[23] and the court case could potentially end up as one almighty brawl, leaving the judge confused and unable to clearly see the path that Merkel hoped to lead him along. Merkel knew that in Bolt he had a mighty opponent, as he himself admitted:

> What the action [against Bolt] was about was two [news-paper] articles, which were very cleverly and brilliantly con-structed by Andrew Bolt, where he was in effect saying that fair skinned Aboriginal people have a choice between identify-ing with their European Heritage and the Aboriginal heritage. The effect of the articles was to suggest that they'd chosen to identify as Aboriginal to, in effect, give themselves financial advantage, to feather their nest. The real sting was that they weren't genuine Aborigines but they were just taking that identification so they'd get better opportunities.[24]

What was Merkel to do to rattle Bolt, hoping to get him off guard and disorientating his mind, prior to sending in counsel assisting, Herman Borenstein SC, for the final attack? Bring in the Nazis of course.

As a way of smearing Bolt's views and delegitimising his journalism, Merkel, in his opening address to the court, 'played the Nazi card', the *reductio ad Hitlerum*[25] technique, well known as an attempt to invalidate someone else's argument on the basis that a similar idea was promoted or practised by Adolf Hitler or the Nazi Party. First coined by political philosopher Leo Strauss in 1953, *reductio ad Hitlerum* is a type of *ad hominem* attack, or a fallacy of irrelevance, that is

---

[23] Bolt was a speaker at a 2017 book-launch. He arrived late, flustered and holding his stained jacket. At the venue entrance he had been set upon by two hooded men, with one more filming, who had attacked him with a sticky dye. In his self-defence he had 'beaten the shit out of' one of them - the other accomplice had run off like a coward before Bolt could 'sink the boot in'. The film-man kept recording because that was meant to be the real prize - Andrew Bolt humiliated on film, cowering and pleading for mercy before two righteous 'St George' heroes after 'slaying' the 'racist Bolt dragon'. Unfortunately for these lacklustre 'knights' of the Far Left, they picked the wrong dragon.[8.10]

[24] This paragraph also very concisely sums up what the whole case was about. Ron Merkel in conversation with Lizzie O'Shea, *Snodger Media*, 2016[8.11].

[25] Latin for 'reduction to Hitler'.

used to smear an opponent by implying guilt by association.[26]
It is a tactic often used to derail arguments because such comparisons tend to distract and anger the opponent, which in
Bolt's case they were certainly successful in doing.[27]

To many other observers however, Merkel from that point
on greatly tarnished his credibility. Was his case so weak, or
so desperate, that he needed to bring in old Adolf as an additional 'counsel assisting'? The disappointment, and indeed
sadness that many felt for an advocate of Merkel's standing,
to believe he had to stoop so low as to slur Bolt during the
opening address, only increased as Merkel played a full hand
of Nazi cards - accusing Bolt of having a 'eugenics approach'
and falsely claiming Bolt believed 'you have got to have two
Aboriginal parents and look very black' to be Aboriginal.

Merkel continued with, 'this kind of thinking led to the
Nuremberg race laws in 1935'. Merkel made sure the court,
and the media, knew what these laws entailed by spelling them
out:

> the definition of Jewish, is that you had to have three Jew-
> ish grandparents and be a participating member in a Jewish
> community. That is the beginning. But the point I am mak-
> ing, as this pure eugenics approach, even in Nazi Germany,
> accepted some relevance of you being part of a community. It
> is an extraordinary concept in a time warp to go back to this,
> how you look and what kind of blood you've got.[28]

It was an appalling slur against Bolt, and irrelevant to the
proceedings. Merkel wasn't looking for the truth, or sympathy
for his client. What he really wanted to do from the outset was
to rattle Bolt and give his 'shock-trooper', Herman Borenstein
SC, a better chance at breaching Bolt's defenses. It was a
strategy that appeared to work.

---

[26] *Wikipedia: Reductio ad Hitlerum*

[27] Andrew Bolt blogpost: 'Mark Leibler responds. The law may have been 'misapplied'
against me and the slur was 'outrageous'', *Herald Sun*, 12 Dec 2013.

[28] *Eatock v Bolt*, Trans. Proc., Fed. Court (Vic) O/N 160844, Day One, 28 March
2011, p16-7.

On Day 2 of the trial, Bolt was in the witness box stating:

> Can I just ... suggest that it has been put to me in the state-
> ments handed to you, and in the cross-examination it is im-
> plied, that I am a racist, eugenics, the Nazi stuff, when as
> my articles insist, I am attacking racism. That is my point of
> view. I have been anti-racist all along.[29]

Bolt elaborated further outside the court, as reported by the
ABC:

> Newspaper columnist Andrew Bolt was boiling with anger
> when he entered the witness box on the second day of a racial
> vilification case, stung by comparisons of his articles with
> Hitler's Nazi Germany. The controversial News Ltd commen-
> tator is being sued under the *Racial Discrimination Act* by a
> group of Aborigines over a series of articles he wrote in 2009
> ... Bolt listened on Monday as Ron Merkel, QC, the counsel
> for the nine Aborigines bringing the class action, said his ar-
> ticles on racial identity took a eugenics approach and echoed
> the Nuremberg laws of 1935. While Mr Bolt had been warned
> by Justice Mordecai Bromberg not to use his testimony as a
> public forum, the journalist vented his anger before his cross-
> examination today. He said any statement linking him to the
> Nuremberg laws and the Holocaust "were false and grossly of-
> fensive". "Mr Merkel crossed the line," Bolt said, adding that
> he was a vigorous opponent of the eugenics movement.[8.12]

Merkel, in one of his retirement legacy interviews, claimed
that, "If I look back on my many, many years in the law, the
one thing I've learnt is that principle counts, and ... the ends
will never justify the means."[30] One wonders how Bolt would
have responded to this statement, coming only a few years
after he experienced first hand the pointy end of Merkel's idea
of 'principle'. As an advocate in a tough case, has Merkel
never used a 'means' to justify an 'ends'?

This is a topic that will be explored in the following sections.

---

[29] *Eatock v Bolt*, Trans. Proc., Fed. Court (Vic) O/N 160844, Day Two, 29 March
2011, p28.

[30] Michael Gordon, 'SMH in Lunch with Ron Merkel', *Sydney Morning Herald*, 29
Aug 2014.

8.2.2 Merkel or Bolt - Who is the Real Race Promoter?

Just to show how illogical, inappropriate and indeed intellectually bereft it was for Merkel to use *reductio ad Hitlerum* against Bolt and his opinions, consider the following hypothetical scenario where the 'Nazi card' has been used against the real-life actions of Justice Merkel, as he was in 1998.

But first the scene needs to be set with an illustration of events that frequently occurred in Nazi Germany. On a night in November 1938, a young German Jewish woman, newly wed, described what happened when there was a knock at her door:

> My terrified father-in-law had opened the door to two SA men, who entered our bedroom, telling my husband to dress to be taken to the local prison .... I helped him to put warm clothing on. We did not speak although I could feel myself and my husband trembling. In less than ten minutes both Gunter (my husband) and his sixty-eight year old father had been taken away in the police van ... while l tried to comfort my aged mother-in-law, who was crying uncontrollably.

Her father-in-law was released after a few days, as he was a veteran of the First Word War, so his 'papers' were sufficient to get him released and free to be part of the community of the 'German race' - at least for the time being. But she found out later that her husband had been taken to Sachsenhausen, the concentration camp for Jewish prisoners, just outside of Berlin.[8.13] In Nazi Germany, one's community acceptance, what jobs you could apply for, whether you could vote, and even one's freedom or life, could be determined by what papers, permits, or certificates you held.

Fast forward to 1998 and imagine you are Debbie Oakford, the Tasmanian Aboriginal woman from Chapter Two who applied to join the Tasmanian ATSIC electoral roll. There is an ominous knock at your door, which you open, only to be served with a subpoena to attend the Federal Court and appear before 'SS Bundesrichter' Ron Merkel[31] to answer questions as to your ancestry and race. For in fact, a Federal Court action has been initiated to determine whether you, Debbie Oakford, are an 'Aboriginal person' as defined as being 'a person of the Aboriginal *race* of Australia'. You are shocked that a word such as 'race' has been entered into recent legislation[32] and is being used to determine your eligiblity to vote in modern Australia, but this is what in fact happened (See Chapter 2.1). As Herr Merkel goes through the paperwork before him, sorting out who is, and who isn't, a 'member of the Aboriginal race of Australia' you begin to tremble with fear as he calls out your name. It appears that the archivist from 'Gestapo' Headquarters in Hobart[33] has researched your family history and unfortunately you do not have sufficient 'connections' in your ancestry to be classed as being 'a person of the Aboriginal race'. Herr Merkel rejects your racial claim and finds you are ineligible to join the ATSIC electoral roll. You are disenfranchised, much to the satisfaction of the 'purer' bred members of the 'Aboriginal race' who have been watching proceedings in court that day. Herr Merkel then moves on to the other trembling applicants standing before him, carefully sifting and analysing their claims and papers. Ultimately two are rejected and the other nine are given a stamp of approval by Herr Merkel, satisfied that their stories and papers are sufficiently in order to show the 'racial reality' that they are in fact of the Aboriginal race.

Beyond putting a Nazi slant to the proceedings, none of

---

[31] Apologies to Mr Merkel, but this hypothetical is simply being used to illustrate the unnecessary pain and hurt that playing the Nazi-card in an argument can bring, as occurred with his slurs against Bolt. Merkel's *reductio ad Hitlerum* in *Eatock v Bolt* also nicely fits Godwin's Law, which contends that Hitler and Nazi comparisons appear in arguments only at the point when arguers could no longer present their views in constructive ways and therefore resorted to demonizing their opponents (*see Wikipedia: Godwin's Law.*)

[32] Aboriginal and Torres Strait Islander Commission Act 1989, No. 150 of 1989 - SECT 4(1): *In this Act, unless the contrary intention appears: 'Aboriginal person' means a person of the Aboriginal **race** of Australia.*

[33] Apologies to Ms Robyn Eastley, Senior Archivist in the Tasmanian Archives Office, who was commissioned to research Debbie Oakford's ancestry in *Shaw v Wolf*, 1998.

this is made up. Justice Merkel *did* hear the case against Ms Oakford under the Aboriginal and Torres Strait Islander Commission Act 1989 which required him to ascertain her 'race'. He *did* have the legal power to adjudicate and sort out these people according to their race. He *did* give a stamp of approval to those standing before him who had convinced him of their racial *bona fides*. Is this not unlike the power that the Gestapo exercised in deciding the racial groupings of the people brought before its officers and judges?

The point is that it was such a cheap shot by Merkel to try and smear Andrew Bolt and his *opinions* with the Nazi race card, given that Merkel himself *actually enforced laws*, not just opinions, that determined the racial status of real Tasmanian people. Merkel then went further and excluded those people he determined did not fit the required racial profile under the ATSIC legislation. In administrative terms, how was Justice Merkel's judgement to exclude Debbie Oakford from one aspect of her society, because of her lack of race credentials, all that different from when the Nazis excluded German Jews from parts of German society because of their race credentials?

And to illustrate just how pernicious Merkel's legacy is, consider the hiring policies of Australia's so-called premier scientific organisation, the Commonwealth Scientific and Industrial Research Organisation (CSIRO). In December 2024, the CSIRO was still using race-based criteria to advertise for applicants for Indigenous Time at Sea Studentships, based in Hobart, Tasmania. The positions were only open to applicants of a particular race:

> CSIRO considers the filling of this position is intended to constitute a special/equal opportunity/affirmative measure under section 8(1) of the *Racial Discrimination Act 1975* (Cth). The position is therefore only open to Aboriginal and/or Torres Strait Islander people with Australian Citizenship. The successful applicant will be required to provide evidence to confirm that they are an Aboriginal and/or Torres Strait Islander person.[8.14]

Returning to the *Eatock v Bolt* trial, in closing submissions it was reported that:

> Ron Merkel QC, for the [Eatock] nine, said the articles attacked not only those mentioned in them but also young Aborigines who, because of "youth, inexperience or psychological vulnerability", were vulnerable to attacks on them. He said if young people had aspirations to be like those challenged in the articles, it would help solve the problems of Aboriginal disadvantage also highlighted by Bolt. "So, it's a double assault on this group," Mr Merkel said. "It's an assault on their own self respect ... their own pride, but it's also an assault on how they will see others viewing them. "What he has done in these articles, absolutely unintentionally, but the consequence of writing these articles is to pull down the kind of **pillars that are the role models for the future."** [8.8](emphasis added.)

With hindsight, one of the ironies of this case is that two of Merkel's claimed 'pillars that are the role models for the future' turned out to be anything but - Eatock turned out to be a fake Aborigine, and may have even perjured herself if she knew deep-down that her story, and her sister Joan's oral history, were fabricated. And now languishing in gaol as a convicted thief and fraudster, Geoff Clark was found to have been offending for years around the time of the Bolt trial.[8.15] Is Merkel suggesting these two people were good role models for a new generation of 'fair-skinned' Aborigines? And more importantly, if Bolt had not had his wings clipped by Merkel's advocacy, perhaps the Aboriginal community might have suffered less at the hands of people like Clark. Perhaps Bolt's free speech had a part to play in shining more light on Clark's activities, but after his humiliating loss in court, Bolt and other commentators and investigators understandably lost courage and started to self-censor. They dared not ask potentially 'offensive' questions of the increasing number of 'fair-skinned' Aborigines who now seem to be turning up all over Australia. As *Dark Emu Exposed* has shown, many of these newly identifying 'fair-skinned' Aborigines appear to be fakes.

8.2.3   Did Merkel's Ends Justify His Means?

If I look back on my many, many years in the law, the one thing I've learnt is that principle counts ... The ends will never justify the means and that is something our respective governments simply don't understand ... It's all ends-driven and the means don't matter and I think that's a fundamental flaw – and tragic at the human level.

Ron Merkel QC [34]

It is no secret that we live in an era when politics is all about polls, populism, spin and winning elections and government. In that process, expedience will invariably triumph over principle. The ends will justify the means and the myths created by that process will count far more than the realities. And I want to explore that problem ... to hopefully demonstrate the point that principle is certainly struggling for oxygen in the political domain.

Ron Merkel QC [35]

There are some troubling aspects about the way Ron Merkel QC ran the *Eatock v Bolt* case. It may only be speculation, but it is almost as if the case was a deliberate set-piece - all the armaments, players and ground-work were very carefully selected and strategically placed to defend a new citadel that was being built to protect a new class of Australians in the making, the 'white Aborigines'. An uncharacteristically off-guard Andrew Bolt, going about his daily tabloid business, walked in to investigate and became totally enmeshed by the trip-wires and the grenades he set off. He only emerged two years later, in a daze after his defeat.

The set-piece worked brilliantly - it scared off any other inquiring minds who might have been keen to investigate the massive rise in fake and 'white Aborigines' who were beginning

---

[34] Michael Gordon, 'SMH in Lunch with Ron Merkel', *Sydney Morning Herald*, 29 Aug 2014 - 'As with many refugee cases that have gone to the High Court in recent years, a central issue is whether the end justifies the means, a topic that Merkel, the son of a Russian father and Polish mother, feels very strongly about. "If I look back ... "

[35] Ron Merkel, 'Oration, Human Rights: Myths and Realities in the Year 2012', 11 Dec 2012, p1.[8.9]

to engulf many aspects of Australian society.

Other commentators were firmly convinced something was going on. In 2016, five years after Bolt's court loss, Simon Breheny, the then director of the Legal Rights Project at the Institute of Public Affairs (IPA) noted:

> political activists and their lawyers have come to realise that section 18C can be used to aggressively pursue political goals. The case against Bolt was not merely a group of offended individuals making a legal complaint in an effort to remedy personal loss. It is possible that the complainants could have made out a defamation suit against Bolt. But the case was pursued using 18C as a battering ram because of the negative perception that would be created by a breach of the Racial Discrimination Act ... Too often the law is being used opportunistically. Section 18C is being used not as a shield but as a weapon. In silencing, or threatening to silence, opponents in a debate using legal means, complainants remove the possibility of debate. It's unhealthy and it's undemocratic.[36]

To further elaborate, as Merkel himself [8.9] and his solicitors [8.16] both acknowledged, the original complaint against Bolt came not from Pat Eatock but apparently, from 'a group of Victorian Aboriginal law students [who] felt particularly humiliated and intimidated by the Bolt articles. It was the Aboriginal Law Students' Society who actually initiated the case.'[37]

This is believable, but why weren't one or more of these students involved in lodging the original complaint with the AHRC? The complaint form only had Pat Eatock listed as the complainant, and the 'Eatock Nine' as a representative group of 'other Aboriginal persons who were likely to be offended, etc.'[8.17] These were publicly known successful Aboriginal people, but no students were among them. And why didn't more of the Eatock Nine become direct applicants along with Pat? She was taking all the legal risk herself by suing Bolt

---

[36]Simon Breheny, 'Repeal section 18C, the 'Andrew Bolt' law: it stifles free speech', *The Australian*, 5 Feb 2016.

[37]Ron Merkel, 'Oration, Human Rights: Myths and Realities in the Year 2012', 11 Dec 2012, p22.[8.9]

and the HWT. Was the liability and stress of being a lead applicant too much of a risk perhaps for any of the others, as it most certainly would have been for a young, asset-less student just starting their career? Imagine if they had lost the case and been lumped with a massive costs order. Perhaps it was thought that Pat, as a frail, elderly, asset-less pensioner, really had nothing to lose, and backed as she was by a *pro bono* legal team, had all to gain if she could play the victim and sympathy cards skillfully? If she lost, she could just declare bankruptcy.

This is perhaps where the evidence suggests that Merkel may have put on his blinkers so as to give himself a clear sight to the 'ends' of humiliating Bolt, without being distracted by the 'means' along the way. Given Merkel's quotations above, professing his adherence to principle over expediency, and his strong record with regard to this in other cases, in *Eatock v Bolt* he clearly fell short - very short. His use of Pat Eatock as the 'witness for the prosecution' was raw expediency, given that even a small amount of research would have revealed that her own principles in this case were certainly wanting.

Just imagine for a moment we enter a hypothetical parallel universe, a better world, where Ron Merkel QC had rigidly adhered to his principles over expediency and his belief that the ends never justifies the means. How might have this hypothetical Ron Merkel run the case?

This Merkel still agreed to take on the case of the offended students, and he has selected Pat Eatock, one of Bolt's subjects, as the best candidate to lead the legal action. Pat comes to his office and starts providing the witness statement that will become Merkel's key piece of evidence on Day 1 of the trial.[38]

She tells Merkel that her grandmother, Lucy, was Aboriginal and born in Carnarvon Gorge in an 'Aboriginal birthing

---

[38] *Eatock v Bolt*, Trans. Proc., Fed. Court (Vic), O/N 160844, Mon 28 Mar 2011, Day One, p51ff.

place' - Merkel quickly checks the authoritative *Australian Dictionary of Biography* which instead tells him that 'Lucy Harriet Eatock was born in Springsure, Queensland, and registered as the ninth child of **Scottish-born** parents Alexander Wakenshaw and his wife Jane Lindsay, née Cousins.'[8.18] There is no mention that she was Aboriginal. Merkel notes the word 'registered', so he tells his clerk to go off to the records office with $25 from petty cash to buy the birth registration certificate. It confirms that both her parents were born in Scotland. Merkel gives Pat a perplexed look - no Aboriginality there, so he begins to wonder if Pat is mistaken or just making the story up.

Pat continues her statement, telling Merkel about her greatgranduncle, Adam Wakenshaw, who she claimed had 'slave sex partners or assistants', and who she suspects is really Lucy's father. Merkel thinks to himself, 'that sounds a bit melodramatic', but makes a note to get the clerk to follow that up, thereby finding the proof in a newspaper report that Adam was in Victoria, 1,800 kilometres south of Springsure at the time of Lucy's conception. So he can't have been her father (see Chapter 4.1). Merkel's suspicions of Pat's tale grows. She is now around 75 years old and in frail health but tells him she remembers a schoolyard story of when she was a 5-year-old: "This is when I first encountered my Aboriginality ... Because we had a white mother and fair skin, my sisters and I were put in to where the white kids' played ... When the school realised that my father was Aboriginal, they took us out of the white kids' playground and put us in the black kids' playground."

Maybe this is true, but do five-year-olds really remember and indeed understand such things as segregation? Merkel wonders how he can corroborate such a story from the memory of an elderly woman. The validity of her claims causes him further concern when she continues with, "I was 14 when I first identified myself in public as an Aboriginal person."[39]

---

[39] *Trial transcripts ibid.*, p52.

But hadn't she already admitted that she had done that at age five?

Pat continues to recount her chronology - "in 1957 I married [and] became a housewife to look after my children. In 1973 I commenced tertiary studies at ANU and in 1975 I was the International Women's Year reporter on campaigning and went as a delegate to a non-governmental forum in Mexico City." Merkel gets Pat to pause for a moment while he asks, "Pat, what about the years between 1957 and 1973? You really need to tell me what was going on in your life at that time so I can get the complete picture of your life as an Aboriginal person." She retraces her steps and, as she describes her life in the 1960s, Merkel starts to feel a little tense:

> we got married and we lived in housing commission accommodation. One day my neighbour started talking negatively about Aboriginals ... I stopped and said, "You can't say that, I'm Aboriginal, you know." She had not realised I was Aboriginal. We had a huge fight and she told me to "get back to my bloody gunyah." A gunyah is one type of Aboriginal bush hut. After that fight everyone in our street appeared to have become aware that I was Aboriginal. I had never denied my Aboriginality.[40]

Perhaps Merkel thinks back to his own time in the 1960's, and wonders, 'that's a little strange – back then we all pretty much recognized who the Aboriginal families were, but Pat is telling me now her local community only recognized her as such after she told them she identified as Aboriginal.' He also recalled the words of Pat, in her filmed interview,[41] relating how she felt after this argument with her neighbour:

> and this was the first time I'd made a statement about, you know, "I'm Aboriginal" you know; and up until that point in time, you know - it had never - it was a part of me but it was [deep] down [inside of me] and it wasn't on the surface.

Merkel asks Pat to elaborate a bit more on her Aboriginal

---

[40] *ibid.*, p56.
[41] see [4.28]

identity during these crucial years:

> In the 1960s I went to hear Faith Bandler speak at a meeting.
> It was the first time I had heard how hugely difficult life was
> for rural and remote Aboriginal communities. It was at this
> meeting I decided I had to be pro-active about my Aboriginal-
> ity. I did not really have a choice whether to identify because
> it was not someone else's oppression, this was my sense of
> oppression ... No one can be healthy mentally or physically if
> they do not recognise who and what they are. Aboriginality
> has nothing to do with skin colour, Aboriginality is in the
> heart. The reality is once you publicly identify as Aboriginal
> there is no going back. We have no choice.[42]

Then Pat adds:

> During the 1960s I was unable to be very active around Abo-
> riginal issues because I was a suburban housewife who had
> five children in less than seven years, with the youngest child
> suffering severe disabilities. After this youngest child was ac-
> cepted into the care of the State in 1971, it was only then that
> I was able to become more active in Aboriginal issues.[43]

Merkel's tension mounts at Pat's reasoning for her self identification and her patchy declaration of it publicly, the lack of
recognition by her local community that she was Aboriginal,
and her lack of involvement in Aboriginal issues prior to 1972,
for weren't these the main concerns in Bolt's offending article?:

> In 1972, Pat Eatock ... officially became the first Aborigine
> to stand for federal parliament in the ACT, even though she
> looked as white as her Scottish mother ... Indeed, Eatock
> only started to identify as Aboriginal when she was 19, after
> attending a political rally, so little did any racial difference
> matter to her before her awakening to far-Left causes.[44]

Bolt, it seems, was much more accurate in his assessment of
Pat's life than the re-imagined version she was now relating to
Merkel, for Merkel's excellent research clerk had just returned
from the National Archives of Australia with Pat's Australian

---

[42] *Trial transcripts ibid.* p56.
[43] *ibid.*, p58.
[44] Andrew Bolt, 'It's so hip to be black', *Herald Sun*, 15 Apr 2009.

Security Intelligence Organisation (ASIO) files.[45] These were declassified and made public in 2005, some six years prior to Eatock's affirmed witness statement being read out in court.

As Merkel reads the ASIO files, his anxiety begins to increase about his client's claims that in the 1960s she was just 'a suburban housewife who had five children', with no time to be 'more active in Aboriginal issues'. One ASIO memo from this period instead confirms Pat seemed to have plenty of time and energy to be 'more active' with the political issues of her European heritage. She was an active member of the Communist Party of Australia (CPA), that very 'white' and very Western ideology:

> **Secret: Priority To Canberra from HQ - June Patricia Eatock:**
> The following provides a summary of the security history of the aforenamed to be shown to the Office of Aboriginal Affairs (Mr Dexter) as discussed:
> **June 1965** - attended a school at the Communist Party of Australia (CPA) on the subject of "Party of the Working Class." **1965-1969** - Attended several meetings of the Liverpool CPA branch and attended, or held, social functions for CPA members. **April 1970** - Applied for a job at the CPA bookshop. **May 1970** - In conversation referred to herself as the Honorary Secretary of the Liverpool Moratorium Committee. **July 1970** - It was reported by another CPA member that she would be replaced in her position at the CPA bookshop as her work was not satisfactory. **November 1970** - On a list of CPA Activists [list redacted].[8.19] (abbreviated and emphasis added.)

The same ASIO file recorded how Pat's activist interests expanded to include militant feminism from 1971, and it was **only from 1972 onwards** that her interests appear to morph into Aboriginal activism:

> **May 1971** - Attended a National Women's Liberation Conference held at Minto NSW. **January 1972** - Wrote an article for the CPA discussion journal "Praxis" on proportional "Spe-

---

[45] National Archives of Australia (NAA): June Patricia Eatock, A6119, 3641, 19 July 2005.

cial interest" representation (e.g. Women, Blacks, Youth) at
CPA Committees, conferences, etc. Attended a CPA school
at Minto on the subject of "Marxist Theory and Evolution."
February 1972 - Spent three days at the Aboriginal Embassy, Canberra. **March 1972** - Attended the Sydney District Conference of the CPA and was elected as a delegate to
the CPA National Congress. Contacted CPA Headquarters to
make arrangements connected with her desire to attend the
annual conference of the Federal Council for the Advancement
of Aborigines and Torres Strait Islanders (FCAATSI) **April
1972** - Attended the FCAATSI Conference in Alice Springs.
May 1972 - Attended a Canberra planning meeting for the
Moratorium for Black Rights during which it was reported
that she had spoken very forcefully and criticized Aboriginal
reluctance to use violence in any confrontation with the authorities. Since **March 1972** - Five by-lined articles in the
CPA newspaper "Tribune" have been attributed to her. All
of these pertain to Aboriginal matters.

Merkel begins to worry that the judge might come to think
that Pat's political trajectory from CPA member, to militant
feminist and finally onto 'political Aborigine', as Bolt had suggested, makes his client just look like an activist seeking a
cause. If she needs to claim that she is Aboriginal as part of
that progression, perhaps so be it. The ASIO files certainly
are more evidence to support what Bolt had written about
Merkel's client, but which she is now telling Merkel deeply of-
fends her. Bolt had suggested she was one of the:

> 'white Aborigines' - people who out of their multi-stranded
> but largely European genealogy, decide to identify with the
> thinnest of all those strands, and the one that has contributed
> least to their looks. Yes, the Aboriginal one now so fashion-
> able among artists and academics.[46] [Eatock] the white Abo-
> rigine – or "political Aborigine" ... thrived as an Aboriginal
> bureaucrat, activist and academic, leading the way for [oth-
> ers].[47]

Perhaps Merkel, should have been feeling a little tense at the
prospect of having to stand up in court to read Pat's witness

---

[46] Andrew Bolt,'White fellas in the black', *Herald Sun*, 21 Aug 2009.
[47] Andrew Bolt,'It's so hip to be black', *Herald Sun*, 15 Apr 2009.

statement as the affirmed truth? So far as the 1960s were concerned, Pat Eatock comes across solely as a communist activist. It is only much later, from 1972, that she begins to portray herself as an Aboriginal activist, and others begin to recognised her as such. Another ASIO file is telling:

> Patty [Pat Eatock] has recently arrived in Canberra, possibly from Sydney and is at present living in Hughes ACT with her two children. She has no husband, wears her hair in a tight bun, and badly needs dental treatment. She claims to be part Aboriginal but if so this is not evident and by references made by her appears to be associated with the Black Moratorium group in Sydney ... the purpose of the Moratorium for Black Rights was to bring the situation of the Aboriginals to the public ... the organisers hope to hold a demonstration ... at Parliament House. After the newspaper correspondent had left [the meeting], it was decided that the demonstration should be militant.[48]

A further worrying May 1972 ASIO memo implies Merkel's client was inciting Aboriginal violence against the authorities. The ASIO agent described the foundation of the 'Action Committee' where, "Patty [Eatock] appeared to take control of this committee and advocated the revolutionary approach to any action taken. Patty stated that if the blacks do not achieve their aim they will 'eat the whites.'"[49]

By 26 July 1972, Pat Eatock was well on the radar at ASIO, where a Current Intelligence Brief had been prepared summarising her as a person of interest:

> since June 1965, EATOCK has come to attention mainly as a result of her attendance at ... CPA Branch meetings. However, it is only since early 1972 that EATOCK, who claims to be part-Aboriginal, appears to have taken an interest in Aboriginal affairs ... it was reported that she had spoken very forcefully, criticising Aboriginal reluctance to use violence in confrontation with authorities. In mid-April 1972, EATOCK, who had previously resided in Sydney, moved to Canberra where she now has a temporary position with the

---

[48] [8.20], p1.
[49] see [8.20], p2.

Office of Aboriginal affairs. It is likely that her involvement
with the 'Embassy' increased correspondingly, however the recent newspaper references to her position as 'secretary-treasurer'
are the first indications that EATOCK has had any close connection with the 'Embassy.'[8.21]

Perhaps Ron Merkel might have read these files with rising
concern. On the one hand he thinks they confirm that his
client is, by mid-1972 at least, identifying herself publicly as
Aboriginal, although people such as her neighbours and the
ASIO agents don't automatically see her that way. But what
of her actions, lifestyle and claims in the years prior? No
mention of her Aboriginality appears during her CPA days.
Bolt's articles claim she 'only started to identify as Aboriginal'
after she became politicised, which the ASIO files seem to
support. Merkel might have just wondered why she wasn't
publicly acknowledged as Aboriginal during the 1960s.

Merkel then scans a biographical piece on Pat in *The Age*
of 6 March 1987, where she says:

In early 1972 Bobbi Sykes and I were invited to speak to a
group of Canberra women about land rights, the Aboriginal
embassy and other issues to Aboriginal women ... [at this
time] I arrived in Canberra, penniless with a five-month-old
baby - to stay.[8.22]

It can only be speculated whether or not Merkel knew what the
Aboriginal community knew; namely that Bobbi Sykes was a
fake Aborigine,[50] and, as many Aboriginal people will admit,
fakes hang around with and promote other fakes, especially
where there are employment or monetary gains to be had.
Perhaps the most senior Aboriginal bureaucrat at that time,
Charles Perkins, recognised something wasn't quite right when
he criticised both Pat Eatock and Bobbi Sykes, as reported by
The Canberra Times in 1973:

---

[50]See *Wikipedia: Roberta Sykes*. Even today, the 'Aboriginal industry' can't bring
itself to admit that 'Aboriginal' icon Roberta 'Bobbi' Sykes was actually a liar
about her own Aboriginality; she was in fact the daughter of a white mother and
most likely an African-American serviceman. The University of Melbourne craftily
describes her not as a capital 'I', but rather a small 'i', indigenous Australian, which
would include all citizens born in Australia, Aboriginal or not. [8.23]

> Mrs Pat Eatock replied on Friday night to criticism by Mr Charles Perkins, an acting assistant secretary with the Department of Aboriginal Affairs, of herself and Ms Bobbi Sykes. Speaking at a VIEW Club luncheon, Mr Perkins said he was "embarrassed and frustrated by the proclamations and actions of these two women" and that they had caused shame to all Aborigines. Mrs Eatock said it was unfortunate that Mr Perkins misunderstood the activities of Ms Sykes and herself because they were doing things to help Aboriginal people.[8.24]

It is very easy to see that a 'penniless' single mum like Pat Eatock might have been tempted to play along and fake her own ancestry, especially when, in 1972, she openly told a reporter at the *Canberra Times*:

> "I want to pick up one of the government's scholarships for Aborigines. Sooner or later Aboriginal people are going to have to re-write the history books, because there is so much which has not been mentioned. I guess I'd like to be one of them." When asked whether she would work for Aborigines through the Government if she completed an Arts degree, Mrs Eatock replied, "no ... whatever I do around Aboriginal issues I will do in my own way because, I think, working for the Government would be a betrayal." [The reporter then perceptively took her comments to their logical endpoint] She sees no inconsistency in accepting Government aid for her education and re-training. "The Government missed the opportunity to educate me when it wouldn't have cost them so much. It conditioned me to the housewife and mother role as it did other girls, pressuring them to leave school early."[8.25]

The self-entitlement of the communist activist Pat Eatock is breath-taking. Her selfish 'ends' are all that matters, no matter what the 'means'.

Perhaps Ron Merkel may not have found much solace either if he had read The Age newspaper reports of Wednesday 26th and Thursday 27th of July 1972 where, although Pat Eatock is clearly identifying herself as an Aboriginal, she is also running dangerously close to being seen to 'incite violence' and perhaps racial hatred as well:

Another mass rally to try to re-stablish the Aboriginal 'embassy' opposite Parliament House will be held next Sunday ... "The embassy will be re-established or Australia will have its own Sharpeville" [The massacre in 1960, when police opened fire on a crowd of black demonstrators in South Africa] the secretary-treasurer (Mrs P. Eatock) said yesterday. The 'embassy' was pulled down by police during a violent demonstration last Thursday.[8.26]

Earlier Mrs Eatock sent a telegram to the Minister for Aborigines (Mr Howson) [that] ... called on Mr Howson to meet them to discuss various immediate issues "in an effort to prevent bloodshed and violence that will otherwise occur on Sunday." [8.27]

Perhaps Merkel may have seen a potential problem looming here. He is about to walk into court and accuse Andrew Bolt of vilifying his client in print because of her race, yet here is evidence that Pat Eatock herself, on the face of it, is guilty of a much worse 'crime' of inciting violence amongst Aboriginal people. Perhaps this would have been devastating if Bolt's legal team had known this? Meanwhile, Pat continues making her statement:

A lot of my Aboriginal identity has been formed by negative experiences of being Aboriginal. When I was growing up, my parents were always really scared that our Aboriginality would be discovered and that the children would be taken away.[51]

By way of contradiction, Pat had earlier claimed that at the age of five, "when the school realised that my father was Aboriginal, they took us out of the white kids' playground and put us in the black kids' playground". If Pat's witness statement is to be believed, then why hadn't they been, 'taken away' at that time, as Pat claimed her parents feared? But perhaps maybe Pat is just making the whole story up?

The doubt continues, given that it was well known that in many cases, 'the *Commonwealth Franchise Act 1902 (Cth)*

---

[51] *Eatock v Bolt*, Trans. Proc., Fed. Court (Vic) O/N 160844, Mon 28 Mar 2011, Day One, p53.

specifically excluded Aboriginal people from voting in federal elections. Only Aboriginal people who were already enrolled to vote in New South Wales (NSW) prior to 1901 could vote in a Federal election. This changed in 1949 so that an Aboriginal man enrolled to vote in NSW could enrol to vote at the federal level'.[8.28] Yet here was Pat's own father, Roderick Eatock, along with his mother Lucy, on the 1933 electoral roll in NSW, when he was 24 years old.[8.29] Having been born in 1909, how could that be if he was Aboriginal and had not been on the electoral role prior to 1901? Maybe Roderick and his mother weren't actually Aboriginal after all?

Perhaps Bolt was right - Pat's family had just been a typical working class Australian family and Pat only 'identified' as Aboriginal later in life? Maybe Merkel might have begun to wonder whether his client was subconsciously (or craftily) putting an 'Aboriginal slant' on everything that she claimed. With her next embellishment, Merkel might have been sure of it:

> "My dad's brothers were abused for being Aboriginal." Pat continued. "One of his brothers was found dead in a dry creek bed near Tenterfield. He had died of Strychnine poisoning. I heard that in the earlier days it was common for Aboriginal people to be given flour with Strychnine poisoning in it. While growing up I experienced other incidents of what I now know to be discrimination."

This should have been easy for Merkel to corroborate. Murders were well documented and there must have been a coronial inquiry. Even though deliberate flour poisoning may have happened in isolated cases on the frontier in the 1800s, did it occur in the 1920's in NSW? A relatively simple check reveals the easily found coroner's report and a newspaper record of the event. Pat's claim is readily revealed as false. Merkel's client is clearly an 'unreliable witness'. Eatock has apparently used the classic technique of the hoaxer or fraudster to spin a fake narrative that merely projects one or two snippets of the truth as a way of fooling her audience or victim. Here is the truth of the poisoning story:

> An inquiry was held at the Court House on Saturday morning by the coroner (Mr H. L. Walker) concerning the death of George Leichhardt Eatock, whose body was found in a bore drain at Jew's Lagoon Station [near Narrabri] on 3rd April. 1926. In deceased's trousers' pocket, a bottle containing strychnine was found ...
>
> Adam Eatock, said the deceased was his brother and he was born in Queensland. He left Sydney eight weeks ago on account of his nerves. He saw the letter he wrote for [getting the] poison strychnine, saying he wanted to poison foxes to get skins to make furs for his sister. His mother [Lucy Eatock] had sent him strychnine.
>
> The Coroner found that deceased died from 'strychnine poisoning administered by himself, but whether accidentally or otherwise, the evidence adduced did not enable him to say'.[8.30], [8.31]

If the above information had been known by Bolt's counsel, Neil Young QC, then Merkel would also soon know that the testimony of his witness would be thoroughly discredited. A little research down in the archives by Young would have effectively picked off each of Eatock's claims as lies, fabrications or gross embellishments. Young could have waved this documentary evidence under Eatock's and Merkel's noses for her, and his, credibility to collapse.

Fortunately for Merkel's case, that wasn't going to happen.

8.3   Neil Young QC

Counsel for the Defence of Andrew Bolt

> *For reasons best known to its lawyers, the Herald Sun chose*
> *to argue that Bolt's columns weren't likely to offend anybody*
> *and/or that if they did it wasn't on the grounds of their*
> *race, colour etc. Both are self-evidently absurd propositions.*

Jonathan Holmes[52]

> *The legal team defending Bolt is led by Neil Young QC, one*
> *of Melbourne's finest lawyers whose daily fee is substantial.*

Chris Merritt[53]

Unfortunately, in this case, Neil Young's advocacy turned out
to be a disappointment. Reading through the court transcripts, at a number of points one could be forgiven for feeling
like metaphorically grabbing Young by the shoulders and, with
a good shake, yell "Come on man, wake up, can't you see where
you should be taking this line of inquiry?"

On Day 1, as he was cross-examining Pat Eatock, why
hadn't it occurred to Young to spend a mere \$24.70 at the
Queensland Births Deaths and Marriages Records Office to
obtain a copy of Lucy Wakenshaw's birth record? As an affirmed Pat sat in the witness box, Young could have just read
it out and politely pointed out to Pat that Lucy's birth had occurred at the family home in Springsure, not in some 'Aboriginal birthing place' in Carnarvon Gorge 172 kilometres away,
as Ron Merkel, on Pat's behalf, had told the court that morning. And why was Pat claiming that grandmother Lucy was
Aboriginal when the birth record clearly noted that both her
parents had been born in Scotland?

Similarly, it is most surprising that for a court case that
was rumoured to have cost \$1.5 million to run, Young hadn't

---

[52]Jonathan Holmes [journalist and presenter of ABC TV's *Media Watch*], 'Bolt,
Bromberg and a profoundly disturbing judgment', 30 Sept 2011.[8.32]

[53]Chris Merritt, 'A question of principle rather than money', *The Australian*, 2 Apr
2011.[8.33]

commissioned a professional genealogist for say, $5,000, to search the Queensland archives and locate William Eatock's birth record as the *Dark Emu Exposed* researchers had done. This would have provided the clinching evidence to show that Pat's grandfather wasn't Aboriginal at all - he was in fact born William Rose, with a father from the West Indies and a mother from Scotland. A relieved Andrew Bolt should have heard from Young's lips that Murray Gleeson-style phrase, 'Well your Honour, I've destroyed her case. I must win'. But Young made no attempt to follow this line of inquiry, and no such words passed his lips.

At another stage of the the cross-examination there came a point where Eatock admitted other members of her family did not identify as Aboriginal. Instead of inquiring further, Young just pulled up and said, "nothing further" and sat down, much to the horror of his anxious client. Young should have inquired of Eatock, 'Why don't your other family members identify as you do, Pat?' Did they know something that Pat had not so far shared with the court? Even without any birth or marriage certificates, Young knew that Pat had married her first cousin, Ronald Adam Eatock, in 1957 - Merkel had told the court as much when he presented her witness statement. Pat's husband "was the son of Richard Alexander Eatock, one of my father's brothers," Merkel related. Thus Pat and her husband shared the same grandparents, William and Lucy Eatock. Young didn't need to be a genealogist himself to open this door and see where Pat's testimony would lead the court. Young could have asked politely, 'Did Pat's husband believe their shared grandparents were Aboriginal as she did? Was her husband raised as Aboriginal? Did he suffer school-yard taunts and was he forced to play "in the black kids' schoolyard" as Pat claimed she had been? Did he identify as Aboriginal as well? How did they view their marriage - was it between two Aboriginals or was it a mixed, or solely a white marriage?' Perhaps, unlike Pat, her husband didn't believe his grandparents William and Lucy had actually been

Aboriginal. The answers will never be known because Young failed to ask these questions.

Perhaps Neil Young QC didn't even want this case? He appeared to some to want to get through the proceedings with a minimum of fuss, perhaps without being seen to question an Aboriginal woman's claims to her ancestry. Perhaps his mind was elsewhere; maybe still at the golf-course?[54]

Or perhaps it was deeper than that. One wonders whether he was rattled even before the trial had begun when two of the applicants, Dr Wayne Atkinson and his brother Graham, made an allegation that there was a 'conflict of interest' in the appointment of Young as counsel for the HWT and Andrew Bolt in the case. It was alleged that the Atkinson brothers were concerned that:

> Neil Young QC had represented us as the key legal counsel for the *Yorta Yorta v State of Victoria & Ors* in our appeal to the High Court, December, 2002 ... Mr Young QC has a clear conflict to act in the circumstances of this case for the reasons outlined. As plaintiffs seeking a fair trial and justice before this court and as previous clients as Yorta Yorta Traditional Owners we do not consent to him acting against us in the upcoming Federal Court action. This should result in Mr Young QC doing the honourable thing by returning the brief.

> **- Dr Wayne Atkinson**[8.34]

Mr Young certainly appeared unfocused and not at the top of his game at times, as Pat exposed when questioned by Young, to the chuckling delight of her court supporters:

Mr Young: When was it that you and your sister Joan started to do research on your family history?

Pat Eatock: That's two questions.

---

[54] As reported by court observer Michael Connor: "The hearing ran across two weeks. One side was passionate about what they were doing. On the Monday of the second week the opposing lawyers were early in the courtroom and were chatting together. Merkel and his team had spent the weekend working on the case. Young told them he had spent the day before playing golf." ('The White Aborigines Trial', *Quadrant Online*, 1 Nov 2011.)

Ouch! Pat could still show she had a sharp mind and was not afraid of authority. Of course, Young had made a fundamental slip-up here by asking a 'compound question' of his witness - a question that 'simultaneously poses more than one inquiry and calls for more than one answer.'[8.35]

In a film clip of a post-trial interview, it certainly seemed that Young had an air of quiet resignation that he had expected to lose the case. Young blamed his client:

> The primary reason why the judge rejected the defence was that Bolt's articles were factually inaccurate, as he found in a number of respects, and secondly that Bolt had expressed the articles in a way which was somewhat inflammatory and unnecessarily critical, and they weren't expressed in a way which was to minimize the risk of offending people of a particular racial origin.[8.36]

With *fait-accompli* music playing in background, and Young lamenting it was all Bolt's own fault, the film-clip's camera zooms in on the page in the final judgement where Bromberg J states, "By their pleadings, both Mr Bolt and HWT have admitted that Ms Eatock did and does genuinely self-identify as an Aboriginal person".[55]

One can imagine Bolt watching this interview now and angrily firing off an email to his former counsel, 'Hey, don't blame me. It was YOUR job to discover and present to the court the FACT that Pat Eatock was a fake as the evidence now clearly shows. She really was a 'white Aborigine' and 'looked as white as her Scottish mother,' as I had claimed. Your poor defence strategy allowed the judge to believe a falsehood - that she was Aboriginal'. With hindsight, Bolt could see that his 'stitch-up' was well underway on Day 1 of the trial.

And then a few other snippets of information came to light. It has been said that Mr Young might be something of a connoisseur of Aboriginal art and is believed to keep a substantial collection of Aboriginal art in his chambers. He

---

[55] *Eatock v Bolt* [2011] at 65.

also appeared to be an active participant in Melbourne's art and culture establishment.[8.37] His wife is also reported to be the Honorary Consul-General for Iceland in Australia,[56] so presumably Mr Young would frequent some high-brow and diplomatic functions. These are all praiseworthy applications of one's time, but within this section of 'Melbourne society', reputation and the company one keeps, is all.

It has been suggested by some that in accepting such an admittedly controversial client as Andrew Bolt, a barrister might risk being seen, in some social circles, to 'dirty his hands'. The fact that the case would necessarily involve exposing the claims of an Aboriginal woman and challenging her integrity, made it doubly risky for one's reputation in polite company at a time of increasing 'virtue signaling' on all things Indigenous. Australia was approaching a time when any public figure was just one thoughtless comment, tweet or joke away from ostracism and permanent cancellation. Perhaps, with the benefit of hindsight, that was a possible aim of the prosecution's strategy - to damage Bolt's reputation to such a degree and 'put him back in his box' that he would no longer dare comment on Aboriginal identity.

Melbourne society is very particular - like the moralising Victorians, to which the state is linked by name, Melbourne's socialites would run a mile from anyone they thought had the potential to sully their good name. A person's social diary would drain very quickly of invitations to Melbourne's social events if there was even a whiff of an association with the 'wrong people'. It was a credit to Young's professionalism that he did indeed accept this brief, but nevertheless, one can't help but wonder whether it did restrain, subconsciously or otherwise, the vigorousness of his advocacy to some degree. Was he ashamed of his client?

Of course, the above thoughts on whether the social niceties of Melbourne's judge and lawyer-loaded upper classes might

---

[56] *Wikipedia: Neil Young QC.*

have had an effect on the apparent poor showing of Young in defending Bolt is mere speculation. But the question still goes begging - why was Neil Young's line of defence of Bolt, in the words of Bolt's old sparring partner at the ABC, Jonathan Holmes,[57] "self-evidently absurd"?[8.32]

Why was it that on Day 1 of the proceedings, Young didn't see that a line of inquiry that pressed Pat Eatock on her claims to Aboriginality was one way to go in defending Bolt? Young showed no sign of recognising Pat for who she really was, one of those old classic Aussie ratbags, opportunists who would say and do outrageous things, anything for attention or action (some might think of Lidia Thorpe today?[58]) The Melbourne and Sydney of the 1960s, 70's and 80's was a mixing cauldron of aspirational working and lower middle classes, bursting forth as a wave of starry-eyed people - the hippies, feminists, Whitlam's graduates, opportunistic activists, strivers, social justice activists and even 'race-shifters' intent on making a New Society, while grabbing a bigger share of money and power along the way. Pat Eatock seemed to be part of this. The foment of the changing times gave her an opportunity to re-invent herself, as she openly described in a 1977 interview.[8.38]

But Neil Young QC seemed to have missed all this. If he had forensically listened to Pat's interview, or watched her film clips,[8.39] [8.40] he too might have recognised the real Pat Eatock and consequently been much more circumspect in accepting the claims she made.

However, there is one more small piece in this puzzle that goes some way to explaining why Andrew Bolt perhaps did not get the vigorous defence in court from Young he may have been looking for. In a close reading of the court transcripts there is a slight hint that Justice Bromberg may have warned off Mr Young from taking a particular line of enquiry, one which his client had anxiously expected his counsel to take.

---

[57]Bolt. A., *The many errors of Jonathan Holmes...*, *Herald Sun*, 7 May 2013
[58]Krishani Dhanji, 'AFP investigates Lidia Thorpe's claim she would "burn down" Parliament House', *Guardian Online*, 13 Oct 2025.

Some six months after the trial ended, Justice Bromberg delivered his written judgement that contained a critical finding: "It is important that nothing in the orders I make should suggest that it is unlawful for a publication to deal with racial identification including challenging the genuineness of the identification of a group of people."[59]

But this is not what His Honour had said in court, as reported by trial observer and historian Michael Connor:

> On the morning of Day 5, Bromberg said to Bolt's counsel, Neil Young QC: "Well, I don't think you will have a lot of trouble persuading me that any entrée into the debate as to who should be regarded as an Aboriginal would offend the Act."[60]

Given this direction by Bromberg J, maybe Bolt was right now to view the trial as a 'stitch-up'? His Honour had warned Bolt's counsel off pursuing a potentially fruitful line of enquiry: is Pat Eatock actually Aboriginal? In his written judgement, Bromberg J appears to contradict this verbal guidance given to Young during the case by now concluding it would not actually 'offend the Act' and would not have been unlawful to 'challenge' or 'debate as to who should be regarded as an Aboriginal'.

On that day in court, Mr Young QC demurred, and his client lost the best chance he had at exposing Eatock's false testimony as a 'white Aborigine', a fake with no Aboriginal ancestry at all.

---

[59] *Eatock v Bolt* [2011] at 461.
[60] Michael Connor, 'The White Aborigines Trial', *Quadrant Online*, 1 Nov 2011. Confirmed in *Eatock v Bolt*, Trans. Proc., Fed. Court (Vic) O/N 160844, 1 Apr 2011, Day 5, p360.

8.3.1   Just How Offendable was Pat Eatock?

I first read Bolt's article when someone rang me or sent me a message, and then I found it on the internet. When I saw it I was horrified. It was absolutely disgusting. I was angry and upset. I felt sick in the stomach.

I believe that Bolt's articles, the subject of these proceedings, are absolutely racist, and I was and remain deeply, deeply, offended. I have read each of the imputations and say [they are] quite offensive to me, and absolutely untrue, insofar as they relate to me.

Pat Eatock[61]

Of course as we know there's an extraordinary ability of people to take offense when it suits them and to indicate that this offence has occurred even before they fully felt it. Being offended is a dramatic capacity of human beings. It's a histrionic ability - you begin by pretending you're offended, you get a response, then you feel you are really offended and eventually you've worked yourself up into a state of anger which you cannot control.

Roger Scruton[62]

As Merkel read out Pat's witness statement, they both wanted Justice Bromberg to believe she was indeed 'deeply offended' by the words in Bolt's articles. Now maybe she was, but then again, maybe she wasn't - perhaps she was faking her feelings about being offended, just as much as it is now known she was faking her Aboriginality.

Young could have probed Eatock more on just how offended she really was. If he could show she wasn't really offended in any meaningful way, her case would be weakened. So why did Young not show the court the pugnacious side of Pat Eatock, the tough communist and political activist, who verbally gave as good as she got? Why did he allow her to portray herself to the court as some respectable, sweet little old

---

[61] *Eatock v Bolt*, Trans. Proc., Fed. Court (Vic) O/N 160844, Mon 28 Mar 2011, Day One, p58-9.
[62] See citation [6.21] by QR Code.

lady on a mobility scooter who was 'deeply offended' by Bolt's words, words that in previous years she would most likely have just rebuffed and moved on?

In 1972 while on a visit to Alice Springs, Pat Eatock was hurled some offensive abuse by a 'little old, very English, lady', abuse that she not only brushed off but went on further and *published herself* for all the world to see:

> The experience involved a little old, very English, lady shrivelled by the Centralian sun to several shades darker than me, who called me an "impudent half-breed" and "that arrogant woman from Canberra who has come up here to make trouble".[8.41]

This quotation indicates that in 1972 Pat Eatock was not shy about discussing her own skin colour, or that of her alleged abuser. Similarly, in a 1987 feature in the *Melbourne Age*, Eatock goes on the record to freely rebroadcast commentary about a challenge to her Aboriginality, the same type of challenging commentary that, in 2011 from Andrew Bolt, she would claim 'deeply offended' her:

> At the Women and Politics Conference in 1975 ... I was under constant attack from my Aboriginal sisters. Tolerance - if not complete forgiveness - was extended to me for my political consciousness of my working classness and femaleness, as well as my Aboriginality. But then a sister started a rumour that I was not Aboriginal at all. This charge was not made easier by originating from a sister-by-blood (my biological sister) in a futile attempt to retain her Queensland country town eminence as a member of the Junior Chamber of Commerce and president of the local Parents and Citizens Association. (Years later my mother accused me of 'destroying' my sister's life by 'coming out' as an Aborigine: my sister was forced to retreat into the anonymity of Brisbane's suburbia!)[8.22]

These quotations were an invitation for Young to push the door a little more open into the claims of Pat Eatock. He could have questioned whether an old experienced political fighter like Pat *really was offended* by Bolt's words, given she had dealt with such claims before. And why did so many other people, beyond his client, also seem to doubt her claim to genuine Aboriginality, including her own sister?

Maybe Neil Young QC didn't fully understand the world of Aboriginal politics and race relations. Perhaps that was a door he did not have the skills, or the determination, to push open, given his advertised professional specialties were 'commercial law practice, with substantial experience in corporations law, banking and finance, competition, taxation, mining and energy law and intellectual property'.[8.42]

Or maybe he knew exactly what needed doing, but his hands were tied by society's timidity when it came to critiquing anything to do with Aboriginal Australia, as concluded by court observer, historian Michael Connor:[63]

> In court the defence [by Neil Young] was constrained by political correctness and the straitjacket on free speech which already exists and which prevents the honest examination of Aboriginality — except if you are Aboriginal. The defence did not question the claimed Aboriginality of the litigants even though this was what the prosecution said the case was about. Let me rewrite that sentence and change one word: The defence **could** not question the claimed Aboriginality of the litigants even though this was what the prosecution said the case was about.

In the end, a bewildered Andrew Bolt found himself standing in court, alongside Neil Young QC and his metaphorically tied hands, as Justice Bromberg read out the reasons for Bolt's court loss. Had Young, as one rumour alleged it, expected the case to be lost but then ultimately be won on appeal? Not such a fanciful idea given the track record of the judgements by the 'frolicking' judge, Justice Bromberg, being overturned on appeal (see Chapter 8.1).

But the HWT decided quite quickly not to appeal the ruling,[64] thereby cementing in the minds of many members of the public that Bolt was 'guilty as charged'. As Bolt had

---

[63]Michael Connor, 'The White Aborigines Trial', *Quadrant Online*, 1 Nov 2011.
[64]Editorial, 'No appeal in Andrew Bolt case', *Herald Sun*, 20 Oct 2011.

recognised, he had needed to win the case first up 'in the court of public opinion' - a win on appeal was useless to him, the damage to his reputation had been done.[65]

8.4   The Aboriginal Law Students' Society

The Originators of the AHRC Complaint Against Bolt

> *The Bolt case ... You all know what it was about. It was interesting, and not well known, that the main reason for the case was that a group of Victorian Aboriginal law students felt particularly humiliated and intimidated by the Bolt articles. The Aboriginal Law Students' Society actually initiated the case and the nine Aboriginal people who gave evidence were Aboriginal leaders, professors, artists and writers ... were highly successful ... but felt a duty to the younger generation to stand up and say, you shouldn't have to be answerable to the world around you for being a fairer, rather than a darker, skinned Aboriginal person.*

Ron Merkel QC[66]

Locating any information regarding the society specifically known as The Aboriginal Law Students' Society, of whom Ron Merkel QC refers to as the original initiators of the AHRC complaint, has not been possible. However, Merkel was probably referring to a Victorian Incorporated Association known as the Indigenous Law Students and Lawyers Association of Victoria Inc., which was formed in 2006. Subsequently, it changed its name in 2007 to *Indigenous Law Students and Lawyers Association of Victoria Tarwirri Inc.* and then proceeded to acquire charity status under the Australian Charities and Not-for-Profits Commission.[67] In its latest published

---

[65] After the loss, I understand that Bolt turned down the HWT's offer to appeal - the stress and damage had been too great for him to contemplate repeating the process for another year or two. (Bolt, *pers. comm.*) As would be shown a decade later with the Cardinal George Pell case, a vindicating win on appeal, even in the High Court, takes such a massive toll that would-be appellants in non-criminal cases must really wonder whether it is worth it.

[66] Ron Merkel, 'Oration, Human Rights: Myths and Realities in the Year 2012', 11 Dec 2012, p11 & p22.[8.9]

[67] This is confirmed by one of Pat Eatock's co-applicants, Anita Heiss, confirming

financial statement, Tarwirri reports that it has revenues of $289,500, of which some 93%, or $271,000, is due to taxpayer-funded government grants.[8.43]

According to the Rules of the Association for Tarwirri, membership is based on race: 'A person is eligible to be a Full Member of the Association if the person is (1) an Indigenous Person, where Indigenous Person means a person who is of Australian Aboriginal and Torres Strait Islander descent; and identifies as an Australian Aboriginal or Torres Strait Islander; and is accepted as such by the community in which he or she lives or has lived.' As proof of 'descent' all the Association requires is a 'Confirmation of Aboriginal and/or Torres Strait Islander descent' (without defining exactly what that would entail) or simply 'signatures of two other existing Association members nominating you for membership'.[8.44]

Photographs of the members, published on the Tarwirri website, lend support to Merkel's claim that, 'a group of Victorian Aboriginal law students felt particularly humiliated and intimidated by the Bolt articles' and 'shouldn't have to be answerable to the world around [them] for being a fairer, rather than a darker, skinned Aboriginal person.' The photographs are of predominately 'fair-skinned' people whose claims to real, meaningful Aboriginality would certainly be expected to raise questions from a readership such as Bolt's.[8.45]

Many Australians would look at these apparently competent, ambitious and educated students, who appear to be fully assimilated into mainstream Victorian society, and wonder why they would need special, race-based recognition or financial and employment support. As Bolt indicated in his articles, his concern was that funding based on one's race is divisive and runs the risk of diverting funds from other Victorian students in real need, or from aspiring real Aboriginal students in remote and disadvantaged communities. The photographs

---

that an "Aislinn Martin (Tarwirri)" was part of her legal team. (Anita Heiss, 'Bolt decision: Anita Heiss hopes for more responsible media', *Crikey*, 28 Sept 2011.)

only reinforce suspicions within some of Bolt's readership that
there could be a rort going on by some Victorians to obtain
Aboriginal benefits when they only have a thin strand of Aboriginal descent, or perhaps none at all.

8.5   Joel Zyngier

Solicitor for the Prosecution

> *I was there at the beginning, and I was there at the end. I was
> in the courtroom when wit and humour became a race crime.
> I saw the torture they inflicted on Andrew Bolt for his wrong
> ideas and the pleasure they got from hurting him. I heard
> meanness and I saw hatred on people's faces—but they weren't
> the ones on trial. During the lunch break on the first day a
> woman said loudly, "I'm interested in anything against Bolt.
> This time he has bitten off more than he can chew." Back in
> the courtroom Eatock's solicitor, **Joel Zyngier**, greeted her
> with a kiss.*

Michael Connor[68]

In May 2009, a few weeks after Andrew Bolt's infamous 'white
Aborigines' articles appeared in the *Herald Sun*, a young Indigenous law graduate suggested to his or her employer at
the time, Holding Redlich Lawyers in Melbourne, that here
was an important matter that the firm should consider taking
up.[8.16]

The legal newsletter, *Probono News*, reported that the
unnamed Indigenous lawyer subsequently convinced Holding
Redlich that 'at issue [was] whether certain articles written
by Bolt ... had breached s.18C of the Racial Discrimination
Act 1975 by expressing views about them because of [their]
race, colour and/or ethnic origin.' Holding Redlich national
pro bono coordinator Linda Rubinstein said 'the lawyers and
applicants in this case are all acting entirely in the public interest.' The action wasn't 'seeking damages' but rather it was

---

[68]Michael Connor, 'The White Aborigines Trial', *Quadrant Online*, 1 Nov 2011.

aimed at protecting 'racial minorities from discrimination and the way in which legitimate social issues can be discussed'. The legal team was said to include:

> Lawyers **Joel Zyngier** and Natalie Dalpethado from Holding Redlich, [who] have put in a lot of the work on the matter recently, working closely with counsel ... [where] all the legal services for the applicants have been provided without charge to the applicants, and that includes senior counsel **Ron Merkel QC**, **Herman Borenstein SC**, supported by junior counsel, Claire Harris and Phoebe Knowles and the services of Holding Redlich as solicitor on the record. ([8.16] emphasis added.)

Given the huge amounts of personal unpaid time involved in *pro bono* cases, something extra is required to maintain commitment over the course of a case. This extra is often a 'passion' to make difference, or a drive to right an historical injustice for the clients involved. Perhaps the lawyers from Holding Redlich maintained their passion to see this case through to the end by drawing upon their senior counsel Ron Merkel's undoubted 'passion for human rights'. He was certainly known to be passionate about issues affecting Aboriginal people, as reported by the *Sydney Morning Herald* in 2014:

> Perhaps surprisingly, Merkel's passion for human rights did not come directly from his migrant parents ... Rather, Merkel's interest in taking on unpopular causes and pursing a legal career was fueled in Year 12 at Melbourne High, where two "sensational" teachers pushed him to think and write about subjects he had never reflected on (like the plight of Aboriginal and Torres Strait Islander people)...
>
> Merkel immersed himself in a range of land rights and discrimination cases, and he looks back on the period as a kind of tipping point. "Justice had been used as a weapon against Aboriginal people since colonisation. Now it was being used as something that could support them." [69]

This case would provide a young solicitor like Zyngier with a very professional entry into how Merkel used justice 'as a

---

[69] Michael Gordon, 'SMH in Lunch with Ron Merkel', *Sydney Morning Herald*, 29 Aug 2014.

weapon [not] against Aboriginal people [but] as something that could support them'. And perhaps there was an additional benefit that helped maintain momentum in the case. To *be seen* to be undertaking such a case might provide the lawyers with social justice credentials greatly admired if one moved in politically Left or liberal-minded circles. As the woman demonstrated at the trial when she exclaimed for all to hear, "I'm interested in anything against Bolt. This time he has bitten off more than he can chew", there were those who wore their anti-Bolt attitude as a badge of honour. Perhaps when this woman was 'greeted with a kiss' in court by Zyngier it was a recognition that he too was such a badge wearer.

Bolt's commentary is very 'triggering' to those of the political Left, especially academics. This is illustrated by how frequently his words are critiqued, criticised, ridiculed and even attacked in articles posted on the popular online academic magazine, *The Conversation.*[8.46] One academic, Steve Mickler, the Professor of Communication Studies and Head of the School of Media, Creative Arts and Social Inquiry at Curtin University in Western Australia even published a diatribe on Bolt's commentary, in which he made extraordinary claims:[70]

> The rights of First Nations peoples are 'racist', left-wing activists are 'fascists' and immigration has become tantamount to a 'foreign invasion'. These are some of the core concepts found in the daily demagoguery of 'Australia's most read' social and political commentator, Andrew Bolt. They are routinely packaged as being underpinned by patriotism, conservative values and egalitarian principles. Yet, as this book argues, Bolt's commentary frequently resonates with the ideas and sentiments of the Far Right — ultra-nationalism, cultural chauvinism and a reactionary hostility to progressive thought.[71]

Professor Marcia Langton AO has also been critical of what she has labelled Bolt's, 'shock jock' business practice.[72] These

---

[70]Steve Mickler, *Andrew Bolt, the Far Right and the First Nations - Deconstructing a Demogogue*, University of Western Australia Publishing, 2017.

[71]Mickler was emailed in an attempt to discuss his claims but no answer was received.

[72]'Andrew Bolt is a very successful businessman ... his business model uses the shock

academics are entitled to argue that Bolt was a 'shock jock'[73] and his tone could be perhaps even offensive to some, but one needs to look beyond any perceived 'incivility' of Bolt's wording - beyond the 'clickbait' used by tabloid journalism to drive traffic - and instead focus on Bolt's core message. It was Bolt alone who identified a rising trend of white Australians choosing to identify as Aboriginal and soaking up resources, which Bolt warned would come at the expense of genuine Aboriginal people in real need. It was also Bolt's courage in exposing fake Aboriginal academics that has now prompted other academics[74] and commentators[75] to finally come forward and denounce, directly or indirectly, these fake Aborigines and the damage they were causing.

Unfortunately, the undoubtedly well-meaning desire by Zyngier to help Aboriginal people who are disadvantaged or discriminated against now appears to have been derailed by his belief that prosecuting on behalf of Pat Eatock was the way to do it. For not only did Eatock turn out to be not Aboriginal in any meaningful way, as Bolt had correctly claimed, but another of the 'fair-skinned' Aborigines that Zyngier's weapon-

---

jock practice of alarming the audience on a matter that causes resentment among ordinary Australians with an instance of a particular outrage against their standards of decency. The claims that he makes need not be true, but they need to cause anger among his audience and identify the enemy presenting a threat to the norms of this audience ... He reports that his audience size is estimated at 300,000. Bolt presents himself as a fearless truth-teller, defying the state, the judiciary and, most important, the purveyors of politically correctness in defence of common sense. Offence is at the core part of his business model.' - Marcia Langton, 'Keeping Andrew Bolt in business', *The Saturday Paper*, 22 Mar 2014.

[73] Bolt is hardly a 'shock jock' in the league that radio hosts Alan Jones, Derryn Hinch (who became a parliamentarian) or Stan Zemanek were. Surprisingly we never hear of the academic Left criticising the likes of say, the non-conservatives, Clementine Ford, Lidia Thorpe and Yassmin Abdel-Magied, who by all accounts have said and done things much more 'shocking' than Bolt ever has.

[74] Moore, T., & Pybus, C., 'Myth-making Isn't the Right Way to 'Indigenise' Our Universities', *Quillette*, 26 June 2022; See Peter Sutton & Keryn Walshe in *Wikipedia: Farmers or Hunter-Gatherers?*; Geoffrey Blainey in Frank Chung, 'Author Bruce Pascoe's best-selling Aboriginal history book Dark Emu debunked', *news.com online*, 12 Jun 2021.

[75] Nyunggai Warren Mundine, 'Where was scrutiny of Bruce Pascoe's claims in Dark Emu?', *The Australian*, 24 Jun 2021; Henry Ergas, 'Scholarly light cast on Dark Emu claims', *The Australian*, 18 Jun 2021. See also - Patrick McCauley, 'Why Did Exposing 'Dark Emu' Take So Very Long?', *Quadrant online*, 24 Jul 2021.

isation of justice sought to support, Geoff Clark, turned out
to be a convicted thief and fraudster who is now languishing
in gaol.[8.15]

   Too often in the life of the Left, 'the road to hell is paved
with good intentions'. Ron Merkel had seen this before in a
case where justice was weaponised by 'men of zeal' on behalf
of Aboriginal people in the pastoral industry. In commenting on the 1966 Equal Pay Case, Merkel understood that the
unintended consequences of legal cases can be profoundly dam-
aging:

> The greatest dangers to Indigenous Australians lurk in insid-
> ious encroachment by men of zeal, well-meaning, but without
> understanding...
>
> One of the most egregious and harmful acts caused to Aborig-
> inal people in Australia was the Equal Pay case in the 1960s,
> when the industrial tribunal, in what was plainly perceived
> to be a fair and equitable approach, decided that Aboriginal
> rural workers should have equal pay. The consequence of that
> decision was that it devastated Aboriginal people and com-
> munities in remote areas where the Aborigines had settled
> on their country at cattle stations where they were employed
> as stockmen and domestic help in and around those stations.
> Once they were given the right to equal pay, they were too
> expensive to retain and the stations moved to aircraft and
> other cost saving measures, rather than continuing to employ
> Aboriginal people as stockmen, and domestic help. Those
> communities then lost their employment, lost their life on
> country, and became slum-dwellers in most of the surround-
> ing towns, and that has never changed. It was catastrophic.
> It was well-meaning. It was an insidious encroachment, but
> without understanding the consequences.[76]

It would interesting to know if Merkel had forewarned Zyngier and the other *pro bono* lawyers that these 'well-meaning'
cases, like the one they were about to embark upon with 'zeal'
against Andrew Bolt, could end up being a total disaster for
the clients they sought to benefit. With hindsight, the results from *Eatock v Bolt* have indeed been a disaster for gen-

---

[76]Ron Merkel, 'Oration, Human Rights: Myths and Realities in the Year 2012', 11
   Dec 2012, p12. (see QR code [8.9])

uine Aboriginal people in real need. Their organisations are being infiltrated by large numbers of Australians willing to self-identify as a 'fair-skinned' Aboriginal person. These interlopers, who may or may not have any Aboriginal ancestry, have no fear of exposure after being being given a cloak of protection by Justice Bromberg's judgement. Just as Merkel had observed that the livelihoods of Aboriginal stockmen and domestics had been destroyed by the the white do-gooders from down south in the Equal Wages Pay case,[77] the same is now happening to the livelihoods of genuine, and generally more disadvantaged, Aboriginal people as they compete with their 'fair skinned' brethren for scarce government resources.

The reality of the relations between Aboriginal people and white Australia over the past one hundred and fifty years had been astutely summarised by Commonwealth public servant, the late Jeremy Long. He noted that:

> As it has so often happened in the course of the history of government dealings with Aborigines, the sequence goes something like this: scandals in the North, followed by alarm in the southern capitals about stories of what was going on "up North" ... Reports of incidents involving conflict between Aboriginal and other people [and] reports of mistreatment and ill-treatment of Aborigines ... produce a response that "something ought to be done". This results in pressure on governments - governments are embarrassed, questions are asked in London, as well as Sydney, Melbourne and other cities - particularly pressure on the Federal Government.[78]

Nothing has changed in modern Australia. The knee-jerk responses are still the same, with reports of 'incidents involving conflict' having money thrown at them by Canberra[79] and the perceived mistreatment of 'fair skinned' Aboriginal people still eliciting the same response from 'men of zeal' in the southern

---

[77] See Trove: Eric Wicks (ed), 'The Equal Pay Case', *Smoke Signals, Victorian Aborigines Advancement League*, April-June 1965, p15-17.

[78] Jeremy Long, The Go-Betweens, State Library of the Northern Territory, Occasional Paper No. 31, 1992, p1-2.

[79] Matt Garrick, 'Details of $250m in promised funding for Alice Springs, "amid a crime wave" in Central Australia to be revealed in federal budget', *ABC News*, 9 May 2023.

capitals that 'something ought to be done'. In the 'mistreatment' claimed by the fake Aborigine, Pat Eatock, that 'something' meant launching a legal case against Andrew Bolt in 2011.

However, fourteen years later, the evidence shows that Bolt was correct after all and the legal action against him was in fact a great injustice: *there was* an increasing trend of white Australians choosing that minor strand of their ancestry (even if it wasn't there) to self-identify as Aboriginal and claim resources that were intended for genuine Aboriginal people in real need.[80] The continuing failures in the *Closing the Gap* measures is further evidence in support of Bolt's analysis that funds were not getting to the most deserving.[81] Had Bolt's ability to speak freely on these matters not been curtailed by 'men of zeal', like Ron Merkel and Joel Zygnier, there is every possibility that the disastrous course race relations has taken in Australia over the past decade may have been averted.[82] But instead, Bolt was 'stitched up' for stating the obvious, with commentary that turned out to be prescient and true:

> that's modern race politics at our universities and anywhere else where grants and privileges are now doled out. Hear that scuffling at the trough? That's the sound of black people being elbowed out by white people shouting, "but I'm Aboriginal too." They are the 'white Aborigines' - people who out of their multi-stranded but largely European genealogy decided to identify with the thinnest of all those strands ... the Aboriginal one.[83]

---

[80] *See also* Pauline Hanson, 'Why Cut the NIAA?', *One Nation*, 4 Mar 2025.

[81] Productivity Commission Media Release, 'Annual Data Compilation Report' - National Agreement on Closing the Gap, 30 Jul 2025: "The latest ... performance ... in *Closing the Gap*, shows mixed progress, with [only] four of 19 targets on track ... Outcomes are continuing to worsen in four targets: adult imprisonment; children in out-of-home care; suicide, & children's development. Outcomes are improving but not on track in: life expectancy; healthy birth-weights; year 12 or equivalent qualifications; tertiary qualifications; youth engagement; and appropriately sized housing. Outcomes are improving and on track in four targets: preschool program enrollments; employment; and land mass and sea country subject to legal rights and interests.

[82] Dana Morse, 'Survey finds "significant" rise in racism towards Indigenous people in past decade', *ABC News*, 24 Jun 2025.

[83] Andrew Bolt, 'White fellas in the black', *Herald Sun*, 21 Aug 2009.

For References link - see QR code on page (xv)

References

[8.1]   Andrew Dodd. *The Law Report interview on Bolt court case.* 4 Oct 2011.

[8.2]   Dale Smith. *The Law Report interview on Bolt court case.* 4 Oct 2011.

[8.3]   Glenn Martin. *When Journalists go off on a frolic', AJOA.* 21 Aug 2021.

[8.4]   Tobias Lonnquist. *The Trend Towards Purposive Statutory Interpretaion.*

[8.5]   Amanda Stoker. *Labor appoints the most 'radical' hard-left activist as president of the ALRC, SkyNews.* 25 June 2023.

[8.6]   Ron Merkel. *The Law Report, ABC Radio.* 23 May 2006.

[8.7]   Herman Borenstein SC. *Biography, Vic Bar.* 2024.

[8.8]   SBS. *Bolt articles insulting, court hears.* 5 April 2011.

[8.9]   Ron Merkel QC. *Human Rights Oration.* 11 Dec 2012.

[8.10] Youtube. *Andrew Bolt Attacked.* 2017.

[8.11] SnodgerMedia. *Education Film - Eatock v Bolt.* 2016.

[8.12] ABC. *Angry Bolt rejects 'eugenics' claim.* 29 March 2011.

[8.13] Lisa Pine. *Nazi Family Policy 1933-1945.* Berg Oxford, 1997, p162-3.

[8.14] CSIRO. *CSIRO Indigenous Employment.* 2025.

[8.15] ABC. *Former ATSIC head Geoff Clark jailed.* 29 Nov 2024.

[8.16] HoldingRedlich. "REPORT:Racial Discrimination vs. Free Speech Test Case Being Run Pro Bono". In: *Probono News* 65 (April 2011).

[8.17] Pat Eatock. *AHRC Complaint Form Eatock v Bolt.* 13 April 2010.

[8.18] Hall Greenland. *Australian Dictionary of Biography - Lucy Harriet Eatock.* 2005.

[8.19] *ASIO File-Eatock, June Patricia Volume 1, 1965 - 1974, NAA: A6119, 3641.*

[8.20] *ASIO MEMO - Pat Eatock, incitement to violence, NAA A6119, 3641.* 5 May 1972.

[8.21] *ASIO Current Intel Brief-Pat Eatock, NAA A6119, 3641.* 26 July 1972.

[8.22] The Age. *This Feeling of Lost Power.* 6 March 1987.

[8.23] University of Melbourne. *Roberta Sykes Indigenous Education Foundation: The Roberta Sykes Scholarship.*

[8.24] Canberra Times. *Reply to Critic.* 23 July 1973.

[8.25] Canberra Times. *Mrs Eatock Going to ANU.* 21 Nov 1972.

[8.26] The Age. *Embassy sets crisis day.* 26 July 1972.

[8.27] The Age. *Aboriginal Representatives meet Minister.* 27 July 1972, p5.

[8.28] The Indigenous Law Centre. *Aboriginal peoples' right to vote in NSW 1823-present.*

[8.29] *Electoral Rolls for Roderick Eatock 1933.*

[8.30] Narrabri North Western Courier. *Coroner's Enquiry - Death of G L Eatock.* 30 April 1925 p2.

[8.31] *NSW Coroner's Record Book 1925, Entry No. 580, third line.*

[8.32] Jonathan Holmes. *Bolt, Bromberg and a profoundly disturbing judgment.* 30 Sept 2011.

[8.33] Chris Merritt. *A Question of principle rather than money.* 2 Apr 2011.

[8.34] Dr Wayne Atkinson. *Conflict of Interest.* undated.

[8.35] Gavin Silbert SC. *Ethical Cross Examination podcast at 00:17.* 2023.

[8.36] Neil Young KC. *Post-Trial Interview with Neil Young QC.* 2016.

[8.37] NGV. *Neil Young QC, NGV Foundation Board Member.* 2019-2020.

[8.38] Youtube. *Pat Eatock being interviewed about her political life and her father, Roderick Eatock.* 1977.

[8.39] Youtube. *Pat Eatock with a Version of her Declaring her Aboriginality.* ca1990s?

[8.40] Youtube. *Pat Eatock speaks of her early political life of as a black, feminist, activist.* ca1990s?

[8.41] Pat Eatock. *A (Racist) Town Like Alice, The Tribune.* 25 April 1972.

[8.42] Neil Young KC. *New Chambers Biography.* 2025.

[8.43] ACNC. *Excerpt of Charity Staus for Tarwirri Inigenous Law Students and Lawyers of Victoria.* 2024.

[8.44] Tarwirri. *Indigenous Law Students and Lawyers Assoc. - Application Form: Annexure A.* 2024.

[8.45] Tarwirri. *Indigenous Law Students and Lawyers of Victoria.* 2024.

[8.46] The Conversation. *Articles on Andrew Bolt.* Accessed 1 Jan 2025.

Part III

Chapter 9

Legacies of *Eatock v Bolt*

> *Occasionally a case arises which makes the word*
> *Kafkaesque appear to be a description of fact rather than*
> *fiction. The present is such a case.*

Former Justice Ron Merkel[1]

Just imagine that instead of it being 1914, Franz Kafka, the novelist from Prague, finds himself writing in Melbourne 100 years into the future. His work is still the same fusion of realism and the fantastic, featuring protagonists facing bizarre or surrealistic predicaments and incomprehensible bureaucratic powers. He had followed the bizarre *Eatock v Bolt* trial in the local newspapers - the chief complainant turns out to be a total fake, supported by an establishment determined to crush the man who has pointed out the obvious. Franz loads his typewriter and begins:

The Trial

Franz Kafka

Chapter One

Someone must have been telling lies about Andrew B., he knew he had done nothing wrong but, one morning, he was arrested...

---

[1] Speaking with regard to an immigration case in 1997.[9.1] p14.

And so the futuristic edition of Kafka's novel opens, with the same words but a new protagonist, about 'a case which makes the word *Kafkaesque* appear to be a description of fact rather than fiction'. *The Trial*, one of Kafka's major works, and perhaps his most pessimistic, was a surreal story of an ordinary young man who finds himself caught up in the mindless bureaucracy of the law, resulting in a constant struggle against an unreasoning and unreasonable authority.[2] It is often considered to be an imaginative anticipation of totalitarianism.[3] So deft was Kafka's prose at detailing nightmarish settings in which characters are crushed by nonsensical, blind authority, that writers began using his name as an adjective, Kafkaesque, a mere sixteen years after his death. Ron Merkel was still doing the same sixty years later to describe some immigration cases. With what we now know, Merkel could well have been speaking of Bolt's case too.

With hindsight, not only was Andrew Bolt's defeat in court a descent into his own Kafkaesque nightmare, it was also just another step for all Australians on the road to the totalitarianism of Aboriginalisation - towards a society where the national flag would become just a 'flag of convenience', relegated to its third place; a nation where ideologues and activists would welcome citizens to their own, but now increasingly Indigenous country; where Australia, 'always was, always will be' Aboriginal land, as some activists claim it has been for 250,000 years before Cook;[4] and a place where ordinary people are expected to suspend their intelligence and accept a 'white' Australian with very distant or even no Aboriginal ancestry as being fully 'Aboriginal' with special rights, privileges and funding. Kafka would have understood that his novel was now non-fiction in modern Australia.

Thirteen years after *Eatock v Bolt*, and with the spectacular loss of the 2023 Voice referendum and the failure of the

---

[2] *The above synopsis is paraphrased and based on Wikipedia: Kafkaesque.*
[3] *Britannica Online: Franz Kafka.*
[4] Dampney, J. & Otto, T., 'Not for white people', *NT News Online*, 16 Sept 2024.

Misinformation Bill in 2024, ordinary Australians are finally waking up to being on 'the road to totalitarianism'. Perhaps this is part of the valuable legacy of *Eatock v Bolt* - history will show that the shock of Bolt's loss became one of the first of many, subtle, subconscious turning points where ordinary Australians began to realise their country is being hijacked and changed by a number of subversive, ideological minorities. Many Australians do not like what they saw in the Bolt case; hopefully the push-back will continue to gather momentum.

9.1 A Positive Outcome from *Eatock v Bolt*

9.1.1 Methodology in Exposing Modern-Day 'Fakes'

The genealogical work presented by *Dark Emu Exposed* in exposing fakes has earned the wrath of some very high-profile critics. Professor Marcia Langton AO for example, has rebuked the *Dark Emu Exposed* website in her defence of the ancestry claims of Professors Bruce Pascoe[9.2] and Lisa Jackson Pulver.[9.3]

Why then has not *Dark Emu Exposed* also been dragged before the AHRC to justify its claims, which perhaps the subjects may find as 'offensive, insulting and humiliating' as Bolt's articles were to Pat Eatock and her group of 'white Aborigines'? The reason can be found in the *Eatock v Bolt* judgement itself. After Justice Bromberg's decision, the two opposing camps of public opinion raced off to their respective ideological corners without really understanding the consequences of what he had determined.

The winners had their biases confirmed that Bolt was a 'racist', and anyone who questioned the ancestry or motives of a 'fair-skinned' Australian claiming to be Aboriginal was a 'racist' too. This is the line that Professor Langton appears to have taken. Those on the losing side hollered that Bolt's, and

by implication all Australians', free speech would henceforth
be seriously curtailed simply because the judge did not like
the 'tone' or 'manner' of Bolt's articles. This explained the
position of organisations such as the Institute of Public Affairs,
who believed:

> You can't pretend to believe in freedom of speech ... because
> ... Section 18D doesn't restore the egregious breach of freedom
> of speech contained in section 18C when a judge is able to
> rule that exemptions don't apply because your tone is not
> acceptable.[5]

These are the two polar positions that most commentators and
the public took upon learning of Bolt's loss in court. However, a close reading of the 470-paragraph judgement, along
with Melbourne University Law Professor Adrienne Stone's
insightful review,[6] provided a legally acceptable methodology
for undertaking the exposure of fake Aboriginal claimants in
the future.

As Professor Stone observed:

> Bromberg J was at pains to point out that nothing in the
> orders [I] make should suggest that it is unlawful for a publi-
> cation to deal with racial identification including challenging
> the genuineness of the identification of a group of people. I
> have not found Mr Bolt ... to have contravened s18C simply
> because the Newspaper Articles dealt with subject matter of
> that kind. I have found a contravention because of the man-
> ner [and 'tone'[7]] in which that subject matter was dealt with.[8]

This guidance meant that *Dark Emu Exposed* can legally comply with Bromberg J's findings by:

---

[5]Simon Breheny, 'Opinion: Section 18C Must Go As It Curbs Freedom Of Speech',
Institute of Public Affairs, 14 Oct 2016.

[6]*Eatock v Bolt* [2011] FCA 1103; Adrienne Stone, 'The Ironic Aftermath of Eatock v
Bolt'. *Melbourne University Law Review*, Vol. 38, 2015, p926-42.

[7]"In relation to the sub-group constituted by the individuals named in the Newspaper Articles, the language, tone and gratuitous asides contained in the Newspaper
Articles were likely to have contributed to the likely offence, insult and humiliation
of the people in that group." – Bromberg J, *Eatock v Bolt* [2011] 197 FCR 261, [415].

[8]Stone, A. (2015) *op cit.*, p937, citing *Eatock v Bolt* [2011] 197 FCR 261, 364–5 [461].
Also listen here to Professor Stone. [9.4]

- only selecting subjects who have made public claims of Aboriginality and have received publicly funded benefits based on those claims. Thus, there should be a 'public interest' defence available;

- undertaking genealogical research using qualified staff, in good faith, diligently and accurately, and based on factual evidence like official records;

- contacting the subjects to give them ample opportunity to refute, or suggest amendments to, the findings prior to publication;

- publishing the findings in such detail and balance that readers can make up their own minds regarding those findings or 'challenges', and

- expressing or publishing the findings in a 'manner' and 'tone' that is not uncivil.

To date, this guidance seems to have worked - *Dark Emu Exposed* has continued to publicly expose fakes but none of the subjects investigated have sent a Concerns Notice (for defamation) nor launched any complaints at the AHRC. This outcome would appear to be an example of what Stone described as 'the Ironic Aftermath of *Eatock v Bolt*', namely that:

> contrary to what was frequently heard during this public debate, it is possible to engage in offensive, insulting, or even humiliating and intimidating speech on questions of race, provided the circumstances fall within ... the defences in s 18D [which] are extensive and they significantly qualify the operation of s 18C in a wide range of contexts that are important to public debate. Artists, academics, journalists, public commentators and anyone who can show 'a genuine purpose in the public interest' can rely on s 18D.[9]

The ABC's Jonathan Holmes came to a similar conclusion:

> Let's suppose for a moment that some or all of ... the 'light-skinned Aborigines' named in his columns had sued Andrew Bolt and News Ltd for defamation. It seems to me that most of them could easily argue that they had been defamed and ... if Bolt had pleaded the defences of truth and fair comment, he might not have succeeded, because his research was so sloppy.

---

[9] Adrienne Stone (2015) *op cit.*, p937.

The facts in his articles were not, in legal terms, 'truly stated'.

But let's suppose for a moment that he had been far more diligent than he seems to have been and that the facts he adduced in the columns were substantially accurate; that he got the ancestry and upbringing of the 'fair-skinned Aborigines' that were his targets right; that he accurately described the jobs they had held and the qualifications needed to get them; and so on.

Then, in my view, he should have been able to succeed with a fair comment defence against defamation. The court doesn't have to have liked his opinions, or thought them reasonable, or in any other way approved of them. It's enough that Bolt honestly held the views he outlined, and they are based on true facts.[10]

Thus, it is important to appreciate that Bromberg J was saying that any publication can 'deal' - do research, conclude, discuss and publish findings, facts and opinions - in 'challenging the genuineness of the identification of a group of people' *provided* one does not do it in a 'manner' - by 'the language, tone and structure' - that would contravene s 18C (using conduct that 'humiliated, offended, insulted or intimidated' by reason of 'race, colour or ethnic origin.)

This finding by Bromberg J provides the legal legitimacy, as far as potentially contravening the Racial Discrimination Act (RDA) is concerned, underpinning the genealogical work published by Andrew Bolt or *Dark Emu Exposed*. When a public person relies upon their family genealogy to define or further their career, or to make public policy decisions that affect the wider community, then that person should be open to others, such as *Dark Emu Exposed*, critiquing their genealogical claims without the threat of running foul of the RDA. This protection has now been established by Justice Bromberg.

Thus, *Eatock v Bolt* may have actually resulted in a fair balance being achieved in the free speech versus discrimination debate regarding Aboriginality. Public figures can now have the genuineness of their beliefs regarding their own Abo-

---

[10]see QR Code [9.14]

riginal identity 'challenged' by critics using commentary and opinion with good faith, acting in the public interest, as long as they avoid making erroneous assertions unsupported by facts.[11] Defamation laws also provide an additional measure of protection to the reputations of the aggrieved.

This interplay between being able exercise one's free speech to challenge a public person's claims to Aboriginality, using factual research findings produced in good faith in the public interest, versus that person's ability to seek redress under the RDA and defamation laws, was to play out in the very high-profile case of the Attorney General of South Australia.

9.1.2 'Challenging' The Hon. Kyam Maher

In 2022, with the election of Peter Malinauskas's Labor government, Kyam Maher was sworn in as South Australia's first Aboriginal Attorney General.

It wasn't long before *Dark Emu Exposed* began receiving emails from Aboriginal people in South Australia expressing doubts about Maher's claims to Aboriginality. The story began to unfold publicly in early 2023 on Andrew Bolt's, 'The Bolt Report' on *Sky News Australia*, a partial transcript of which is produced as follows:

Bolt: It's now three weeks since I showed you [Bolt's audience] documents and other evidence suggesting that South Australian Attorney General Kyam Maher's claims to be Aboriginal is almost certainly false. I wrote the same in newspapers around the country[12] but "hello?", three weeks later where's Kyam Maher to tell me I'm wrong and to say, "hey no, here are the proofs"?

As I showed you, skilled genealogists from *Dark Emu Exposed* found the available records for Maher, who claims to be an

---

[11][9.5] at 381, 382 & 392.

[12]Andrew Bolt, 'White media turns a blind eye to 'fake' Aboriginals - The strangest thing is that no one dares ask politician Kyam Maher if he – like thousands of other Australians – is pretending to be what he's not.', *Herald Sun*, 27 Feb 2023.

initiated Aborigine. They do not show a single Aboriginal ancestor ... Maybe, I mean, I could be wrong but the weird thing is that Maher suddenly doesn't want to talk at all about being Aboriginal. Not many people dare ask him either, which is odd. I mean, he is South Australia's top legal figure. Shouldn't they at least ask – Are you what you say?

But huge credit to, of all things – an ABC journalist!, **David Bevin** - for trying last week, although Maher simply would not respond:

David Bevan: Are you going to respond to those...

Kyam Mayer (*interrupting*): No, no I'm not David.

Bevan: You're not going to...

Maher: No.

Bevan: You're not going to dignify them?

Maher: Absolutely not!

long silence while Bevan carefully considers his next question

Bevan: Are you going to sue?

Maher: Um, I'm, I'm just not going to dignify some of the, and it has been exceptionally disappointing some of the things that, in a whole range of areas we've seen, you know, some of this debate descend into; and I know it's a topic that you brought up before David and is it, you know, is it really worth it if we're going to see some of the commentary we hear as part of this and yeah I think it actually is worth it...

Bolt: Not the answer I'd expect from an Aboriginal man who can prove it. Bevan tried again:

Bevan: But, if you and the Premier have brought your, for want of a better word "ancestry" into the public arena doesn't it follow that you should be open to questions about it, as unpleasant as this is...

Maher (*interrupting*): Yeah, nah/nup, it's not something I brought into the public arena, David, it's others who have brought it in and um, and if, if...

Bevan (*emphatically interrupting*): But you did!

Maher: it's not a path that I'm going to go down and uh, if it's a path that commentators want to go down with, with people of the Jewish Community, the Vietnamese community, they're welcome to, but it's not something I'm going to commentate on.

Bolt: Pardon? His Aboriginality is not something he's put in the public arena? I mean really, he's traded on it! His post with Aboriginal face paint. He's given interviews about it.[13]

The above set of exchanges perfectly illustrates the positive outcomes from the findings of *Eatock v Bolt*. Two political commentators, Bolt and Bevan, raised publicly the topic of 'challenging the genuineness of the identification' of one of Australia's most legally powerful people, the Attorney General of South Australia, in regard to his own declared identification as an Aboriginal man. Bolt and Bevan were protected by Justice Bromberg's ruling - they were 'commenting' or providing an 'opinion' on well-researched 'facts', they adopted a civil 'tone' and 'manner', and they gave Maher an opportunity to respond and present his side of the story, and even, as suggested by Bevan, to sue for defamation, or to ignore his critics, as the case may be. To date Maher has chosen the latter path - no one has received any proof from Maher or his office to support his claims of Aboriginal descent, nor has to date a Concerns Notice been received by any of the parties involved.

The implication that listeners and viewers were likely to have drawn from these exchanges was that Maher was at best avoiding the questions because he actually had no proof to back up his claims of Aboriginality or, at worst, he knew he was mistaken to believe that he was of Aboriginal descent.[14]

---

[13]See full *Bolt Report* here:[9.6]

[14]Or, more perversely, perhaps Maher simply closed his mind off to the issue so as not to, as he says, 'dignify' the commentators with an answer. One always has to keep in mind our disclaimer (see front page (ii)) - perhaps Maher does have Aboriginal ancestry that he has discovered by say, DNA analysis, but which is

This is important. It doesn't get more worrying for Australians than this; as a Minister of the Crown, Maher appears to be either 'reckless' in that he is making serious claims about his own ancestry without first exercising some basic scholarship, by himself or with the aid of a genealogist, to actually determine if in fact he is truly of Aboriginal descent; or more worryingly, some might wonder whether he has potentially committed an offence by knowingly making false statements regarding his Aboriginal ancestry.

Some people might have wondered why there were no media photographs of Kyam Maher, SA's first Aboriginal Attorney General and Aboriginal Affairs Minister, putting his own ballot paper into the ballot box during the historic SA First Nations Voice election. Traditionally, a classic media photoshoot is for politicians to be photographed in their local voting booths, smiling alongside their spouse, as they push the voting form through the slot of the ballot box. But not in the case of Kyam Maher - no such photograph of the historic first elections for the SA Voice to Parliament has come to light despite an extensive search. Why not?

Surely Maher has a Certificate of Aboriginality or a signed Statutory Declaration that confirms his status as a 'First Nations Person', thus giving him the right to vote in the Aboriginal elections? One would imagine that voting without either of these would lead a person to be open to a charge of fraud.

---

undocumented by records, and he wishes to keep this as a family secret. This is fully understandable if he was just a private citizen. But he is a state Attorney General who emphasised his claimed Aboriginality when he was appointed. He then legislated the South Australia First Nations Voice Act 2023 [9.7], an Act that brought into existence a form of electoral 'apartheid' - a race-based, additional political 'platform for Aboriginal and Torres Strait Islander people to be better heard by government so that they have more of a say in the decisions that affect their lives.' (from *Preamble of the Act*) Maher is therefore making public policy that affects all South Australians, Aboriginal and non-Aboriginal alike, so the appearance of his own claims to Aboriginality becomes crucial to upholding the very integrity of the legislation that he introduced. Additionally, the research into Maher's claims for Aboriginality originally partially arose in response to a request from the family of the late Anangu man, George Kenmore, from APY Lands.[9.8] The family and other Anangu elders were deeply disturbed by Maher's alleged efforts to become an initiated Anangu man despite his having been born in PNG and having no real family or cultural connections to APY Lands.

Certainly the South Australian Premier, Peter Malinauskas, must be confident that Maher has all his 'paperwork' in order, as he alluded to in a discussion with Senator Jacinta Nampijinpa Price on the ABC's *Q&A* program.[9.9] Yet, one person who was a little confused by Maher's evasiveness was the Hon. Nicola Centofanti, the Leader of the Liberal Opposition in the SA Legislative Council. For on the 9th of April 2024, she rose in the chamber and asked Maher a direct question that had been troubling many observers:

> My question is to the Minister for Aboriginal Affairs regarding the South Australian Aboriginal Voice to Parliament elections. Did the minister cast his democratic right in the South Australian Aboriginal Voice to Parliament elections and, if so, in which region did the Minister for Aboriginal Affairs cast his vote?

Maher's answer was worthy of a masterful politician:

> Similarly to, for example, the Governor at state elections not casting a vote in the state elections, as the minister responsible I didn't cast a vote but I very much look forward to when I am not the minister and can cast my vote in these elections.[9.10]

This is a surprising reason given that during the 2023 Voice Referendum the Federal Minister for Indigenous Australians, Aboriginal woman Linda Burney, openly posed for photographs as she inserted her Yes-marked ballot into the voting box.[15] Presumably she had no qualms, as both an Aboriginal woman and the minister responsible, in voting in a Voice to Parliament related referendum. Further probing by the South Australian Opposition a month later only provided another opportunity for Maher to elaborate on his reason for not voting in his own legislated Voice elections:

> I have had a number of discussions with a range of people about the operations of the Voice and general protocols in

---

[15] Amber Schultz, "...inside the polling centre Burney proudly held up her ballot paper marked 'Yes'. Burney said she had 'butterflies' in her stomach while casting her vote, but was optimistic about the referendum outcome", *WAtoday Online*, October 14, 2023.

terms of democratic institutions. As I have said, my advice was that in state elections, by convention, the Governor does not vote, and I made the decision, as the person who is responsible for the administration of the legislation and ultimately that act, that I would not vote in these elections. As I have said in response to the question before, I very much look forward to my participation in the First Nations Voice voting in years to come when I am not the minister responsible.[16]

Kyam Maher was holding his ground and, as he told Karla Grant on her SBS *Living Black* program[9.11], he was not going to 'dignify' challenges to his self-identity with a detailed answer, no matter who raised them. Australians can read into this what they will.

9.2   A Mixed Outcome from *Eatock v Bolt*

9.2.1   Drawing a Line Under Free Speech

Citizens in a modern state believe the right to free speech is a good thing, even a fundamental human right. However, it comes on a spectrum - all societies draw lines on this spectrum as to where free speech ends and, for example, where blasphemy, criminal incitement, defamation or just plain bad manners, start. Cross that line and one's free speech is promptly curtailed, resulting in one being shamed, ostracised, cancelled, dragged into court, perhaps bankrupted, jailed, or even put to death in some countries. There is no right to absolute free speech.

Whilst the notorious *Eatock v Bolt* case was principally about statutory Aboriginality - just who is and who isn't Aboriginal - it was also an argument about where on the free speech spectrum this line should be drawn.

On one end of the spectrum there was a group of 'fair-skinned' Aboriginal people and their supporters, including a

---

[16]Response to a question from The Hon. L.A. Henderson, *Parliament of South Australia Hansard*, Thursday 2 May 2024.

group of *pro bono* lawyers, who were apparently intent on 'stitching up' Andrew Bolt. He was a man who they perceived had crossed the line so far, and so often, that he needed to be brought down and cancelled. They no longer wanted to be offended by Bolt and his commentary and demanded the line be redrawn much further up the spectrum. In that way, they would be free to pursue their lives, identity, ideology and politics unhindered, as the new class of 'fair-skinned Aboriginal people'.

At the other end of the spectrum was Bolt and his usual supporters. But there as also a group of free speech advocates; a motley crew of commentators - from the Left and the Right - who had come together in agreement on this issue to support, not so much Andrew Bolt the personality,[17] but rather Andrew Bolt's right to say what he liked, even if he ended up being highly offensive, or even charged with defamation, sprayed with sticky dye by protesters, yelled at for being a racist, or just plain hated for all time. They believed he deserved a fundamental right to free speech and it was up to him alone to calculate the consequences, not the legal fraternity down at the Federal Court flicking through their copies of the Racial Discrimination Act.[18]

Arguably, Bolt was correct to challenge, even to offend and humiliate, with witty, sarcastic and gratuitous language, the ancestry claims of a public figure like Pat Eatock. She clearly was a 'white Aborigine' and a 'ratbag' who was having a lend of credulous Australians. If Bolt honestly believed her claims for funds and resources from the tax-payer were not in the public interest, he was entitled to say so, even if that

---

[17]One commentator called Bolt "an offensive, myopic, aggressively ignorant buffoon whose popularity I have yet to find a decent explanation for - in short, Andrew Bolt is a total flogger. And [yet] I hope he wins the case".[9.12]

[18]In the wake of Bolt's loss, some excellent articles appeared from journalists, lawyers and other commentators that encapsulated what really was at stake in this court case. All agreed something important happened on 28 September 2011 and the pros and cons can be read here: Pro-Bolt - [9.13],[9.14], [9.15], [9.12], Listen to Dale Smith[9.16] and Andrew Dodd[9.17]; Anti-Bolt - [9.18], [9.19], [9.20], [9.21]; More Balanced - [9.22] and listen to Adrienne Stone.[9.4]

made his commentary sound highly offensive to some. But
Bolt's methodology was faulty to some degree. Although he
was in many ways ultimately to be vindicated, back in 2009
he hadn't done his homework properly. Critical parts of his
research were wanting, so he couldn't adequately defend himself in court. The fact that his counsel didn't help with the
'absurd'[19] defence meant that Bolt's case was ultimately lost.
Commentator David Marr, writing an opinion piece in the
Sydney Morning Herald the day after Bolt's conviction, had a
point:

> Freedom of speech is not at stake here. Judge Mordecai
> Bromberg is not telling the media what we can say or where
> we can poke our noses. He's attacking lousy journalism. He's
> saying that if Andrew Bolt of the Herald Sun wants to ac-
> cuse people of appalling motives, he should start by getting
> his facts right. Bolt was wrong. Spectacularly wrong. In
> two famous columns in 2009 he took a swipe at "political"
> or "professional" or "official" Aborigines who could pass for
> white but chose to identify as black for personal or political
> gain, to win prizes and places reserved for real, black Abo-
> rigines and to borrow "other people's glories". But Bolt's
> lawyers had to concede even before this case began in the
> Federal Court that nine of these named "white Aborigines"
> had identified as black from childhood. All nine came to court
> to say they didn't choose this down the track but were raised
> as Aborigines. Their evidence was not contested by Bolt or
> his paper. So as we say in the trade: no story.[20]

Yet as we now know, with regard to at least the lead applicant
Pat Eatock, David Marr has turned out to be as wrong today
as he had accused Bolt of being wrong the day after the court
decision. Everyone connected to this case who 'conceded' that
simply by *claiming* she 'identified as black from childhood'
was sufficient evidence and proof that Eatock *was* Aboriginal
has allowed a great injustice to Bolt to occur. However, legal
proceedings are not about justice - they are about advocating

---

[19] Jonathan Holmes, 'Bolt, Bromberg and a profoundly disturbing judgment', 30 Sept
2011. See QR Code [8.32].
[20] David Marr, 'In black and white, Andrew Bolt trifled with the facts', *SMH*, 29 Sept
2011.

your case on the day and winning, according to what the law says is right and wrong. Bolt lost his case on 28 September 2011 but today he is winning one 'white Aborigine' case after another. History will show that the fundamental points raised by Bolt were correct even if, as Marr correctly pointed out, he pushed these points home by using 'mockery, derision and sarcasm.' But aren't they the valid tools of trade of a tabloid journalist trying to turn the attention of his society onto an even greater injustice - that being perpetrated upon genuine Aboriginal people in real need?

9.2.2 Good Tone Versus Bad Tone

Since his loss in court, it does appear that Andrew Bolt has re-toned his manner and moved his journalistic style a notch or two from the 'tabloid' side towards the 'investigative' side with regard to his Aboriginality investigations. Nevertheless, this has not restricted Bolt's ability to expose even more 'white Aborigines' as fakes in academia, politics and the arts, than he did previously. Bolt has probably heeded the few kernels of wisdom or hints that were to be found in Justice Bromberg's findings, even if overall the court case was a 'stitch-up', given the false claims of the main witness for the prosecution, Pat Eatock.

A good summary of Justice Bromberg's hints (in bold below) was published immediately after Bolt's loss by his newsprint competitor, *The Age*, and not without some glee of editorial *schadenfreude* one suspects:

> Everyone, quipped the late Daniel Patrick Moynihan, Democratic Party senator for New York, is entitled to his own opinion, but not **his own facts** ... the reaction of Herald Sun columnist Andrew Bolt to this week's Federal Court judgment against him suggests he would struggle to grasp Moynihan's point.

> Bolt, who was taken to court under the Racial Discrimination Act (RDA) by Pat Eatock, an Aborigine, over his published comments on some fair-skinned Aborigines, including her, has

since sought to portray himself as a martyr to the cause of free speech. It is a stance that is only credible if the right to free speech is construed as including a right to utter **malicious falsehoods**. Ms Eatock and eight other fair-skinned Aborigines testified that they had been offended by ... Bolt [who] suggested that they need not have identified as Aboriginal, because of their appearance and mixed ancestry, but had **chosen** to do so ... because of career opportunities open to people as Aboriginal leaders and advocates. The implication was that the fair-skinned Aborigines he named had done just that. Bolt denied he intended readers to draw such an inference. "I'm not saying any of those I've named chose to be Aboriginal for anything but the most heartfelt and honest of reasons," ... "I certainly don't accuse them of opportunism, even if full-blood Aborigines may wonder how such fair people can claim to be one of them and in some cases take black jobs." This **disclaimer** did not impress Justice Mordecai Bromberg, who described it in his judgment as "**an exculpatory device** ... rather than a genuine attempt to counter the contrary messages that the article otherwise conveys ...

Justice Bromberg noted Bolt's "**liberal use of sarcasm and mockery**" ... the **style** of Bolt's writing ... led to the finding against him ... the articles ... were riddled with **factual errors**. They were not people who had made a **conscious choice to become Aborigines**, but who had identified as such since earliest childhood ... In court, Bolt conceded that he had **not checked details** ... **with the persons he wrote about**, but instead relied on Google searches for information. The RDA contains provisions protecting freedom of expression, which ... would allow commentators such as Bolt to deal with questions of "**racial identification, including by challenging the genuineness of the identification of a group of people**". Bolt **forfeited** that protection, however, because of the **manner** in which he approached the subject ... What is called freedom of the press is but an instance of the broader **right of freedom of speech and expression**, on which **liberal democracy depends**. When those who invoke that right do so by **distorting or suppressing the facts**, however, they do not uphold liberal freedoms ... Commentators are obliged to **get the facts right**.

The Age Editorial[21]

---

[21] Editorial: 'Free speech was not the loser in the Bolt case', *The Age*, 30 Sept 2011.

Over recent years Bolt appears to have squarely addressed these criticisms. Now when he discusses 'white Aborigines' he tells his audience that he adds to his own investigations by citing the research of professional genealogists and researchers at organisations such as *Dark Emu Exposed* so as to make sure he gets his facts right.

He also tells his readers and viewers that he contacts the persons he will write about to check details before publication, for example:

> Again, maybe there's a mistake, but when dark-emu-exposed.org showed [Professor Bronwyn] Carlson their findings, they first got a threatening lawyer's letter. When they asked again for evidence, they got no response.

> I emailed Carlson a couple of times with my own questions, but also got no response, although her biography on the university website has since been changed to delete her claim to be "an Aboriginal woman".[9.23]

Just as importantly, he now includes a disclaimer that there may be a hidden or unrecorded Aboriginal ancestor which the researchers don't know about, and he gives the person a chance to respond, for example:

> First a caveat: publicly available genealogies of the people I mention show no Aboriginal ancestors, but could be wrong. Maybe there's, say, an illegitimate birth that professional genealogists from dark-emu-exposed.org somehow missed.

> ... Margo Neale, an adjunct professor of the Australian National University, and senior Indigenous curator at the National Museum of Australia [professes to be Aboriginal]. Again, there's no Aboriginal ancestor in her genealogical records that we can find. So I wrote to her, asking: "Who is your Aboriginal apical ancestor, the first one from whom you base your claim to be Aboriginal?"

> She replied: "Aboriginal histories, as you know, can indeed be tricky particularly if one relies on western records during the long period of disruption and displacement ... Aboriginal births, deaths and marriages were largely unrecorded outside missions and pastoral properties in earlier days at least, or inaccurately recorded."

I asked again: "So which Aboriginal ancestor had their birth
inaccurately recorded?" She never replied. I know of more
such academics, many in Aboriginal jobs. Shouldn't universities demand more proof?

Unfortunately, it appears that Bolt has to some extent sacri-
ficed some of the turns of phrase that Justice Bromberg dis-
approvingly called 'mocking' and 'gratuitous'. These biting
phrases of clarity are the bread-and-butter of tabloid journalism in that they take the reader straight to the main point of
the article.

When Bolt talked about the 'political Aborigine', the 'professional Aborigine' and 'an official Aborigine and hired as
such', everyone knew exactly what he meant. Australians read
about and see such people every day at work or on the news
as they 'invent such racist and trivial excuses to divide' while
'scuffling at the trough', all the whiles asking us to 'surrender
my reason and pretend white is really black, just to aid some
artist's self-actualisation therapy'.

Bolt exhorted his readers to understand 'that way lies
madness, where truth is just a whim and words mean nothing'
and that 'a privileged white Aborigine snaffles that extra' and,
by 'seeking power and reassurance in a racial identity, is not
just weak [but is] a borrowing of other people's glories' that
will ultimately divide our country. 'At its worst, it's them
against us'.

These were some of the quotations of Bolt's that were dis-
approvingly cited by Bromberg J in his judgement[22]; and if
Bolt has begun to self-censor after his loss, his readership and
viewers are the poorer for it. But after his adverse judgement,
Bolt genuinely had to modify his 'tone' and 'style' if he was
to keep out of trouble while carrying on exposing the systematic racism and fakery that is the modern 'white Aboriginal'
industry.[23]

---

[22]See [9.5] at 414.

[23]The mellowing of Bolt's punchy descriptors reflect a general trend in Australian
journalism towards playing it safe and thus becoming boring. In 2023 the *Walkley*

One benefit of Bolt's new modified tone and more measured investigative style is that representatives of real Aboriginal organisations, such as long-standing Land Councils, were more willing to appear on *Sky News Australia* and 'The Bolt Report'. At the height of the racial discrimination action against Bolt in 2011, it would have been hard to imagine the Chief Executive Officer (CEO) of the Sydney-based Metropolitan Local Aboriginal Land Council (MLALC) appearing as a guest on 'The Bolt Report'. But in 2024 that is exactly what its current CEO, Nathan Moran, did.[9.25] Perhaps 'The Bolt Report' is now seen as an ally by Aboriginal organisations in the campaign to expose the fakes. It also might suggest that the problem of fakes has been rapidly increasing in the last few years.

From a positive perspective, Bolt's strike-rate in exposing many 'white Aborigines' as fakes has increased dramatically, as has the public awareness of just how big the problem is. Bolt's advocacy has probably played a significant part in questions now being asked in parliaments as to how we determine who is and who isn't an Aborigine. This came to the fore when the then Liberal Opposition Leader, Peter Dutton, tabled a set of questions to Prime Minister Albanese asking how the Voice body would work within the Constitution, as proposed in the 2023 referendum:

> Will the Government clarify the definition of aboriginality to determine who can serve on the body [known as the Voice]?[9.26]

The ABC was also prompted to start to allow the issue to be aired in programs such as *Q&A* [9.9] and *SBS Insight*.[9.27]

Awards retired the category of 'Headline, Caption and Hook' due to low entries in recent years. Are Australians never to see winners again like: "Headless Body in Topless Bar"; "Sneddon Died on the Job"; nor encourage new entries like, "Noel Pearson Thinks He's the Last Male on Earth - everyone else is a C***", and no chance that the Bruce Pascoe Hitler parody will ever get a Logie - see[9.24]

9.3 The Fakes: Who, Where, How & Why

The phenomenon of some prominent academics and politicians seemingly taking huge risks to declare they are 'Aboriginal', when in fact they aren't, is fascinating. Examination of their family genealogies indicates they are all mistaken. As delicious as the ideologically-based feeling might be for a 'gotcha' moment - exposing some prominent 'Aboriginal' claimant living on the public purse - the primary motivation driving *Dark Emu Exposed* is not just revealing 'who are' and 'where are' the fakes.

Rather, of even more interest is the 'how' and the 'why' of what the fakes, and by extension Bolt's 'white Aborigines', are doing. What motivates such people to be part of Bolt's 'trend' of Australians greatly embellishing or even faking their Aboriginality? And how can the public believe anything they say if they are so mistaken, or potentially even consciously lying, about who they really are?

One possible explanation of this phenomenon lies with an experienced academic from New Zealand, where race, identity and politics have been battling each other for much longer and harder than in Australia.

9.3.1 Neotribal Elites and Their Fair-skinned Aboriginal Accomplices

> *Who controls the past controls the future.*
> *Who controls the present controls the past.*
>
> **- George Orwell, *1984***

It is worth taking the time to ask a couple of pertinent questions: Why has there been such an apparent increase in the number of successfully assimilated or 'fair-skinned' Aboriginal people entering the public square, with their loud activist statements and claims? And, why does there seem to be a very noisy 'ideological minority'[24] within this group who are constantly complaining about Closing the Gap, so-called intergenerational trauma, and a claimed lack of a voice, power or funding for Aboriginal peoples, when they and their organisations seem to be doing very well indeed?

The phenomenon of the 'ideological minority' has been studied in depth by New Zealand scholar, Professor Elizabeth Rata.[25] She refers to this group as the 'neotribal ethnic elites'. While her fields of study are principally the indigenous elites in New Zealand, Fiji, Malaysia and the United States, her research would appear to have some direct application in Australia. For example, Professor Rata has observed:

> The worldwide ethnic and indigenous movements of the last three decades of the twentieth century were intended to achieve social justice, economic redistribution and greater political participation for peoples marginalised initially during colonisation ... These goals have remained elusive for the vast majority. But why, despite the extravagant rhetoric, has this happened?

By rephrasing her question into an Australian context, she would be asking: "But why, despite the extravagant rhetoric, haven't we Closed the Gap between mainstream Australians and the most disadvantaged of the Aborigines living in remote communities?"[26]

---

[24] Think Michael Mansell, Noel Pearson, Marcia Langton, Bruce Pascoe, Megan Davis, Senator Lidia Thorpe, former Senator Pat Dodson, Pat Anderson, Thomas Mayo, Geoff Clark, Linda Burney, Kyam Maher, Bronwyn Carlson and Tom Calma, to name but a few.

[25] Professor of Critical Studies in Education at the University of Auckland and Co-chair of the Inter-University Academic Freedom Council which provides support and advice to academics from all New Zealand universities. Her research includes the study of race, ethnicity and education, specifically the effects of racial categorisation on educational policy and the curriculum. Her original theory of neotribal capitalism provides the foundation for an extensive and ongoing research programme into racial politics. Neotribal capitalism is about elite emergence and the ways in which traditionalist ideology and re-tribalist politics are used, with New Zealand as the example, to privatise public resources and acquire non-democratic political power. (*University of Auckland:* https://profiles.auckland.ac.nz/e-rata).

[26] However, Australia is different to Rata's other Indigenous populations in that for 80% or so of Australians of Aboriginal descent, the 'gap' has closed. The relative disadvantage of Aboriginal Australians is only a reality for the remaining 20% who reside principally in regional and remote communities.

In a 2006 paper, *The Political Strategies of Ethnic and Indigenous Elites*,[27] Rata provided a scholarly analysis of what
Bolt would go on to warn about just three years later - the
rising 'trend' of an ethnic elite (his 'white Aborigines') whose
main aim seems to be a quest for personal economic and political power rather than delivering help to genuine Aboriginal
people in real need. Instead, as Bolt has often told his readership and viewers, their actions would only lead to divisions
within our society based on race and ethnic resentment. Rata's
scholarship serves as an academic framework to support Bolt's
real-life observations. Rata also found that:

> the reason for the relative failure of ethnic and indigenous mo-
> bilisation to achieve its promised results[28] is due to two main
> factors. First, in government responses to ethnic mobilisation
> and, second, the emergence of elites from within the policies
> and practices of the government responses.[29]

Insightfully, she believes this 'elite emergence' came about by
the government responses that allowed the creation of:

> ethnic socio-political categories within the nation-state [which],
> as a result, have built institutional and permanent boundaries
> between racial groups. Public policy is a significant contrib-
> utor to this boundary-making process ... In the process of
> ethnic boundary making, the brokerage between the leaders
> of the ethnic and indigenous movements and their respec-
> tive governments transformed the leaders into a self-interested
> class of elites, with economic and political ambitions that are
> no longer representative of the entire ethnic group's inter-
> ests.[30]

This is why Bolt and his views were a problem to the emergence of this new class of Aboriginal elites. Here they were
trying to *broker* and build a new ethic *boundary* between themselves and the rest of Australia, and this pesky journalist kept

[27]Rata, E. (2006). 'The Political Strategies of Ethnic and Indigenous Elites'. In Rata,
E. and Openshaw, R.(Eds.). *Public Policy and Ethnicity - The Politics of Ethnic
Boundary Making.* London, UK: Palgrave Macmillan. pp40-53.
[28]- for that remaining 20% of Aboriginal Australians -
[29]Rata (2006), *ibid.,* p40.
[30]Rata (2006), *ibid.* p40.

calling them out for what they really were, as Pat Eatock's counsel Ron Merkel QC told the court:

> And what these articles [of Bolt's] are saying is, these people aren't really Aborigines. And they're in the trough, and they're taking – their snouts in the trough, and putting other Aboriginal people, the real Aboriginal people that Mr Bolt thinks should be getting all the benefits, they're taking away these benefits.[31]

Exactly! Ron Merkel has succinctly summed up the whole case accurately by just applying some common sense. And that is why Bolt was a problem - every time Merkel's clients and the other ethnic elites added a few more bricks to their new boundary walls, he would come in with his common sense and kick them out.

Bolt was street-wise enough in 2009 to see that, despite the extravagant rhetoric, the Closing the Gap initiative of 2008 and its goals would never be achieved if the system was overwhelmed by an increasing 'trend' of 'white Aborigines' with their 'snouts in the trough'.

Rata recognised that to overcome critics like Bolt, and 'entrench ethnicity as a political category and, with that entrenchment, to cement their own privileged positions', these emergent ethnic elites needed to find a strategy. The first strategy they were to adopt was:

> the cultural production of a neotraditionalist ideology which enabled the elite to make a spurious claim for continuity with an 'authentic' tribal past. As a result, the elite claimed economic resources and political partnership as the inheritance of that past.[32]

In Australia, this would manifested itself in the explosion in the number of ceremonies, festivals, books, ABC/SBS/NITV programs, films, educational resources, grants and awards that stressed a new-found understanding and appreciation of the so-called 65,000-year-deep history of Aboriginal peoples and

---

[31] *Eatock v Bolt*, Trans. Proc., Fed. Court (Vic), Mon 28 Mar 2011, Day One, p9.
[32] Rata (2006), *ibid.*, p41.

their culture. This strategy is constantly asserted, often with no evidence, that ancient practices are still practiced today - the public needs to be indoctrinated to believe that the culture of the Old People of the tribal past was alive within the new custodians, the 'white Aborigines'. This was admitted as much by one of Australia's most influential members of who a Rata-minded person might see as a member of the ethnic elite, Professor Marcia Langton AO, from the University of Melbourne. She told the *Guardian* in 2019, that she wanted:

> Australian children, especially Indigenous children, to know that contemporary Aboriginal ... communities are **strong, resilient, rich and diverse** ... They [need] ... to learn about our cultures, societies and history so that they go out into the world with a **respect** for the first peoples of Australia and **everything they have achieved** ... we know that human history on this continent began at least **60 millennia before Lieutenant Arthur Phillip** and the First Fleet arrived. Moreover, because of the knowledge of human economic activity that **Bruce Pascoe** ... reveal[s] in *Dark Emu*, the impact of the hundreds of generations of the first peoples who lived here **before the British** came is critical to understanding the places where Australians live **today.** We know from [Pascoe's] account, based on fascinating evidence, that Aboriginal and Torres Strait Islanders produced food with unique **agricultural and aquaculture** methods, they created material culture and toolkits that were ingenious and appropriate to their lifestyles and environments, they managed the land through changes in climate and geography ... and developed artistic and design traditions and legal, religious and social institutions of great subtlety and beauty. There were extensive **trade routes** that criss-crossed the country, some **still used today**. The evidence of this is all around us today, much of it still practised and preserved, and increasingly better understood. Books, films, documentaries, art exhibitions, cultural festivals, music, theatrical and dance performances, and the ongoing ceremonial and ritual activities have made this available to a global audience. Aboriginal ... people maintain knowledge traditions with their own philosophies and epistemologies that originated in ancient Australia. Many of these knowledge **traditions continue today**.[33] (emphasis added.)

---

[33]Marcia Langton, 'Fire, water and astronomy: Aboriginal and Torres Strait Islander

This explains why there has been such a concerted campaign to constantly expose the Australian public to 'Aboriginality' - from renaming of capital cities on the weather maps, to concocted 'ceremonies' with lots of smoke and the waving of gumleaves, to indigenous flags and cultural warnings being posted on all government websites and, most insidiously, by 'Indigenising the school curriculum', amongst many other initiatives.

For an advocate like Langton to be successful in this cultural production and spurious claim - that city-based Aboriginal elites had an inheritance and continuity with an authentic and ancient tribal past - she needed 'experts'. These had to be respectable Aboriginal academics who could broker 'the process of ethnic boundary making', between the leaders of the ethnic and indigenous movements, like Langton herself, and governments, business, academia and the media. If the elite Indigenous movement was to achieve the economic and political recognition, ambitions and inheritance that they craved, they would have to put forward a convincing story to government and the public.

But, as Bolt was inconveniently able to routinely show, the 'experts' that Langton chose in her attempts to build an authentic tribal past, often turned out to be just 'white Aborigines' or worse still, total fakes, pushing some concocted story about Aboriginal Australia.[34] For example, Professor Langton chose self-proclaimed Aboriginal man, **Bruce Pascoe**, to be her 'expert' on all things relating to Aboriginal 'agriculture'. Unfortunately for Langton, her academic colleagues contradicted her by roundly debunking Pascoe's theory that pre-colonial Aborigines were 'farmers'.[35] The mainstream me-

---

culture comes to life in the classroom', *The Guardian Online*, 11 Apr 2019.

[34] Scholars are beginning to study this trend: see Terry Moore and Carol Pybus, "Myth-making Isn't the Right Way to 'Indigenise' Our Universities", *Quillette online*, 26 Jun 2022; Pennycook G, *et al*, "On the reception and detection of pseudo-profound bullshit", *Judgment and Decision Making*, 10(6), 2015, p549-563.

[35] (a) Dr Ian Keen: "Professor Marcia Langton is reported to have said that *Dark Emu* 'is the most important book on Australia and should be read by every Australian'. Again, coming as it does from an eminent scholar, this is an unexpected

dia piled in, signaling it was all over for Pascoe and his theory.[36] Embarrassingly, Langton had even gone on the record, as part of the elites' cultural production agenda, to praise Pascoe in the upper-middle-class magazine, *Gourmet Traveller*:[37]

> **Interviewer:** How did you feel reading Bruce Pascoe's book *Dark Emu*, and his assertion that Indigenous Australians were the first people in the world to bake bread?
>
> **Langton:** *Dark Emu* is a profound challenge to conventional thinking about Aboriginal life on this continent. He details the Aboriginal economy and analyses the historical data showing that our societies were not simple hunter-gatherer economies but sophisticated, with farming and irrigation practices. This is the most important book on Australia and should be read by every Australian.

And challenge the authenticity of Langton's 'white Aborigines' Bolt certainly did, to devastating effect. Firstly Bolt had a ratings field-day in exposing the hoax that was Bruce Pascoe and his *Dark Emu*.[9.28] This contributed greatly to derailing the phenomenal growth that Pascoe and his *Dark Emu* story[9.29] had achieved up until about 2020. This further weakened Langton's ability at cultural production given her very public support for Pascoe.[9.2]

Langton had welcomed an 'Aboriginal' Pascoe when he took up a coveted Professorship of Enterprise at her prestigious University of Melbourne.[9.30] Yet today, the university's website appears to have quietly dropped any mention of Pascoe's

---

judgement". - *Foragers or Farmers: Dark Emu and the Controversy over Aboriginal Agriculture, Anthropological Forum*, 5 Jan 2021, p2; (b) Peter Sutton and Keryn Walshe in *Farmers or Hunter-gatherers? The Dark Emu Debate* 'accuse Pascoe of a "lack of true scholarship", ignoring Aboriginal voices, dragging respect for traditional Aboriginal culture back into the Eurocentric world of the colonial era, and "trimming" colonial observations to fit his argument. They write that while *Dark Emu* "purports to be factual" it is "littered with unsourced material, is poorly researched, distorts and exaggerates many points, selectively emphasises evidence to suit those opinions, and ignores large bodies of information that do not support the author's opinions"- (*Stuart Rintoul, see fn34*); and c) See the ABC documentary *The Dark Emu Story* (ABC iview) as Langton and other commentators reflect on the conflict over Bruce Pascoe's authenticity.

[36] Stuart Rintoul, 'Debunking Dark Emu: did the publishing phenomenon get it wrong?', *Sydney Morning Herald*, 12 Jun 2021.

[37] Tran Lam Lee, 'Marcia Langton: How I Eat', *Gourmet Traveller*, 21 Jun 2018.

claim to Aboriginality - he is now just referred to as, 'a writer and farmer'.

Another 'Aboriginal' expert Professor Langton relied upon in her support of the Indigenisation of politics and culture in Australia was Adjunct Professor **Margo 'Ngawa' Neale**. She was chosen to be the editor for Langton's co-authored book *The Way of the Ancestors*, one of the books in the Indigenous series *First Knowledges* produced by international publisher Thames & Hudson.[38] Bolt metaphorically kicked out another brick from the racial boundary wall Langton was busily trying to build when he exposed Neale as just another Aboriginal fake.[9.31]

And so it continued, with Bolt now setting his sights on **Professor Kerrie Doyle** from Western Sydney University.[39] He publicised evidence showing she was a complete fake, having been born in Papua New Guinea to white parents and not, as she had claimed, from the Winninninni tribe - an entirely fictitious tribal name.[40] Unfortunately for Langton, Kerrie Doyle had acknowledged the professor in her PhD thesis:

> Professor Marcia Langton and the post-graduate research team at the University of Melbourne have also greatly contributed to this journey [of Doyle's through her PhD at ANU and then onto Oxford on an Indigenous scholarship]. I have been fortunate enough to have been given opportunities to increase my academic ability by the Aurora Scholarship program and the Roberta Sykes Scholarship program.[9.32]

It seems that, once again, Langton had been mentor to an 'Aboriginal' academic who ultimately turned out to be a fake. This is very concerning because if a highly regarded Aboriginal academic such as Langton could be fooled by all these fakes, what hope was there for the average Australian in deciding

---

[38]Langton, M., & Corn, A., 'The way of the Ancestors', *Thames & Hudson*, 2023.

[39]Andrew Bolt, 'New fake claims by Professor Kerrie Doyle obviously absurd, Professor Kerrie Doyle, who claims to be a member of the "Winninninni" tribe', *Herald Sun*, 4 Jan 2023.

[40]No such tribal name exists in Norman Tindale's, *Aborginal Tribes of Australia*, 1974 - see QR Code [4.14].

just who is, and who isn't, Aboriginal?

Doyle had been a recipient of a Roberta Sykes Scholarship - colloquially known as the 'Tar-Brush Scholarship' ('white' applicants can go in and emerge as proud [insert tribal name here] 'fair-skinned' Aboriginal scholars). The scholarships are administered by the **Aurora Education Foundation Ltd** and are a perfect example of what Professor Rata and Andrew Bolt were warning about more than a decade ago.

9.3.2   Neotribal Elites and The Aurora Foundation

> *Every great cause begins as a movement,*
> *becomes a business, and turns into a racket.*

Eric Hoffer[41]

On a balmy evening in 2023, down on the waterfront of Sydney Harbour, the Aurora Education Foundation was celebrating its end-of-year reception. This registered charity[42] has had a long and successful history since its inception fifteen years ago if its mission statement is to be believed:

> Our role is to inspire First Peoples in their education journey and connect them with educational and career opportunities that enable them to realise their potential.

> Aurora supports students and scholars to achieve unparalleled outcomes and shift the conversation to one of proud and talented students with limitless potential. In order to achieve systemic change, we are committed to an authentic and trusted approach, evidence-based decision making and a long-term focus.[9.33]

This sounds like a worthy cause, and certainly the Foundation regularly receives high praise, for example from Australia's High Commission in London,[43] but is it true to its mission of

---

[41] 1960s American longshoreman and commentator.

[42] ACNC Registered: Aurora Education Foundation Ltd, ABN 28158391363

[43] Australian High Commission in the United Kingdom: 'In partnership with the Australia-United Kingdom Chamber of Commerce, we welcomed the Aurora Ed-

supporting genuine Aboriginal students and scholars in need? Did the organisation's operation match its rhetoric?

Anyone who was familiar with the educational plight of many Aboriginal students in regional and remote Australia might have been unsettled by the appearance of the student recipients being feted at the harbour-side reception and the apparent largese shown to the Foundation's staff and guests in attendance. Although Bolt had been very blunt when he penned his offending two articles regarding the 'professional Aborigine' who required of Bolt to 'surrender [his] reason and pretend white is really black', it was easy to understand what Bolt had meant by looking at the seemingly privileged 'fair skinned' Aboriginal people at the Aurora reception.[44] Bolt's concerns that 'when a privileged white Aborigine then snaffles that extra, odds are that an underprivileged black Aborigine misses out on the very things [like a good education] we hoped would help them most.'[45] If he had attended the reception, Bolt would have clearly seen that his phrase, the 'white Aborigine' raised the same concerns down on Sydney Harbour that evening as it had in his articles more than a decade previously.[46]

The pretence was complete on reading the summary of Aurora's 2023 financial statement.[9.35] The charity boasted an income of nearly $10 million per year, with $6 million of that coming from the Australian taxpayer as government grants, and a further $3.5 million as tax-deductible donations and be-

---

ucation Foundation to Australia House to celebrate 15 years of education pathways for First Nations Australian students. In 2010, there had never been an Aboriginal or Torres Strait Islander person studying full-time at the University of Oxford or University of Cambridge. 80 First Nations scholars have now completed their studies at Oxbridge and other world-leading universities with the support of an Aurora Education scholarship', *Facebook*, 25 October 2024. (As detailed in Section 9.3.1, fake Aboriginal scholar, Kerrie Doyle had been one of the first of Aurora's Oxford graduates).

[44] See photographs of the attendees at the 2023 End of Year Reception.[9.34]

[45] Andrew Bolt, 'White fellas in the black', *Herald Sun*, 21 August 2009.

[46] The photo on Aurora's Mission Statement, of seemingly middle-class white kids on an adventure camp, certainly raises questions as to whether this is really an organisation helping genuine Aboriginal students obtain a good education.[9.33]Unless of course it is the definition of who is an 'Aboriginal' that has changed.

quests from well-meaning Australians or organisations. However, on the expense side, the salaries for the 57 full-time employees and 46 casual and part-timers (103 people to handle a modest budget of $10 million) consumed half the budget - with some $5 million per year going out as 'employee expenses' to fund this harbour-side gravy train of largely 'white Aborigines'.

And what of the actual grants and donations to students? These appeared to be only some $600,000 for use in Australia and just under $1 million for use overseas. This expenditure on students amounts in total to only about 16% of the charity's revenue, arguably a very poor level of efficiency (i.e. 84% of the charity's income is consumed in overheads).

The overt political advocacy of the Aurora Foundation, which is largely a publicly funded charity, is also of concern. Reading the Foundation's statement advocating support for a Yes vote in the 2023 Voice referendum, it is not immediately apparent how this advocacy is of any value to its primary legal function under its charity status, which is 'support[ing] Aboriginal and Torres Strait Islander students to realise their full time education and employment potential':

WHY AURORA EDUCATION FOUNDATION SUPPORTS A VOICE TO PARLIAMENT
We stand together to support the Voice to Parliament. This is a positive and meaningful change to build on a strong foundation and start something even greater – to create a better system where First Nations people can thrive in whatever path they choose. At Aurora ... we talk about the need for change – change that unravels **two centuries of systematic and structural barriers** so that our kids can thrive in whatever path they choose. Change that's **informed by Indigenous peoples for Indigenous peoples, because nobody understands what's best for us more than we do.** As an Indigenous organisation, we need to have these conversations because the laws that govern **the continent now known as Australia** were developed without its **First Peoples**. It is **a system designed by non-Indigenous people for non-Indigenous people.** It is **a Constitution**

that **does not recognise the presence of Aboriginal and Torres Strait Islander peoples before colonisation.** We are the **oldest living civilisation on earth,** with 65,000 years of knowledges, cultures and kinship. Our Elders have sustained our people and this continent for millennia, in ways that are only now being grasped by Western history and science. **We are the experts in what's best for us** – we always have been. This is as true for education and employment as it is for **every facet of our lives.** A referendum on establishing an Indigenous Voice to Parliament ... is an opportunity to recognise Indigenous peoples in the history of this continent, and a way to solidify an **Indigenous voice on matters that impact us.** At Aurora, we support this change. We support the Uluru Statement from the Heart. And we support an Indigenous Voice to Parliament ... we believe this is our opportunity to hold the line for generations to come – to learn from the spirit and courage of our Elders, many of whom have long **fought for self-determination** and Constitutional recognition ... Our vision is a society in which **First Peoples determine their own aspirations.** At Aurora, we support a 'yes' vote. We hope you will join us.[9.36] (emphasis added.)

The above highlighted phrases suggest that the Aurora Foundation might be really nothing more than an Aboriginal activist advocacy group masquerading as a student educational organisation. Even more worryingly is that many of these political statements and demands are based upon race. This is an illustration of Professor Rata's observations[47] that the strategy of the neotribal elites is to make spurious claims for a continuity with an authentic tribal past (i.e. activists today claim they are the direct inheritors of 65,000 years of civilisation despite the fact that culturally, socially and genetic they are overwhelmingly of European heritage.)[48] and then claim political recognition of group rights under Australia's Constitution, while at the same time demanding self-determination rights. If successful, these rights would be afforded to no other citizens in Australia, thus making Aboriginal people a 'new and spe-

---

[47]See Section 9.3.1

[48]In any case, Anatomically Modern Humans (AMH) have only been on the continent of Australia some 50,000 years[9.37] and Aboriginal societies were not 'civilizations'.

cial class' of Australian - recognised with power-sharing within the Constitution because of their race, but then free to 'self-determine' and create their own political path to statehood, also because of their race. This is a formula for the break-up of the Commonwealth of Australia along the lines of a race-based, apartheid system.

Furthermore, the 'racist' claims made by the Aurora Foundation that 'change needs to be informed by Indigenous peoples for Indigenous peoples because nobody understands what's best for us more than we do' is deeply concerning. Despite lacking in any rational common sense, this mindset creates a direct link between race and knowledge and between blood and politics. It is in direct opposition to the mindset of a liberal, democratic and pluralist society based on equality for all citizens regardless of their race, ethnicity, colour or creed. Aurora's claims are as ludicrous as saying that only men should have a say in government policy that affects men because 'nobody understands what's best for men more than men do'.[49]

Professor Rata was particularly concerned about the weaponisation of ethnicity as a threat to modern liberal democracies:

> While the untrammelled ambitions of all elites pose a threat to the liberal-democratic ideals of social justice, fair economic distribution and accountable politics, those of ethnicised elites pose the greater threat.

> This is the case because ethnic elites advocate foundational groups (i.e. collectives united by non-dissolvable bonds such as kinship or ethnicity and not reducible to individuals) over individual citizenship, along with tribal or ethnic political

---

[49] Does Aurora really want to take Australia back to the race-based thinking of Nazi Germany in 1935?: '*So, when we speak of related blood, we mean the blood of those races that are determinative for the blood of the peoples who since time immemorial have a closed settlement area in Europe. Therefore, the members of the European peoples ... are essentially of related blood. However, one has to exclude the foreign-blooded, who can be found among every European people, such as the Jews and the human beings with a Negroid blood-impact.*' - A quotation from the Nazi Party lawyer and State Secretary in the Reich Interior Ministry Wilhelm Stuckart's definition of 'related blood'. Reverse the terminology and substitute 'Aboriginal' for 'European', 'Australia' for 'Europe' and consider British settlers as the 'foreign-blooded' within Australia and the Aurora sentiment is not that different from that of Nazi Germany. (See *Wikipedia: Nazi racial theories, Stuckart, Wilhelm (1935)*).

structures as the framework for the range of regulatory institutions and practices that bind people into the foundational collective.

The result is that only those people who share the same racial or ethnic ancestry can belong to the socio-political structure. The creation of these structures does, in fact, make racial divisions permanent as boundaries are erected around ethnicised categories to institutionalise ethnic divisions.[50]

These words of Rata's precisely sum up the racial divisions being created in Australia by organisations such as Aurora, the various Uluru Statement committees, Reconcilliation Australia and the various state's Aboriginal Treaty organisations. Bolt's pleading words were also as relevant quayside on Sydney Harbour in 2023 as they were back in 2009 when he wrote them:

Let's go beyond racial pride. Beyond black and white. Let's be proud only of being human beings set on this land together, determined to find what unites us and not to invent such racist and trivial excuses to divide. Deal?[51]

9.4   If It Wasn't So Serious, It Would be a Big Joke

When you venture out as a comedian into that rather provocative borderland, it's not just because you want to provoke. You do it because you want to discover truths, explore the point at which it starts to hurt, reveal hypocrisy. Why mustn't we eat other? Why mustn't we go to bed with our sister? Why mustn't we kill each other or steal? Nothing is fixed.

Frank Hvam, a Danish comedian[52]

One could easily just make a few word changes and put these sentiments into the mouth of Andrew Bolt to reveal something about free speech in modern Australia:

---

[50]Rata, *op. cit.*, p41.
[51]Andrew Bolt, 'It's so hip to be black', *Herald Sun*, 15 April 2009.
[52]Rose, F. *The Tyranny of Silence*, Cato, 2014, p28.

When you venture out as a tabloid journalist into that rather provocative borderland, it's not just because you want to provoke. You do it because you want to discover truths, explore the point at which it starts to hurt, reveal hypocrisy. Why mustn't we fake being Aboriginal? Why mustn't we divide Australians based on race? Why mustn't we lie to, or steal from, the taxpayer? Nothing is fixed.

Hvam was speaking in 2005 with regard to the:

limits of humor in an age of [Islamic] religious fundamentalism and terror. Rejecting the idea that anyone could dictate what he was allowed to be funny about, Hvam nevertheless had to admit that a little self-censor had wormed its way inside his own mind ... [He] was not a man to respect a taboo, but he had found himself making an exception in the case of Islam: "I realized that I wouldn't have the guts to mock the Koran on television. For me, this was a frustrating discovery, because I was brought up to believe that we all have the right to say whatever we want. I find it hugely provoking that there are people who are threatening enough to make me keep my mouth shut."[53]

Bolt's articles should be seen in a similar light. They were written 'in a context in which the breaking of a taboo is considered to be progressive rather than intended to offend or attack a minority.' In this case, Bolt is confronting head-on Australian society's taboo of publicly challenging a person's claim to Aboriginality. He alone was entering the 'provocative borderland' to 'discover truths' and to 'explore the point at which it starts to hurt [and] reveal hypocrisy.' He was asking the transracial equivalent of, can a man put on a frock and some lippy and call himself a woman? - can a white woman put on an Aboriginal-print T-shirt and call herself Aboriginal?[54]

---

[53] *ibid.*, p27-8.
[54] The comparison here is not intended to be flippant, but rather is offered as an example of 'tabloid-speak' that goes to the heart of a complex and contentious issue. The idea of conflating transgenderism with transracialism is highly controversial and 'offensive, humiliating and intimidating' to some (see the critical response to Rebecca Tuvel's, 'In Defense of Transracialism', *Hypatia: A Journal of Feminist Philosophy*, Spring 2017, 32 (2), p263–278.)

Perhaps author Salman Rushdie summed it up best when discussing his own freedom of speech controversy:

> The only answer you can give from my side of the table is that everyone has a right to tell their story in any way they wish. This goes back to the question of what sort of society we want. If you wish to live in an open society, it follows that people will talk about things in different ways, and some of them will cause offense and anger. The answer to that is matter-of-fact: OK, you don't like it, but there are lots of things I don't like either. That's the price for living in an open society. From the moment you begin to talk about limiting and controlling certain expressions, you step into a world where freedom no longer reigns, and from that moment on, you are only discussing what level of un-freedom you want to accept. You have already accepted the principle of not being free.[55]

Publicly, Bolt's questioning of the 'white Aborigines' suffered a reversal for ten years as the controlling woke puritans deemed such free speech as being unacceptable. But, like any fad, woke is now starting to fade. The media programmes where many 'white Aborigines' were welcomed over the last decade - the ABC's *Q & A* and *The Drum*, and Ten's *The Project* - have all been cancelled.

Bolt is now coming back, his free speech restored, and his valid critiques of 'white Aborigines' and their assorted hangers-on are now being regularly published. He is making them look like the big joke that they are. And the public are starting to laugh too when they see Winninninni Aboriginal woman Professor Kerrie Doyle pick up her clap sticks and rap out a tune by Pemulwuy, or Professor Dennis Foley, in Aussie Bogan fishing attire, tells Australians that, along with another dozen academics, he too is Aboriginal.[9.38]

---

[55]Rose (2014), *op. cit.*, p5.

9.5   Revisiting the Legality of *Eatock v Bolt*

> *The law is a foreign country; they do things differently there.*
>
> **A man in the street**[56]

In February 2025, Gavin Silbert KC[57] was commissioned to write an opinion on what the consequences, if any, would be for the findings in *Eatock v Bolt*, given that Pat Eatock was mistaken to believe she was of Aboriginal descent.

Four questions were asked of Silbert KC and his opinions were as follows:

On the basis that Ms Eatock was not Aboriginal l am asked to answer the following four questions:

(i) Would she still have standing in bringing the action against Mr Bolt and the Herald and Weekly Times under the Racial Discrimination Act 1975 (Cth)?

(ii) All parties, including Mr Bolt, at the time of the trial accepted that Ms Eatock was of Aboriginal descent. This was also affirmed in her witness statement. Would this acceptance as a fact when it was not correct potentially alter the findings against Mr Bolt?

(iii) Is there any mechanism, appeal or otherwise, to have the matter reheard or re-examined based on the new evidence regarding Ms Eatock's Aboriginality?

(iv) Did Ms Eatock have standing at all to initiate proceedings under the Racial Discrimination Act 1975 (Cth)? What ramifications may there be with regard to the validity of the judgment if she did not in fact have standing to commence proceedings?

Question (i) - *The answer to this question is Yes.* - "Having found that each of the nine individuals were Aboriginals the fact that it can now be proved that Ms Eatock was not an Aboriginal does not affect the finding in relation to the group. An individual finding in relation to Ms Eatock may well be challengeable but the finding in relation to the group stands.

---

[56] A paraphrase of the first line of L.P. Hartley's, *The Go-Between*, 1953.

[57] Gavin Silbert KC, former Chief Crown Prosecutor in Victoria, 2008-2018.[9.39]

As a nominal applicant on behalf of the group Ms Eatock had *locus standi* to pursue the action."

Question (ii) - *The answer to this question is No.* - "The judgement is based on findings of fact which are not susceptible to challenge on appeal, irrespective of the Aboriginality of Ms Eatock. Had Ms Eatock been permitted to pursue a personal offence claim then the result would have been open to challenge."

Question (iii) - *The answer to this question is No.* - "The result cannot be challenged by either appeal to the Full Federal Court or by any other mechanism."

Question (iv) - *Ms Eatock had locus standi, or standing, to bring the proceeding on behalf of the group.* - "The judge's findings will stand. Even carving out the issue of Ms Eatock's Aboriginality any person nominated by the other eight individuals to bring the group proceeding under section 18C was competent to do so."

- Gavin Silbert KC[58]

Silbert's assessment confirms what lawyer Nicholas Kirby wrote on the case in *Barnews* in 2012:[9.41]

> The way Ms Eatock pleaded her case, the issue was not whether or not she was reasonably likely to be offended, but, instead, whether the identified class of persons (i.e. fair-skinned Aboriginals)[the 'group'] were reasonably likely to be offended. Bromberg J found that such a reasonable likelihood existed.[59]

Thus, once the case proceeded, it was the *group* that had standing - *locus standi*. Even if Pat Eatock was 'disqualified' for not actually being Aboriginal and a legitimate member of the group, the group action could still proceed. Only a narrow window of opportunity had existed for Bolt's defence to stop the 'stitch-up' from getting underway in the first place. By exposing Eatock as a fake early on the defence may well have prevented the whole sorry saga from continuing. Nevertheless, had Eatock been excluded, then another from the 'group' would have been required to come forward as the lead

---

[58]Gavin Silbert KC, Owen Dixon Chambers, 7 March 2025. [*Full Opinion here* [9.40]]
[59]See *Eatock v Bolt* at 270 to 273.

complainant. Whether any of them had as 'convincing' a story as Eatock and would have done so is open to speculation.

But as is now known, Bolt's legal team didn't spend their first week or two down in the archives discovering Pat Eatock's real genealogy and past history. Her fakery did manage to get the 'fair-skinned Aboriginal' group through the court's front door and from then on Bolt's 'stitch-up' was irreversible. She had performed brilliantly.

It is not recorded if any of the jubilant *'pro bonoes'* in Eatock's legal team ever reflected on Ron 'St George' Merkel's mantra, "The ends will never justify the means".[60]

For References link - see QR code on page (xv)

References

[9.1]   John McMillan. *Federal Court v Minister for Immigration [1999] AIAdminLawF 8.* 1999, 22 AIAL Forum 1, p14.

[9.2]   Prof. Marcia Langton AO. *A Defence of Bruce Pascoe's Aboriginality - on Youtube.* 2021.

[9.3]   Prof. Marcia Langton AO. *A Defence of the Aboriginality of Lisa Jackson Pulver - on Youtube at 03:15.* 2023.

[9.4]   Adrienne Stone. *The Law Report interview on Bolt court case.* 4 Oct 2011.

[9.5]   *Eatock v Bolt [2011] FCA 1103.* Sept. 28, 2011.

[9.6]   The Bolt Report. *Andrew Bolt: AG Kyam Maher won't answer questions.* 2023.

[9.7]   SA Government. *First Nations Voice Act 2023, South Australia.* 2023.

[9.8]   George Kenmore. *George Kenmore Family Twitter (X) account exposing Kyam Maher.*

[9.9]   ABC Q&A. *Peter Malinauskas Premier of SA redefines Aboriginality with Senator Jacinta Nampijinpa Price.* 2023.

[9.10] Parl. South Australia Hansard. *Question to Kyam Maher - Voting in First Nations Voice, 9 Apr 2024.*

---

[60]Michael Gordon, 'SMH in Lunch with Ron Merkel', *Sydney Morning Herald*, 29 Aug 2014.

[9.11] NTIV. *Kyam Maher and his Aboriginality. Karla Grant on NITV Living Black.* 2024.

[9.12] Luke Walladge. *In defence of Andrew Bolt.* 20 Sep 2010.

[9.13] Andrew Dodd. *The Bolt decision will have implications for us all.* 28 Sept 2011.

[9.14] Jonathan Holmes. *Bolt, Bromberg and a profoundly disturbing judgment.* 30 Sep 2011.

[9.15] Jonathan Holmes. *True enemies of free speech.* 31 Mar 2011.

[9.16] Dale Smith. *The Law Report interview on Bolt court case.* 4 Oct 2011.

[9.17] Andrew Dodd. *The Law Report interview on Bolt court case.* 4 Oct 2011.

[9.18] Editorial National Times. *Bolt's 'freedom of speech' crusade won't right his wrongs.* 20 Oct 2011.

[9.19] Greg Barnes. *Even Bolt's freedom of speech isn't an absolute right.* 29 Sept 2011.

[9.20] David Marr. *In black and white, Andrew Bolt trifled with the facts.* 29 Sept 2011.

[9.21] The Age Editorial. *Free speech was not the loser in the Bolt case-Commentators are obliged to get the facts right.* 30 Sept 2011.

[9.22] Chris Merritt. *A Question of principle rather than money.* 2 Apr 2011.

[9.23] Andrew Bolt. *Academics claim to be Aboriginal. HeraldSun.* 4 Aug 2024.

[9.24] Youtube. *The Emu Wars.* 2021.

[9.25] The Bolt Report. *Nathan Moran on fake Aborigines.* 2 Sept 2024.

[9.26] Peter Dutton. *18 Questions on the Voice. The Australian.* 7 Jan 2023.

[9.27] SBS Insight. *Community Leaders warn many who claim to be Indigenous could be 'fakes'.* 18 Oct 2022.

[9.28] Andrew Bolt. *Bruce Pascoe - Bolt Report Youtube collection.* 2109-2025.

[9.29] Andrew Bolt. *Debunking Dark Emu and Bruce Pascoe - The Bolt Report.* 2019ff.

[9.30] University of Melbourne. *Marcia Langton endorses Bruce Pascoe at Melbourne Uni.* 2 Sept 2020.

[9.31] Andrew Bolt. *Margo Neale - a Fake on the Bolt Report.* 2024.

[9.32] Kerrie Doyle. *Psychological distress and community exclusion in Indigenous communities. PhD Thesis, ANU, 2017.* 2017.

[9.33] Aurora Education Foundation Ltd. *Mission Statement.* 2023.

[9.34] Aurora Education Foundation Ltd. *Photographs of End of Year Function.* 2023.

[9.35] Aurora Education Foundation Ltd. *Excerpt of Financial State-ment 2023*. 2023.
[9.36] Aurora Education Foundation Ltd. *Voice Statement*. 2023.
[9.37] JF O'Connell. *When did Homo sapiens first reach Southeast Asia and Sahul?* 21 Aug 2018.
[9.38] Andrew Bolt. *Academics Choosing to be Aboriginal in 2025.* 11 Mar 2025.
[9.39] Gavin Silbert KC. *Biography*. 2025.
[9.40] Gavin Silbert KC. *Opinion - Eatock v Bolt*. 7 March 2025.
[9.41] Nicolas Kirby. *Media responsibility under the Racial Discrimination Act*. Bar News Winter 2012, p30-2.

Chapter 10

Epilogue

People buy counterfeit products to signal positive traits, to themselves and others. Counterfeits, however, have an additional property, in that they signal an aspiration to be something one is not - for example, to feel wealthier than one's income would warrant. [They also] cause people to be not admirable but unethical, generating in them a feeling of a counterfeit self that leads them to behave unethically. [The] desired signals ('I am an admirable person') may conflict with actual signals ('I am a fake') ... Although the wearer intends them to signal positive traits, wearing counterfeits can in fact send a negative signal to the self.

Francesca Gino: 'The Counterfeit Self: The Deceptive Costs of Faking It'.[1]

The previous chapters were concerned with exposing the problems that fake and 'white Aborigines' pose for Australian society, and how one investigative critic, Andrew Bolt, was censured for daring to use his free speech to expose these issues. This Epilogue concludes with how these issues arose and what, as a society, Australians might do to correct them.

---

[1]Francesca Gino, *et al*, 'The Counterfeit Self: The Deceptive Costs of Faking It', *Psychological Science*, 21(5), 2010, p712–720.

10.1   Why Do We Have Fake and White Aborigines?

The most likely answer is esteem (both self and from others), along with fame, fortune, power and control, with at least three personality types at play, as described below.

The 'Tom Ripley' Phenomenon

First are the metaphorical 'Tom Ripley' types[2] - characters at the individual level who are willing to take on an assumed identity, in this case an Aboriginal one. They will, to varying degrees, discard, hide and even publicly trash their own ethnic and family history and then adopt a fake or greatly embellished Aboriginal identity. It is almost as if they would prefer to be a counterfeit somebody instead of a real nobody. Although this phenomenon is not new,[3] the rise of social media and identity politics in a hyper-marketing world has greatly encouraged and facilitated these Aboriginal counterfeits.

Many think the most [in]famous example in Australia is the fake Aboriginal man, Bruce Pascoe, whose *Dark Emu* (2014) book became a best-selling hoax, an Antipodean version of Erich Von Daniken's *Chariots of the Gods?*(1968), or Paul Ehrlich's, *The Population Bomb* (1968). All three of these authors turned out to be successful peddlers of a fascinating hoax. They were excellent storytellers, believable and, most importantly, the public were susceptible at that particular time to the message that the hoax conveyed. Often people bought the books because *they wanted the story to be true.*[4]

Historian, Professor Tom Griffiths described the *Dark Emu* phenomenon perfectly:

---

[2]See *Wikipedia: Tom Ripley.* [n.b. not for the fictional Ripley's murderous tendency but rather for his ability to be someone he was not.]

[3]See Grey Owl in 1925 Canada & Wanda Koolmatrie in 1990s Australia.

[4]Von Daniken's 1968 book coincided with public interest in space travel and aliens - the moon landing was one year later. Erlich built on the anxieties of Rachel Carson's *Silent Spring* (1962) and the obvious rapid population increases in the Third World.

> Pascoe is a writer but also a performer, an orator, a dedicated storyteller in the old style ... Earlier this year I was in a university lecture hall packed with hundreds of young people who had come out on a dark winter night to listen to the author of *Dark Emu*, and they were enthralled. You could have heard a pin drop. At the end of the speech the crowd erupted in an ovation for several minutes. Whatever Bruce Pascoe is saying, Australians clearly want to hear it now.[5]

Pascoe's concocted story about Aboriginal agriculture in *Dark Emu* was a hoax that was eagerly lapped up by a public who desperately wanted, because of social justice and/or political concerns for Aborigines, to believe that the British settlement (the 'invasion') of Australia was illegal. The British, as the hoax would unfold, failed to see the Aborigines as 'farmers' - Indigenous peoples who 'mixed their labour with the soil' - as had been recognised by treaties in New Zealand and North America with their respective Indigenous peoples. But this hoax could only be successful to the public if it was told by an authentic voice - the voice of an Aborigine.

The public had failed previously to take the bait when pretty much the same story was told by Rupert Gerritsen in 2008 in his book, *Australia and the Origins of Agriculture*. This is despite the fact that:

> Pascoe cites him [Gerritsen] as a scholar who languished in obscurity because his theories contradicted the mainstream view. "Rupert should have got all the credit for *Dark Emu*," [Pascoe] says candidly, a sentiment that gets ready agreement from Gerritsen's brother Rolf, a professor of economic and indigenous policy studies at Charles Darwin University. "Ninety per cent of Bruce's book is taken from my brother's research," Rolf Gerritsen says with a chuckle, adding that this is not to belittle Pascoe's considerable achievement in popularising complex issues and shifting the national conversation about indigenous history.[6]

---

[5] Tom Griffiths, 'Reading Bruce Pascoe', *Inside Story*, 26 Nov 2019.

[6] Richard Guilliatt, 'Bruce Pascoe, the man behind Dark Emu. Academic conflict accidentally turned Bruce Pascoe into our most influential indigenous historian', *The Australian*, 25 May 2019.

Similarly, for historian Bill Gammage's 2011 book, *The Biggest Estate on Earth: How Aborigines made Australia.* Although this book had much wider acceptance, and very much higher book sales, than Gerritsen's, it still never achieved the best-seller status of *Dark Emu.* Perhaps this was because Pascoe had 'read the market' and knew what was required to be successful - *Dark Emu* had to be written by an Aboriginal, not 'whitefellas' like Gerritsen and Gammage.[7] As anthropologist Peter Sutton astutely observed:

> if he'd [Pascoe] been a white farmer from Mallacoota, they would have just said, well, how does he know? But there are people who believe that knowledge comes with your blood from birth. That's obviously bullshit. So to claim Aboriginality, you know, is a big deal. And that's why it's humming at the moment. People were more relaxed about the issue when the payoff was not big. But now the payoff is big. You can get ahead in academia, the arts, the public service if you've got an Aboriginal identity.[10.2]

Pascoe understood what was required because he had heeded some good advice, twenty years prior. Veronica Sen of *The Canberra Times* was in the vanguard of the identity politics wave that was about to engulf Australia. With hindsight, it appears her review of Pascoe's 1988 book, *Fox*, might have planted the idea of 'race-shifting' into his head:

> One is conscious that the ideas, fears and longings of *Fox* are, as here, described for him, from the outside, and with an overlay of a white author's interpretation. Pascoe is, after all, imagining the psyche of an Aboriginal person; and it is not possible for him to convey all that the concept of 'my people' would mean to, say, Colin Johnson or Sally Morgan. He writes as a humane, informed liberal, but as a white man as well.[8]

To many, the career of Bruce Pascoe looks like that of a man

---

[7]The first publisher who rejected Pascoe's manuscript, noted he 'had consistently stated a desire to be part that emerging corpus of published works in that area'. (i.e. Gammage's book, Aboriginal 'farming', 'land management' and 'agriculture').[10.1]]

[8]Veronica Sen, 'Searching for Identity', *The Canberra Times*, Saturday 23 July 1988, p20. (nb. If Pascoe really was an Aboriginal man, why didn't he get the *The Canberra Times* to correct their description of him as a 'white author'?)

willing to fake it to be a somebody (an Aboriginal best-selling author), rather than remain a genuine nobody (a forgotten school teacher from Mallacoota and the editor of an obscure journal of short stories)'.[9]

Unfortunately, for every very public Bruce Pascoe there are probably several hundred or more small-time 'Tom Ripleys' - young and old white Australians who now identify as Aboriginal but who have no Aboriginal ancestry at all. Many of them are just succumbing to a fad, probably no different to when their parents and grandparents became Hare Krishnas, joined the Trotskyists, or a Nimbin hippy community - they 'felt lost' and craved a sense of belonging, the attention, esteem, importance, love or any one of a number of other reasons. Depending on one's political or worldview, these less public types are either sad or inspiring.

The Ideologue

The second type of personality at play is the ideologue - the person, political party or the institution that wants to progress the Aboriginalisation of Australia as a part of a grab for power to further their own political goals. Such people often harbour an element of resentment against ordinary Australians. From its earliest foundation, modern Australia is now unique in the world as a mass civilisation created from little more than bare earth a mere 237 years ago. It was a new world where the masses, who had never really had a chance to do anything on their own, could get the opportunity at building something for themselves on a clean slate, underpinned by the best institutions available at that time, British ones. From the outset,

---

[9]Patrick Connel (*Canberra Times*) described Pascoe on **26 March 1983** as a "russet-bearded Celt". On **23 July 1988** Veronica Sen (*Canberra Times*) describes him as a "white man" unable to "imagin[e] the psyche of an Aboriginal person; and it is not possible for him to convey all that the concept of 'my people' would mean to" a real Aboriginal writer. By year's end Pascoe appears to have 'race-shifted': Rod Usher (*The Age*) wrote on **3 Dec 1988**: "Apart from the fact that he has some Aboriginal blood in his veins, Pascoe still wants..." And so is born in 1988 - in the literary sense - the proud Yuin, Bunurong and Tasmanian Aboriginal man, Bruce Pascoe, from Mallacoota.

Australia was an array of working peoples - convicts, immigrants and the native-born - who were initially governed by a small elite of administrators in the Colonial office, and subsequently by local politicians and public servants. There was no pre-existing ruling class, aristocracy, landed gentry or resident sovereign. From its egalitarian beginnings, Australians have forged a rich country with a large middle class. No one class of people had been able to assert themselves as an aristocracy or an intellectual elite that saw itself as being in charge of everyone else. Apart from an ever-changing establishment of well-connected individual politicians and the wealthy, Australia did not have a ruling class as such.[10]

The Aboriginalisation movement is but the latest attempt by a new lobby group to fill the political void traditionally occupied in other societies by a ruling class. This time, the idea is to do it by establishing an hereditary Aboriginal aristocracy in Australia. The 2023 Voice referendum was in fact an attempted soft coup with the aim of installing a powerful Aboriginal lobby group deep within our constitution that would have acted as a new ruling class. No laws would pass in Australia without the approval of this Aboriginal 'House of Lords', a new hereditary aristocracy based on birth, race and ancestry. The fakes play a crucial role in facilitating these political campaigns, given their strong intellectual and media skills and their professional placement within important institutions. Many genuine yet unscrupulous Aboriginal people not only tolerate but support the fakes. They understand the skills the fakes bring to their 'cause' of establishing this Aboriginal polity and aristocracy within Australia.

---

[10]This is despite many attempts by historical lobby groups to create one, such as the NSW Corp during the Rum Rebellion, the Squattocracy and NSW's Bunyip Aristocracy for example. The 'establishment' in Australia has historically consisted of largely of powerful individuals and families whose influence does not survive long-term as it would in an inter-generational class structure. However, since the 1970s a new class of university educated intellectuals, who today populate the political parties, the law, government and the institutions, are well on their way to forming a new elite or class. This class has come to dominate the United Kingdom (where it is known as the 'blob') and large parts of Europe (as the EU bureaucracy) and ultimately may be successful in Australia as well.

Follow the Money

The third personality at play are the commercial interests - the individuals, corporations and institutions that can profit from the rise of the Aboriginalisation of Australia and its attendant list of fakes and 'white Aborigines'.

For example, Bruce Pascoe's hoax theories were avidly promoted not just by political ideologues, but also by a publishing industry desperate for new and divergent book sales. Major publishers routinely publish the works of fake Aborigines with apparently no questions asked.[11] In summing up the poor book sales for 2019, Mark Rubbo, managing director of the leading independent bookstore chain *Readings*, is reported as saying:

> "I'm hoping it's a blip. It wasn't a great publishing cycle. There wasn't one book that everyone had to have." Readings' top book at Christmas was *Dark Emu* by Bruce Pascoe, a 2014 book on Aboriginal agriculture that sold 115,300 copies in 2019, possibly fanned by an attack from conservative commentator Andrew Bolt... "I am very proud of its sales; it's an important book, but I have never experienced a five-year-old book as my Christmas bestseller before. And unfortunately it's a $20 book." [12]

Universities too are commercial ventures where government subsidies for Aboriginal students and staff flow freely. Putting to one side any ethical and moral dilemmas, which appears to be quite easy for some universities, one can understand for example the commercial attractiveness of some $2.3 million per year in government grants for the 110 Aboriginal staff and 339 Aboriginal student enrolments at the University of Sydney. It appears this university does not want to probe too deeply in determining how many of these people are in fact fakes.[10.3]

---

[11] For example: Bruce Pascoe by Hardie Grant and Black Inc, Bronwyn Carlson by Routledge, Margo Neale by Thames & Hudson, amongst others.

[12] Shona Martyn, 'I'm hoping it's a blip: sales down in difficult year for publishing industry', *Sydney Morning Herald*, 10 Jan 2020.

In some ways however, it should be no surprise to see the rise of a 'genre' of fake Aborigines and a new class of white 'fraudsters' eager to remake themselves as 'fair-skinned Aborigines'. As perhaps the world's most successful multi-ethnic immigrant nation, issues of race, identity, class, money and political power have always been foremost in shaping who we really are as Australians. Each of the various ethnic groups, compounded by differing cultural, economic and political goals *within* each of these groups, means there is much competition for the attention of policy makers, the voters and the consumer. This often means Australians can be very susceptible to the hoax, as author and former literary editor of the *Times* in London, Melissa Katsoulis, observed:

> What is it about Australia? A country whose ratio of literary hoaxes to genuine literary successes is so high must surely be guarding a fascinating cultural secret. Or is the Antipodean profusion of writerly tricks merely the result of a publishing scene desperate for a short-cut to established literary identity? It is telling that every single one of Australia's hoaxes involve race. Nino Culotta's books are about Italian immigrants; Norma Khouri writes about Islamic honour killings; Marlo Morgan and Wanda Koolmatrie both ape Aboriginals (albeit from diametrically opposing viewpoints); the unsavoury Helen Demidenko was inspired by the openly white supremacist context of her upbringing to write a fake memoir in support of Nazi soldiers. Even the most famous of them all, the Ern Malley poems, were created by a pair of young Anglo-Saxon fogies who wanted to poke fun at a trendy Jewish poetaster and his modernist crowd.[13]

The delicious irony of Katsoulis' 2010 book, *Telling Tales - A History of Literary Hoaxes,* is that it was published by Hardie Grant, who also published fake Aboriginal man, Bruce Pascoe, one of the most successful Australian hoax writers in recent times. And the 2014 *Dark Emu* was all about race, thereby confirming Katsoulis' 2010 observation: "It is telling that every single one of Australia's hoaxes involve race".

---

[13] Melissa Katsoulis, *Telling Tales - A History of Literary Hoaxes,* Hardie Grant, 2010, p123.

Just as worrying are the greater number of low-profile Australians who are faking their Aboriginality. Simply by deciding to 'tick the box' and putting on an Aboriginal T-shirt, a whole new vista of opportunity will open up for these fakes that is not available to non-Aboriginal Australians. For example, the universities are falling over themselves offering $50-60,000 annual student scholarships, and around to $100-200,000 per year for jobs, to those willing to claim they are Aboriginal.[10.3] For anyone who can fake it, or even just convince themselves they *might* have some distant Aboriginal ancestor, the temptation to tick the box is often irresistible.

The Destruction of Trust and Duty - The Rise of Cheating

For many people the revelation that Pat Eatock was a fake only serves as further evidence that the Progressive Left can only push their agenda ahead by cheating. Whether it is a structurally-biased poll of 6,315 residents to force through a change of a council's name from Moreland to the alleged Aboriginal name, Merri-bek, in Melbourne,[14] or the perception that the federal government refused to provide equal funding to both the Yes and No cases for the 2023 Voice referendum,[15] there is a sense by many ordinary Australians that the noble Australian concepts of fairness, a 'fair go' and meritocracy are being overturned. There will ultimately be a backlash as Australians will not accept the resulting sectarianism that this bias and identity politics of the Left is producing. In his 2009 articles Andrew Bolt voiced this backlash, which was firmly suppressed by Justice Bromberg in the 'stitch-up' that was *Eatock v Bolt*. But the dismal failure of the 2017 Uluru Statement from the Heart, which failed to garner enough support from the wider public, and the defeat of the 2023 Voice Referendum, indicated that the backlash against the 'fair-skinned Aboriginal' activist class, the neotribal elites, was effectively

---

[14]'Moreland Council votes to change name to Merri-bek', ABC online, 3 Jul 2022.

[15]Labor approves $9.5m for 'facts of the voice' not funding de-facto yes campaign, The Guardian online, 6 Mar 2023

underway. The backlash and then the pushback still has many
years of conflict ahead but the booing of Welcome to Country's will only get louder[16] as the box-ticking fakes surge to
ever increasing numbers in each census.

The unfolding polarisation of views in Australia is deeply
disturbing to some intellectuals. For example, there should
be a genuine sympathy for the lament of well-meaning conservative activists such as **Damien Freeman** who advocate
for a middle-path 'settlement' in the reconcilliation between
the races in Australia. Unfortunately for Freeman, the reconciliation process was hijacked by a lobby group of Aboriginal
activists, a number of whom are 'white Aborigines' or even
fakes. Australians are a commonsense, street-wise people and
could see the Voice as a soft-coup in action. However, they are
not of sufficient intellectual bent to understand, let alone agree
to, Freeman's more complicated vision of what he thinks a successful reconciliation would mean. In a 2024 *Quadrant* article,[17] Freeman correctly observed that Australia's politics had
become polarised - 'on the left of the political spectrum, we
find identity politics; on the right, the rise of populism. These
make it increasingly difficult to find common ground.' Whilst
Freeman's observation is correct, what he misses is that the
polarisation is caused by the radical Left pushing so far away
from the Centre of Australian politics that it can then look
back at the Centre and accuse it of being the populous Right.
As the referendum results show, the majority of Australians,
now labelled as the 'populous Right' recognised the misinformation, disinformation and cheating that emanated from the
Yes campaign. And they recognised racism when they saw it,
and so voted No.

Another observer of the politics of race is author, commentator and *Quadrant* contributor, Kel Richards, whose observations regarding the Voice are edifying:

---

[16]'Storm's Welcome to Country cancelled',Sydney Morning Herald, 25 Apr 2025.
[17]Damien Freeman, 'Wrecking the Voice', *Quadrant Online* 5 Dec 2024.

...there is only one race - the human race. All those superficial racial distinctions are just that - superficial. When the indigenous Voice referendum was put to Australian voters on October 14, 2023, the implication was that the roughly 800,000 Australians who identify as indigenous could be treated as a single, homogenous group. The unexamined (and mentally lazy) assumption behind the referendum proposal was that everyone in the 'indigenous' racial category was sufficiently alike as to have the same problems, the same concerns, and the same political needs. The assumption was that an Aboriginal academic at Sydney University was, in all relevant respects, similar to a barely literate Aboriginal resident of a remote community outside Alice Springs. But it was clear to common sense that the Aboriginal academic would have far more in common with fellow academics at the same university than with the resident of the remote community living on government welfare. That is why common sense rejected the Voice proposal by 60 per cent to 40 per cent in the outcome of the referendum. We need to learn to treat racial categories as unimportant. Race does not matter.[18]

Richards was saying in 2024 exactly what Bolt was saying in his allegedly offensive articles back in 2009: race does not - and should not - matter, so stop trying to divide Australians based on race. Intellectually and morally, Andrew Bolt, Kel Richards and the common sense of many of the Australian people in the street are way ahead of the likes of Pat Eatock, Ron Merkel and surprisingly, Damien Freeman too.

10.2 A Legislative Pushback

10.2.1 Legal Consequences of Being a Fake

At the individual level, there is very little in the way of legal consequences for being suspected of being, or even exposed as, a fake Aboriginal person. During investigations by *Dark Emu Exposed*, where suggestions were made that the subjects were mistaken to believe they were of Aboriginal descent, in all cases except for one, the subjects in question simply brushed

---

[18]Kel Richards, 'Recognising Racism', *Quadrant Online*, 11 June 2025.

off the allegations and carried on. The exception was Professor Bronwyn Carlson, whose Macquarie University online biography was modified to remove mention that she was 'an Aboriginal woman'.[10.4] Carlson nevertheless appears to be continuing in her university position much as before. Others have just made general public statements that the questioning of their Aboriginality does not dignify a response. The South Australian Attorney-General, The Hon. Kyam Maher is in this category (See Section 9.1.2). In response to challenges by both Bolt and *Dark Emu Exposed* others such as the Labor Federal Member for Robertson, Dr Gordon Reid, double-down by reaffirming under parliamentary privilege their claim to Aboriginality.[10.5],[10.6]

At the height of the 'Dark Emu Wars' in 2020, a complaint was made in a letter to the Home Affairs Department by Aboriginal businesswoman Josephine Cashman concerning allegations that the *Dark Emu* author, Bruce Pascoe, falsely claimed to be Indigenous. The Home Affairs Minister at the time, Peter Dutton, referred the matter to the Australian Federal Police (AFP).[19] After a short investigation, the AFP found that 'no Commonwealth offence' had been committed by Pascoe and the AFP had now 'finalised this matter' and the investigation stopped.[20] Importantly, the AFP stated that Pascoe's 'Aboriginality was not relevant in determining whether a Commonwealth offence had been committed' and so those inquiries had not been undertaken.[21]

In the numerous cases of complaints[22] being lodged with either Office of the Registrar of Indigenous Corporations (ORIC) or the various state Independent Commission Against Corruption (ICAC) concerning allegations that certain people are

---

[19] Adam Morton, 'Peter Dutton's office referred complaint accusing Bruce Pascoe of falsely claiming to be Indigenous to AFP', *Guardian Online*, 11 Jan 2020.

[20] 'AFP finds "no Commonwealth offence" following allegations against Bruce Pascoe, *SBS News Online*, 24 Jan 2020.

[21] 'Complaint Dark Emu author Bruce Pascoe lied about Aboriginal heritage "finalised" by AFP', *ABC News Online*, 24 Jan 2020.

[22] Several personal communications to this author under confidentiality.

fakes, it would appear that none have been successful unless actual criminal fraud can be demonstrated. If a person is a fake but have in their possession any supporting evidence such as a Certificate of Aboriginality, or a claimed family tree indicating an Aboriginal apical ancestor, then the authorities will not act even if these documents are suspected of being bogus.

It is only in the most egregious of cases where a sufficient number of respected Aboriginal people complain and evidence indicates a criminal conviction is achievable (e.g. a definitely forged Certificate of Aboriginality and admissions of guilt) that cases are undertaken to the full extent of the law. One such case is that of Ashley Brown in the Northern Territory who admitted to forging his Certificate of Aboriginality. A huge amount of work was necessary to collect the evidence to a criminal case burden of proof standard, resulting in a 38-page report by the Northern Territory's Independent Commissioner Against Corruption (ICAC). Brown was exposed and found to be a fake but, other than being dismissed from his Aboriginal identified position, it is not known what penalty, if any, Brown has suffered as a result of his false claim to Aboriginality.[10.7]

Understandably, authorities are reluctant to assign the valuable resources required for the complex investigation of cases such as Ashley Brown's, and so these prosecutions are quite rare - and the fakes know it.

10.2.2   The Racial Financial Discrimination Act 2030

- Aiming for Net-Zero race-based funding by 2030.

One way to thwart the rise in the misallocation of resources to fake and undeserving white Aborgines is to eliminate all government funding based on race. If all legislation was aimed at funding on the basis of need, rather than race or ethnicity, there would be massive increases in service delivery productivity and consequential outcomes for those Australians in real need. This is such a common sense proposal. Australian taxpayers is quite happy to pay taxes for grants, welfare and other social services to Australians in real need, regardless of their race, ethnicity or culture.

As a thought experiment, perhaps consider initially removing from the Department for Indigenous Australians any responsibility for welfare or economic outcomes. All these responsibilities should be rolled into the same government departments that serve the rest of the Australian population. There might be a case for a small separate bureaucracy to handle legal and cultural matters relating to Aboriginal Australia such as Native Title and specific issues concerning remote and very remote Aboriginal communities, for example.

To really drive the point home that race-based funding is not to be undertaken, perhaps Australia might consider legislation against the use of government funds going to recipients based on race. Consider the following draft Act:

> THE RACIAL FINANCIAL DISCRIMINATION ACT 2030
> Proposal - *Offensive financial behaviour because of race, colour or national or ethnic origin.*
>
> (1) It is unlawful for a person or an organisation to provide, otherwise than in private, funds derived from governments, whether state or federal:
>
> (a) to a recipient besed upon the race, colour or national or ethnic origin of that recipient;
>
> (2) It is unlawful for a person or an organisation to advertise for, or call for, otherwise than in private, applicants to apply for funds derived from governments, whether state or federal where part of the application process relies upon the race, colour or national or ethnic origin of that applicant.

10.2.3 Legislation as Part of the Higher Education Support Act 2003

The Higher Education Support Act 2003 was enacted, 'to support a higher education system' in Australia, whereby the 'university system is largely funded through Government research and teaching grants and student fees supported by a

Government-backed loan scheme'.[23] Specifically, the Act provides for 'grants for assisting Indigenous persons' [Section 3.5 (1)(aa)][10.9];

One way to overcome the corrosive and demoralising effects that fake Aboriginal students and staff are having within the university sector is to amend the Act in a way that forces universities to improve their application processes. This could be words to the effect of removing an individual's Statutory Declaration as being sufficient evidence of Aboriginal descent. Nor would the word of two 'suitably qualified' referees be acceptable as evidence of an applicant's *bona fides*. Instead, universities should be required to obtain from students and staff, who are applying for Indigenous funding or employment, independently certified genealogical evidence which clearly shows their apical Aboriginal ancestors[24] and/or a Certified Certificate of Aboriginality from an Aboriginal corporation which is registered with the Office of the Registrar of Indigenous Corporations (ORIC).[10.11] Some will claim that because their ancestors were of the so-called stolen generations, the genealogical records are lost so it will be difficult for them to prove their Aboriginality. This is an often used misdirection predominately put out by fakes as a justification as to why they can't document their claimed Aboriginality. There may be a few rare cases where this might be true, but if a person claims their ancestor was one of the stolen generations, then they must have that person's name. This can then lead them to the extensive name data bases within the various organisations such as LinkUp, AIATSIS and regional land councils and corporations and family groups. If they really are of Aboriginal descent they invariably will be able to link themselves to an apical Aboriginal ancestor. As the genealogical studies of *Dark Emu Exposed* show, if a person has their parents' marriage certificate they can essentially trace their family tree.

---

[23] Other funding sources include state government funding, overseas student fees, investment income and income from contract research and consultancy.[10.8]

[24] For example from a qualified genealogist, or the *ntscorp* for NSW residents.[10.10]

Problems caused by breaks in the family tree, due to adoptions and out-of-wedlock births, complicate the research, but are not insurmountable. For the very few who cannot confirm their apical Aboriginal ancestor, the conclusion might not be that 'the records are lost', but rather, 'you are mistaken to think you are Aboriginal'.

Finally, even though there may be some unscrupulous Indigenous Corporations who might provide Certificates of Aboriginality to fake applicants, this proposed amendment to the Act would go a long way to curtail the fakes at, for example the University of Sydney, where it is alleged that large numbers of students and staff are only relying on self-identification via a Statutory Declaration as evidence of their Aboriginality.

10.2.4   Is it Time for a Bran Nue DNA?

> *nothing I would rather be,*
> *than to be an Aborigine!*
> **Bronwyn Carlson**[25]

Not a week passes without the *Dark Emu Exposed* website receiving an email from an irate reader who believes the only solution to the fakes and frauds is to require DNA testing prior to any Australian receiving a taxpayer-funded benefit meant for Aboriginal people.

What these readers would like is for the generally accepted Three-Part Rule,[26] the definition of statutory Aboriginality, to be modified as follows (in bold):

An Aboriginal or Torres Strait Islander is:

- a person of Aboriginal or Torres Strait Islander descent, **as determined by an approved genetic test,**

- who identifies as an Aboriginal or Torres Strait Islander, and

- is accepted as such by the community in which he (she) lives.

---

[25] In a film review: Bronwyn Carlson,'Bran Nue Dae review: exceptional singing and music obscure the political heart of this classic Australian musical', *The Conversation*, 20 Jan 2020.

[26] See [2.4]

As logical and efficient as this might sound to many people, it is in fact the last thing any society should contemplate. The mandatory DNA testing of citizens, a form of racial profiling so as to scientifically classify people into various ethnic groups or classes, leads down a very dark road towards racial totalitarianism.

The profiling and classifying of citizens is an easy road for governments to begin to travel down. At the time of writing, the UK Labor Party Prime Minister, Sir Keir Starmer, has stated, 'You will not be able to work in the United Kingdom if you do not have digital ID.'[27] This is an extraordinary demand for a British Labor leader to make. He is telling his rank and file that, unless they hand over their personal data and biometrics to a massive database run by a government-backed tech company, they will not be able to access the one sovereign thing a working man owns - his labour; his ability to work.

Sometimes political leaders and their advisors are so far removed from the day-to-day reality of their citizens they can willingly just take a step along the path to a totalitarianism[28] without even realising the consequences of their actions. To illustrate how easily governments, often with good intentions, can make these errors, it is worth returning to the insightful quote of Brian Lapping from his 1987 book, *Apartheid - A History*. Lapping had first hand experience that South Africans were:

> not uniquely evil or racist or authoritarian people. They did not go suddenly wrong in 1948, when the National Party came to power and imposed a rigid form of racial segregation; they went wrong because every previous step along the fatal road had seemed to work. When they launched into full-blown apartheid it seemed to nearly all of them the only way forward.

---

[27]'You will not be able to work in the United Kingdom if you do not have digital ID', *Sky News Australia*, 26 Sept 2025.

[28]Such as the racial totalitarianism of Nazi Germany, the political totalitarianism of police states in various Latin American countries in the 1970s, the totalitarianism of the Soviet Union and even very much milder versions such as occurred in 'lockdown Melbourne' during COVID.

To some Australians, the proposal - 'You will not be able to receive Aboriginal benefits if you do not have DNA ID' - might sound like a logical, efficient and fair way to ensure taxpayer funds allocated to Aboriginal people would not be siphoned off by fakes and frauds. Indeed, this proposal surfaces every few years, such as when Mark Latham, a then NSW One Nation politician, launched such a policy initiative during the 2019 NSW State election. He received plenty of media coverage, some supportive in that it was not overtly critical,[29] but much that was adverse.[10.12]

Understandably, mandatory DNA testing is a very controversial subject. But here is the problem, as elucidated by Gary Johns, Close the Gap Research chairman, on *The Bolt Report*:

> The law is that you have to prove descent [of Aboriginality]. Now how do you measure descent in a culture that doesn't have a written record, often? You have to prove it by blood or now a DNA test. So if you want to have a race-based system whereby you get benefits because of your ancestry then at some stage you have to measure. So I'm saying nothing more than this is already the law. The big hit though is that I would rather none of these embarrassing discussions because there should be no race-based programs and no race-based benefits and then we could dispense with the whole nonsense of blood and DNA and measurement and identity.[30]

Despite the confused indignation of his critics,[31] Johns was saying he *didn't* want DNA testing to become necessary but, if Australia's policies with regard to Aboriginal welfare and

---

[29]Stephen Johnson, 'Australians claiming to be Aboriginal will be forced to undergo DNA testing', *Daily Mail Online*, 10 March 2019.

[30]The Bolt Report, *Sky News Australia*, 23 Jul 2023. See also another quotation: "If benefits or programs are to be awarded based on race, then race will have to be measured ... If the current three-part test on Aboriginality is to remain then just as Aborigines insist in Native Title claims, blood will have to be measured for all benefits and jobs", Gary Johns, 'The Burden of Culture: How to Dismantle the Aboriginal Industry and Give Hope to its Victims', Quadrant Books, 2022, p440.

[31]Roberts, G., 'Voice No camp responds to Gary Johns's call for Aboriginality "blood tests" for welfare payments', *ABC*, 25 Jul 2023; Butler, J., 'Gary Johns refuses to quit no campaign over "outdated" views on Indigenous benefits', *Guardian online*, 24 Jul 2023.

benefits continue, that would likely be the inevitable result to keep the system legal in the face of tightening budgets and the massive increase in fakes rorting the system. Johns' solution is to scrap the current systemically racist system whereby benefits are paid on the basis of race, and instead adopt an equity-based system where all Australians, regardless of race or ethnicity, receive benefits based on need.

Johns' point of view can't be ignored - a reckoning is coming, as has already begun in women's sport. After a decade of agonising over the effects of trans-women destroying the 'fairness and the integrity of the female competition',[32] World Athletics has introduced chromosome testing for female athletes - cheek swabs and dry blood-spot tests - in order to maintain 'the integrity of competition'. The test will indicate the presence of the male Y chromosome. Critics of the announcement believe that 'athletics is heading into a "really tricky space" with the introduction of chromosome testing'.[33]

The risk for Australia is that ultimately it will venture further into such a 'tricky space' where the courts will be forced to decide if, and under what terms, DNA testing for Aboriginality is admitted. It is already happening in some court actions[34] and, as precedents are set, DNA evidence could well become the norm. As the slow legislative creep of South Africa's apartheid system showed, where 'every previous step along the fatal road had seemed to work', DNA testing for Aboriginality, may seem as being 'the only way forward' for Australians. If that turns out to be the case, Australian society will be the poorer for it - 'systemic racism' will have been firmly entrenched.[35]

---

[32] Kim, J., 'Transgender track and field athletes can't compete in women's international events', *NPR Online*, 24 Mar 2023.

[33] De Silva, C., 'Australian Olympian Linden Hall concerned as World Athletics announces chromosome testing of female athletes', *ABC News*, 26 Mar 2025.

[34] See the complex cases of *Roos v. Winnaa Pty Ltd*, FWC 3568 [2018] and *Fair Work Commission v. Winnaa Pty Ltd*, FWC 3568, C2017/371 [2018] cited in Watt, Kowal & Cummings (2020), p140 (see Further Reading at chapter end.)

[35] An excellent summary of the status of genetic testing in Aboriginal Australia: Watt, E., Kowal, E., & Cummings, C., 'Traditional Laws Meet Emerging Biotechnolo-

A final warning comes from Chris Merritt, Vice President of the Rule of Law Institute of Australia and *The Australian* newspaper's Legal Affairs Contributor. His words during the 2023 Voice referendum debate regarding the classing of Australians by race also ring true for the proposal for the DNA testing for Aboriginality:

> the last thing we want in this country are race laws, race tribunals determining who is an Aborigine and who is not. I don't think we want to go there ... you take a wrong turn and you abandon the equality of citizenship and you hit all this nonsense. Race laws are just an abomination and they should form no part of the Australian statute.[36]

For References link - see QR code on page (xv)

References

[10.1] AIATSIS. *FOI on Bruce Pascoe's Dark Emu manuscript.* 24 Jan 2012.

[10.2] ABC. *Peter Sutton on Dark Emu Documentary.* 2024.

[10.3] James Willis. *Sydney Uni fails plan to tighten 'bogus' Indigenous guidelines. Daily Telegraph.* 17 Oct 2024.

[10.4] Dark Emu Exposed website. *Professor Bronwyn Carlson Removes Aboriginal claim from university portal.* 2024.

[10.5] Youtube. *Gordon Reid reaffirms his Aboriginality under Parliamentary Privilege.* 2023.

[10.6] Youtube. *Gordon Reid's ancestry investigated.* 2023.

[10.7] ICAC NT. *Investigation into the conduct of Ashley Brown, Public Statement.* Oct 2020.

[10.8] Universities Australia. *How Universities are Funded.* accessed 2025.

[10.9] Comm. Gov. *Higher Education Support Act 2003.* accessed 2025.

[10.10] ntscorp. *Example of an ntscorp family geneaology.*

[10.11] ORIC. *Office of the Registrar of Indigenous Corporations.* accessed 2025.

[10.12] ABC Media Watch. *DNA Testing of Aboriginal Australians? One Nation's DNA test.* 2019.

[10.13] Chris Merritt. *No Place for Race in Our Constitution.* 2023.

---

gies...', *Human Organization*, Vol. 79, No. 2, 2020. (Download available online.)
[36]Listen to Chris Merritt's admirable commentary in this film clip - [10.13]

Chapter 11

APPENDIX - Definitions and Methodology

Legal discourse in the courts is probably the least promising field in which to explore the concepts of [Aboriginal] identity. It projects interrelated individual and communal realities on to a pointillist landscape of disputes and 'matters'

Robert French AC[1]

In the Introduction to this book, the questions were asked, 'just who is, and who isn't, Aboriginal today?' and, 'should it even matter'? Obviously how Australia's Aboriginal people describe their own identity, or see themselves, in terms of their own family, community, culture or society is their own business. It should not be the subject of a book such as this.

However, the moment an Australian who claims to be Aboriginal steps into the public square and seeks to make an economic or a political demand on the taxpayer and/or Australian society *because* of their Aboriginality, the issue of that Aboriginality becomes a matter of public interest and very much a concern of this book. Back in 2009, Andrew Bolt also thought this way, but two years later found himself in a Kafkaesque nightmare, undergoing as Justice French had pre-

---

[1]Former Chief Justice of the High Court of Australia. See ([2.3] p18.)

dicted, 'legal discourse in the ... least promising field in which to explore the concepts of [Aboriginal] identity', the Federal Court.

The following definitions and the methodology presented in this book will hopefully assist any future Bolt-minded public commentators to avoid their own Kafkaesque nightmare under the Racial Discrimination Act. All they need to do when faced with a perfectly white-looking Australian, who claims to be Aboriginal and is demanding access to a benefit from the taxpayer that is expressly reserved for Aboriginal people, is to very politely, in a civil tone and manner ask - "Who are your apical Aboriginal ancestors?" or "Where is the evidence to show that you are really of Aboriginal descent?"

If the person cannot provide the details it is completely acceptable to begin to doubt the authenticity of any of their claims to statutory Aboriginality.

11.1 Definitions

11.1.1 A New Identifier

identify (*verb*)[2]

> **1.** to recognise or establish as being a particular person or thing; attest or prove to be as claimed or asserted; **2.** psychology to associate (one or oneself) with another person or group of people by identification; **3.** identify as, to consider oneself to be part of a particular group or category.

A New Identifier is defined as a descendant of an Aboriginal or Torres Strait Islander of mixed ancestry who has ostensibly assimilated into Australian mainstream society but has recently and often very publicly identified as being reconnected with their Indigenous ancestors. This may be by discovering previously unknown ancestors, or forging connections with known ones. They prioritise (choose) their Aboriginal ancestry over

---

[2]Unless otherwise specified *The Macquarie Dictionary* definitions have been used.

any other ancestry or heritage they may carry. Many have made this change in their racial identification later in life. Some have tried to establish Indigenous community, culture and rights with varying degrees of success. Many have tried to obtain Certificates of Aboriginality, but some have not been recognised and accepted by the Aboriginal community. It is a requirement that the person actually have *some* Indigenous ancestry or very strongly believe that they do.[3]

11.1.2 A Box-ticker

A box-ticker is defined as an Australian who:

> **1.** flippantly, negligently, recklessly, opportunistically or maliciously 'ticks-the-box' on a form to indicate their identity as an Aboriginal or Torres Strait Islander person without the ancestral basis to make that claim; **2.** verbally agrees to, or promotes themselves as, or lets others treat them as, being a person of Aboriginal and Torres Strait Islander descent when there is no basis in fact for that belief.

A box-ticker is at best reckless in that they knowingly have not attempted to determine the facts of their ancestry by competent genealogical research or, at worst, they are opportunistic, malicious and even fraudulent, given they are fully aware they have no Aboriginal ancestry, but nevertheless they seek to gain advantage by identifying as an Aboriginal person.

11.1.3 A Person of Aboriginal Heritage

heritage (*noun*)

> **1.** that which comes or belongs to one by reason of birth; an inherited lot or portion [Middle English (h)eritage, from Old French, from *heriter* inherit, from Late Latin.]

A person of Aboriginal or Torres Strait Islander heritage who

---

[3] Based on the work of Deakin University anthropologists, Elizabeth Watt and Emma Kowal, 'To be or not to be Indigenous? Understanding the rise of Australia's Indigenous population since 1971', *Ethnic and Racial Studies*, Vol. 42, No. 16, 2019, p63-82.

definitely has Aboriginal or Torres Strait ancestry, however distant, but they may or may not want to *solely* identify as an Aboriginal or Torres Strait Islander. Some describe themselves as 'part-Aboriginal' or as having, for example, an Aboriginal great-great-grandmother, and others make no mention at all of their heritage. They do not necessarily formally or publicly identify as Aboriginal for the purposes of obtaining services, funding or employment positions restricted to Aboriginal people.

This is analogous to how many Australians with other heritages describe themselves - they are 'Aussie-Greek, or claim 'my grandparents came from Vietnam', or 'one of my ancestors was an Irish convict'. They are Australian-born but openly acknowledge having a source of a particular ethnic heritage. However, unlike the 'white Aborigines' and box-tickers, these Australians would not generally identify as solely, for example, Greek, Vietnamese or Irish.

11.1.4   The Mistaken

There are some fake Aboriginal people who are genuinely mistaken about their ancestry. They have a genuine belief their family's oral history is true, but they haven't undertaken the necessary research to confirm it. Others delude themselves with a self-serving and unresearched belief that they *might be* Aboriginal, and so therefore *they are* Aboriginal. In 2002, historian Cassandra Pybus touched on this aspect of choosing to be Aboriginal, in the aftermath of the *Shaw v Wolf* case in Tasmania:

> People may discover something, that indicates to them, that it's possible that they've got Aboriginal ancestry. Now some people might just put that aside and say well that's interesting, but for some other people it's like a conversion - they then convert to being Aboriginal and along with this comes a lot of notions about spirituality and a special relationship to the land.[4]

---

[4]See ABC, *Four Corners*, Chapter 2 reference at QR Code [2.5], 0:00 to 2:10.

A more recent example is that of Tasmanian 'Aboriginal' man and photographer, Adjunct Professor Wayne Quilliam. He explained his claims to Aboriginality to Karla Grant on NITV's *Living Black* program:

> It was always our grandmother [who] dropped the sort of hint that we're Aboriginal; where mum would tell us and they'd sort of reinterate [*sic*] in such a way that - they would, they just never come out one day and said we're Aboriginal. It never happened like that. It was always that discussion of, you know, we'd be out hunting and you know the grandfather had talked to us, and that was from the white side of the family my grandfather, my mother's side, we're Aboriginal, and they showed us this old photo of our great-great-great-grandmother and they showed us a birth certificate and basically it was just married to an Aboriginal woman so that's our, that's all the information we've got. 'Cause Tassie [Tasmania] back then, there wasn't the records, the record keeping. There wasn't a lot of information around.[11.1]

Genealogical research by *Dark Emu Exposed* confirmed that Quilliam is mistaken to believe he is 'Aboriginal' on his mother's side of the family.[11.2] Perhaps the family's oral history was misled by the fact that one of Quilliam's ancestors did have 'colour', which the family mistakenly assumed was derived from Aboriginality.[5] Quilliam was contacted for comment, but no response was received.

11.1.5   The Fake

The word 'fake' is the broad term used to describe Australians who claim to be of Aboriginal descent when genealogical records indicate that none of their ancestors were Aboriginal. Some are genuinely mistaken – they believe their family's oral history without doing any further inquiry themselves. Others delude themselves with a self-serving and unresearched belief that *they might* be, and so most likely *they are* Aboriginal.

---

[5]The family's 'colour' appears to be derived from Quilliam's 5x great-grandfather, Robert William Hepburn, who was born in Jamaica in 1782 to a mother, Mary Ann Roy who was said to have been a 'mulatto' - someone of mixed-race heritage and 'coloured'.

And still others are out-and-out frauds - they know they are not Aboriginal (see definition below).

To many, this makes them look like opportunists, people who are willing to 'fake' their Aboriginal identity for some benefit or publicity. Fakes who are in relatively high public positions are particularly egregious given they have the ability and access to resources necessary to undertake the genealogical research required to prove their own Aboriginal ancestry. The likes of author Bruce Pascoe, academic Bronwyn Carlson or politician Kyam Maher are in this category.

From these foregoing groups are explicitly excluded those people of non-Aboriginal ancestry who have been accepted into a traditionally minded, non-city-based Aboriginal community and who make no race-based claims on the taxpayer. This description should also be read in conjunction with the *Disclaimer* on page (ii).

11.1.6 The Fraud

The frauds definitely know they have no Aboriginal ancestry but believe they can get away with their subterfuge. They put on a well-crafted performance that includes Aboriginal-themed clothing, identity badges (such as face-paint, red headbands, possum cloaks, etc), coupled with a few words of a claimed Aboriginal language interspersed with modern iterations like 'mob', capital C - 'Country', 'Siss', 'Bro', 'Uncle' and 'Auntie' which all serve to add cover to their hoax.

The late Eric Willmot was in this category, as was most probably Pat Eatock. Some men have even undergone painful, bloodletting initiations as a way of mentally convincing themselves they are accepted as Aboriginal by the relevant tribe.

11.1.7 Emerging Indigeneity

emerge (*verb*) [emerging]

> **1.** to come forth into view or notice, as from concealment or obscurity; **2.** to come up or arise, as a question or difficulty. [Latin *emergere* rise out.]

Emerging Indigeneity is a term promoted by Professor Bronwyn Carlson of Macquarie University. Her words are noteworthy given that she herself is a fake in the vanguard of an academy pushing for emerging Indigenous rights by a process of 'idea-laundering'.[6]

Carlson describes the phrase 'emerging Indigeneity' as a collective definition for the new perspectives that are emerging regarding what it can mean to be Indigenous in Australia, such as the Queer Indigenous movement, non-traditional Aboriginal musicians, such as DOBBY, who perform in non-authentic genres[7], and Indigenous knowledges, a so-called Aboriginal science and 'ways of knowing'. Emergent Indigeneity is increasingly alluded to with phrases such as 'We acknowledge elders, past, present and emerging'.[11.3]

The curious paradox about the Emerging Indigenity movement is that it seeks to validate and promote new Indigenous identities and thoughts that are clearly socially and culturally based upon modern Western philosophies - a mix of capitalism or Marxism, individualism, non-normative sexualities and genders, environmentalism and spiritualism - by attempting to claim Indigenous 'rights' that are rooted in deep antiquity. This paradox means the movement can progress either one of two ways - its internal contradictions will be so obvious to real Aboriginal people that they and their allies will push back against its inauthenticity and it will fade away, just like the Western fashion fad it really is (as Queers for Palestine so comically illustrated), or else it will morph into a much

---

[6] Roger Karge, 'Macquarie's (Formerly) Indigenous Laundress', *Quadrant Online*, 31 Mar 2025.

[7] Rhyan Clapham, known by his stage name Dobby (stylised as DOBBY), who claims to be a Filipino-Aboriginal Australian musician.

larger movement, inflated by ever increasing numbers of new identifiers, fakes, frauds and mistaken identity's, who will be assisted by sympathetic non-Indigenous facilitators and allies.

11.1.8   Aboriginal Descent

The definition of descent is simply the ancestry (DNA, genetics, lineage) that one inherits from one's parents and ancestors. In the Australian legal sense it is closely related to the term 'race', which in relation to Australian Aborigines, Justice Brennan has described as:

> Membership of a race imports a biological history or origin which is common to other members of the race ... Actual proof of descent from ancestors who were acknowledged members of the race or actual proof of descent from ancestors none of whom were members of the race is admissible to prove or to contradict, as the case may be, an assertion of membership of the race... [G]enetic inheritance is fixed at birth.[8]

11.2   Race

race (*noun*)

> **1.** a group of people sharing genetically determined characteristics such as skin pigmentation or hair texture. [Because the 19th-century classification of humans into distinct races has been qualified scientifically, and has been misused, many 'progressives' now prefer to avoid this term when referring to a group of humans, and to replace it with another term such as people(s) or community] **2.** the differentiation [i.e. dividing] of people according to genetically determined characteristics: genetic studies of race; discrimination on the grounds of race. **3.** a large class of living beings: the human race; **4.** a group of people sharing a language or culture or traditional beliefs or practices: the Scottish or Aboriginal race. [French, from Italian razza race, breed, lineage; origin uncertain.][9]

---

[8]Justice Robert French, 'Aboriginal Identity - The Legal Dimension', *Australian Indigenous Law Review*, Vol. 15, No. 1, 2011, p19.

[9]See also the Oxford English Dictionary: 'beliefs that members of a particular racial or ethnic group possess innate characteristics or qualities'; and Merriam-Webster Third International: 'racism is the assumption that psychocultural traits and capacities

11.2.1 Racism

A useful and practical definition of 'racism' can be found in an article by Australian writer and broadcaster, Kel Richards:

> **Racism consists of dividing people on the basis of race** - the classifying of people based on their racial category and treating their racial category as the most important thing about them.
>
> Racism can be either **Darwinian racism**, or **Marxist racism**.
>
> **Darwinian racism** is based on the notion that some races are more evolved [better] than others. White supremacism is an expression of Darwinian racism.[10]
>
> **Marxist racism** is based on the notion that some races should be preferred over other races (so as to right some perceived historical injustice and/or to promote 'equity' between the races). This Marxist idea of racial preference can be clearly seen in the Black Lives Matter movement.[11]
>
> Darwinian racists and Marxist racists heartily loathe each other. Darwinian racists accuse Marxist racists of practising 'replacement' — of aiming to 'replace' white people with black in the social structure. Marxist racists accuse Darwinian racists of arrogant hatred of non-white races. Both types of racism are built on the same foundation — the same core error of mistakenly believing that racial characteristics define a person. Both believe that racial differences vastly outweigh common humanity. That which distinguishes one race from another is not shallow and skin-deep (they assume) but is at the very foundation, heart and soul of each human being. If you are of one race, then you are fundamentally different from every other race. Most of you — not just your skin colour, hair colour, eye shape, and so on - will be deeply unlike persons from another race.[12](emphasis added.)

This definition goes to the heart of Bolt's critique of the 'fair-skinned Aboriginal people', the 'white Aborigines'. Bolt was pointing out they were defining themselves, relative to the rest

are determined by biological race and that races differ decisively from one another'. [cited in Richards, footnote 12.]

[10]See 'race' definition (1) in 11.2 above.

[11]See 'race' definition (2) in 11.2 above, which supports an understanding of 'Marxist racism' as an act of differentiating or dividing people on the basis of race without necessarily commenting on inferiority or superiority.

[12]Kel Richards,'Recognising Racism', *Quadrant Online*, 11 Jun 2025.

of the community, primarily and fundamentally based on their race; they were a 'proud [insert tribal name here] man/woman' first, followed then by their career and personal characteristics. For example, two of the 'white Aborigines' who took Bolt to court are still today identifying themselves in 'Marxist racism' terms:

> **Dr Anita Heiss AM. DLitt.** is a proud member of the Wiradyuri nation of central New South Wales and one of Australia's most prolific and well-known authors publishing across genres including non-fiction, historical fiction, commercial fiction and children's fiction. (from Heiss's personal webpage)[11.4]]

> **Larissa Behrendt** – a Euahleyai-Gamillaroi woman – is an award winning author and an award winning filmmaker. She is the author of several books and writes and directs for film and television. She is also a lawyer and an academic based at the University of Technology Sydney. She is the host of Speaking Out on *ABC Radio*.(from Behrendt's personal webpage.)[11.5]

Richards goes on to note:

> That's the error both types of racism make. And that's why I am proposing that the best definition of racism is 'dividing people on the basis of race'. Because division between races lies at the heart of both Darwinian racism and Marxist racism ... this belief says that people are distinguished from one another not by culture, or community influence, or intelligence, or upbringing, but by DNA - by inherited racial characteristics. This deep (and unchangeable) division of the human race according to racial categories is what all racism consists of. And this division can express itself as a claim of superiority (Darwinian racism) or of an entitlement or preference (Marxist racism).

This Marxist racist view of humanity is what Bolt was writing about in his 'offensive' articles. He wanted his readership to understand that race does not matter - that racial category is a minor, not a major, component in the identity of an individual. That is what Martin Luther King Jr was arguing in his famous 'I Have a Dream' speech in Washington on March 28

1963,[11.6] in which he made the bold assertion, for that time, that the colour of one's skin does not matter - other characteristics of each person matter far more.

11.2.2   Race as a Social Construct

In Australia today the word 'race' is predominately used to describe social and legal ideas. When people claim that 'race is a social construct', what they mean is that it is a word-idea that has been made up, invented or constructed to describe some social observations, legal facts, or indeed a way to vilify other individuals or groups by discrimination (racism). Such people claim that the scientific basis of race has been discredited; that is, it is no longer valid to use race to *biologically* or *physically* classify individuals or groups of people based on their perceived race or racial differences (see Macquarie definition in section 11.2). But these same people then go on to use race in the Marxist sense to divide Australians into the oppressed, the Aborigines, and the oppressor, the white (or any other non-Aboriginal) Australians.

This new use of the word 'race' is just another 'social construct' that has allowed it to be 'weaponised' in many political and sociological situations.

11.2.3   Race Prejudice as a Group Position

How are we going to get rid of racism...?
Stop talking about it.
US Actor Morgan Freeman[13]

In 1958, Herbert Blumer of the University of California, Berkeley, wrote a prescient paper about racial prejudice that seems to fit perfectly with an Australia of sixty-seven years later.[14]

---

[13]Excerpt from a 2005 interview with reporter Mike Wallace on the US *60 Minutes* program.[11.7]

[14]Blumer, H., 'Race Prejudice as a Sense of Group Position', *The Pacific Sociological Review*, Vol. 1, No. 1, Spring 1958, pp3-7.

Blumer observed that traditionally the idea of racial prejudice was 'dominated by the idea that such prejudice exists fundamentally as a feeling or set of feelings lodged in the individual'. These feelings were things like 'antipathy, hostility, hatred, intolerance, and aggressiveness.'[15] However, he believed that it wasn't *individuals* who were the main driver of prejudice but rather *groups* were to blame:

> race prejudice is fundamentally a matter of relationship between racial groups [which] therefore presupposes, necessarily, that racially prejudiced individuals think of themselves as belonging to a given racial group.[16]

This logic then led Blumer to posit that once a racial group forms, it begins to see racial prejudice coming not from isolated racists but rather from other groups. This then means:

> a scheme of racial identification is necessary as a framework for racial prejudice. Moreover, such identification involves the formation of an image or a conception of one's own racial group and of another racial group, inevitably in terms of the relationship [between] such groups.

US Academic Kate Fitzgerald argues that this insight by Blumer - that race is group-based (structural) rather than individual - has become the 'foundational idea for most of the major sociological perspectives on race today.'[17] That would appear to be the case in Australia too. In an earlier Australia of the 1970s and 80s, overt racism was generally *seen*[18] to manifest itself as derogatory and racist comments and exclusionary actions, *by individuals*, in pubs, shops, at work and at social gatherings and occasionally in the media. In those days it was generally understood that the particular person was deemed to be racist, not the institution, nor his or her family, club

---

[15] *ibid.*, p3. (Resentment could probably be added as well.)

[16] *ibid.*, p3.

[17] Fitzgerald, K., 'The Continuing Significance of Race: Racial Genomics in a Postracial Era', *Humanity & Society* Vol. 38(1), 2014, p55.

[18] Even though there is some validity to the argument that governments and organisations were also racist at that time, past history may indicate that racism was still seen, or perceived to be, largely a problem of racist individuals, even if they were members or representatives of those organisations.

or employer. By the late 1960s, all of the major examples of overt structural and institutional racism (mainly as exclusion or segregation policies) had been overturned via the ending of the White Australia Policy, the granting of full citizen rights to Aborigines in amendments to the various Franchise Acts, and from changes brought about through the 1967 referendum.

Public attitudes against racist remarks had began to change significantly and over the next two decades real strides were made by friends, colleagues and family to ostracise those deemed to be racist - behaviour began to change, as unacceptable attitudes and language were called-out both privately and in the media. Prime Minister Bob Hawke's claim in his 1988 Australia Day Speech rang true and seemed to reflect the success of all the country's collective hard work in suppressing sectarianism and racism: "In Australia, there is no hierarchy of descents, there must be no privilege of origin."

But then a strange thing happened. Just as Australians thought overt racism was diminishing and Andrew Bolt's dream of a 'colour-blind' society was within our grasp, Blumer's 'group racism' began to reappear. An identifiable date for this turnaround is 1991, the year of the release of the *Report of the National Inquiry into Racist Violence in Australia*, by the then Human Rights and Equal Opportunity Commission of Australia (HREOC).[11.8]

The HREOC's 576-page report can be likened to a manifesto for group racism. It formed one of the foundational documents for the Labor government's Racial Discrimination Amendment Bill 1992, which led to amendments of the original Racial Discrimination Act 1975. The Act's name was amended (some might say weaponised to suit the times) to the Racial Hatred Act 1995 and the new sections 18C and D were added, the very sections that had Bolt 'stitched up' in court sixteen years later.

The Inquiry into Racial Violence Report (perhaps 'manifesto') articulated all the new racial groups to whom violence was said to have been directed - specifically Aboriginal people (p38), Torres Strait Islanders (p46), people of Non-English speaking backgrounds (p47), Chinese workers (p48), South Sea Islanders (p49), Southern and Eastern European Immigrants (p50), Asian Australians (p140), Jews (p142) and Arab Australians (p145). The pro-racists were also given 'group' status[19] as were the much larger number of anti-racists, who the report also perversely categorised as victimised groups.[20]

A careful observer might wonder at the huge disparity of the anti-racism forces (in number, resources and lobbying power) compared with the three ratbag and inconsequentially small pro-racism organisations cited. Were these racist groups all that consequential, or were the report's authors trying to make organised racism a bigger force than it really was? Was there a gravy-train of anti-racism business and political influence for lobby groups to be had here? Was the oft heard phrase 'structural racism' just a way to keep Australians and their society permanently accused of being racist? Perhaps so, and Blumer's thesis is once again useful in describing what may have been happening in modern Australia:

> a major influence in public discussion is exercised by individuals and groups who have the public ear and who are felt to have standing, prestige, authority and power. Intellectual and social elites, public figures of prominence, and leaders of powerful organizations are likely to be the key figures in the formation of the sense of group position and in the characterization of the subordinate group.[21]

The next time a report arises of someone haranguing Australia for being racist, focus on the author's status. Is that person speaking as an individual or as the representative of a group? Invariably, it would seem that the majority of the racist com-

---

[19] The 'organised racist groups' were identified as National Action (p198), the Australian Nationalist Movement (p199) and the League of Rights (p145).

[20] Anti-Racist Community Groups (p181), Other Community Groups (p183), Churches (p185), Public Authorities, Politicians and Public Figures (p189), Journalists and Academics (p191), Writers to the Editors of Newspapers (p193), and even people said to be carrying Land Rights or Anti-Apartheid Stickers (p145).

[21] Blumer, *op.cit.*, p6.

mentary is presented as group racism, rather than individual racism.[22]

But then Blumer also points to a way of *reducing* group racial prejudice in society:

> The sense of group position dissolves and race prejudice declines when: events touching on relations are not treated as 'big events' and hence do not set crucial issues in the arena of public discussion; or when the elite leaders or spokesmen and women do not define such big events vehemently or adversely; or where they define them in the direction of racial harmony; or when there is a paucity of strong interest groups seeking to build up a strong adverse image for special advantage. Under such conditions the sense of group position recedes and race prejudice declines.[23]

Australian society too is at the mercy of these elites, spin-doctors (spokesmen and women) and the media. They decide what is to be a 'big event' in racial discourse. *Eatock v Bolt* was deemed at the time to be one such 'big event', carefully set up and orchestrated to fool the public into believing Australia's media was steeped in structural racism.

Unfortunately, the public are not only frequently fooled but are also complicit when they over-respond in a viral way to these 'big events', the provocations of the elites and the 'clickbait' of the media. Sadly, it would seem that Australia will not be heeding Morgan Freeman's advice anytime soon about how to stop group racism - to simply 'stop talking about it'.

---

[22]For example, the racist slur against footballer Adam Goodes by an *individual* teenage girl spectator was repackaged and weaponised as *group* racism - Indigenous sportsmen vs the Australian Football League (AFL), all spectators, Australia in general and the right-wing media (Melissa Davey, 'Adam Goodes should apologise, says mother of girl who called him an ape', *Guardian Online*, 30 Jul 2015.); and googling 'racism in Australia' brings organisations representing *groups* to the top of the listing: Amnesty International, the Human Rights Commission (the renamed HREOC), Reconcilliation Australia amongst many others. Even the independent Aboriginal commentator and author, Stan Grant, speaks of racism in Australia on behalf of a group - 'his people' (Stan Grant, 'Racism and the Australian dream, *The Ethics Centre*, 24 Jan 2016.)

[23]Blumer, *op.cit.*, p7.

11.2.4   Aboriginalisation

Aboriginalisation is here defined as a politically inspired process by which identified Aboriginal people are given preferential employment in certain roles within organisations or institutions; and standing is given to Aboriginal ideas, customs, culture and intellectual concepts on a par with, or in replacement of, traditional Western culture, thinking, experience and science. Aboriginalisation is driven by the UN-endorsed ideology of Indigenous Self-determination.

Aboriginalisation is a danger to Australia because it is a *regressive* ideology - it seeks to open up Australia's political, legal, economic and social institutions to admit so-called 'Indigenous knowledges'. These 'Indigenous ways of knowing' are a dangerous mixture of fragmentary aspects of ancient Aboriginal customs mixed with largely concocted 'New Age' interpretations of Aboriginal culture. They are regressive because they are undemocratic;[24] are a direct challenge to equality before the law;[25] they promote separateness or *apartheid* in the justice system,[26] and they are sexist with regard to the cultural separation boys and girls/men and women in many aspects of society (the separation of men's and women's business).[27] Aboriginalization is a direct threat to the *progressiveness* of Australian society that has been successfully demonstrated since the time of first settlement in 1788.[28]

---

[24] See the failed race-based 2023 Voice referendum.

[25] Janet Albrechtsen, 'The hustle for special rights is a hoax', *The Australian*, 26 Nov 2025.

[26] Yoorrook Justice Commission of Victoria, Criminal Justice Report, 'First Peoples must have decision-making power, authority, control and resources in the criminal justice system as these relate to them', 2025.

[27] Listen to podcast excerpt on the inability of 14-year-old school boys to be taught by young, white, female teachers - [11.9] and the separation of men's and women's business especially in Aboriginal Muslim communities - [11.10].

[28] For a detailed study of the reasons why Aboriginal culture is largely 'unfit for purpose' in the twenty-first century see Gary Johns, 'The Burden of Culture', *Quadrant Books*, 2022, Chapters 8 to 11.

11.2.5 Methodology

The apparent family trees that have been presented in this
work are constructed through a detailed investigation of each
of the apparent family branches that make up the tree. These
branches are known as 'through lines' and each contains documentary links to notes and records that provide the continuity
between each level of ancestor in each of the branches. By
ensuring that documentary proof (birth, death and marriage
records and/or confirmed and verified records, e.g. newspapers or government reports) have been located linking a person
in the branch to his or her parents and his or her child, this
methodology confirms that the links all the way through to the
penultimate ancestor are maintained, thus proving the genealogy of the family based on the records and evidence available
at the time of the research.

If all branches in the family tree lead back to ancestors
who can be shown to have been born overseas, this suggests
that none of the family's ancestors were of Aboriginal descent.

Once it is decided to publish the apparent family tree the
usual practice is to contact the subject directly by email invit-
ing that person to respond with any concerns and the opportunity to suggest corrections or amendments if warranted. This
usually occurs two to four weeks prior to publication.

As Pat Eatock passed away in 2015, a close family member was contacted instead. The family member strongly re-
futed the research that indicated Pat Eatock was mistaken to
believe she was of Aboriginal descent. Despite several email
exchanges, in which the family member threatened legal action, no suggestions were offered as to why the research might
be wrong, nor was any evidence offered that Pat Eatock was
in fact Aboriginal.

Consequently, the decision to publish the apparent Family
Tree of William and Lucy Eatock, and thus Pat Eatock, was
taken on the basis that the findings of Justice Bromberg's have

been complied with, namely:

> it is [not] unlawful for a publication to deal with racial iden-
> tification including challenging the genuineness of the identi-
> fication of a group of people ... provided the publication does
> not use a language, tone and structure that would contribute
> to the unlawful manner in which the subject matter [challeng-
> ing a person's claim to Aboriginality] was dealt with.

The research has been undertaken in good faith to a level that
would satisfy the Briginshaw principal (see next section) and
the findings were published in the public interest, given the
notoriety and influence that the *Eatock v Bolt* case has had on
free speech and race relations in Australia.

11.3   The Briginshaw Principle

The Briginshaw principle is the idea that 'the strength of evidence necessary to establish facts on the balance of probabilities, may depend on the nature of what is sought to be proven'.
In particular it holds that cogent or strict proof is necessary to
support a judicial finding of serious allegations, such as fraud,
sexual assault or anti-discrimination (and challenges to a person's identity, ancestry or paternity for example), due to the
relative seriousness of those types of civil allegations. It also
stresses that the balance of probabilities is the applicable standard of proof in all civil proceedings, subject to statute.[29]

Merkel J, in *Shaw v Wolf*,[11.11] dealt with the issue of the
onus and standard of proof to be applied in the cases where
there was dispute as to which party was obliged to make the
case of Aboriginality or non-Aboriginality. He found that the
party making the claim that someone was 'not an Aboriginal person' *had the onus of establishing the proof* of that allegation. Importantly, Merkel J considered 'the importance
and gravity of the consequences flowing from a finding as to
whether a person is or is not an Aboriginal person.' He con-

---

[29] *Wikipedia - Briginshaw principle.*

cluded that 'it is appropriate to apply the Briginshaw standard to the issue of whether the [claimants] have established that a particular respondent is not an Aboriginal person'.[30]

Consequently, based on Merkel J's finding, the onus of establishing the proof that a particular person is mistaken to believe they have Aboriginal descent rests with the author of *Witness for the Prosecution*. The apparent family trees that have been constructed and published in this book have therefore been prepared to a standard that would satisfy the Briginshaw Principle. This involved using qualified genealogists and researchers who sourced information from family members themselves, yet always corroborated that information by reference to publicly available documents and archival sources. The draft apparent family tree was checked and reconfirmed as being accurate by a separate, independent qualified genealogist. The findings were then sent to the person under study, the person claiming Aboriginal descent, to allow that person the opportunity to comment and advise of any corrections as need be, prior to publication.

For References link - see QR code on page (xv)

References

[11.1] NITV. *Wayne Quilliam's Mistaken Aboriginality, Karla Grant, NITV Living Black*. 24 Nov 2014.

[11.2] Dark Emu Exposed website. *Is Adjunct Professor Wayne Quilliam Mistaken to Believe that he is Aboriginal?* 4 Mar 2025.

[11.3] Bronwyn Carlson. *The Politics of Identity Who counts as Aboriginal today? AIATSIS*. 2016.

[11.4] Anita Heiss. *My Story & Career*. 2025.

[11.5] Larissa Behrendt. *About Me*. 2025.

[11.6] Youtube. *Martin Luther - I have a dream speech*. 1963.

[11.7] 60 Minutes Program USA. *Morgan Freeman on Black History Month and Racism*. 2005.

---

[30] Rachel Connell, 'Who is an Aboriginal Person?': Shaw v Wolf', *Indigenous Law Bulletin*, 4(12), 1998, p20.

[11.8]   AHRC. *Report of the National Inquiry into Racist Violence in Australia. Human Rights and Equal Opportunity Commission.* 1991.

[11.9]   ABC Podcast. *People vs the Drought.* c2018.

[11.10] The Safi Bros Podcast. *Aboriginal Elder and Muslim Uncle Andrew Hassan Gardiner.* 2025.

[11.11] *Shaw v Wolf FCA 389; 83 FCR 113.* 1998.

Acknowledgements

This book would not have been possible without the group of courageous, yet by necessity anonymous, academic and Aboriginal informants, all of whom in this time of 'cancel culture' have been constant sources of evidence, advice and peer-review. I thank many colleagues for the conversations and the advice offered during the long writing process. The depth of research accumulated in this book is due to the diligent work of researchers and genealogists Lorraine Newland, Kaye Vernon, J. Hunter and NG, and I am grateful for their perseverance in this project. Also, a thank you to Johanna Craven and Dr David Barton for editing, critical review and publishing assistance; and to Tim Barber at *Dissect Designs* for the excellent book cover design.

The methodology adopted by *Dark Emu Exposed* is derived from the historiography of the late Keith Windschuttle. Keith was one of the first to see that his history profession was being corrupted, as he warned in 1994 with his book, *The Killing of History*. Fast forward thirty-one years and here I am, solving a basic historical question - were Pat Eatock and her paternal grandparents Aboriginal as she, the historians and her lawyers all claimed them to be - using techniques I learnt from studying Keith's historiography, a trainee-ship for which I will ever be grateful.

Finally, I would like to thank Andrew Bolt for initiating the inquiry that led to this book, plus *The Bolt Report*, *Herald and Weekly Times* and *Sky News Australia*, for having the legal courage to regularly publish the findings of the investigative work by *Dark Emu Exposed* on the many fake Aborigines who have been uncovered to date.

Roger Karge

Index